D1401820

The Definitive Guide to SQLite

Michael Owens

Apress®

The Definitive Guide to SQLite

Copyright © 2006 by Michael Owens

ISBN-13: 978-1-59059-673-9

ISBN-10: 1-59059-673-0

Printed and bound in the United States of America 9 8 7 6 5 4 3 2 1

Lead Editors: Jason Gilmore, Keir Thomas
Technical Reviewer: Preston Hagar
Editorial Board: Steve Anglin, Ewan Buckingham, Gary Cornell, Jason Gilmore, Jonathan Gennick, Jonathan Hassell, James Huddleston, Chris Mills, Matthew Moodie, Dominic Shakeshaft, Jim Sumser, Keir Thomas, Matt Wade
Project Manager: Beth Christmas
Copy Edit Manager: Nicole LeClerc
Copy Editor: Liz Welch
Assistant Production Director: Kari Brooks-Copony
Production Editor: Katie Stence
Compositor: Susan Glinert
Proofreader: April Eddy
Indexer: Toma Mulligan
Artist: Kinetic Publishing Services, LLC
Cover Designer: Kurt Krames
Manufacturing Director: Tom Debolski

Distributed to the book trade worldwide by Springer-Verlag New York, Inc., 233 Spring Street, 6th Floor, New York, NY 10013. Phone 1-800-SPRINGER, fax 201-348-4505, e-mail orders-ny@springer-sbm.com, or visit http://www.springeronline.com.

For information on translations, please contact Apress directly at 2560 Ninth Street, Suite 219, Berkeley, CA 94710. Phone 510-549-5930, fax 510-549-5939, e-mail info@apress.com, or visit http://www.apress.com.

The source code for this book is available to readers at http://www.apress.com in the Source Code section.

To my family: Gintana, Natalie, and Riley
To my parents: Larry and Nancy
And to my grandfather: C. R. Clough

Contents at a Glance

Contents

Foreword

When I first began coding SQLite in the spring of 2000, I never imagined that it would be so enthusiastically received by the programming community. Today, there are millions and millions of copies of SQLite running unnoticed inside computers and gadgets made by hundreds of companies from around the world. You have probably used SQLite before without realizing it. SQLite might be inside your new cell phone or MP3 player or in the set-top box from your cable company. At least one copy of SQLite is probably found on your home computer; it comes built in on Apple's Mac OS X and on most versions of Linux, and it gets added to Windows when you install any of dozens of third-party software titles. SQLite backs many websites thanks in part to its inclusion in the PHP5 programming language. And SQLite is also known to be used in aircraft avionics, modeling and simulation programs, industrial controllers, smart cards, decision-support packages, and medical information systems. Since there are no reporting requirements on the use of SQLite, there are without doubt countless other deployments that are unknown to me.

Much credit for the popularity of SQLite belongs to Michael Owens. Mike's articles on SQLite in The Linux Journal (June 2003) and in The C/C++ Users Journal (March 2004) introduced SQLite to countless programmers. The traffic at the SQLite website jumped noticeably after each of these articles appeared. It is good to see Mike apply his expository talents in a larger work: the book you now peruse. I am sure you will not be disappointed. This volume contains everything you are likely to ever need to know about SQLite. You will do well to keep it within arm's reach.

SQLite is free software. *Free* as in *freedom*. Though I am its architect and principal coder, SQLite is not my program. SQLite does not belong to anyone. It is not covered by copyright. Everyone who has ever contributed code to the SQLite project has signed an affidavit releasing their contributions to the public domain and I keep the originals to those affidavits in the fire-safe at my office. I have also taken great care to ensure that no patented algorithms are used in SQLite. These precautions mean that you are free to use SQLite in any way you wish without having to pay royalties or license fees or abide by any other restrictions.

SQLite continues to improve and advance. But the other SQLite developers and I are committed to maintaining its core values. We will keep the code small—never exceeding 250KB for the core library. We will maintain backward compatibility both in the published API and the database file format. And we will continue to work to make sure SQLite is thoroughly tested and as bug-free as possible. We want you to always be able to drop newer versions of SQLite into your older programs, in order to take advantage of the latest features and optimizations, with little or no code change on your part and without having to do any additional debugging. We did break backward compatibility on the transition from version 2 to version 3 in 2004, but since then we have achieved all of these goals and plan to continue doing so into the future. There are no plans for a SQLite version 4.

I hope that you find SQLite to be useful. On behalf of all the contributors to SQLite, I charge you to use it well: make good and beautiful things that are fast, reliable, and simple to use. Seek forgiveness for yourself and forgive others. And since you have received SQLite for free, please give something for free to someone else in return. Volunteer in your community, contribute to some other software project, or find some other way to pay the debt forward.

Richard Hipp
Charlotte, NC
April 11, 2006

About the Author

MICHAEL OWENS is the IT director for a major real estate firm in Fort Worth, Texas, where he's charged with the development and management of the company's core systems. His prior experience includes time spent at Oak Ridge National Laboratory as a process design engineer, and at Nova Information Systems as a C++ programmer. He is the original creator of PySQLite, the Python extension for SQLite. Michael earned his bachelor's degree in chemical engineering from the University of Tennessee in Knoxville.

Michael enjoys jogging, playing guitar, snow skiing, and hunting with his buddies in the Texas panhandle. He lives with his wife, two daughters, and two rat terriers in Fort Worth, Texas.

About the Technical Reviewer

PRESTON HAGAR has a broad range of computer skills and experience. He has served as a system administrator, consultant, DBA, programmer, and web developer. He currently works for one of the largest single office real estate companies in the country, where he focuses on programming and database administration. He is lead developer and maintainer of iBroker3, a QT/C++ real estate software suite that manages all facets of a real estate business. Preston is also author of PNF and a partner in Linterra, a consulting company whose primary focus is to provide Linux server solutions for small- to medium-sized businesses.

Preston enjoys skiing and playing tennis. He lives with his wife in North Richland Hills, Texas.

Acknowledgments

First and foremost, thanks to my family for putting up with all the nights, weekends, vacations, and holidays that I have spent working on this book. I recall seeing so many instances in other books where authors beg the forgiveness of their loved ones, and now I understand why.

Thanks to my employer and hunting buddy, Mike Bowman, for his support throughout this project, and for the years of satisfaction that have come from using open source software to run the company. He's given me the most enjoyable job I've ever had.

I am grateful to Jamis Buck, Roger Binns, Wez Furlong (Dr. Evil), and Christian Werner for their comments on the various language extensions. I am also greatful to Vladimir Vukicevic for telling me how the Mozilla project uses SQLite, Eric Kustarz for his input on NFS, as well as David Gleason and Ernest Prabhakar at Apple for information on Mac OS X.

I am deeply indebted to Richard Hipp, the creator of SQLite, for his feedback from reviewing countless drafts, answering endless emails at all hours of the day, and for being very supportive throughout the project. His suggestions, advice, and encouragement made all the difference.

Thanks to Stéphane Faroult for his input on the book, especially the relational model and SQL chapters. Thanks also to Jonathan Gennick who from the start has patiently but firmly forced me to confront my addiction to passive construction. An ongoing battle it is.

Thanks to all the great people who write open source software. All of the code for this book was developed using open source software: Gentoo and Ubuntu Linux, KDE, GCC, Emacs, Firefox, OpenOffice, Ruby. . . the list goes on. I want to specifically thank the creators of the Dia drawing program. It has been invaluable for creating the conceptual illustrations for this book. I am also greatful to my colleague, John Starke, for introducing me to it.

To all the people at Apress, who have consistently provided me with more support than I could ever need and then some. Thank you! Jason, Keir, Beth, Liz, Katie, and Julie, you have all been a pleasure to work with.

Finally, to my wife, Gintana, who's been my partner in crime for 14 years now. You are the reason I ever stuck with anything, the reason I even tried.

CHAPTER 1

■■■

Introducing SQLite

SQLite is an open source embedded relational database. Originally released in 2000, it was designed to provide a convenient way for applications to manage data without the overhead that often comes with dedicated relational database management systems. SQLite has a reputation for being highly portable, easy to use, compact, efficient, and reliable.

An Embedded Database

SQLite is an *embedded* database. Rather than running independently as a standalone process, it symbiotically coexists inside the application it serves—within its process space. Its code is intertwined, or *embedded*, as a part of the program that hosts it. To an outside observer, it would never be apparent that such a program had a relational database management system (RDBMS) on board. The program would just do its job and manage its data somehow, making no fanfare about how it went about doing so. But inside, there is a complete, self-contained database engine at work.

One advantage of having a database server inside your program is that no network configuration or administration is required. Both client and server run together in the same process. This reduces overhead related to network calls, simplifies database administration, and makes it easier to deploy your application. Everything you need is compiled right into your program.

Consider the processes found in Figure 1-1. One is a Perl script, another is a standard C/C++ program, and the other is an Apache process with PHP, all using SQLite. The Perl script imports the DBI::SQLite module, which in turn is linked to the SQLite C API, pulling in the SQLite library. The PHP library works similarly, as does the C++ program. Ultimately, all three processes interface with the SQLite C API. All three therefore have SQLite embedded in their process spaces, and all three are independent database servers in and of themselves. Furthermore, even though each process represents an independent server, they can still operate on the same database file(s), as SQLite uses the operating system to manage synchronization and locking.

Today there is a wide variety of relational database products on the market specifically designed for embedded use—products such as Sybase SQL Anywhere, InterSystems Caché, Pervasive PSQL, and Microsoft's Jet Engine. Some vendors have retrofitted their large-scale databases to create embedded variants. Examples of these include IBM's DB2 Everyplace, Oracle's 10g, and Microsoft's SQL Server Desktop Engine. The open source databases MySQL and Firebird both offer embedded versions as well. Of all these products, only two are both open source and unencumbered by licensing fees: Firebird and SQLite. Of these remaining two, only one is designed exclusively for use as an embedded database: SQLite.

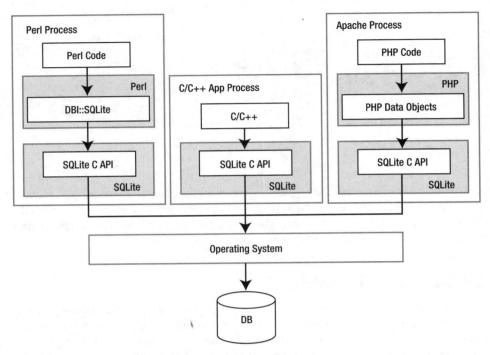

Figure 1-1. *SQLite embedded in host processes*

A Developer's Database

SQLite is quite versatile. It is a database, a programming library, and a command-line tool, as well an excellent learning tool that provides a good introduction to relational databases. There are indeed many ways to use it—in embedded environments, websites, operating system services, scripts, and applications. For programmers, SQLite is like digital duct tape, providing an easy way to bind applications and their data. Like duct tape, there is no end to its potential uses. In a web environment, SQLite can help with managing complex session information. Rather than serializing session data into one big blob, individual pieces can be selectively written to and read from individual session databases. SQLite also serves as a good stand-in relational database for development and testing: there are no external RDBMSs or networking to configure, or usernames and passwords to bother with. SQLite might also serve as a cache, hold configuration data, or because of its binary compatibility across platforms, even work as an application file format.

Besides being just a storage receptacle, SQLite can serve as a purely functional tool as well for general data processing. Depending on size and complexity, it may be easier to represent some application data structures as a table or tables in an in-memory database. This way, you can operate on the data relationally, using SQLite to do the heavy lifting rather than having to write your own algorithms to manipulate and sort data structures. If you are a programmer, imagine how much code it would take to implement the following SQL statement in your program:

```
SELECT AVG(z-y) FROM table GROUP BY x
  HAVING x > MIN(z) OR x < MAX(y)
  ORDER BY y DESC LIMIT 10 OFFSET 3;
```

If you are already familiar with SQL, imagine coding the equivalent of a subquery, compound query, GROUP BY clause or multiway join—in C. SQLite embeds all of this functionality into your application with minimal cost. With a database engine integrated directly into your code, you can begin to think of SQL as a domain-specific language in which to implement complex sorting algorithms in your program. This approach becomes more appealing as the size of your data set grows or as your algorithms become more complex. What's more, SQLite can be configured to use a fixed amount of RAM and then offload data to disk if it exceeds the specified limit. This is even harder to do if you write your own algorithms. With SQLite, this limit is instituted with a single SQL command.

SQLite is also a great learning tool for programmers—a cornucopia for studying computer science topics. From parser generators, tokenizers, virtual machines, B-tree algorithms, caching, program architecture, and more, it is a fantastic vehicle for exploration of many well-established computer science concepts. Its modularity, small size, and simplicity make it easy to present each topic as an isolated case study that any one individual could easily follow.

An Administrator's Database

But SQLite is not just a programmer's database. It is a useful tool for system administrators as well. It is small, compact, and elegant like a regular expression or a Unix utility such as find, rsync, or grep. SQLite has a command-line utility that can be used within shell scripts. However, it works even better with a large variety of scripting languages such as Perl, Python, and Ruby. Together the two can help with a wide variety of tasks, such as aggregating log file data, monitoring disk quotas, or performing bandwidth accounting in stateful firewalls. Furthermore, since SQLite databases are ordinary operating system files, they are easy to work with, transport, and back up.

Also, SQLite is a convenient learning tool. It is an ideal beginner's database with which to learn about relational concepts. It can be installed quickly and easily on almost any platform, and its database files share freely between them without the need for conversion. It is full featured but not daunting. And it—both the program and the database—can be carried around on a floppy disk or Universal Serial Bus (USB) stick.

SQLite History

SQLite was conceived on a battleship... well, sort of. SQLite's author, D. Richard Hipp, was working for General Dynamics on a program for the U.S. Navy developing software for use on board guided missile destroyers. The program originally ran on Hewlett-Packard Unix (HPUX) and used an Informix database as the back-end. For their particular application, Informix was somewhat overkill. For an experienced database administrator (DBA), it could take almost an entire day to install or upgrade. To the uninitiated application programmer, it might take forever. What was really needed was a self-contained database that was easy to use and that could travel with the program and run anywhere regardless of what other software was or wasn't installed on the system.

In January 2000, Hipp and a colleague discussed the idea of creating a simple embedded SQL database that would use the GNU DBM B-Tree library (gdbm) as a back-end, one that would require no installation or administrative support whatsoever. Later, when some free time opened up, Hipp started work on the project, and in August 2000, SQLite 1.0 was released.

As planned, SQLite 1.0 used gdbm as its storage manager. However, Hipp soon replaced it with his own B-tree implementation that supported transactions and stored records in key order. With the first major upgrade in hand, SQLite began a steady evolution, growing in both features and users. By mid-2001 many projects—both open source and commercial alike—started to use it. In the years that followed, other members of the open source community started to write SQLite extensions for their favorite scripting languages and libraries. One by one, new extensions—an Open Database Connectivity (ODBC) interface followed by extensions for Perl, Python, Ruby, Java and other mainstays—fell into place and testified to SQLite's wide application and utility.

SQLite began a major upgrade from version 2 to 3 in 2004. Its primary goal was enhanced internationalization supporting UTF-8 and UTF-16 text as well as user-defined text-collating sequences. While 3.0 was originally slated for release in summer 2005, America Online provided the necessary funding to see that it was completed by July 2004. Besides internationalization, version 3 brought many other new features such as a revamped C API, a more compact format for database files (a 25 percent size reduction), manifest typing, Binary Large Object (BLOB) support, 64-bit ROWIDs, autovacuum, and improved concurrency. In spite of the many new features, the overall library footprint was still less than 240 kilobytes. Another improvement in version 3 was a good code cleanup—revisiting and rewriting, or otherwise throwing out extraneous stuff accumulated in the 2.*x* series.

SQLite continues to grow feature-wise while still remaining true to its initial design goals: simplicity, flexibility, compactness, speed, and overall ease of use. At the time this book went to press, SQLite added enforcement of CHECK constraints. Next on the docket are recursive triggers and foreign keys. What's next after that? Well, it all depends. Perhaps you or your company will sponsor the next big feature that makes this little database even better.

Who Uses SQLite

Today, SQLite is used in a wide variety of software and products. It is used in Apple's Mac OS X operating system as a part of their CoreData application framework. It is also used in the system's Safari web browser, Mail.app email program, RSS manager, as well as Apple's Aperture photography software. SQLite can be found in Sun's Solaris operating environment, specifically the database backing the Service Management Facility that debuted with Solaris 10, a core component of its predictive self-healing technology. SQLite is in the Mozilla Project's mozStorage C++/JavaScript API layer, which will be the backbone of personal information storage for Firefox, Thunderbird, and Sunbird. SQLite has been added as part of the PHP 5 standard library. It also ships as part of Trolltech's cross-platform Qt C++ application framework, which is the foundation of the popular KDE window manager, and many other software applications. SQLite is especially popular in embedded platforms. Much of Richard Hipp's SQLite-related business has been porting SQLite to various proprietary embedded platforms. Symbian uses SQLite to provide SQL support in the native Symbian OS platform. SQLite is also a core component in the new Linux-based Palm OS, targeted for smart phones. It is also included in commercial development products for cell phone applications.

Although it is rarely advertised, SQLite is also used in a variety of consumer products, as some tech-savvy consumers have discovered in the course of poking around under the hood. Examples include the D-Link Media Lounge, Slim Devices Squeezebox music player, and the Philips GoGear personal music player. I recently saw online that some clever consumers found a SQLite database embedded in the *Complete New Yorker* DVD set—a digital library of every issue of the *New Yorker* magazine—apparently used by its accompanying search software.

You can find SQLite as an alternate back-end storage facility for a wide array of open source projects such as Yum—the package manager for Fedora Core, Movable Type, DSPAM, Edgewall Software's excellent Trac SCM and project management system, and KDE's Amarok audio player, to name just a few. Even parts of SQLite's core utilities can be found in other open source projects. One such example is its Lemon parser generator, which the `lighttpd` web server project uses for generating the parser code for reading its configuration file. Indeed there seems to be such a variety of uses for SQLite that Google took notice and awarded Richard Hipp with "Best Integrator" at O'Reilly's 2005 Open Source Convention.

Architecture

SQLite has an elegant, modular architecture that takes some rather unique approaches to relational database management. It consists of eight separate modules grouped within three major subsystems (as shown in Figure 1-2). These modules divide query processing into discrete tasks that work like an assembly line. The top of the stack compiles the query, the middle executes it, and the bottom handles storage and interfacing with the operating system.

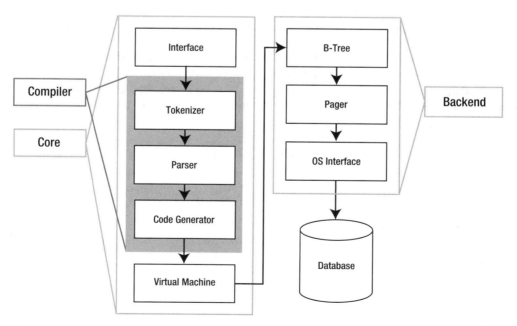

Figure 1-2. *SQLite's architecture*

The Interface

The interface is the top of the stack and consists of the SQLite C API. It is the means through which programs, scripting languages, and libraries alike interact with SQLite.

The Compiler

The compilation process starts with the tokenizer and parser. They basically work together to take a Structured Query Language (SQL) statement in text form, validate its syntax, and then convert it to a hierarchical data structure that the lower layers can more easily work with. SQLite's tokenizer is handcoded. Its parser is generated by SQLite's custom parser generator, which is called Lemon. The Lemon parser generator is designed for high performance and takes special precautions to guard against memory leaks. Once the statement has been broken into tokens, evaluated, and recast in the form of a parse tree, the parser passes the tree down to the code generator.

The code generator translates the parse tree into a kind of assembly language specific to SQLite. This assembly language is made up of instructions that are executable by its virtual machine. The code generator's sole job is to convert the parse tree into a complete mini-program written in this assembly and hand it off to the virtual machine for processing.

The Virtual Machine

At the center of the stack is the virtual machine, also called the virtual database engine (VDBE). The VDBE works on byte code—like a Java virtual machine or scripting language interpreter. The VDBE's byte code (or virtual machine language) consists of 128 opcodes, which are all centered around database operations. The VDBE is a virtual machine designed specifically for data processing. Every instruction in its instruction set either accomplishes a specific database operation (like opening a cursor on a table, making a record, extracting a column, or beginning a transaction) or manipulates the stack in some way to prepare for such an operation. All together and in the right order, the VDBE's instruction set can satisfy any SQL command, however complex. Every SQL statement in SQLite—from selecting and updating rows to creating tables, views, and indexes—is first compiled into this virtual machine language, forming a standalone program that defines how to perform the given command. For example, take the statement

```
SELECT name FROM episodes LIMIT 10;
```

This compiles into the VDBE program shown in Listing 1-1.

Listing 1-1. *VDBE Assembly*

```
0   Integer         10   0
1   MustBeInt        0   0
2   Negative         0   0
3   MemStore         0   1
4   Goto             0   15
5   Integer          0   0
6   OpenRead         0   2
7   SetNumColumns    0   4
8   Rewind           0   13
```

```
 9  MemIncr        0  13
10  Column         0   3
11  Callback       1   0
12  Next           0   9
13  Close          0   0
14  Halt           0   0
15  Transaction    0   0
16  VerifyCookie   0 190
17  Goto           0   5
18  Noop           0   0
```

The program consists of 18 instructions. These instructions, performed in this particular order with the given operands, will return the name field of the first ten records in the episodes table (which is a part of the example database included with this book).

In many ways the VDBE is the heart of SQLite: all of the modules above it work to create a VDBE program, while all modules below it exist to execute that program, one instruction at a time.

The Back-end

The back-end is made up of the B-tree, page cache, and OS interface. The B-tree and page cache (pager) work together as information brokers. Their currency is database pages, which are uniformly sized blocks of data that, like freight cars, are made for transportation. Inside the pages are the goods: more interesting bits of information such as records and columns and index entries. Neither the B-tree nor the pager has any knowledge of the contents. They only move and order pages; they don't care what's inside.

The B-tree's job is order. It maintains many complex and intricate relationships between pages, which keeps everything connected and easy to locate. It organizes pages into tree-like structures (hence the name), which are highly optimized for searching. The pager serves the B-tree, feeding it pages. Its job is transportation and efficiency. The pager transfers pages to and from disk at the B-tree's behest. Disk operations are by far the slowest thing a computer has to do. Therefore, the pager tries to speed this up by keeping frequently used pages cached in memory and thus minimizes the number of times it has to deal directly with the hard drive. It uses special techniques to guess which pages will be needed in the future and thus gambles on the B-tree's behalf to keep pages flying as fast a possible. Also in the pager's job description is transaction management, database locking, and crash recovery. Many of these jobs are mediated by the OS interface.

Things like file locking are often implemented differently in different operating systems. The OS interface provides an abstraction layer that hides these differences from the other SQLite modules. The end result is that the other modules see a single consistent interface with which to do things like file locking. So the pager, for example, doesn't have to worry about doing file locking one way on Windows and doing it another way on different operating systems such as Unix. It lets the OS interface worry about this. It just says to the OS interface "lock this file," and the OS interface figures out how to do that based on the operating system it happens to be running on. The OS interface not only keeps code simple and tidy in the other modules, but it also keeps the messy issues cleanly organized in one place. This makes it easier to port (adapt) SQLite to different operating systems—all of the OS issues that must be addressed are clearly identified and documented in the OS interface's API.

Utilities and Test Code

Miscellaneous utilities and common services such as memory allocation, string comparison, and Unicode conversion routines are kept in the utilities module. This is basically a catchall module for services that multiple modules need to use or share. The testing module contains a myriad of regression tests designed to examine every little corner of the database code. This module is one of the reasons SQLite is so reliable: it performs a lot of regression testing.

SQLite's Features and Philosophy

SQLite offers a surprising range of features and capabilities despite its small size. It supports a large subset of ANSI SQL92 (transactions, views, check constraints, correlated subqueries, and compound queries) along with many other features found in relational databases, such as triggers, indexes, autoincrement columns, and the LIMIT/OFFSET clause. It also has many unique features, such as in-memory databases, dynamic typing, and something called conflict resolution (explained in a moment).

As mentioned at the beginning of this chapter, SQLite has a number of governing principles or characteristics that serve to more or less define its philosophy and implementation. Let's expand on these issues next.

Zero Configuration

From its initial conception, SQLite has been designed with the specific absence of a DBA in mind. Configuring and administering SQLite is as simple as it gets. SQLite contains just enough features to fit in a single programmer's brain, and like its library, requires as small a footprint in the gray matter as it does in RAM.

Portability

SQLite was designed specifically with portability in mind. It compiles and runs on Windows, Linux, BSD, Mac OS X, commercial Unix systems such as Solaris, HPUX, and AIX, as well as many embedded platforms such as QNX, VxWorks, Symbian, Palm OS, and Windows CE. It works seamlessly on 16-, 32-, and 64-bit architectures with both big and little endian byte orders. Portability doesn't stop with the software either: SQLite's database files are as portable as its code. The database file format is binary compatible across all supported operating systems, hardware architectures, and byte orders. You can create a SQLite database on a Sun SPARC workstation and use it on a Mac or Windows machine—even cell phone—without any conversion or modification. Furthermore, SQLite databases can hold up to 2 terabytes of data (limited only by the operating system's maximum file size) and natively support both UTF-8 and UTF-16 encoding.

Compactness

SQLite was designed to be lightweight and self-contained: one header file, one library, and you're relational, no external database server required. Everything—client, server, virtual machine—packs into a tidy quarter megabyte, which at the moment is smaller than the home page of the publishers of this book: www.apress.com (the home page weighing around 260 kilobytes). If you really work at it and disable unneeded features at compile time, you can further shrink the library down to under 170 kilobytes (on x86 hardware compiled with the GNU C compiler). Furthermore, there is a proprietary version of SQLite that is as small is 69 kilobytes, capable of running on smart cards (see the "Additional Information" section for more details).

Equally compact are SQLite databases. They are ordinary operating system files. Regardless of your system, all objects in your SQLite database—tables, triggers, schema, indexes, and views—are contained in a single operating system file. Furthermore, SQLite uses variable-length records, allocating only the minimum amount of data needed to hold each field. A 2-byte field sitting in a varchar(100) column only takes up 3 bytes of space, not 100 (the extra byte is used to record its type information).

Simplicity

As a programming library, SQLite's API is one of the simplest and easiest to use. The API is both well documented and intuitive. It is designed to help you customize SQLite in many ways, such as implementing your own custom SQL functions in C. Better yet, the open source community has a created a vast number of language and library interfaces with which to use SQLite. There are extensions for Perl, Python, Ruby, Tcl/Tk, Java, PHP, Visual Basic, ODBC, Delphi, Microsoft .NET, Smalltalk, Ada, Objective C, Eiffel, Rexx, Lisp, Scheme, Lua, Pike, Objective Camel, Qt, WxWindows, REALBASIC, and others. An exhaustive list can be found on the SQLite Wiki: www.sqlite.org/cvstrac/wiki?p=SqliteWrappers.

Architecturally, SQLite has a modular design. This design includes many innovative ideas that enable it to be full featured and extensible while at the same time retaining a great degree of simplicity throughout its code base. Each module is a specialized, independent system that performs a specific task. This modularity makes it much easier to develop each system independently, and to debug queries as they pass from one module to the next—from compilation and planning to execution and materialization. The end result is that there is a crisp, well-defined separation between the front-end (SQL compiler) and back-end (storage system), allowing the two to be coded independently of each other. This design makes it easier to add new features to the database engine, is faster to debug, and results in better overall reliability.

Flexibility

Several factors work together to make SQLite a very flexible database. As an embedded database, it offers the best of both worlds: the power and flexibility of a relational database front-end, with the simplicity and compactness of a B-tree back-end. With it, there are no large database servers to configure, no networking or connectivity problems to worry about, no platform limitations, no baroque APIs to learn, and no license fees or royalties to pay. Rather, you get simple SQL support dropped right into your application.

Liberal Licensing

All of SQLite's code is in the public domain. There is no license. No claim of copyright is made on any part of the core source code. All contributors to this code are required to sign affidavits specifically disavowing any copyright interest in contributed code. Thus there are no legal restrictions on how you may use the source code in any form: you can modify, incorporate, distribute, sell, and use the code for any purpose—commercial or otherwise—without any royalty fees or restrictions.

Reliability

But the source code is more than just free; it also happens to be well written. SQLite's code base consists of about 30,000 lines of standard ANSI C, which is clean, modular, and well commented. It is designed to be approachable, easy to understand, easy to customize, and generally very accessible. It is easily within the ability of a competent C programmer to follow any part of SQLite or the whole of it with sufficient time and study.

Additionally, SQLite's code offers a full-featured API specifically for customizing and extending SQLite through the addition of user-defined functions, aggregates, and collating sequences along with support for operational security.

While SQLite's modular design significantly contributes to its overall reliability, its source code is also well tested. Whereas the core software (library and utilities) consists of about 30,000 lines of code, the distribution also includes an extensive test suite consisting of over 30,000 lines of regression test code, which covers over 97 percent of the core code. That is, over half of the SQLite project's total code is devoted exclusively to regression testing. Another way of saying this is for every line of database code written, there is approximately one line of test code written as well.

Convenience

SQLite also has a number of unique features that provide a great degree of convenience. These include dynamic typing, conflict resolution, and the ability to "attach" multiple databases to a single session.

SQLite's dynamic typing is somewhat akin to that found in scripting languages (e.g., "duck typing" in Ruby). Specifically, the type of a variable is determined by its value, not by a declaration as employed in statically typed languages. You could say that where most database systems work like statically typed languages, SQLite works like a dynamically typed language. That is, most database systems restrict a field's value to the type declared in its respective column. For example, each field in an integer column can hold only integers. In SQLite, while a column can have a declared type, fields are free to deviate from them, just as a variable in a scripting language can be reassigned a value with a different type. This can be especially helpful for prototyping: since SQLite does not force you to explicitly change a column's type, you need only change how your program stores information in that column rather than continually having to update the schema and reload your data.

Conflict resolution is another unique feature. It can make writing SQL, as easy as it is, even easier. This feature is built into many SQL operations and can be made to perform what I call "lazy updates." Say you have a record you need to insert, but you are not sure whether one just like it already exists in the database. Rather than write a SELECT statement to look for a match, and then recast your INSERT to an UPDATE if it does, conflict resolution lets you say to SQLite, "Here, try to insert this record, and if you find one with the same key, just update it with these values instead." Now you've gone from having to code three different SQL statements to cover all the bases (i.e., SELECT, INSERT, and possibly UPDATE) to just one: INSERT ON CONFLICT REPLACE (...). Better yet, you can build this conflict resolution into the table definition itself and dispense with the need to ever specify it again on future INSERT statements. In fact, you can dispense with ever having to write UPDATE statements to this table again—just write INSERT statements and let SQLite do the dirty work of figuring out what to do using the conflict resolution rules defined in the schema.

Finally, SQLite lets you "attach" external databases to your current session. Say you are connected to one database (foo.db) and need to work on another (bar.db). Rather than opening a separate connection and fumbling back and forth between them, you can simply attach the database of interest to your current connection with a single SQL command:

```
ATTACH database bar.db as bar;
```

All of the tables in bar.db are now accessible as if they existed in foo.db. You can detach it just as easily when you're done. This makes all sorts of things like copying tables between databases even easier than it already is.

Performance and Limitations

SQLite is a speedy database. But the words "speedy," "fast," "peppy," or "quick" are rather subjective, ambiguous terms. To be perfectly honest, there are things SQLite can do quicker than other databases, and there are things that it cannot. Suffice it to say, within the parameters for which it has been designed, SQLite can be said to be consistently fast and efficient across the board. SQLite uses B-trees for indexes and B+-trees for tables, the same as most other database systems. For searching a single table, it is as fast if not faster than any other database on average. Simple SELECT, INSERT, and UPDATE statements are extremely quick—virtually at the speed of RAM (for in-memory databases) or disk. Here SQLite is often faster than other databases, as it has less overhead to deal with in starting a transaction or generating a query plan, and it doesn't incur the overhead of making a network call to the server. Its simplicity here makes it fast. As queries become larger and more complex, however, query time overshadows the network call or transaction overhead, and the game goes to the database with the best optimizer. This is where larger, more sophisticated databases begin to shine. While SQLite can certainly do complex queries, it does not have a sophisticated optimizer or query planner. It knows how to use indexes to be sure, but it doesn't keep elaborate table statistics. If you perform a 17-way join, SQLite will join the tables and give you the result. What it won't do is try to determine optimal paths by computing various alternate query plans and selecting the fastest candidate, as you might expect from Oracle or PostgreSQL. Thus if you are running complex queries on large data sets, odds are that SQLite is not going to be as fast as databases with sophisticated query planners.

So there are situations where SQLite is not as fast as larger databases. But many if not all of these conditions are to be expected. SQLite is an embedded database designed for small to medium-sized applications. These limitations are in line with its intended purpose. Many new users make the mistake of assuming that they can use SQLite as a drop-in replacement for larger relational databases. Sometimes you can; sometimes you can't. It all depends on what you are trying to do.

In general, there are three major variables that define SQLite's main limitations. These variables are:

- **Concurrency**. SQLite has coarse-grained locking, which allows multiple readers but only one writer at a time. Writers exclusively lock the database during writes and no one else has access during that time. SQLite does take steps to minimize the amount of time in which exclusive locks are held. Generally, locks in SQLite are kept for only a few milliseconds. But as a general rule of thumb, if your application has high write concurrency (many connections competing to write to the same database) and it is time critical, you probably need another database. It is really a matter of testing your application to know what kind of performance you can get. I have seen SQLite handle over 500 transactions per second for 100 concurrent connections in simple web applications. But even the notion of a transaction is vague. Transactions are a function of the number of records being modified, as well as the number and complexity of the queries involved. Acceptable concurrency all depends on your particular application, and can only be determined empirically by direct testing. In general, this is true with any database: you don't know what kind of performance your application will get until you do real-world tests.

- **Database size**. While SQLite's databases can scale to 2 terabytes, there are memory (RAM) costs associated with large databases. When SQLite begins a transaction, it allocates a bitmap for tracking dirty pages, which assists in managing its rollback journal. To do this, it requires 256 bytes of RAM for every 1MB of database. Thus, when databases become very large, the size of the bitmap allocated in each transaction can become significant. A 100GB database would require 25MB of RAM to be allocated before each transaction. This directly affects the rate at which transactions can be performed regardless of their complexity. So in reality, the practical limits on database size are in the tens of gigabytes. They can be much bigger, but keep in mind that the overhead associated with transaction startup will increase linearly with the database size.

- **Networking**. While SQLite databases can be shared over network file systems, the latency associated with such file systems can cause performance to suffer. Worse, bugs in network file system implementations can also make it error prone. If the file system's locking does not work properly, two clients may be allowed to simultaneously modify the same database file, which will almost certainly result in database corruption. It is not that SQLite is incapable of working over a network file system because of anything in its implementation—indeed, it uses standard locking mechanisms such as POSIX advisory locks on Unix and the equivalent system calls on Windows. Rather, it is simply impossible for SQLite to officially confirm that any given network file system is without bugs that may adversely affect its operation. It has been claimed that certain network file system implementations (such are Solaris NFS v4) work just fine and reliably implement the requisite locking mechanisms needed by SQLite. However, the SQLite developers have neither the time nor resources to certify that any given network file system works flawlessly in all cases. Therefore, the official position is that it is safe to use SQLite over a network file system only if there is no more than one connection operating on a given database at a time—which is to say when no locking is required.

Again, most of these limitations are intentional—they are a result of SQLite's design. Supporting high write concurrency, for example, brings with it great deal of complexity and this runs counter to SQLite's simplicity in design. Similarly, being an embedded database, SQLite intentionally does not support networking. This should come as no surprise. In short, what SQLite can't do is a direct result of what it can. It was designed to operate as a modular, simple, compact, and easy-to-use embedded relational database whose code base is within the reach of the programmers using it. And in many respects it can do what many other databases cannot, such as run in embedded environments where actual *power consumption* is a limiting factor.

While SQLite's SQL implementation is quite good, there are some things it currently does not implement. These are as follows:

- **Foreign key constraints.** Foreign keys are the foundation of referential integrity in relational databases. While SQLite parses them, it currently does not have support for foreign keys. It does support check constraints, and foreign key support is estimated to be completed by sometime in 2006.

- **Complete trigger support.** There is some support for triggers but it is not complete. Missing features include FOR EACH STATEMENT triggers (currently all triggers must be FOR EACH ROW), INSTEAD OF triggers on tables (currently INSTEAD OF triggers are only allowed on views), and recursive triggers—triggers that trigger themselves. Recursive triggers are needed in order to implement foreign key constraints.

- **Complete ALTER TABLE support.** Only the RENAME TABLE and ADD COLUMN variants of the ALTER TABLE command are supported. Other kinds of ALTER TABLE operations such as DROP COLUMN, ALTER COLUMN, and ADD CONSTRAINT are not implemented.

- **Nested transactions.** SQLite allows only a single transaction to be active at one time. Nested transactions allow for fine-grained control over larger, more complex operations in that parts of a transaction can be defined and rolled back in case of an error rather than the entire transaction.

- **RIGHT and FULL OUTER JOIN.** LEFT OUTER JOIN is implemented, but RIGHT OUTER JOIN and FULL OUTER JOIN are not. LEFT OUT JOIN can be implemented as a right outer join by simply reversing the order of the tables and modifying the join constraint. Furthermore, FULL OUTER JOIN can be implemented as a combination of other relational operations supported by SQLite.

- **Updatable views.** VIEWs in SQLite are read-only. You may not execute a DELETE, INSERT, or UPDATE statement on a view. But you can create a trigger that fires on an attempt to DELETE, INSERT, or UPDATE a view and do what you need in the body of the trigger.

- **GRANT and REVOKE.** Since SQLite reads and writes an ordinary disk file, the only access permissions that can be applied are the normal file access permissions of the underlying operating system. GRANT and REVOKE commands in general are aimed at much higher-end systems where there are multiple users who have varying access levels to data in the database. In the SQLite model, the application is the main user and has access to the entire database. Access in this model is defined at the application level—specifically, what applications have access to the database file.

In addition to what is listed here, there is a page on the SQLite Wiki devoted to reporting unsupported SQL. It is located at www.sqlite.org/cvstrac/wiki?p=UnsupportedSql.

Who Should Read This Book

As SQLite has many uses, it also has many audiences. Whether you are a programmer, web developer, systems administrator, or just casual user looking to learn about relational databases, this book aims at helping you understand and get the most out of your particular use for SQLite.

SQLite is a terrific database to start on if you are new to relational databases. For new database users, this book assumes nothing. If you have never touched a relational database before, if you have never issued a single SQL statement, this book will help you not only get started with SQLite but also become a competent user of SQL. It will prepare you to get the most out of SQLite, as well as provide you with a good foundation with which to move on to larger relational systems and explore more advanced features and topics.

For programmers, this book assumes only that you know the programming language in which you intend to use SQLite. Furthermore, it does more than document APIs. If anything, that is the least of what it does, as API documentation only illustrates how an interface works. As with any database, you have to have some idea of how that database works internally to get the most out of it. Every database has unique architectural aspects, specific relational features, and important limitations, all of which good programmers learn about and take into consideration when writing their code. SQLite, though simple and straightforward, is no exception. As a programmer, you need to know something about how it processes data internally to get it to work well with your application. This book shows you how. It covers the API and explores how it works in relation to SQLite's architecture, allowing C programmers, web developers, and scriptwriters alike to write more informed code. This helps you better understand not only what SQLite can do, but also what it can't. Your knowledge of the architecture will tell you better than any list of rules when SQLite is or isn't a good fit for what you are trying to accomplish. You'll know if, when, and where you need to consider another approach.

And that underscores one of the most important aims in this book: to teach concepts over recipes—to adequately address both how and why. There simply is no substitute for conceptually understanding how something works. To that end, this book includes both historical and theoretical material where appropriate to help frame complicated, technical, or abstract concepts. At the same time, it tries to be ruthlessly practical. Intermixed in the writing are many figures and examples designed specifically to illustrate the topics at hand and provide real-world value.

To help accommodate both those who want to know why in addition to those who want to know how, the theoretical and the practical are arranged orthogonally in chapters. Those who don't care for theory can simply skip past the theoretical chapters. While the practical chapters draw on some of this material, they are in no way dependent upon them.

How This Book Is Organized

This book is divided into three parts: SQLite the database, SQLite the programming library, and reference material. The database aspects of SQLite are covered in Chapters 2, 3, and 4. The programming aspects of SQLite are covered in Chapters 5–8. A brief chapter outline is as follows:

Chapter 1, "Introducing SQLite," introduces the main features of SQLite, its origin and history, as well as the scope and objectives of this book.

Chapter 2, "Getting Started," covers how to obtain and use SQLite. It illustrates how to get SQLite in binary and source form, as well as how to compile and build it on a variety of platforms. It explains how to use the SQLite command-line utility to create and work with databases.

Chapter 3, "The Relational Model," provides some background behind SQL. It illustrates the historical and theoretical basis that led to the formation of SQL and helps explain why it is the way it is today. It highlights the 30-year history of the relational model in the context of Codd's famous 12 rules.

Chapter 4, "SQL," provides a complete introduction to SQL as implemented by SQLite. It assumes no prior experience with SQL. It starts with the fundamentals and works through constructing complex queries and explores every aspect of all commands in SQLite's SQL implementation.

Chapter 5, "Design and Concepts," lays the groundwork for programming with SQLite. It illustrates the SQLite API, its architecture, and how the two work in relation to one another. It addresses important topics related to programming such as transactions and locking. It provides programmers of all languages with a clear understanding of how SQLite works internally and what to keep in mind when writing programs that use it.

Chapter 6, "The Core C API," covers the part of the SQLite C API related to executing queries. From connecting to databases, executing queries, obtaining data, and managing transactions, this chapter covers all parts of the API related to query and data processing.

Chapter 7, "The Extension C API," covers the remaining part of the C API devoted to customizing and extending SQLite. SQLite provides facilities for implementing user-defined SQL functions, aggregates, and collations. This chapter illustrates how to implement each of these features and provides practical examples of their use.

Chapter 8, "Language Extensions," uses the basic concepts outlined in Chapter 5 and provides a concise introduction to SQLite programming in six popular languages: Perl, Python, Ruby, Java, Tcl, and PHP.

Chapter 9, "SQLite Internals," explores the inner workings of SQLite. It is a high-level overview of the source code and provides a glimpse into how the major subsystems are implemented. This provides programmers with a deeper understanding of SQLite's design decisions, assumptions, and trade-offs, as well as a point of departure for developers who want to work on SQLite.

Finally, complete references for the SQLite C API and SQL syntax are included in the appendices.

DATABASE EXAMPLES

The example databases accompanying this book are available online and can be downloaded from the Apress website (`www.apress.com`). Each database is in SQL format and you can simply follow the procedures covered in Chapter 2 to create them using the SQLite command-line program. The example databases are further explained and illustrated as they are introduced in this book.

The source code for all examples is also available online. All examples compile and run on both Windows and Unix. For each example, makefiles are included for Unix environments and Visual C++ projects have been created for Windows users. MinGW users can use the Unix makefiles.

Additional Information

The SQLite website has a wealth of information, including the official documentation, mailing lists, Wiki, and other general information. It is located at `www.sqlite.org`. The SQLite community is very helpful, and you may find everything you need on SQLite's mailing list. Additionally, SQLite's author offers professional training and support for SQLite, which includes custom programming (porting to embedded platforms, etc.), and enhanced versions of SQLite, which include native encryption and extremely small versions optimized for embedded applications. More information can be found at `www.hwaci.com/sw/sqlite/prosupport.html`.

Summary

SQLite is not to be confused with other larger databases like Oracle or PostgreSQL. Whereas dedicated relational databases such as these are electronic backhoes, SQLite is a digital Swiss Army Knife. Whereas large-scale dedicated relational databases are designed for thousands of users, SQLite is designed for thousands of uses. It is more than a database. Although a tool in its own right, it is a tool for making tools as well. It is a true utility, engineered to enable you— the programmer, user, or administrator—to quickly and easily shape those disparate piles of data into order, and manipulate them to your liking with minimal effort.

SQLite is public domain software. Free. You can do anything with it or its source code you like. No licenses, no install programs, no restrictions. Just copy and run. It is also portable, well tested, and reliable. It has a clean, modular design that helps keep the system simple, easy to develop, and easy to debug. In addition to good design, it has good testing. There is more code written to test SQLite than there is SQLite code to test. It should not be too surprising, then, that SQLite has proven itself to be a solid, reliable database over its five-year history.

Finally, SQLite is fun. At least I think so. It is a unique and interesting piece of software that I have found many uses for over the years. I hope that you will find it equally useful and enjoyable.

If you have any comments or suggestions on this book or its examples, please feel free to send me an email at `sqlitebook@gmail.com`. I will also keep additional information related to the book at `www.mikesclutter.com`.

CHAPTER 2

■■■

Getting Started

On the whole, it's easy to begin using SQLite no matter what operating system you are using. For the vast majority of users, SQLite can be installed and running with a new database in hand in under 5 minutes, regardless of experience. This chapter covers everything you need to know in order to install SQLite and work with databases. You will have a working knowledge of where to obtain SQLite software or source code and how to install or compile it on multiple platforms. By the time you finish this chapter, you will have a new SQLite database with tables, views, and indexes that you can query, back up, and restore. Furthermore, you will learn everything you need to know about managing SQLite databases, including how to create, view, and examine their contents. Finally, you will be introduced to several tools with which to work with SQLite in various environments. This chapter does include some examples that use SQL to introduce the SQLite command-line program. If you are not yet familiar with SQL, you should still be able to follow the examples without much trouble. SQL is addressed in detail in Chapter 4.

Where to Get SQLite

The SQLite website (www.sqlite.org) provides both precompiled binaries of SQLite as well as source code. Binaries are available for both Windows and Linux.

There are several binary packages to choose from, each of which is specific to a particular way of using SQLite. The binary packages are as follows:

- **Statically linked command-line program (CLP).** This version of the SQLite command-line program has the database engine compiled in and is a self-contained, standalone program. This provides a convenient way to work with SQLite databases from the command line without having to worry about whether or not the SQLite shared library is installed on your system or located in the right place.

- **SQLite dynamic link library (DLL).** This is the SQLite database engine packaged into a shared library, or Windows DLL. Use this with programs that dynamically link to SQLite. This form makes it easier to upgrade SQLite without having to recompile the software that depends on it.

- **Tcl extension.** This is a Tcl extension library that enables you to connect to SQLite from within the Tcl language. SQLite's author, Richard Hipp, happens to be the author and maintainer for the Tcl extension.

SQLite's source code is provided in two forms that vary by platform. One form is for compiling on Windows and the other is for compiling on POSIX platforms such as Linux, BSD, and Solaris. The source code itself does not differ between source distributions. Rather, the two distributions simply include different conveniences that make it easier to work within their respective environments. The Windows distribution, for example, has the preprocessing and code generation performed by GNU Autoconf and other associated Unix build tools already added to the source files, freeing Windows users from having to bother with them.

SQLite on Windows

Whether you are using SQLite as an end user, or you are writing programs that use it, SQLite can be installed on Windows with a minimum of fuss. In this section, we will cover all the options—from installing the available binary packages to building everything from source using the most popular compilers. Let's start with the easy things first and progress to things more technically challenging.

Getting the Command-Line Program

The SQLite command-line program (hereafter referred to as the CLP) is by far the easiest way to get started using SQLite. Follow these steps to obtain the CLP:

1. Open your favorite browser and navigate to the SQLite home page: `www.sqlite.org`.

2. Click the download link on the top right of the page. This will take you to the download page.

3. Under the section *Precompiled Binaries For Windows*, there should be a file whose name is of the form `sqlite-3_x_y.zip`, where *x* and *y* are the minor version numbers. There should be a comment beside it that reads *A command-line program for accessing and modifying SQLite databases*. Download this file to a temporary folder.

4. Unzip the file. In Windows XP and Me, you can right-click on the file and a context menu should appear. Select Extract All from the menu. This will bring up the Windows Extraction Wizard. Follow the instructions and extract the file to a folder of your choosing. The wizard will then place a copy of the statically linked CLP in the specified folder. The file's name should be `sqlite3.exe`. If you have an older version of Windows, you may need to obtain a compression utility, such as WinZip (`www.winzip.com`), to unzip the file. To run the CLP from any directory in the Windows shell, you need to copy it to a folder that is in your Windows system path. A suitable default that should work on all versions of Windows is the `\windows\system32` folder on your root partition (`C:\` for most systems).

Note If you don't know what your Windows system path is, here is how to find it. Click Start ➤ Control Panel. (If you are using Windows XP, look at the Control Panel dialog box at the left side of the window. It will either say "Switch to Classic View" or "Switch to Category View." If you see the former, then click it. This will put the view into Classic View.) Double-click the System icon. In the resulting dialog box, select the Advanced tab and click the Environmental Variables button. In the System Variables list box, double-click the Path entry. This will open the Edit System Variables dialog box. The Values text box contains a long list of paths delimited by semicolons. All of the folders listed here are part of your system path. You can add an additional folder to this path if you like by simply appending a semicolon to the end of the line and typing the new path.

5. Open a command shell. You can do this different ways, depending on your version of Windows. Using the Windows Start menu, select Start ➤ Run. Type cmd in the Open drop-down box (or command if you are using a version of Windows 98/Me). Click OK (Figure 2-1). This will open a Windows command shell. If this doesn't work, try going to Start ➤ All Programs ➤ Accessories ➤ Command Prompt.

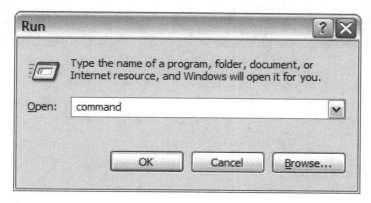

Figure 2-1. *Opening a Windows command shell*

6. Within the shell, type sqlite3 on the command line and press Enter. This should bring up a SQLite command prompt. (If you get an error, then the sqlite3.exe executable has not been copied to a folder in your system path. Recheck your path, and place a copy of the program somewhere within it.) When the SQLite shell appears, type .help on the command line. This will display a list of commands with their associated descriptions similar to the one in Figure 2-2. Type .exit to exit the program. You now have a working copy of the SQLite CLP installed on your system.

Figure 2-2. *The SQLite shell on Windows*

If you are especially eager to work with SQLite at this point, you may want to skip ahead to the section "The CLP in Shell Mode;" the next few sections are geared to developers who want to write programs that use SQLite.

Getting the SQLite DLL

The SQLite DLL is used for software that has been compiled to link dynamically to SQLite. Most software that uses SQLite in this fashion usually includes its own copy of the SQLite DLL and installs it automatically with the software.

If you are going to be programming with SQLite, using the DLL is probably the easiest way to start. The SQLite DLL can be obtained as follows:

1. Go to the SQLite home page, www.sqlite.com. On the upper right of the page, click the download link. This will take you to the download page.

2. On the download page, find the section *Precompiled Binaries For Windows*.

3. Locate the DLL zip file. This file will have the description *This is a DLL of the SQLite library without the TCL bindings*. The filename will have the form sqlitedll-3_x_y.zip, where *x* and *y* are the minor versions. If you want Tcl support included, select the file with the name of the form tclsqlitedll-3_x_y.zip.

4. Download and unzip the file. The extracted contents should include two files: the actual DLL file (sqlite3.dll) accompanied by another file called sqlite3.def. The SQLite DLL provided here is thread safe. That is, it was compiled with the THREADSAFE preprocessor flag defined. You can therefore use this DLL in multithreaded programs.

In order to use the DLL, it needs to be either in the same folder with programs that use it or placed somewhere in the system's path (see the note on the Windows System path in the previous section).

If you want to write programs that use the SQLite DLL, you will need to create an import library with which to link your programs. This is quite simple to do using the sqlite3.def mentioned earlier. If you are using Microsoft Visual C++, open a shell, change the directory to the SQLite distribution, and simply run the command

```
LIB /DEF:sqlite3.def
```

If you are using MinGW (see the section "Building SQLite with MinGW" later in this chapter), run the command

```
dlltool --def sqlite3.def --dllname sqlite3.dll --output-lib sqlite3.lib
```

Running either of these commands will create an import library called sqlite3.lib with which you can link your programs. By linking your programs to this import library, they will load and use the SQLite DLL upon execution.

Compiling the SQLite Source Code on Windows

Building SQLite from source within Windows is straightforward. Depending on the compiler you are using and what you are trying to achieve, there are several approaches to compiling SQLite. The most common scenarios on Windows include using either Microsoft Visual C++ or MinGW. Both are addressed here. Information on how to compile SQLite with other compilers can be found on the SQLite Wiki (www.sqlite.org/cvstrac/wiki?p=HowToCompile).

The Stable Source Distribution

Stable versions of SQLite's source code can be obtained in zip files from the SQLite website. Bleeding-edge versions can be obtained from anonymous CVS. Unless you are familiar with CVS, using the source distribution is the easiest way to go. To download a stable source distribution, follow these steps:

1. Go to the SQLite website, www.sqlite.org. Follow the download link, which will take you to the download page.

2. On the download page, find the Source Code section.

3. The first two files should be zip files containing the source code for Windows. The file you want to download should have a name with the form sqlite-source-3-*x_y*.zip, where *x* and *y* are the minor version numbers. The important thing here is that you want sqlite-source-3-*x_y*.zip, which corresponds to SQLite version 3, not sqlite-source2-*x_y*.zip, which corresponds to SQLite version 2.

Note The Windows zip archive and the other (POSIX) tarballs on the download page differ slightly in their contents. While they contain identical source code, the SQLite distribution uses some POSIX build tools (sed, awk, etc.) to dynamically generate some C source code in the build process. These build tools are not available by default on Windows systems. Therefore, the Windows source archive includes all of the preprocessing and generated code as a matter of convenience to Windows users who lack the build support infrastructure of Unix. This is why Windows users should use the zip archives rather than the POSIX tarballs on the download page. It is still possible to build the tarballs on Windows, but you need the requisite POSIX build tools (which are included in the MSYS/MinGW distributions covered in a moment).

---

4. Extract/unzip the file to a directory of your choosing. The extracted contents will be the complete SQLite version 3 source code for Windows.

Anonymous CVS

If you want to play with the latest features or participate in SQLite development, then retrieving SQLite from anonymous CVS makes the most sense. Anonymous CVS provides read access to the CVS repository—you can check out the code but you cannot commit any changes you may make in your local copy back to the repository. CVS allows you to maintain the absolutely latest version of the SQLite source code. If you want, you can keep your copy of the code synced up to the day, hour, or minute to stay current with changes as they are committed. Thus, if you see an important bug fix or feature posted that you want to take advantage of, all you need to do is perform a CVS update and recompile your copy of the code. Also note that the version in CVS corresponds to that found in the POSIX tarballs: it still requires the code-generation and preprocessing steps before the code can be built under Windows. You must therefore have the requisite POSIX build tools mentioned in the previous note in order to build SQLite from CVS on Windows.

Obtaining SQLite from CVS on Windows is perhaps easiest by using WinCVS. WinCVS (shown in Figure 2-3) is a well-written graphical application that makes working with CVS repositories easy and intuitive. WinCVS can be obtained at www.wincvs.org.

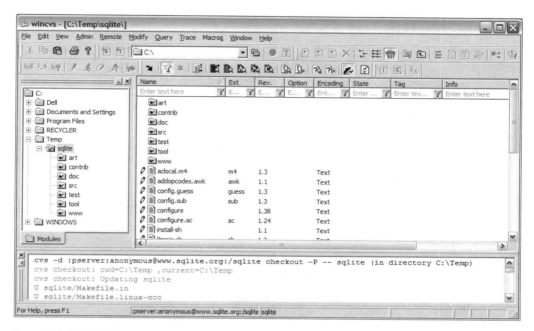

Figure 2-3. *WinCVS*

Once it's installed, you can configure WinCVS to connect to SQLite's CVS repository as follows:

1. Create a folder in which to check out the SQLite source code (e.g., C:\Temp).

2. Open WinCVS. On the left pane, navigate to the folder you created.

3. From the main menu, select Admin ➤ Login. In the CVSROOT text box, type :pserver:anonymous@www.sqlite.org:/sqlite, and click OK. This will bring up a dialog box requesting the home folder. Use the folder you created earlier (C:\Temp in this example). Next a password dialog box will appear. For the password, enter "anonymous", and click OK. If you log in successfully, then the output pane will display the following:

```
cvs -d :pserver:anonymous@www.sqlite.org:/sqlite login
Logging in to :pserver:anonymous@www.sqlite.org:2401:/sqlite

***** CVS exited normally with code 0 *****
```

4. In the main menu, select Remote ➤ Checkout Module (Figure 2-4). In the Module Name And Path On Server box, type sqlite. In the CVSROOT box, type :pserver:anonymous@www.sqlite.org:/sqlite.

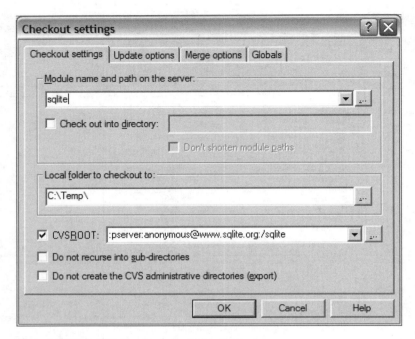

Figure 2-4. *WinCVS Checkout Settings dialog box*

5. Note that the Local Folder To Checkout To text box should already contain the path to the folder you created to store the source code. Click OK. You should see a long list of files appear in the output pane, the first part of which looks like this:

```
cvs -d :pserver:anonymous@www.sqlite.org:/sqlite checkout -P sqlite (in
directory C:\Temp\sqlite)
cvs checkout: cwd=C:\Temp\sqlite ,current=C:\Temp\sqlite
cvs checkout: Updating sqlite
U sqlite/Makefile.in
U sqlite/Makefile.linux-gcc
U sqlite/README
U sqlite/VERSION
U sqlite/aclocal.m4
```

Once completed, the latest version of SQLite should be checked out in your local SQLite folder.

Building the SQLite DLL with Microsoft Visual C++

To build the SQLite DLL from source using Visual C++, follow these steps:

1. Start Visual Studio. Create a new DLL project within the unpacked SQLite source directory. Do this by going to File ➤ New ➤ Project. Under Project Types (Figure 2-5), select Visual C++ Projects, and then select Win32. Choose the Win32 Project template. In the Location text box, enter the folder name that contains your SQLite source folder. In this example, it would be C:\Temp. In the Name text box, enter the name of the folder containing the SQLite source code—sqlite in this example. This will create the Visual C++ project inside the existing SQLite source folder (C:\Temp\sqlite). Click OK.

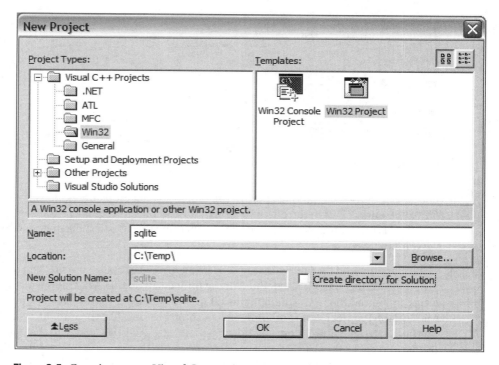

Figure 2-5. *Creating a new Visual C++ project*

2. Next, the Win 32 Application Wizard will automatically open (Figure 2-6). Choose Application Settings and set the application type to DLL. Be sure to check the Empty Project box. Click Finish, and this will create a blank DLL project.

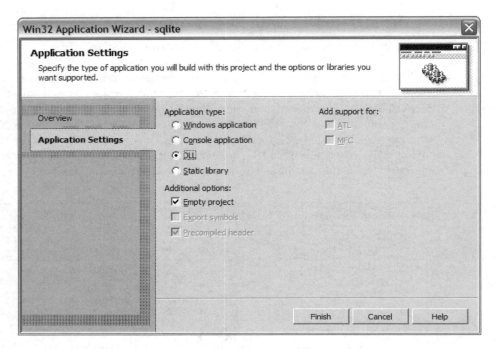

Figure 2-6. *The Win32 Application Wizard*

3. Add SQLite source files and headers to the project. Select Project ➤ Add Existing Item. Add all .c and .h files in the directory except for two files: tclsqlite.c and shell.c. (The first is for Tcl support; the second is for creating the SQLite shell, neither of which we want in this case.)

4. If you want to build the DLL with thread safety, you need to make sure that you have the preprocessor flag THREADSAFE defined in the project. To do this, select Project ➤ Properties and under the C/C++ item in the left tree view, select Preprocessor (Figure 2-7). Click on the Preprocessor Definitions cell. A small button will appear to the right. Click this button to open the dialog box shown in Figure 2-8. Add THREADSAFE to the bottom of the list and click OK. Also, you will need to make sure that you use the multithreaded Microsoft C runtime library DLL. Specify this by selecting the Code Generation item (Figure 2-7) and under Runtime Library select Multi-threaded Debug (/MTd).

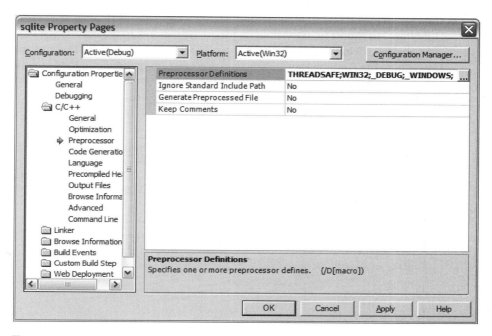

Figure 2-7. *Preprocessor project settings*

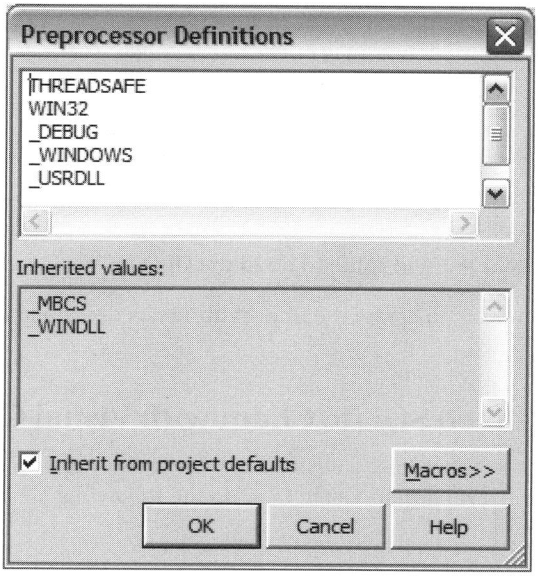

Figure 2-8. *Preprocessor definitions*

5. Specify an export or a module definition (.def) file. This file defines what symbols (or functions) to export (make visible) to programs that link to the library. SQLite's source distribution is kind enough to include such a file (sqlite3.def) for this very purpose. Also within the Property Pages dialog box, select All Configurations in the Configuration drop-down box (Figure 2-9). Then click the Linker folder and click the Input submenu. In the Module Definition File property page, type sqlite3.def. You are now ready to build the DLL.

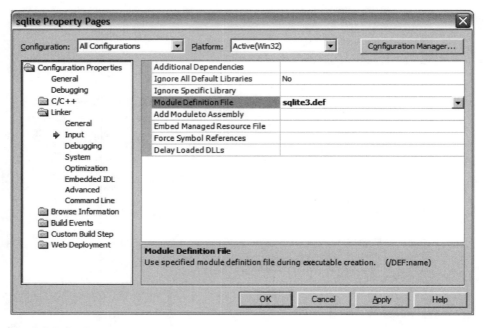

Figure 2-9. *Project properties*

6. From the main menu, select Build ➤ Build sqlite to build the DLL.

7. Once you have built the DLL, be sure to create the import library as described in the section "Getting the SQLite DLL."

Building a Dynamically Linked SQLite Client with Visual C++

The binary for a static CLP is available on the SQLite website, but what if you want a version that uses the SQLite DLL? To build such a version in Visual C++, do the following:

■**Note** Many of the steps are very similar to the process of building a DLL, mentioned earlier—you may want to use some of the figures listed there for reference.

---

1. From the main menu, select File ➤ New ➤ Project. Under Project Types, select Visual C++ Projects, and then select Win32. Choose the Win32 Project template. Name the project (shell, for example) and click OK.

2. After this, the Win 32 Application Wizard will automatically open. Choose Application Settings and set the application type to Console Application, and be sure to check the Empty Project box. Click Finish to create a blank executable project.

3. Next you want to add the SQLite shell source file. Select Project ➤ Add Existing Item. In the dialog box that appears, add the source file shell.c.

4. Tell Visual C++ to link against the SQLite DLL. Select Project ➤ Properties. In the dialog box that appears, select All Configurations in the Configuration drop-down box. Next select the Linker folder. Select the Input submenu and within the Additional Dependencies property page, add sqlite3.lib. You are now ready to build the program. Note that the SQLite DLL needs to be either in the same directory as the command-line program or in the Windows system path.

■**Note** If you build the SQLite DLL with threading enabled or you obtain the DLL from the SQLite website, you need to use the multithreaded Microsoft C runtime library DLL when building the CLP. To do this, refer to the second half of step 4 in "Building the SQLite DLL with Microsoft Visual C++." It contains two informative figures that make it easy to set this option.

Building SQLite with MinGW

MinGW (www.mingw.org) is a very nice distribution of the GNU Compiler Collection (GCC) for Windows. It also includes freely available Windows-specific header files and libraries that you can use to create native Windows programs that do not rely on any third-party C runtime DLLs. Put simply, it is a free C/C++ compiler for Windows, and a very good one at that. It is usually used in conjunction with MSYS, which is a portable POSIX environment that makes Unix users feel at home on Windows. Together, the two provide a powerful environment with which to compile and build software on Windows. With this build environment, you can build both the tarball archives as well as the source directly from CVS.

To build the SQLite DLL from source with MinGW, do the following:

1. Open your favorite browser and navigate to the MinGW website: www.mingw.org.

2. On the left side of the page, click the Download link, which will take you to the main download page.

3. On the download page, look for the FileList section. There will be a link to SF File Releases page, which at the time of this writing is located above the long listing of files. Follow that link. It will take you to the SourceForge download page for MinGW. Scroll down to the MinGW section and download the latest release (MinGW-5.0.2.exe at the time of this writing).

4. After downloading the file, click Back a few times to return to the initial SourceForge download page. Look for the MSYS section and download the current version (MSYS-1.0.11-2004.04.30.exe at the time of this writing).

5. Install MinGW, followed by MSYS. The MinGW installer will prompt you for a mirror site. Choose the one that is closest to you. In the next dialog box (the Choose Components dialog box shown in Figure 2-10), make sure you also select the second option—g++ compiler—in addition to the default (if you forget you can always rerun the MinGW installer and select this component). Select the defaults for all other screens. Double-click the respective files, which will invoke installers for each package. Follow the directions provided by the installers.

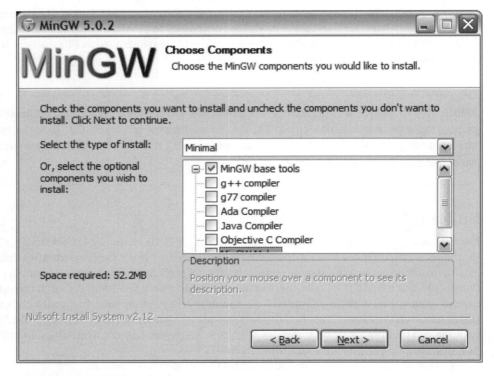

Figure 2-10. *MinGW installation components*

6. Download the Linux/Unix SQLite source code distribution. Navigate to www.sqlite.org and click on the download link. On the download page, find the Source Code section. The file you are looking for is the POSIX source distribution and should have a name of the form sqlite-3.*x*.*y*.tar.gz, where *x* and *y* are the minor version numbers (at the time of this writing, the current filename is sqlite-3.3.4.tar.gz). In Unix parlance, this kind of source archive is called a *tarball* (akin to a Windows zip file). Download the tarball and place it in a temporary directory (e.g., C:\Temp).

7. MSYS will have placed an icon on your desktop. Double-click that icon to open the environment.

8. Navigate to your temporary directory in which you downloaded the SQLite source distribution. Since this is a Unix-like environment, you will need to use Unix file system conventions. For example, to get to c:\Temp, you would type cd /c/Temp.

9. Unpack the SQLite tarball. Issue this command:

   ```
   tar -xzvf sqlite-3.3.4.tar.gz
   ```

10. Move into the unpacked directory:

    ```
    cd sqlite-3.3.4
    ```

11. Create the Makefile. For a single-threaded DLL, run

    ```
    ./configure
    ```

12. If you want to create a multithreaded DLL, run

    ```
    ./configure --enable-threads
    ```

13. Build the source:

    ```
    make
    ```

14. Create the SQLite DLL:

    ```
    dllwrap --dllname sqlite3.dll --def sqlite3.def *.o
    ```

15. Create the import library:

    ```
    dlltool --def sqlite3.def --dllname sqlite3.dll --output-lib sqlite3.lib
    ```

You now have a functional SQLite DLL and import library. To build a version of the SQLite CLP that links against the SQLite DLL you just created, within the MSYS environment run the command

```
gcc -I . src/shell.c -o sqlite3.exe sqlite3.lib
```

Now from Windows Explorer, navigate to the temporary folder and double-click on sqlite3.exe. You now have a working SQLite CLP, which uses the SQLite DLL you created.

SQLite on POSIX Systems

SQLite compiles and builds identically on POSIX systems such as Linux, Mac OS X, FreeBSD, NetBSD, OpenBSD, Solaris, and others. SQLite binaries can be obtained in a variety of ways depending on the particular operating system.

Binaries and Packages

If you are using Mac OS 10.4 ("Tiger") or greater, you already have SQLite installed on your system. If not, there are several routes you can take to install it. The easiest way is to use one of the following Mac-specific package management systems, all of which include packages or ports for SQLite:

- **Metadistribution.** Metadistribution is a Gentoo-based package management system based on Gentoo's Portage. All packages are fetched from the Internet and built from source using a single command, `emerge`. You can find the Mac version at `www.metadistribution/macos/`.

- **Fink.** Fink is a Debian-based package management system that uses Debian utilities such as `dpkg`, `dselect`, and `apt-get`, in addition to its own utility—`fink`. You can download Fink from `http://fink.sourceforge.net`. With Fink, it is possible to install straight from precompiled binaries. No compilation step is needed.

- **Darwin Ports.** Darwin Ports is a package system written in Tcl, which like Metadistribution, installs from source. More information can be obtained from `http://darwinports.opendarwin.org`.

BSD users will have no trouble installing SQLite either. FreeBSD, OpenBSD, and NetBSD all have packages and/or ports for SQLite, all of which are very easy to install. As I write this, each distribution has ports for very recent versions of SQLite 3.*x*.

Solaris 10 uses SQLite as part of the OS; however at the time of this writing it uses version SQLite 2.*x*. An easy way to install SQLite in Solaris (and other open source software as well) is to use Blastwave's `pkg-get` utility. Blastwave is a Debian-based package management system for Solaris that makes installing free software on Solaris simple. You can get more information on Blastwave from `www.blastwave.org`.

As mentioned earlier, binaries for Linux are available directly from the SQLite website. The download page on SQLite's website provides the following binaries:

- **Statically linked command-line program.** The filename is of the form `sqlite3-3.x.y.bin.gz`, where *x* and *y* are the minor version numbers.

- **Shared library.** Two forms of the shared library exist. One form includes the Tcl bindings; the other does not. The name of the shared library with Tcl bindings has the form `tclsqlite-3.3.x.y.so.gz`, where again *x* and *y* are the minor version numbers. The name of the shared library without Tcl bindings is of the form `sqlite-3.x.y.so.gz`. Note that the shared libraries provided are not thread safe. If you need a thread-safe version, you will have to compile the library from source. See the section "Compiling SQLite from Source" for more details.

- **SQLite Analyzer.** This is a command-line program that provides detailed information about the contents of a SQLite database. You'll find information on this program in the section "Getting Database File Information."

Various RPM-based Linux distributions may include RPMs for SQLite, but may not include the most recent versions. Fedora and Mandriva don't appear to include RPMs for SQLite at all. Perhaps the best way to find the most recent versions of SQLite in RPM form is to consult the Internet. RPM PBone Search (`http://rpm.pbone.net`) and RPMFind (`http://rpmfind.net`) are two good places to start.

Debian-based distributions will have no trouble getting up-to-date versions of SQLite. SQLite 3 packages are available online in both Ubuntu and Debian repositories, among others.

Compiling SQLite from Source

Compiling SQLite from source on POSIX systems follows very closely the MinGW instructions given earlier for the Windows platform (actually it is more the other way around; MinGW installation apes Linux source installation!). To build SQLite on POSIX systems, you need to ensure that you have the GNU Compiler Collection (GCC) installed, including Autoconf, Automake, and Libtool. Most of the systems already discussed include all of these by default. With this software in place, you can build SQLite by doing the following:

1. Download the Linux/Unix SQLite tarball (source code) from the SQLite website. At the time of this writing, the current version is `sqlite-3.3.4.tar.gz`. Place it in a directory (e.g., `/tmp`).

2. Navigate to your build directory:

   ```
   cd /tmp
   ```

3. Unpack the SQLite tarball:

   ```
   tar -xzvf sqlite-3.3.4.tar.gz
   ```

4. Move into the unpacked directory:

   ```
   cd sqlite-3.3.4
   ```

5. Create the Makefile:

   ```
   ./configure
   ```

6. If you want to create a multithreaded shared library, run

   ```
   ./configure --enable-threads
   ```

7. Other options, such as the installation directory, are also available. For a complete list of configure options, run

   ```
   ./configure --help
   ```

8. Build the source:

   ```
   make
   ```

9. As root, install:

   ```
   make install
   ```

You now have a functional SQLite installation on your system that includes both the SQLite shared library and a dynamically linked CLP (which uses the SQLite shared library). If you have GNU Readline installed on you system, the CLP should be compiled with Readline support. Test it out by running it from the command line:

```
root@linux # sqlite3
```

This will invoke the CLP using an in-memory database. Type `.help` for a list of shell commands. Type `.exit` to close the application, or press Ctrl+D.

Working with SQLite Databases

The SQLite CLP is the most common means you can use to work with and manage SQLite databases. It runs on as many platforms as the SQLite library, so learning how to use it ensures you will always have a common and familiar way to manage your databases. The CLP is really two programs in one. It can run from the command line to perform various administration tasks, or it can be run in shell mode and act as an interactive query processor.

The CLP in Shell Mode

Open a shell and change directory to some temporary folder—say C:\Temp if you are on Windows or /tmp if you're in Unix. This will be your current working directory. All files you create in the course of working with the shell will be created in this directory.

■**Note** To get a command line on Windows, go to Start ➤ Programs ➤ Accessories ➤ Command Prompt.

To invoke the CLP as in shell mode, type sqlite3 from a command line, followed by an optional database name. If you do not specify a database name, SQLite will use an in-memory database (the contents of which will be lost when the CLP exits).

Using the CLP as an interactive shell, you can issue queries, obtain schema information, import and export data, and perform other miscellaneous database tasks. The shell will consider any statement issued as a query, except for commands that begin with a period (.). These commands are reserved for specific shell operations, a complete list of which can be obtained by typing .help as shown:

```
mike@linux tmp $ sqlite3
SQLite version 3.3.4
Enter ".help" for instructions
sqlite> .h
```

```
.databases              List names and files of attached databases
.dump ?TABLE? ...       Dump the database in a SQL text format
.echo ON|OFF            Turn command echo on or off
.exit                   Exit this program
.explain ON|OFF         Turn output mode suitable for EXPLAIN on or off.
.header(s) ON|OFF       Turn display of headers on or off
.help                   Show this message
.import FILE TABLE      Import data from FILE into TABLE
.indices TABLE          Show names of all indices on TABLE
.mode MODE ?TABLE?      Set output mode where MODE is one of:
                          csv       Comma-separated values
                          column    Left-aligned columns.  (See .width)
                          html      HTML <table> code
                          insert    SQL insert statements for TABLE
```

```
                          line    One value per line
                          list    Values delimited by .separator string
                          tabs    Tab-separated values
                          tcl     TCL list elements
.nullvalue STRING         Print STRING in place of NULL values
.output FILENAME          Send output to FILENAME
.output stdout            Send output to the screen
.prompt MAIN CONTINUE     Replace the standard prompts
.quit                     Exit this program
.read FILENAME            Execute SQL in FILENAME
.schema ?TABLE?           Show the CREATE statements
.separator STRING         Change separator used by output mode and .import
.show                     Show the current values for various settings
.tables ?PATTERN?         List names of tables matching a LIKE pattern
.timeout MS               Try opening locked tables for MS milliseconds
.width NUM NUM ...        Set column widths for "column" mode
```

```
sqlite>.exit
```

You can just as easily type .h for short. Many of the commands can be similarly abbreviated, such as .e—short for .exit—to exit the shell.

Let's start by creating a database that we will call test.db. From the command line, open the CLP in shell mode by typing the following:

```
sqlite3 test.db
```

Even though we have provided a database name, SQLite does not actually create the database (yet) if it doesn't already exist. SQLite will defer creating the database until you actually create something inside it, such as a table or view. The reason for this is so that you have the opportunity to set various permanent database settings (such as page size) before the database structure is committed to disk. Some settings such as page size and character encoding (UTF-8, UTF-16, etc.) cannot be changed once the database is created, so this interim is where you have a chance to specify them. We will go with the default settings here, so to actually create the database on disk, we need only to create a table. Issue the following statement from the shell:

```
sqlite> create table test (id integer primary key, value text);
```

Now you have a database file on disk called test.db, which contains one table called test. This table, as you can see, has two columns:

- A primary key column called id, which has an autoincrement attribute. Wherever you define a column of type integer primary key, SQLite will apply an autoincrement function for the column. That is, if no value is provided for the column in an INSERT statement, SQLite will automatically generate one by finding the next integer value specific to that column.

- A simple text field called value.

Let's add a few rows to the table:

```
sqlite> insert into test (value) values('eenie');
sqlite> insert into test (value) values('meenie');
sqlite> insert into test (value) values('miny');
sqlite> insert into test (value) values('mo');
```

Now fetch them back:

```
sqlite> .mode col
sqlite> .headers on
sqlite> SELECT * FROM test;
```

```
id          value
----------  ----------
1           eenie
2           meenie
3           miny
4           mo
```

The two commands preceding the SELECT statement (.headers and .mode) are used to improve the formatting a little (both of which are covered later). We can see that SQLite provided sequential integer values for the id column, which we did not provide in the INSERT statements. While on the topic of autoincrement columns, you might be interested to know that the value of the last inserted autoincrement value can be obtained using the SQL function last_insert_rowid():

```
sqlite> select last_insert_rowid();
```

```
last_insert_rowid()
-------------------
4
```

Before we quit, let's add an index and a view to the database. These will come in handy in the illustrations that follow:

```
sqlite> create index test_idx on test (value);
sqlite> create view schema as select * from sqlite_master;
```

To exit the shell, issue the .exit command:

```
sqlite> .exit
C:\Temp>
```

On Windows, you can also terminate the shell by using the key sequence Ctrl+C. On Unix, you can use Ctrl+D.

Getting Database Schema Information

There are several shell commands for obtaining information about the contents of a database. You can retrieve a list of tables (and views) using .tables [pattern], where [pattern] can be any pattern that the SQL LIKE operator understands (we cover LIKE in Chapter 4 if you are unfamiliar with it). All tables and views matching the given pattern will be returned. If no pattern is supplied, all tables and views are returned:

```
sqlite> .tables
```

```
schema test
```

Here we see our table named test and our view named schema. Similarly, indexes for a given table can be printed using .indices [table name]:

```
sqlite> .indices test
```

```
test_idx
```

Here we see the index we created earlier on test, called test_idx. The SQL definition or data definition language (DDL) for a table or view can be obtained using .schema [table name]. If no table name is provided, the SQL definitions of all database objects (tables, indexes, views, and indexes) are returned:

```
sqlite> .schema test
```

```
CREATE TABLE test (id integer primary key, value text);
CREATE INDEX test_idx on test (value);
```

```
sqlite> .schema
```

```
CREATE TABLE test (id integer primary key, value text);
CREATE VIEW schema as select * from sqlite_master;
CREATE INDEX test_idx on test (value);
```

More detailed schema information can be had from SQLite's one and only system view, sqlite_master. This view is a simple system catalog of sorts. Its schema is described in Table 2-1. Querying sqlite_master for our current database returns the following (don't forget to use the .mode col and .headers on commands first to manually set the column format and headers):

Table 2-1. *SQLite Master Table Schema*

Name	Description
type	The object's type (table, index, view, trigger)
name	The object's name
tbl_name	The table the object is associated with
rootpage	The object's root page index in the database (where it begins)
sql	The object's SQL definition (DDL)

```
sqlite> .mode col
sqlite> .headers on
sqlite> select type, name, tbl_name, sql from sqlite_master order by type;
```

```
type        name        tbl_name    sql
----------  ----------  ----------  ------------------------------------
index       test_idx    test        CREATE INDEX test_idx on test (value)
table       test        test        CREATE TABLE test (id integer primary
view        schema      schema      CREATE VIEW schema as select * from s
```

We see a complete inventory of test.db contents: one table, one index, and one view, each with their respective SQL definitions.

There are few additional commands for obtaining schema information through SQLite's PRAGMA commands, table_info, index_info, and index_list, which are covered in Chapter 4.

■**Tip** Don't forget that most shells keep a history of the commands that you execute. To rerun a previous command, you can hit the Up Arrow key to scroll through your previous commands.

Exporting Data

You can export database objects to SQL format using the .dump command. Without any arguments, .dump will export the entire database. If you provide arguments, the shell interprets them as table names or views. Any tables or views matching the given arguments will be exported. Those that don't are simply ignored. In shell mode, the output from the .dump command is directed to the screen by default. If you want to redirect output to a file, use the .output [filename] command. This command redirects all output to the file filename. To restore output back to the screen, simply issue .output stdout. So, to export the current database to a file file.sql, you simply do the following:

```
sqlite> .output file.sql
sqlite> .dump
sqlite> .output stdout
```

This will create the file `file.sql` in your current working directory if it does not already exist. If a file by that name does exist, it will be overwritten.

By combining redirection with SQL and the various shell formatting options (covered later), you have a great deal of control over exporting data. You can export specific subsets of tables and views in various formats using the delimiter of your choice, which can later be imported using the `.import` command described next.

Importing Data

There are two ways to import data, depending on the format of the file to import. If the file is composed of SQL, you can use the `.read` command to import (execute) the file. If the file contains comma-separated values (CSV) or other delimited data, you can use the `.import [file][table]` command. This command will parse the specified file and attempt to insert it into the specified table. It does this by parsing each line in the file using the pipe character (|) as the delimiter and inserting the parsed columns into the table. Naturally, the number of parsed fields in the file should match up with the number of columns in the table. You can specify a different delimiter using the `.separator` command. To see the current value set for the separator, use the `.show` command. This will show all user-defined settings for the shell, among them the current default separator:

```
sqlite> .show
```

```
     echo: off
  explain: off
  headers: on
     mode: column
nullvalue: ""
   output: stdout
separator: "|"
    width:
```

The `.read` command is the way to import files created by the `.dump` command. Using `file.sql` created earlier as a backup, we can drop the existing database objects (the `test` table and `schema` view) and reimport it as follows:

```
sqlite> drop table test;
sqlite> drop view schema;
sqlite> .read file.csv
```

Formatting

The shell offers a number of formatting options. The simplest are `.echo`, which echoes the last run command after issuing a command, and `.headers`, which includes column names for queries when set to on. The text representation of null values can be set with `.nullvalue`. For instance, if you want null values to appear as NULL, simply issue the command `.nullvalue NULL`. By default, this value is an empty string. Also, the shell prompt can be changed using `.prompt [value]`:

```
sqlite> .prompt 'sqlite3> '
sqlite3>
```

Result data can be formatted several ways using the .mode command. The current options are csv, column, html, insert, line, list, tabs, and tcl, each of which is helpful in different ways. The default is .list. For instance, list mode displays results with the columns separated by the default separator. Thus, if you wanted to dump a table in a CSV format, you could do the following:

```
sqlite3> .output file.csv
sqlite3> .separator ,
sqlite3> select * from test;
sqlite3> .output stdout
```

The contents of file.csv are now

```
1,eenie
2,meenie
3,miny
4,mo
```

Actually, since there is a CSV mode already defined in the shell, it is just as easy to use it in this particular example instead:

```
sqlite3> .output file.csv
sqlite3> .mode csv
sqlite3> select * from test;
sqlite3> .output stdout
```

and obtain similar results. The difference is that CSV mode will wrap field values with double quotes, whereas list mode (the default) does not.

Putting It All Together

Combining the previous three sections on exporting, importing, and formatting data, we now have an easy way to export and import data in delimited form. For example, to export only the rows of the test table whose value fields start with the letter "m" to a file called test.csv in comma-separated values, do the following:

```
sqlite> .output text.csv
sqlite> .separator ,
sqlite> select * from test where value like 'm%';
sqlite> .output stdout
```

If you want to then import this CSV data into a similar table with the same structure as the test table (call it test2), do the following:

```
sqlite> create table test2(id integer primary key, value text);
sqlite> .import text.csv test2
```

The CLP, therefore, makes it easy to both import and export text-delimited data to and from the database.

The CLP in Command-Line Mode

The CLP can be used from the command line for tasks such as importing and exporting data, returning result sets, and performing general batch processing. It is ideal for use in shell scripts for automated database administration. To see what the CLP offers in command-line mode, invoke it from the shell (Windows or Unix) with the –help switch, as shown here:

```
mike@linux tmp $ sqlite3 -help
```

```
Usage: sqlite3 [OPTIONS] FILENAME [SQL]
Options are:
   -init filename        read/process named file
   -echo                 print commands before execution
   -[no]header           turn headers on or off
   -column               set output mode to 'column'
   -html                 set output mode to HTML
   -line                 set output mode to 'line'
   -list                 set output mode to 'list'
   -separator 'x'        set output field separator (|)
   -nullvalue 'text'     set text string for NULL values
   -version              show SQLite version
   -help                 show this text, also show dot-commands
```

The CLP in command-line mode takes the following arguments:

- A list of options (optional)

- A database filename (required)

- A SQL command to execute (optional)

Most of the options control output formatting except for the init switch, which specifies a batch file of SQL commands to process. The database filename is required. The SQL command is optional with a few caveats.

There are actually two ways to invoke the CLP in command-line mode. The first is to provide a SQL command. However, "SQL command" is somewhat misleading as you can provide SQLite shell commands as well, such as .dump and .schema. Any valid SQL or SQLite shell command will do. When it's provided, SQLite will simply execute the specified command, print the result to standard output, and exit. For example, to dump the test.db database from the command line, issue the command

```
sqlite3 test.db .dump
```

To make it useful, we should redirect the output to a file:

```
sqlite3 test.db .dump > test.sql
```

The file test.sql now contains the complete human-readable (SQL) representation of test.db. Similarly, to select all records for the test table, issue

```
sqlite3 test.db "select * from test"
```

The second way to invoke the CLP in command-line mode is to redirect a file as an input stream. For instance, to create a new database test2.db from our database dump test.sql, do the following:

```
sqlite3 test2.db < test.sql
```

The CLP will read the file as standard input, then process and apply all SQL commands within it to the test2.db database file.

So, in order for command-line mode to be invoked, either a SQL command or an input stream must be provided to the CLP. To further illustrate this, yet another way to create a database from the test.sql file is to use the init option and provide the test.sql as an argument:

```
sqlite3 -init test.sql test3.db
```

The CLP will process test.sql, create the test3.db database, and then go into shell mode. Why? The invocation included no SQL command or input stream. To get around this, you need to provide a SQL command. For example:

```
sqlite3 -init test.sql test3.db .exit
```

The .exit command prompts the CLP to run in command-line mode and does as little as possible. All things considered, redirection is perhaps the easiest method for processing files from the command line.

Database Administration

All database administration tasks can be performed within the shell and on the command line. Typically, the command line is easier to use for many general administration tasks, but it is really a matter of taste. Many of the common database administration tasks have been touched upon through the examples provided thus far. For the sake of completeness, I will nevertheless list the most common tasks along with the typical ways of performing them.

Creating, Backing Up, and Dropping Databases

Backing up a database can be done in two ways, depending on the type of backup you desire. A SQL dump is perhaps the most portable form for keeping backups. The standard way to generate one is using the CLP .dump command. From the command line, this is done as follows:

```
sqlite3 test.db .dump > test.sql
```

Within the shell, you can redirect output to an external file, issue the command, and restore output to the screen as follows:

```
sqlite> .output file.sql
sqlite> .dump
sqlite> .exit
```

Likewise, importing a database is most easily done by providing the SQL dump as an input stream to the CLP:

```
sqlite3 test.db < test.sql
```

This assumes that test.db does not already exist. If it does, then things may still work if the contents of test.sql are different from those of test.db. You will of course get errors if test.sql contains objects that already reside within test.db.

Making a binary backup of a database is little more than a file copy. One small operation you may want to perform beforehand is a database vacuum, which will free up any unused space created from deleted objects. This will provide you with a more compact binary copy:

```
sqlite3 test.db VACUUM
cp test.db test.backup
```

As a general rule, binary backups are not as portable as SQL backups. On the whole, SQLite does have good backward compatibility and is binary compatible across all platforms for a given database format. However, for long-term backups, it is always a good idea to use SQL form. If size is an issue, SQL format (raw text) usually yields a good compression ratio.

Finally, if you've worked with other databases, "dropping" a database in SQLite, like binary backups, is a simple file operation: you simply delete the database file you wish to drop.

Getting Database File Information

As mentioned earlier, the primary means by which to obtain database information is using the sqlite_master view, which provides detailed information about all objects contained in a given database.

If you want information on the physical database structure, you can use a tool called SQLite Analyzer, which can be downloaded in binary form from the SQLite website. SQLite Analyzer provides detailed technical information about the on-disk structure of a SQLite database. This information includes a detailed breakdown of database, table, and index statistics for individual objects and in aggregate. It provides everything from database properties such as page size, number of tables, indexes, file size, and average page density (utilization) to detailed descriptions of individual database objects. Following the report is a detailed list of definitions explaining all terms used within the report. A partial output of sqlite_analyzer is as follows:

```
mike@linux tmp $ sqlite3_analyzer test.db
```

```
/** Disk-Space Utilization Report For test.db
*** As of 2005-May-07 20:26:23

Page size in bytes................... 1024
Pages in the whole file (measured).... 3
Pages in the whole file (calculated).. 3
Pages that store data................. 3          100.0%
Pages on the freelist (per header).... 0            0.0%
Pages on the freelist (calculated).... 0            0.0%
Pages of auto-vacuum overhead......... 0            0.0%
Number of tables in the database...... 2
Number of indices.................... 1
Number of named indices.............. 1
Automatically generated indices....... 0
Size of the file in bytes............ 3072
Bytes of user payload stored......... 26           0.85%
```

```
*** Page counts for all tables with their indices ********************

    TEST................................. 2        66.7%
    SQLITE_MASTER........................ 1        33.3%

*** All tables and indices *******************************************

Percentage of total database.......... 100.0%
Number of entries..................... 11
Bytes of storage consumed............. 3072
Bytes of payload...................... 235           7.6%
Average payload per entry............. 21.36
Average unused bytes per entry........ 243.00
Maximum payload per entry............. 72
Entries that use overflow............. 0             0.0%
Primary pages used.................... 3
Overflow pages used................... 0
Total pages used...................... 3
Unused bytes on primary pages......... 2673          87.0%
Unused bytes on overflow pages........ 0
Unused bytes on all pages............. 2673          87.0%

*** Table TEST and all its indices **********************************

Percentage of total database..........  66.7%
Number of entries..................... 8
Bytes of storage consumed............. 2048
Bytes of payload...................... 60            2.9%
Average payload per entry............. 7.50
Average unused bytes per entry........ 243.00
Maximum payload per entry............. 10
Entries that use overflow............. 0             0.0%
Primary pages used.................... 2
Overflow pages used................... 0
Total pages used...................... 2
Unused bytes on primary pages......... 1944          94.9%
Unused bytes on overflow pages........ 0
Unused bytes on all pages............. 1944          94.9%
```

SQLite Analyzer is provided in binary form on the SQLite website for Linux and Windows. On POSIX platforms, or with MinGW, SQLite Analyzer can be built from the source using the Unix makefile provided. From the build directory, issue the command

```
make sqlite3_analyzer
```

You must, however, have Tcl support configured in the build settings as SQLite Analyzer uses the Tcl extension to perform most of its work. Refer to "Compiling SQLite from Source" for more information.

Other SQLite Tools

There are many other open source and commercial programs available with which to work
with SQLite. Good graphical, cross-platform tools include

- SQLite Database Browser (http://sqlitebrowser.sourceforge.net) is a program developed with Qt. With it users can manage databases, tables, and indexes, as well as import
  and export them. Users can interactively run SQL queries and inspect the results, as well
  as examine a log of all SQL commands issued. Users can also browse tables and modify
  their records.

- SQLite Control Center (http://bobmanc.home.comcast.net/sqlitecc.html) is a cross-
  platform program that uses the wxWindows C++ GUI framework. It does many of the
  same things as SQLite Database Browser, including general management of databases,
  tables, indexes, and triggers. Likewise, it also allows users to edit table data in a grid
  display and construct queries using a syntax-highlighting text editor.

- SQLiteManager (www.sqlabs.net/sqlitemanager.php) is a commercial software package
  designed for working with and administering SQLite. Users can manage database objects,
  execute queries, and save SQL, as well as create reports with flexible report templates.

These are just the cross-platform tools. Many more tools are available that can be used with
PHP and other specific environments. You can find more information on such packages on the
SQLite Wiki (www.sqlite.org/cvstrac/wiki?p=SqliteTools).

Summary

No matter what platform you work on, SQLite is quite easy to install and build. Windows and
Linux users can obtain binaries directly from the SQLite website. Users of many other operating
systems can also obtain binaries using their native—or even third-party—package systems.

The common way to work with SQLite across all platforms is using the SQLite command-
line program (CLP). This program operates as both a command-line tool and an interactive
shell. You can issue queries and do essential database administration tasks such as creating
tables, indexes, and views as well as exporting and importing data. SQLite databases are contained
in single operating system files, so doing things like binary backups are very simple—just copy
the file. For long-term backups, however, it is always best to dump the database in SQL format,
as this is portable across SQLite versions.

In the next few chapters, you will be using the CLP to explore SQL and the database aspects
of SQLite. The next chapter provides a great deal of background to SQL. It is almost entirely
theoretical. However, if you have previously used relational databases and SQL, you may find
it very informative. It provides not only the basic theory underlying SQL but also a good bit of
history as well. If you don't care for theory and want to dive right in, you may want to skip
ahead to Chapter 4, where you will be able to put the CLP to immediate use.

The Relational Model

$\mathbf{S}$QL has a very practical exterior but a very theoretical interior. That interior is the relational model. The relational model came before SQL and created a need for SQL. The power of SQL lies not in the language itself but in the concepts set forth in the relational model. These concepts form the basis of SQL's design and operation.

The relational model is a powerful and elegant idea that has pervaded not only computer science but our daily lives as well, whether we know it or not. Like the automobile, or penicillin, it is one of the many great examples of human thought and discovery that has fundamentally impacted the way the world works. The relational model has spawned a billion-dollar industry, and has become an integral part of almost every other industry. You'll see the relational model at work nearly everywhere that deals with information of any kind—in Fortune 500 companies, universities, hospitals, grocery stores, websites, routers, MP3 players, cell phones, and even smart cards. It is truly pervasive.

Background

The relational model was born in 1969, inside of IBM. A researcher named E. F. Codd distributed an internal paper titled "Derivability, Redundancy, and Consistency of Relations Stored in Large Data Banks," which defined the basic theory of the relational model. This paper was circulated internally and not widely distributed. In 1970, Codd published a more refined version of this paper in *Communications of the ACM* called "A Relational Model for Large Shared Data Banks," which is more widely recognized as the seminal work on relational theory. This is the paper that changed the industry.

Despite the enormous influence of this paper, the relational model in its entirety did not appear overnight, or within the scope of a single historic paper. It evolved, grew, and expanded over time and was the product of many minds, not just Codd alone. For example, the term "relational model" wasn't coined until 1979, nine years after publication of the paper proposing it (see Date, 1999, in the References section). Codd's 12 rules, now famous as the working definition of relational, weren't posited until 1985, appearing in a two-part series published by *Computerworld* magazine. Thus, while there was a seminal paper proposing the general concept, much of the relational model as we know it today is actually the result of a series of papers, articles, and debates by many people over a 30-year period, and indeed continues to develop to this very day. That is also why in some of the various quotes included in this chapter you may see terms such as "data base," which may initially appear to be a typo. They aren't. At the time these statements were made, the terminology still had not congealed and all sorts of various terms were being thrown around.

The Three Components

By 1980, enough was known about the relational model for Codd to identify three principle components:

- **The structural component**: This component defines how information is structured, or represented. Specifically, all information is represented as *relations*, which are composed of *tuples*, which in turn are composed of *attribute* and *value* components. The relation is the sole data structure used to represent all information in the database. Relations as defined in the relational model are derived from relations in set theory, a branch of mathematics, and share many of their properties. They are formally defined in Codd's 1970 paper.

- **The integrity component**: This component defines methods that enforce relationships within and between relations (or tables) in the structural component. These methods are called *constraints*, and are expressed in the form of rules. There are three principle types of integrity: domain integrity, governing values in columns; entity integrity, governing rows in tables; and referential integrity, governing how tables relate to one another. Integrity has no analog in set theory, but rather is unique to relational theory. It was initially addressed in Codd's 1970 paper and greatly expanded upon in the 1980s by Codd and others.

- **The manipulative component**: This aspect defines the methods with which to operate on or manipulate information. Like relations, these operations also have their roots in mathematics. They are formalized in *relational algebra* and *relational calculus* as originally presented in Codd's 1972 paper "Relational Completeness of Data Base Sublanguages."

SQL, likewise, is structured similarly along these lines—so similarly, in fact, that it is hard to talk about SQL without addressing the relational model to some degree, directly or indirectly. It is true that SQL is for the most part a straightforward language, which to many people appears as an island unto itself. But in reality, it is the offspring of the relational model, and in many ways is clearly a reflection of it.

SQL and the Relational Model

This chapter presents the theoretical roots of SQL, and examines the power and elegance behind SQL. It prepares you to deal with SQL not in isolation but in the context of the relational model. If nothing else, it should give you an appreciation for how elegant, powerful, and complex a beast a relational database really is. You may be surprised by what even the most rudimentary relational databases are capable of.

You don't have to read this chapter in order to understand SQL; it merely provides a theoretical and historical backdrop. To this end, I present the theoretical aspects in terms of several influential papers and articles written by Codd between 1970 and 1985 that define the essence of the relational model, along with the ideas and work of other contributors to the field. Two of Codd's papers mentioned here are available online, and are listed in the References section at the end of the chapter. Again, others contributed to the development of the relational model, but this chapter will draw primarily from Codd's work.

This chapter is not an exhaustive treatment of the relational model, or a complete history of it. It is merely an appetizer. The SQL chapter that follows is the main course. This chapter presents only the minimal material needed to get an appreciation of the origin and theoretical underpinnings of SQL. We illustrate the relational model in terms of both its three components in general and in the context of Codd's 12 rules in particular. The relational model in its full splendor is far beyond the scope of this book, and I have neither the qualifications nor the stamina to fully describe it. See the References section at the end of this chapter if you want to learn more. The rules as they are presented here are taken directly from Codd's October 14, 1985, *Computerworld* article.

The Structural Component

The structural component of the relational model lays the foundation upon which the other components build. It defines the form in which information is represented. It is defined by the first of Codd's 12 rules, which is the cornerstone of the relational model.

The Information Principle

The first rule, called the *Information Rule*, is also known as the *Information Principle*. It is defined as follows:

> **1. The Information Rule.** *All information in a relational data base is represented explicitly at the logical level and in exactly one way—by values in tables.*

Date summarizes this rule as follows:

> *The entire information content of the database is represented in one and only one way, namely as explicit values in column positions in rows in tables.*

There are two import expressions here: "logical level" and "values in tables." The logic level, or logical representation, refers to the way that you, the user, see the database and information within it. It is a kind of ideal worldview for information. The logical level is a consistent, uniform depiction of data, which has two important properties:

- The view presented in the logical level consists of tables, made up of rows, which in turn are made up of values.

- The view is completely independent of the database system—the technology (software or hardware) that enables it.

The logical representation is a world unto itself, which is completely distinct from how the database is implemented, or how it stores data physically, or how it operates internally. These latter components—software, operating system, and hardware—are referred to as the *physical representation*—the technology of the system. If the database vendor decides to store database tables in a different way on disk, the Information Principle mandates that such a change in physical representation can in no way affect or change the logical representation of that data—the way in which you (or your programs) see that data. The logical representation is independent of physical representation. A result of the Information Principle is that it is possible to represent the same information in the same way across multiple database implementations on multiple operating systems on different hardware, as shown in Figure 3-1.

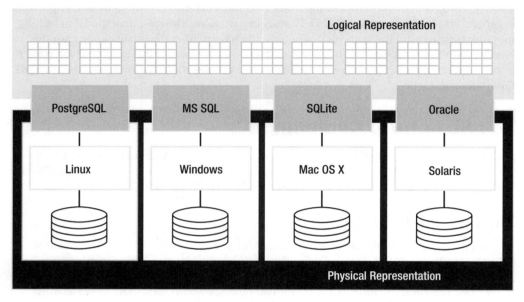

Figure 3-1. *Logical and physical representation*

You can create a relation (or table) in Oracle on Solaris that is represented in exactly the same way as a table in PostgreSQL on Linux, or SQLite on Mac OS X.[1] The Information Principle guarantees you a consistent logical view of information regardless of how the database software is implemented, or the operating system or hardware it runs on.

The Sanctity of the Logical Level

So important are these two constraints in the relational model that they are expanded upon and reinforced in several other rules (8, 9, 11, and 12) so as to eliminate any possible ambiguity. In short, Codd says:

> **8. Physical Data Independence.** *The logical view can in no way be impaired by the underlying software or hardware.*

> **9. Logical Data Independence.** *Application programs and terminal activities remain logically unimpaired when information-preserving changes of any kind that theoretically permit un-impairment are made to the base tables.*

---

1. In reality, this is not 100 percent true (it's more like 95 percent true). There are slight differences in database implementations so that relations in one database may contain features not present in other databases. Nevertheless, they still all adhere to the same general structure: relations made of tuples made of values.

11. Distribution Independence. *Even if the database is spread across various locations, it cannot impact the logical view of data.*

12. Nonsubversion Rule. *The database software may not provide any facility which can subvert the integrity constraints of the logical view.*

The separation of logical from physical was very important to Codd from the outset. In the opening of his original paper he had strong words concerning this separation:

> *Future users of large data banks must be protected from having to know how the data is organized in the machine (the internal representation)… Activities of users at terminals and most application programs should remain unaffected when the internal representation of data is changed and even when some aspects of the external representation are changed.*

The relational model was in part a reaction to the database systems of the day, which closely tied applications to both database implementation and data format on disk. Codd's relational model challenged this:

> *It provides a means of describing data with its natural structure only—that is, without superimposing any additional structure for machine representation purposes. Accordingly, it provides a basis for a high level data language which will yield maximal independence between programs on the one hand and machine representation and organization of data on the other.*

So in the relational model, the Information Principle provides a level of abstraction through which information can be represented in a consistent way. The user sees and works with data exclusively in terms of this logical representation. This representation is completely insulated from the underlying technology. It cannot be undermined, influenced, or affected by it in any way. As stated before, the Information Principle is the foundation of the relational model.

The Anatomy of the Logical Level

The logical level is made up of more than relations. It is made up of *tables, rows, columns,* and *types.* In relational parlance, these are often referred to more formally as *relation variables, tuples, values,* and *domains,* respectively. SQL, for example, uses many of the former, and relational theory tends to use many of the latter. Throughout the literature, however, you will see these terms used almost interchangeably. Even in Codd's papers, both sets of terms are used. Interestingly, there is one term that both lexicons have in common: *relations.* (In case you're wondering, tables and relations are not the same thing; we'll address the difference later in this chapter.)

This big soup of terminology comprises the anatomy of the relational body, which will be explained in detail over the next several sections. The relationships between all of these terms are illustrated in Figure 3-2.

At the center of everything is the relation. It is the central object around which the structural, integrity, and manipulative components of the relational model are built. All of the fundamental operations in the relational model are expressed in terms of relations, and all integrity constraints are defined within relations. Your understanding of the relational model is only as good as your understanding of relations themselves. To have a good grasp of relations, however, you must first understand tuples.

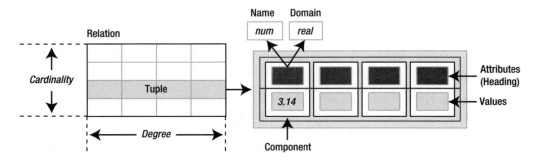

Figure 3-2. *The logical representation of data*

Tuples

A tuple is a set of *values*, each of which has an associated *attribute*. An attribute defines a value's *name* and *domain*. The attribute's name is used to identify the value in the tuple, and its domain defines the kind of information stored within it. The combination of attribute and value is called a *component*. In Figure 3-2, you can see that the first component is named *num*, and that it has a value of 3.14 and a domain of *real* (as in real numbers).

A component is kind of a tidy, self-contained unit of data. It has three essential ingredients: a name, a domain, and a value. Its name gives it identity, its domain a description of its content, and its value the content itself. Together, components aggregate into larger structures such as tables and relations, and their qualities propagate into those structures, imparting to them identity, description, and content as well.

The name and value parts of a component are easy enough to understand, but what exactly is a domain? The word *domain*, like the words *relation* and *tuple*, comes from mathematics. In mathematics, the domain of a function is the set of all values for which the function is defined. Some familiar domains in mathematics are the sets of all integers, rational numbers, real numbers, and complex numbers. Generally, the term *domain* corresponds to a set of permissible values. A domain is sometimes referred to as a *type*, and is synonymous to a data type in programming languages. A domain, especially in the relational sense, also implies a set of operators that can be used to operate on its associated values. For example, common operators associated with integers are addition, subtraction, multiplication, and division.

So the job of a domain is to define a finite or an infinite set of permissible values along with ways of operating on them. In a way, the domain controls or restricts the value of an attribute, but it does so only by providing information. The database actually restricts an attribute's value so that it conforms to its associated domain. As you will see later, this particular restriction is defined in the integrity component of the relational model, and is called *domain integrity*. The group of collective attributes in a tuple is called its *heading*. Just as an attribute defines the properties of its associated value, the heading defines the properties of its tuple.

Relations

A relation, simply enough, is a set of one or more tuples that share the same heading. Just as domains have analogs in programming languages, so do tuples and relations. And even if you are not a programmer, the analogy is quite helpful in illustrating the relationship between tuples, relations, and headings.

For example, consider the relation and its C equivalent shown in Figure 3-3. You could say that a tuple is similar to a C structure. They both are made up of attributes that have a name and a type. As shown in the figure, a C structure's attributes are defined in its declaration, just as a tuple's attributes are defined in its heading. The declaration and heading both provide information about the contents of their respective data structures.

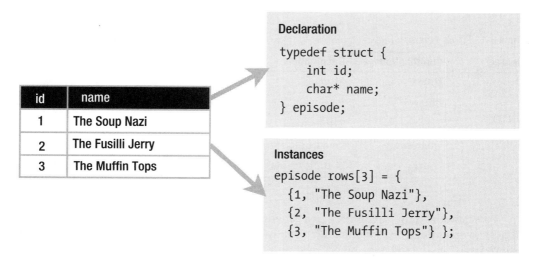

Figure 3-3. *Header as declaration; tuple as instance*

Similarly, a tuple's values are analogous to an *instance* of a C structure. Its values form a composite data structure that corresponds to the attributes defined in its heading. Each value in the structure is identifiable by an attribute name, and each value is restricted by an attribute domain.

Thus, tuples are more than just rows of amorphous values like what you might find in a spreadsheet. They are well-defined data structures with a high degree of specificity over the information within them. They have more in common with constructs in programming languages than with rows in a spreadsheet.

But the analogy doesn't stop there. As also shown in Figure 3-3, a relation is the C equivalent of an array of structures. Each structure in the array along with the array itself shares the same type, just as relations and their tuples share the same heading.

The bottom line is that relations and tuples are highly structured. Furthermore, this structure is defined by their common heading.

Degree and Cardinality

Associated with tuples and relations are the notions of *degree* and *cardinality*. These are just fancy words for width and height, respectively. You could say a relation's width is the number of attributes in its heading. This is called the degree. Its height is the number of tuples it contains; this is called cardinality. These terms are illustrated in Figure 3-2. A relation with four attributes and five tuples would be said to be of degree 4 and cardinality 5.

While tuples don't have cardinality, they nonetheless have their own fancy terms. A tuple of degree 1 is said to be a *unary* tuple. Tuples of degree 2, 3, and 4 are said to be *binary, ternary,* and *quaternary*, respectively. Generally, a tuple of degree N is said to be an N-ary tuple. In fact, the word *tuple* is taken from the N-ary form. In the strictest sense, a unary tuple is called a *monad*, a binary tuple a *pair*, a ternary tuple a *triple*, a quaternary tuple a *tetrad*, and so on, as shown in Table 3-1.

Table 3-1. *Tuple Terminology*

Degree	Qualification	Designation	Example
1	Unary	Monad	1
2	Binary	Pair, twin	(0, 1)
3	Ternary	Triple, triad	(0, 1, 2)
4	Quaternary	Quadruple, tetrad	(0, 1, 2, 3)
N	N-ary	N-tuple (tuple)	(0, 1, 2, ... N)

Typically, the term *tuple* is used as a generic catchall for tuples of all degrees, and using terms like *monad* and *triad* is often more confusing than it is precise. As with tuples, a relation composed of binary tuples is a binary relation. A relation composed of N-ary tuples is an N-ary relation, and so forth.

Mathematical Relations

The notion of a relation in relational theory is taken directly from the relation in set theory, with a few modifications. To really understand relations, as defined in relational theory, you must understand their predecessors in mathematics.

Just as in relational theory, mathematical relations are sets of mathematical tuples. Like mathematical relations, mathematical tuples also differ somewhat from their relational namesakes. In mathematics, tuples are ordered sequences and relations are unordered sets. Sets by their very nature are ambivalent to order. That is, the order of elements in a set does not affect the fundamental identity of that set, whereas the order of items in a sequence does affect its identity.

To begin with, every value in a tuple has a specific domain associated with it. Suppose we have a tuple composed of the following two domains:

- The domain of all integers {...,-1,0,1,...}, denoted by **I**

- The domain of the first names of all Seinfeld characters {'Jerry', 'Cosmo', 'Newman', ...}, denoted by **F**

Now, suppose we have a relation composed of such tuples. The relation then is also composed of the domains **I** and **F** (in that order). The first column of the relation must consist of integer values, and the second column must consist of the first names of Seinfeld characters. Using this as an example, the formal definition of a relation can be expressed as follows:

A relation over I and F is any subset of the cross product of I and F, represented by I×F.

This is a somewhat annoying definition because it defines a relation in terms of another perhaps unfamiliar concept: the *cross product*. The cross product, also called the *Cartesian product*, is quite simple, however. It is the combination of every value in every domain with every value in every other domain. To compute I×F, for example, you take each integer *i* in I, and pair it with each name *f* in F. This yields an infinitely large set of (*i,f*) tuples (binary tuples), as illustrated in Figure 3-4. Note that the figure is somewhat simplistic and depicts the set of all integers as the values to {-1, 0, 1}.

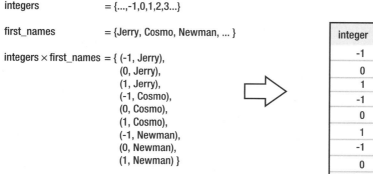

Figure 3-4. *The cross product of integers and Seinfeld character first names*

What does the cross product do here? Why is it used? The cross product of domains **I** and **F** is a set containing every tuple that could ever exist by the combination of these two domains. That is, every tuple that has an integer as its first value and the first name of a Seinfeld character as its second value is contained in the cross product I×F. The cross product is itself just a set, albeit a very big one. It is a set defining the limit of every tuple that could ever be formed from the domains **I** and **F**. That being said, any subset of this cross product is a relation, specifically a "relation over I and F." That is a mathematical relation: any subset of a cross project.

Put more simply, a relation is defined in terms of its constituent domains—it is a portion (or subset) of their cross product. This cross product is a superset containing every possible tuple that could ever appear in the relation. (I know this seems circuitous.) The proper way of expressing a relation is to speak of a *relation R over the domains X, Y, and Z*. If we were to expand our relation to include the domain of all Seinfeld episodes, denoted by **E**, it would then be "a relation *R* over I, F, and E"—represented by I×F×E, which in turn is an even larger set than I×F.

Relational Relations

There is one fundamental difference between tuples in mathematics and tuples in relational theory. In mathematics, the order of values in a tuple is significant; in relational theory it isn't. This is because members (attributes) of relational tuples have names, which are used to identify them. Mathematical ones do not. Therefore, mathematical tuples in relations over I×F are always of the form (*i,f*) because this is the only way to identify them—by ordinal positions. This convention is not needed in relational tuples because they have attributes that have names to identify them, rather than ordinal positions. Order, then, in a relational tuple offers no real advantage. The same applies to relational relations, as they share the same attributes through their common heading.

In his original paper, Codd differentiated mathematical relations (which he called domain-ordered relations) from his relational relations (called domain-unordered relations) by referring to the latter as "relationships":

> *Accordingly, we propose that users deal, not with relations which are domain-ordered, but with relationships which are their domain-unordered counterparts. To accomplish this, domains must be uniquely identifiable at least within any given relation, without using their position.*

Domains (or attributes) are uniquely identifiable through attribute names. Therefore, both column and row order do not matter in the relational model. This is the principal way in which the relations of set theory and the relations of relational theory differ. In all other respects, tuples and relations in the relational theory share all the same properties of their counterparts in set theory.

And that is a relation. It is the fundamental object upon which relational theory is built. If you understand it, you are well on your way to understanding the core mechanics of relational theory. Relational theory is fitted so as to mirror the true mathematical relation as closely as possible. The reason is that the closer the relational model fits the mathematical model, the more it benefits from other facets of mathematics already well established. A prime example is relational algebra, which is part of the manipulative component of the relational model. Many of the operations defined for relations in set theory carry over to relational algebra because relational relations are sufficiently similar. The same is true for relational calculus, which employs methods of formal logic. As Codd put it

> *Moreover, the (relational) approach has a close tie to first-order predicate logic—a logic on which most of mathematics is based, hence a logic which can be expected to have strength, endurance, and many applications.*

Codd recognized not only that the elegance of mathematics is beneficial as a basis to build upon, but that it also offers a vast reservoir of existing knowledge that can be harnessed as well.

Tables: Relation Variables

A relation, though it contains values, is itself just a value, just like an integer or a string. The value of a relation is given by the particular set of tuples it contains. Likewise, the value of each tuple in turn is given by the specific values within it. Thus, the value of a relation is determined by the sum of its parts. Figure 3-5 illustrates this. It depicts three relations, represented by *R1*, *R2*, and *R3*, taken over I×F. Each represents a different value, or relation.

R1, *R2*, and *R3* are not relations but rather *relation variables*. They *represent* relations. Codd referred to them as *named relations*. Date (2003) calls them *relvars*. SQL calls them *tables*. They are also known as *base tables*. The bottom line is that they are simply variables whose values are relations. I will simply refer to them here as tables, as that is what you will be dealing with in SQL.

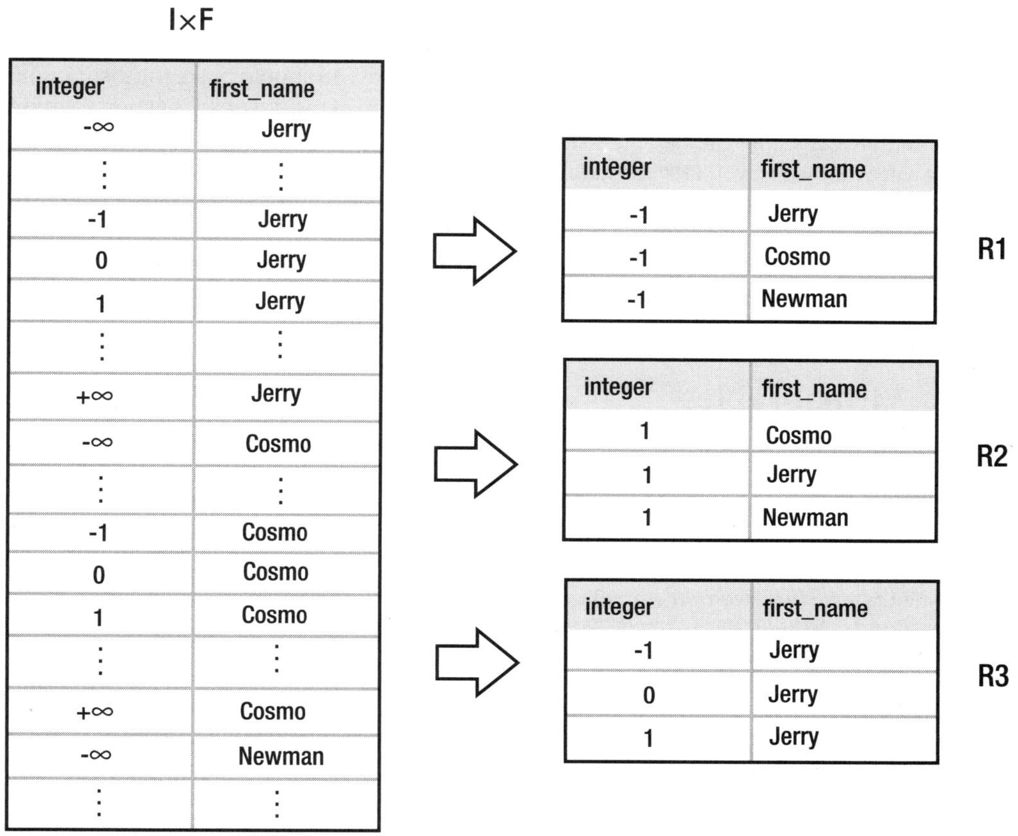

I×F

integer	first_name
-∞	Jerry
⋮	⋮
-1	Jerry
0	Jerry
1	Jerry
⋮	⋮
+∞	Jerry
-∞	Cosmo
⋮	⋮
-1	Cosmo
0	Cosmo
1	Cosmo
⋮	⋮
+∞	Cosmo
-∞	Newman
⋮	⋮

integer	first_name
-1	Jerry
-1	Cosmo
-1	Newman

R1

integer	first_name
1	Cosmo
1	Jerry
1	Newman

R2

integer	first_name
-1	Jerry
0	Jerry
1	Jerry

R3

Figure 3-5. *Relations over I×F*

In practice, the precise meaning of "relation" can sometimes be a bit murky. Relations are often referred to in the same context as tables. However, they are not the same thing. One is a value; the other is a variable. A relation is a *value*, like an integer value is 1, 2, or 3. A table is a variable—to which relations are assigned. Tables, like variables, have both a name and a value. Their name is just a symbol. Their value is a relation. They are no different than variables in algebra, such as x and y in the equation of a line. Tables share all the properties of relations (heading, degree, cardinality, etc.) just as integer variables share the properties of integers.

With this in mind, what does it mean to update or modify a table? If you are familiar with SQL, you probably think of it in terms of modifying a single value, or a few rows. You see it the same as changing cells in a spreadsheet. You modify *parts* of the spreadsheet. You see those parts as individual values. The relational view is different. In the relational view, you don't modify parts of a table. A table is a variable holding an entire relation as its value. If you change anything, you change *the entire relation*—no matter how small the difference might be. You aren't changing a row or column; you are actually swapping one relation with an entirely new one, where the new relation contains the rows or columns you want changed.

I know that it may seem like frivolous semantics. But just as you don't modify part of an integer variable, you don't modify part of a relation variable either. There is nothing wrong with thinking in terms of the SQL view—where you are changing values in a row. It is logically equivalent: in a SQL update, you are articulating the change you want to make in a statement, and that statement produces a new relation. But that is where you should make the distinction: the change produces a *new* relation, not a patched-up version of the old one. That new relation becomes a new value that the table holds.

Be aware that when you talk about tables in a database, you are referring to variables, specifically relation variables—not relations. If a database were composed strictly of relations, then its contents would be fixed values, not subject to change. But databases are dynamic. And the reason is because their contents—tables—are relation variables, which are subject to change. They change by *assigning* those relation variables new relation values, not by adding, subtracting, or changing tuples.

Views: Virtual Tables

Views are virtual tables. They look like tables and act like tables, but they're not. Views are relational expressions that yield relations. It is like saying that the algebraic expression $x+y$ is not a number per se, though it can yield a number if the expression is evaluated, provided we have specific values for x and y. The same is true for views. Codd (1980) described them as follows:

> A view is a virtual relation (table) defined by means of an expression or sequence of commands. Although not directly supported by actual data, a view appears to a user as if were an additional base table kept up-to-date and in the state of integrity with other base tables. Views are useful for permitting application programs and users at terminals to interact with constant view structures, even when the base tables themselves are undergoing structural changes at the logical level...

Logical Data Independence

In one sense, views are simply a matter of convenience. They let you assign a name to a set of operations and treat the result like a relation. They are a kind of shorthand. This is perhaps the most common use of views. Another use was for security. In some systems, views can be used to selectively present parts of tables, while excluding other sensitive or restricted parts. But the original intent of views was much more than these two applications. The main application for views was facilitating what is called *logical data independence*, which is defined as follows:

> **9. Logical Data Independence.** *Application programs and terminal activities remain logically unimpaired when information-preserving changes of any kind that theoretically permit un-impairment are made to the base tables.*

Logical data independence means that applications and users should theoretically be able to see the same logical structure (e.g., the same attributes in a relation), even if it is changed (e.g., an attribute in that relation is moved to another relation). An example is when a relation is decomposed into two relations for the sake of normalization, as described in the section "Normalization."

More precisely, logical data independence means that users and applications *should be able to be* insulated from changes at the logical level of the database. That doesn't mean the database is supposed to automatically shield users and programs from the database administrator (DBA) doing something really bone-headed like dropping a table and going home for the day. Rather, it means that the relational model provides a means for the administrator to bridge the gap if she wants to make substantive changes at the logical level that would impact the logical view seen by users and applications. For instance, if the DBA decomposes a table into two smaller ones, she can create a view that looks like the original table, though it is in reality a relational expression that combines (joins) the two new tables. The users and applications know no differently.

Updatable Views

But logical data independence entails more than just viewing data. Many people who are familiar with views understand them as read-only. However, the relational model clearly states that you should be able to write to views as well, just as if they were ordinary tables. While logical data independence would seem to imply this, Rule 6 makes it explicit:

> **6. View Updating Rule.** *All views that are theoretically updatable are also updatable by the system.*

Rule 6 is essential for logical data independence. "Theoretically updatable" means the view is constructed in such a way that it is theoretically possible to map changes made on it to its respective base tables. That is, if it can be done in theory, the system should be able to do it.

That said, Rule 6 and updatable views (sometimes referred to as materialized views) are not fully supported in all relational databases, simply because they are not easy to implement. Programming a system to know what is "theoretically updatable" in relational algebra and/or calculus is not exactly a weekend project. On the other hand, read-only views are extremely common. In fact, it is almost hard to find relational databases today that don't support them.

The System Catalog

As a database is composed of tables and views, you might at some point wonder how you can find out exactly what is in a given database. As it turns out, a relational database contains tables and views describing its tables and views—information about the information. That is, all tables, views, constraints, and other database objects belonging in a database are registered in what is referred to as the *system catalog*. Per Rule 4:

> **Rule 4. Dynamic On-Line Catalog Based on the Relational Model.** *The data base description is represented at the logical level in the same way as ordinary data, so that authorized users can apply the same relational language to its interrogation as they apply to the regular data.*

The system catalog is subject to the Information Principle: it is required to be represented in a relational format that can be queried in the same way as other relations in the system. This means that even metadata (information about information) in a database has to be represented relationally. In many database products, many of the tables in the system catalog are often implemented as views. The beauty of views and the system catalog is that together they enable you to extend or enhance the catalog itself. You can create your own catalog views that contain information you find useful or informative. Those views in turn may even use catalog tables as a basis.

The Integrity Component

While the structural aspect of the model relates to the structure of information, the integrity aspect relates to the information within the structure. Information can be arranged in relations in a way that gives rise to various relationships, both within columns of a single relation and between columns of different relations. These relationships provide additional structure and indeed add even more information to what is already present.

The integrity aspect of the relational model provides a way to explicitly define and protect such relationships. Although their use in a database is entirely optional, the degree to which they are employed can ultimately determine the consistency of your data.

Primary Keys

Codd's second rule is the starting point of data integrity, and deals with the nature of data within relations. This rule is called the Guaranteed Access Rule and is defined as follows:

> *2. Guaranteed Access Rule. Each and every datum (atomic value) in a relational data base is guaranteed to be logically accessible by resorting to a combination of table name, primary key value and column name.*

The relational model requires that every relation have a primary key. The primary key is the set of attributes in a relation that uniquely identifies each tuple within it. This rule carries with it an important corollary: relations may not contain duplicate tuples.

The Guaranteed Access Rule states that every field (or value in a tuple) in a relational database must be addressable. To be addressable, it must be identifiable. To be identifiable, each tuple must be distinguishable in some way from all other tuples in the relation, which is to say unique (thus, duplicate tuples would violate this constraint).

Uniqueness is the business of the primary key. A key is a designated attribute (or group of attributes) in a relation such that

1. The value (or combined values) of that attribute (or attributes) is unique for every tuple in the relation.

2. If the key is composed of more than one attribute, all of the attributes that define the key must be necessary to ensure uniqueness. That is, every attribute in the key is sufficient to ensure uniqueness, but also necessary as well—if one were absent, then the uniqueness condition would not hold.

If both conditions 1 and 2 are met, then the resulting attribute or group of attributes is a key (also called a candidate key). If condition 1 is met but not condition 2, then the attribute (or group of attributes) is called a *superkey*. It is a key that could stand to lose some weight. That is, it has more attributes than necessary to ensure uniqueness: a smaller key containing fewer attributes could be defined that still guarantees uniqueness.

A relation may have one or more candidate keys. If it does, then which one of them that is defined as the primary key is arbitrary:

> *Whenever a relation has two or more nonredundant primary keys, one of them is arbitrarily selected and called the primary key of the relation.*

The primary key is just a rule that requires that every relation have at least one candidate key. The definition of a primary key serves more as an affirmation of the Guaranteed Access Rule than it does in defining a new relational concept.

Foreign Keys

With keys comes more than simply identification. While keys define relationships between tuples within a single relation (you might say vertically), they can also define relationships between tuples in different relations (horizontally). A key's identification property allows a tuple in one relation to identify (or reference) a specific tuple in another relation by way of a common key value. This is called a *foreign key relationship*. Specifically, a key in one table corresponds to, or references, the primary key in another table (the foreign key), thereby relating the tuples in each table. Take, for example, the foods and food_types tables, as shown in Figure 3-6. Each row in foods corresponds to a distinct food item (Junior Mints, Mackinaw Peaches, etc.), the name of which is stored in the name attribute. Each row in food_types stores various food classifications (e.g., Junk Food, Fruit, etc.). Each row in foods references a row in food_types by using a common key. foods contains a key called type_id, every value of which corresponds to a value in the primary key (id) of the food_types, as illustrated by the arrow in Figure 3-6.

foods   **food_types**

id	name	type_id		id	name
244	Mackinaw Peaches	8		1	Bakery
245	Cheerios	2		2	Cereal
244	Chocolate Bobka	1		8	Fruit
245	Junior Mints	9		9	Junk food

Figure 3-6. *Foreign key relationship between foods and food_types*

From a relational standpoint, this is merely a foreign key relationship. But in reality it is more than that. This relationship models a relationship in the real world. It has a basis in reality, has real meaning, and adds information above and beyond the information contained in the individual tables. Therefore, it is a critical part of the information itself.

It is easy to see that such relationships, if not properly maintained, can be precarious. If an application comes to assume this relationship, and its normal operation depends on the fact that a tuple in foods always has a corresponding tuple in food_types, what happens if someone deletes all the tuples from food_types? Where does that leave the type_id values in the foods tuples pointing to now? What has become of this relationship?

For that matter, what is to stop a user from just ignoring the primary key rule and jamming a thousand identical food_types tuples back into the database? If there is nothing in place to protect and ensure these relationships, they can be as destructive as they are beneficial. Such rules, like laws, are worthless without enforcement.

Constraints

Enter the *constraint*. Constraints are relational cops. They enforce database rules and relation-ships and preserve order in general. They bring consistency and uniformity to information within a database. With constraints, you can rest assured that tuples in the foods table will always reference legitimate tuples in food_types. Primary keys will always exist in tables, and their values will always be unique. This kind of uniformity and consistency is called *data integrity*. It is the integrity component of the relational model.

Constraints work by governing database operations. Like the precogs in *Minority Report*, they stop bad things before they happen. If a user or an application issues a request that would result in an inconsistent relationship or data, the database refuses to carry out the operation and issues an error, called a *constraint violation*. In the relational model, constraints fall into four general classes of integrity:

- **Domain integrity**: Domain integrity is the relationship between attribute values and their associated domains. In the relational model, domain integrity is instituted through *domain constraints*. A domain constraint requires that each attribute value in a tuple exist within its associated domain. For example, if the type_id attribute in the foods table is declared as an integer, then the corresponding values of type_id in all tuples in the foods table must be integer values—not floating-point numbers or strings. Domain integrity is also referred to as *attribute integrity*—it pertains to the attributes of a relation. Domain integrity is not limited to just checking that a given value resides in a given domain. It includes additional constraints as well, such as CHECK constraints. CHECK constraints (which are covered in Chapter 4) can define arbitrarily complex rules on what constitutes a permissible value for a given attribute.

- **Entity integrity**: This form of integrity is mandated by the Guaranteed Access Rule: each tuple in a relation must be uniquely identifiable. Whereas domain integrity is concerned with a relation's attribute values, entity integrity is concerned with its tuples. The term "entity" here is a rather loose term for table. It originates from database modeling (i.e., entity-relationship diagrams). In this particular context, an entity simply refers to anything in the real world that must be represented in a database.

- **Referential integrity**: This form of integrity pertains to relationships between tables, specifically the preservation of foreign key relationships. Whereas entity integrity pertains to tuples in a relation, referential integrity pertains to tuples between relations.

- **User-defined integrity**: User-defined integrity encompasses any form of integrity not defined in the other forms. Many relational databases offer various facilities that go beyond the normal constraint mechanisms. One such example is triggers, which are covered in Chapter 4.

The relational model requires that databases and query languages support integrity constraints. Furthermore, these constraints, like all other data and metadata in the database, must also be defined directly in the database, specifically in the system catalog:

> *10. Integrity Independence. Integrity constraints specific to a particular relational data base must be definable in the relational data sub-language and storable in the catalog, not in the application programs.*

Null Values

Closely associated with data integrity in the relational model is a special value (or lack thereof), which exists both inside and outside of every domain. This special value denotes the *absence* of a value and is called a *null value*, or *null* for short. Nulls are prescribed in Codd's third rule:

> **3. Systematic Treatment of Null Values.** *Null values (distinct from the empty character string or a string of blank characters and distinct from zero or any other number) are supported in fully relational DBMS for representing missing information and inapplicable information in a systematic way, independent of data type.*

There are multiple interpretations for what null values mean. The prevailing view of null seems to be "unknown." But there are others. For example, a tuple containing employee information may have an attribute for the employee's middle name. But not everyone has a middle name. A tuple for a person without a middle name might use a null value for that particular attribute. In this case, the null value doesn't necessarily mean "unknown" but rather "not applicable." Thus, a value may be null because it is either missing (a value exists but was not input) or uncertain (it is not known whether a value exists at all), or it is simply not applicable for the tuple (or employee) in question.

The inclusion of nulls in the relational model has been a source of controversy for many years, and there are people on both sides of the debate who feel very strongly for their positions. Codd, for example, felt the need for nulls:

> *In general, controversy still surrounds the problem of missing and inapplicable information in data bases. It seems to me that those who complain loudly about the complexities of manipulating nulls are overlooking the fact that handling missing information and inapplicable information is inherently complicated.*

Date, Codd's colleague and well-known authority on the relational model, is opposed to them:

> *...we should make it very clear that in our opinion (and in that of many other writers too, we hasten to add), nulls and 3VL are a serious mistake and have no place in a clean formal system like the relational model.*

The "3VL" acronym in the quote stands for "three-valued logic," which corresponds to how nulls are evaluated in logical expressions. This is addressed in Chapter 4.

Normalization

The implication of no duplicate tuples provided by the Guaranteed Access Rule gives rise to an important concept in database design called *normalization*. Normalization concerns itself with the organization of attributes within relations so as to minimize duplication of data. Data duplication, as you will see, has more deleterious effects than just taking up unnecessary space. It increases the opportunity for database inconsistencies to arise. Normalization is about designing your database to be more resistant to the ill effects of thoughtless users and buggy programs.

While based on principles of the relational model, normalization is somewhat a subject (some even say an art) in itself. It can become quite complicated, introducing a considerable amount of new concepts and terminology. A proper treatment of the subject is beyond the scope of this book. What follows is a very brief introduction.

Normal Forms

As stated, the chief aim of normalization is to eradicate duplication. Relations that have duplication removed are said to be *normalized*. However, there are degrees of normalization. These degrees are called *normal forms*. The first degree is called *first normal form*, followed by *second normal form*, and so on. They are abbreviated 1NF, 2NF, 3NF, and so on. Each normal form defines specific conditions a relation must meet in order to be so classified. Thus a relation that meets the conditions of first normal form is said to be "in first normal form." Normal forms build on each other so that higher normal forms require all the conditions of lower forms as prerequisites. For data to be in 2NF, it must also be in 1NF. Essentially, the higher the normal form of a relation, the less duplication it has, and the more resistant it is to inconsistencies. The most common and perhaps most widely used normal form is 3NF, although there are even more advanced normal forms such as Boyce-Codd normal form (BCNF), 4NF, 5NF, and higher. The first three normal forms are easy enough to describe.

First Normal Form

First normal form simply states that all attributes in a relation use domains that are made up of atomic values. The working definition of "atomic" is the same as other disciplines, meaning simply "that which cannot be broken down further." For example, integer values would seem to be atomic, as you can't break them down further. But you could argue that integer values could be decomposed into their prime factors. Atomicity, then, is determined by the method of decomposition, which can be a subjective matter. For all practical purposes, it is the database management system that decides what is atomic. And the domains provided by the system can safely be considered as such.

That said, first normal form basically means that a single attribute cannot hold more than a single value. For example, take the episodes table shown in Table 3-2 in the next section. 1NF states that you couldn't store both the values 1992 and 1993 (two integer values) in a year attribute of a single tuple. It sounds so silly that it can be kind of hard to imagine. But it's that simple. It is so simple, in fact, that you have to work at violating 1NF; most databases won't even give you the means to do it.

Functional Dependencies

To understand second and third normal form, you have to first understand *functional dependencies*. The simple definition of a functional dependency is a correlation between columns in a table. If the values of one column (or set of columns) correlate to the values of another, then they have a functional dependency. More precisely, a functional dependency describes a relationship between two or more attributes in a relation such that the value of one attribute (or set of attributes) can be inferred from the value of another attribute (or attributes) for every tuple in the relation. This is more easily illustrated by example. Consider the table, called episodes, shown in Table 3-2.

There is a functional dependency between season and year. For any given value of season, you will find the same value of year. If you ever come across a tuple with a value of 4 for season, you know the value for year will be 1992. If you know the former, you can determine the latter.

Table 3-2. *The Unnormalized episodes Table*

season	week	year	name
4	1	1992	The Junior Mint
4	2	1992	The Smelly Car
5	1	1993	The Mango
5	2	1993	The Puffy Shirt
6	21	1994	The Fusilli Jerry
6	25	1994	The Understudy

Many times, functional dependencies are a warning sign that duplication lurks within a table. And already you can see in this example how inconsistencies can crop up. If there is in fact a correlation between year and season, what happens to that relationship if someone modifies the first row so that its value for year is 1999 (but fails to do so for the second row)? That relationship has been compromised. It is inconsistent. One tuple with season=4 has year=1992, and another with season=4 has year=1999. How can season 4 have happened in both 1992 and 1999? This is logically inconsistent, and the functional dependency (or lack of sufficient normalization) is what made it possible to introduce this inconsistency. What is even more interesting is that there is no standard integrity constraint designed to guard against this problem. It is purely the result of bad design.

Functional dependencies always involve exactly two sets of attributes: one set (the determinant) determines (or relates to) the value of another (the dependent). Call the attribute(s) making up the determinant *A* and the attribute(s) making up the dependent *B*. With this in place, you can express this relationship using the following two (equivalent) statements:

1. *B* is functionally dependent upon *A*.

2. *A* functionally determines *B*.

There is even a fancy notation for this as well: A → B. The bottom line: for any value of *A*, the value of *B* has some kind of correlation.

Second Normal Form

Second normal form is defined in terms of functional dependencies. It requires that a relation be in first normal form *and* that all non-key attributes be functionally dependent upon *all* attributes of the primary key (not just part of them). Remember that normalization is about cutting out duplication, so while this sounds like an arbitrary rule, it is in fact aimed at weeding out duplication.

You have already seen what duplication looks like when 2NF is not followed, using episodes as an example. The primary key in episodes is composed of both season and week. You know that year is functionally dependent on season, which in turn is only part of the primary key (red-flag). Specifically, for every season=x (e.g., 4) you have the same year=y (e.g., 1992). There is no reason to include the year attribute in the relation if its value is correlated with season. That's duplication. It must go.

So what do you do? You decompose the table into two tables. Cut out `year`, and move it to its own table: call it the `seasons` table. Now `episodes` is decomposed into two tables with a foreign key relationship where `episodes.season` references `seasons.season` (see Tables 3-3 and 3-4).

Table 3-3. *The episodes Table in Second Normal Form*

season	week	name
4	1	The Junior Mint
4	2	The Smelly Car
5	1	The Mango
5	2	The Puffy Shirt
6	21	The Fusilli Jerry
6	25	The Understudy

Table 3-4. *The seasons Table from Normalizing episodes*

season	year
4	1992
5	1993
6	1994

This is like factoring out a common variable in an algebraic expression. Now `episodes` is in 2NF. Furthermore, no information is lost because `year` is functionally determined by `season`. But look what else you get: the new design allows referential integrity to back you up: you have a foreign key constraint guarding this relationship (the correlation between `season` and `year`), which you couldn't get in the previous form. What was previously only implied is now both explicit and enforceable.

Now consider the specific case mentioned earlier where someone modifies the first row. The logical inconsistency is no longer possible: it is impossible to mess up the year, because it is not in `episodes`. If someone changes year=1992 to 1999 in `seasons`, it may be inaccurate, but it is still logically consistent. That is, both rows that refer to it in `episodes` (season=4) will still be in agreement about the year in which season 4 took place. Normalization cannot make you get your facts right, but it can ensure that at least your data is consistent about them.

Second normal form works by tightening the specificity between the primary key and the non-key attributes. If the values of a non-key attribute correlate to only *part* of the primary key, then logically that attribute can introduce duplication. Why? Because only part of a primary key is not unique (*all* of the primary key is required for uniqueness, as mentioned earlier), and a correspondence between two columns, neither of which is unique, opens the possibility for duplication, and duplication invites inconsistency.

Third Normal Form

Third normal form shifts attention from functional dependencies on the primary key to dependencies on any other non-key attributes in a relation. It roots out a special class of functional dependencies called *transitive dependencies*. A transitive dependency is just a chain of two or more functional dependencies spanning two or more attribute groups (two or more correlations). For example, say you have a relation with three sets of attributes, *A*, *B*, and *C*, where *A* is the primary key, and *B* is a candidate key. If $A \to B$ and $B \to C$, then *C* is transitively dependent on *A*: it depends on *A* indirectly through its relationship with *B*. Transitive dependencies harbor duplication. Third normal form dictates that a relation must be in second normal form and also have no transitive dependencies.

To picture this, let's rig the original episodes table to have an integer primary key called id, and the candidate key is now the combination of season and week. This relation is shown in Table 3-5.

Table 3-5. *An Unormalized episodes Table with an Integer Primary Key*

id	season	week	year	name
1	4	1	1992	The Junior Mint
2	4	2	1992	The Smelly Car
3	5	1	1993	The Mango
4	5	2	1993	The Puffy Shirt
5	6	21	1994	The Fusilli Jerry
6	6	25	1994	The Understudy

In this version of episodes, year is functionally dependent on season, which in turn is functionally dependent on id. So we have id → season → year. How do you know this? Work backwards. Ask yourself if you can determine season from id. Yes. Then can you determine year from season? Yes. Therefore, you have a transitive dependency: id functionally determines season and season functionally determines year. To be in third normal form, year, which is functionally dependent on a non-key attribute, must go. And as with the previous example, you relegate year into its own table, again splitting episodes into two tables, as shown in Tables 3-6 and 3-7.

Table 3-6. *The episodes Table in Third Normal Form*

id	season	week	name
1	4	1	The Junior Mint
2	4	2	The Smelly Car
3	5	1	The Mango
4	5	2	The Puffy Shirt
5	6	21	The Fusilli Jerry
6	6	25	The Understudy

Just as in the 2NF example, decomposition made an implicit relationship explicit.

Table 3-7. *The seasons Table from Normalizing episodes*

season	year
4	1992
5	1993
6	1994

Since functional dependencies between non-key attributes are not allowed in a table, you may wonder why it is okay for functional dependencies to exist between keys. The answer is simple: uniqueness. Even if there is a correlation between one key and another, the fact that they are unique guarantees that their correlation is also unique; therefore, no duplication exists.

In the end, 2NF and 3NF aim not to introduce confusing rules, but to seek out and destroy duplication and the inconsistencies that can arise from it. It is essential to proper database design. The more important your data, the more attention you should pay to ensure that your database is properly designed and normalized.

The Manipulative Component

The manipulative component of the relational model defines the ways in which information can be manipulated and changed. It is the dynamic part of the model that connects the data in the logical view to the outside world.

Relational Algebra and Calculus

In his original paper, Codd described a language that could be used to operate on data:

> The adoption of a relational model of data, as described above, permits the development of a universal data sublanguage based on an applied predicate calculus... Such a language would provide a yardstick of linguistic power for all other proposed data languages, and would itself be a strong candidate for embedding (with appropriate syntactic modification) in a variety of host languages (programming, command- or problem-oriented).

This "universal data sublanguage" would have a sound mathematical basis. Codd defined this basis in the form of relational algebra and relational calculus, illustrated in his 1972 paper "Relational Completeness of Data Base Sublanguages." As described in the abstract of that paper:

> In the near future, we can expect a great variety of languages to be proposed for interrogating and updating data bases. This paper attempts to provide a theoretical basis which may be used to determine how complete a selection capability is provided in a proposed data sublanguage independently of any host language in which the sublanguage may be embedded.

A relational algebra and relational calculus are defined. Then, an algorithm is presented for reducing an arbitrary relation-defining expression (based on the calculus) into a semantically equivalent expression of the relational algebra.

Finally, some opinions are stated regarding the relative merits of calculus-oriented versus algebra-oriented sublanguages from the standpoint of optimal search and highly discriminating authorization schemes.

These two "pure" languages—relational algebra and calculus—focused on mathematical theory rather than a particular language syntax. The latter is the job of the "data sublanguage," or "query language," as we know it today. Like the structural part of the relational model, the manipulative part drew heavily from mathematics. Relational algebra has its basis in set theory. Likewise, relational calculus has its basis in predicate calculus. From a computer science perspective, relational algebra can be considered more of a *procedural language* while relational calculus is more of a *declarative language*. The meanings of these terms are explained in more detail in Chapter 4.

As stated in the quote, while the particular forms of expression in the two languages are different, they are nevertheless logically equivalent. That is, any operation in relational algebra can also be expressed in terms of calculus, and vice versa. Another way of saying this is that the two languages have the same *expressive power*—the same fundamental operations can be performed or expressed in either system.

Relational Query Language

Together, relational algebra and calculus serve as a guideline, or a yardstick as Codd describes it, for query languages implemented in relational databases. Any query language that can express all of the fundamental operations set forth in relational algebra and/or calculus is said to be *relationally complete*.

The query language must also address the other aspects (structural and integrity) of the relational model as well. This is summed up in Codd's fifth rule, defined as follows:

> **5. Comprehensive Data Sublanguage Rule.** *A relational system may support several languages and various modes of terminal use (for example, the fill-in-the-blanks mode). However, there must be at least one language whose statements are expressible, per some well-defined syntax, as character strings and that is comprehensive in supporting all the following items:*
>
> *Data Definition, View Definition, Data Manipulation (Interactive and by program), Integrity Constraints, and Authorization, Transaction boundaries (begin, commit, and rollback).*

Additionally, Codd's seventh rule requires that the database (and by extension the query language) not only use relations for storage, manipulation, and retrieval, but also as operands for the purpose of modifying the database:

> **7. High Level Insert, Update, and Delete.** *The system must support set at a time insert, update, and delete operators.*

A user then should be able to insert tuples by providing a relation composed of the tuples to be inserted, and similarly for updating and deleting information within the system. While this rule keeps things consistent—using relations—its primary intent at the time was actually in optimizing database performance. The idea was that in some cases the database could make better optimizations by seeing modifications together as a set than it could by processing them individually.

So, first, a relational database must provide at least one query language that addresses the structural, integrity, and manipulative aspects of the relational model. And with respect to the manipulative aspect, it must be capable of expressing the mathematical concepts set forth in relational algebra and/or calculus. Furthermore, it must accept relations as a means for modifying data in the system. Note that Codd never mandated a particular query language. He only mandated that a relational database provide one and what it must do.

The Advent of SQL

Thus, over the years, there have been multiple competing query languages. However, the most popular and widely adopted of these languages today is undoubtedly SQL. SQL is a relationally complete query language that exhibits aspects of both relational algebra and relational calculus. That is, it has both declarative features (calculus) and procedural features (algebra). In fact, as you will see in the next chapter, SQL includes almost all of the operators defined in relational algebra.

SQL also reflects each aspect of the relational model. Part of its language is dedicated to working with the structural aspect of the model, specifically to creating, altering, and destroying tables. This part of the language is called data definition language (DDL). Within DDL lies also the integrity aspect, allowing the creation of keys and various database constraints. Likewise, part of the language is dedicated to the operational aspect, called data manipulation language (DML). And as stated, it includes ideas from both relational algebra and calculus.

Ironically, despite the clear influence of the relational model on SQL, the current SQL standard does not mention the relational model or use relational terminology.[2] And while SQL is relationally complete, in many ways it falls short of the true power of the relational model. Although it was primarily inspired by relational calculus, some have claimed that there are ways in which SQL also violates it. Furthermore, SQL lacks some relational operations that some consider important, such as relational assignment, and has a number of redundant features. Part of the reason for this was that the organization(s) responsible for creating the SQL standard felt that it was more important to release a standard as early as possible in order to establish a base that database implementations could build upon (Connolly, 2001). Thus, when the initial standard was released in 1987, though practical, it was found wanting in many ways by researchers involved with the relational model (Codd included). Among other things, it omitted some relational operations and included no mention of referential integrity constraints. Subsequent standards filled in some of the gaps here and there, but this seems to have done little to appease its detractors or deter database vendors from "extending" their SQL dialects to include proprietary features.

Entire books and websites are devoted to both SQL's inadequacies as well as what an ideal query language should be. Furthermore, alternative query languages have been proposed and implemented (both before and after SQL) that in the minds of their creators are more expressive and better reflect the principles and intent of the relational model.[3]

---

2. See http://en.wikipedia.org/wiki/Relational_model.
3. Tutorial D is one such example. See www.thethirdmanifesto.com for more information.

Despite its criticisms and shortcomings, however, SQL is what we have to work with. It is undoubtedly the most popular and widely adopted query language in the industry, and given its longstanding dominance in the marketplace, it is unlikely that its position will change any time in the near future.

The Meaning of Relational

Given all this information, what exactly is *relational*? It is a common misconception that relational databases derive the name "relational" from their ability to "relate" a column in one table to a column in another through a foreign key relationship. The true meaning of relational, however, stems from the central structural component of the relational model: the relation, which itself is based on the mathematical concept. First and foremost, a relational database is one that uses relations as the sole structural unit in which to represent information, as mandated by the Information Principle.

A more specific definition of relational, however, is provided by Codd's Rule Zero:

> **Rule Zero.** *For any system that is advertised as, or claimed to be, a relational data base management system, that system must be able to manage data bases entirely through its relational capabilities.*

For a database to be called relational, it must provide all of the facilities required by the relational model. That is, it must conform to all of the other 12 rules. And believe it or not, you have covered every one of them. You therefore should have a good idea at this point what it means to be relational. Don't get too cocky, though, as Codd later expanded the 12 rules to over 300.

Summary

This was a nickel tour through the relational model. While our discussion isn't definitive, my goal was to give you enough history to make the topic enjoyable and enough theory for you to understand some of the thinking behind SQL—why it works the way it does. The relational model has clearly influenced its design and has provided it with a solid theoretical foundation.

The relational model has proven itself over its 30-year history. It has had an enormous impact not only on computing but on the way we do business. Today, it can be found in a wide array of electronic machinery, ranging from mainframes to cell phones.

The relational model was created to provide a logical, consistent representation of data that is independent of hardware and software. The model built on well-founded theory set forth in mathematics. This model provides database users with a consistent, unchanging view of information, powerful methods to operate on it, and mechanisms to protect and ensure its consistency and integrity.

There are many more aspects to the relational model, and much that builds on it. It is the subject of entire books, some of which I have included in the "References" section. While it is a large subject, its core concepts are logical and straightforward. These concepts ground, frame, and form the basis of the subject covered in the next chapter: SQL.

If you are new to SQL and you've patiently endured this chapter, you should have a much easier time grasping the concepts in the next chapter. You will see SQL not as an arbitrary language but as a gateway into a powerful database management system. You will find that its syntax is heavily geared to what you've learned here in this chapter.

References

Codd, E. F. 1970. "A relational model for large shared data banks." *Communications of ACM*, 13(6): 377–387.

Codd, E. F. 1972. Relational Completeness of Data Base Sublanguages in Data Base Systems. In Rustin, R. J. (ed.), *Data Base Systems*, Courant Computer Symposia Series, v. 6. Englewood Cliffs, NJ: Prentice-Hall.

Codd, E. F. 1979. "Extending the Database Relational Model to capture more meaning." *ACM Transactions on Database Systems*. 4(4): 397–434.

Codd, E. F. 1980. Data Models in Database Management. In *Proceedings of the 1980 Workshop on Data Abstraction, Databases and Conceptual Modeling* (Pingree Park, CO, June 23–26, 1980). New York: ACM Press, 112–114.

Codd, E. F. 1982. "Relational database: a practical foundation for productivity." *Communications of ACM* 25(2): 109–117.

Codd, E. F. 1985. "Is your DBMS really relational?," *Computerworld* (Part 1: October 14, 1985, Part 2: October 21, 1985).

Connolly, C. E. B. 2001. *Database Systems: A Practical Approach to Design, Implementation and Management.* Boston: Addison-Wesley.

Date, C. J. 1999. *Thirty Years of Relational: Relational* (series of 12 articles), Intelligent Enterprise 1, Nos. 1–3 and 2, Nos. 1–9 (October 1998 onward). Note: Most installments after the first publication in the online portion of the magazine at www.intelligententerprise.com, accessed on March 16, 2006.

Date, C. J. 2003. *An Introduction to Database Systems*, 8th ed. Boston: Addison-Wesley.

Grimaldi, R. P. 1998. *Discrete and Combinatorial Mathematics*, 4th ed. Boston: Addison-Wesley.

Reiter, R. 1978. On Closed World Data Bases. In Gallaire, H. and Minker, J. (eds.), *Logic and Data Bases*. New York: Plenum, 119–140.

Silberschatz, A., H. F. Korth, and S. Sidharshan. 2002. *Database System Concepts*. New York: McGraw Hill.

■ ■ ■

SQL

This chapter is a complete introduction to SQL in general, and SQLite's implementation of it in particular. It assumes no previous experience with either SQL or the relational model. If you are new to SQL, SQLite should serve as an excellent springboard to entering the world of relational databases. It will give you a good grounding in the fundamentals. While the previous chapter on the relational model was a little theoretical and stuffy, this chapter is much more relaxed and practical. We're not here to prove theories; we're here to get things done. So if you didn't read the previous chapter, that's perfectly fine. You should still have no trouble with the material covered in this chapter. An understanding of the relational model is edifying, but not necessary to learn SQL.

SQL is the sole (and almost universal) means by which to communicate with a relational database. It is a language exclusively devoted to information processing. It is designed for structuring, reading, writing, sorting, filtering, protecting, calculating, generating, grouping, aggregating, and in general managing information.

SQL is an intuitive, user-friendly language. It can be fun to use and is quite powerful. One of the fun things about SQL is that regardless of whether you are an expert or a novice, it seems that you can always continue to learn new ways of doing things (for better or worse). There are often many ways to tackle a given problem, and you may find yourself taking delight in trying to find more efficient ways to get what you need, either through more compact expressions or more elegant approaches, as if solving a puzzle. And you can continue to explore dusty corners of the language you never took notice of before with which to further hone your skills, no matter your experience.

The goal of this chapter is to teach you to use SQL *well*—to expose you to good techniques, and perhaps a few cheap tricks along the way. As you can already tell, there are many different aspects to SQL. This chapter breaks them down into discrete parts and presents them in a logical order that should be relatively easy to follow. Nevertheless, SQL is a big subject and there is a lot of ground to cover. It will take some time and more than one cup of coffee to get through this chapter. But by the time you are done, you should be well equipped to put a dent in a database.

The Relational Model

As you'll remember from Chapter 3, SQL is a consequence of the relational model, which was originally proposed by E. F. Codd in 1969. The relational model requires that relational databases provide a query language, and over the years SQL rose to become the lingua franca.

The relational model consists of three essential parts: form, function, and consistency. Form refers to the structure of information. There is but one single data structure used to represent all information. This structure is called a *relation* (known in SQL as a *table*), which is made up of *tuples* (known in SQL as *rows*), which in turn are made up of *attributes* (known in SQL as *columns*).

The relational model's form is a *logical representation* of information. This logical representation is a pristine, abstract view of information unaffected by anything outside of it. It is like a mathematical concept: clean and consistent, governed by a well-defined set of deterministic rules that are not subject to change. The logical representation is completely independent of the *physical representation*, which refers to how database software stores this information on the physical level (e.g., disk). The two representations are thus distinct: nothing that occurs in the physical level can change or affect anything at the logical level. The logical level is uninhibited by hardware, software, vendor, or technology.

The second essential part of the model—the functional part—is also called the manipulative component. It defines ways of operating on information at the logical level. This was formally introduced in Codd's 1972 paper titled "Relational Completeness of Data Base Sublanguages." It added the functional part to the relational model by defining *relational algebra* and *relational calculus*. These are two formal, or "pure," query languages with a heavy basis in mathematics. Relations, as described in the data model, are mathematical sets (with a few additional properties). Relational algebra and calculus, in turn, build on this model by adding operations from set theory and formal logic, thus forming the functional component of the relational model. So both the form and function prescribed in the relational model come directly from concepts in mathematics. Each derivative, however, adds a little something to better adapt it to computers and information processing.

Query Languages

A query language connects the outside world with the abstract logical representation, and allows the two to interact. It provides a way to retrieve and modify information. It is the dynamic part of the relational model.

Codd intended relational algebra and calculus to serve as a baseline for other query languages. Relational algebra and calculus employ a highly mathematical notation that, while good for defining theory, is not terribly user-friendly in practice. Their purpose was thus to define the mathematical or relational requirements that a more user-friendly query language should support. Query languages that met these minimum requirements were called *relationally complete*. This user-friendly query language then provides a more tractable and intuitive way for a person to work with relational data, while at the same time adhering to a sound theoretical basis.

The Growth of SQL

Perhaps the first such query language that was to be so employed was that of IBM's *System R*, a relational database research project that was a direct outgrowth of Codd's papers. It was originally called SEQUEL, which stands for "Structured English Query Language." It was later shortened to SQL, or "Structured Query Language."

Other companies such as Oracle followed suit (in fact, Oracle beat IBM to market with the first SQL product), and pretty soon SQL was the de facto standard. There were other query languages, such as Ingres's QUEL, but in time SQL won out. The reasons SQL emerged as the standard may have had more to do with the dynamics of the marketplace than anything else. But the reasons why it is special today are perhaps a little clearer. There are (among others) standardization, wide adoption, and general ease of use.

SQL has been accepted as the standard language for relational databases by the American National Standards Institute (ANSI), the International Standards Organization (ISO), and the International Electrotechnical Commission (IEC). It has a well-defined standard that specifies what SQL is and does, and this standard has continued to evolve over the past two decades. To date, five versions of the standard have been published over the years (1986, 1989, 1992, 1999, and 2003). The standards are cumulative. Each version of the standard has built on the previous one, adding new features. So in effect, there is only one standard that has continued to grow and evolve over time. The first versions—SQL86 and SQL89—are collectively referred to as SQL1. SQL92 is commonly referred to as SQL2, and SQL99 as SQL3. The ANSI standard, as a whole, is very large. The SQL92 standard alone is over 600 pages. No one database product conforms to the entire standard. Nevertheless, the standard goes a long way in bringing a great deal of uniformity to relational databases.

SQL's wide adoption today is patently obvious: Oracle, Microsoft SQL Server, DB2, Informix, Sybase, PostgreSQL, MySQL, Firebird, Teradata, Intersystems Caché, and SQLite are but some of the relational databases that use SQL as their query language.

The Example Database

Before diving into syntax, let's get situated with the obligatory example database. The database used in this chapter (and the rest of this book for that matter) consists of all the foods in every episode of *Seinfeld*. If you've ever watched *Seinfeld*, you can't help but notice a slight preoccupation with food. There are more than 412 different foods mentioned in the 180 episodes of its history (according to the data I found on the Internet). That's over two new foods every show. Subtract commercial time and that's virtually a new food introduced every 10 minutes.

As it turns out, this preoccupation with food works out nicely as it makes for a database that illustrates all the requisite concepts. The database tables are shown in Figure 4-1.

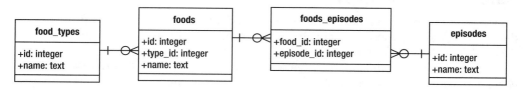

Figure 4-1. *The* Seinfeld *food database*

The database schema, as defined in SQLite, is defined as follows:

```
create table episodes (
  id integer primary key,
  season int,
  name text );
```

```
create table foods(
  id integer primary key,
  type_id integer,
  name text );

create table food_types(
  id integer primary key,
  name text );

create table foods_episodes(
  food_id integer,
  episode_id integer );
```

The main table is foods. Each row in foods corresponds to a distinct food item, the name of which is stored in the name attribute. The type_id attribute references the food_types table, which stores the various food classifications (e.g., baked goods, drinks, or junk food). Finally, the foods_episodes table links foods in foods with the episodes in episodes.

Installation

The food database is located in the examples zip file accompanying this book. It is available on the Apress website (www.apress.com) in the Source Code section. To create the database, first locate the foods.sql file in the root directory of the unpacked zip file. To create a new database from scratch from the command line, navigate to the examples directory and run the following command:

```
sqlite3 foods.db < foods.sql
```

This will create a database file called foods.db. If you are not familiar with how to use the SQLite command-line program, refer to Chapter 2.

Running the Examples

For your convenience, all of the SQL examples in the chapter are available in the file sql.sql in the root directory of the examples zip file. So instead of typing them by hand, simply open the file and locate the SQL you want to try out.

A convenient way to run the longer queries in this chapter is to copy them into your favorite editor and save them in a separate file, which you can run from the command line. For example, copy a long query in test.sql to try out. You simply use the same method to run it as you did to create your database earlier:

```
sqlite3 foods.db < test.sql
```

The results will be printed to the screen. This also makes it easier to experiment with these queries without having to retype them or edit them from inside the SQLite shell. You just make your changes in the editor, save the file, and rerun the command line.

For maximum readability of the output, you may want to put the following commands at the beginning of the file:

```
.echo on
.mode col
.headers on
.nullvalue NULL
```

This causes the command-line program to 1) echo the SQL as it is executed, 2) print results in column mode, 3) include the column headers, and 4) print null values as NULL. The output of all examples in this chapter is formatted with these specific settings. Another option you may want to set for various examples is the .width option, which sets the respective column widths of the output. These vary from example to example.

For better readability, the examples are presented in two different formats. For short queries, I show the SQL and output as it would be shown from within the SQLite shell. For example:

```
sqlite> SELECT * FROM foods WHERE name='JujyFruit' AND type_id=9;

id          type_id     name
----------  ----------  ----------
244         9           JujyFruit
```

Occasionally, as in the previous example, I take the liberty of adding an extra line between the command and its output (in the shell, the output immediately follows the command). For longer queries, I show just the SQL in code format separated from the results by gray lines, as in the following example:

```
SELECT f.name name, types.name type FROM foods f
INNER JOIN (SELECT * FROM food_types WHERE id=6) types
ON f.type_id=types.id;
```

```
name                     type
-----------------------  -----
Generic (as a meal)      Dip
Good Dip                 Dip
Guacamole Dip            Dip
Hummus                   Dip
```

Syntax

SQL's declarative syntax reads a lot like a natural language. Statements are expressed in the imperative mood, beginning with the verb describing the action. Following it are the subject and predicate, as illustrated in Figure 4-2.

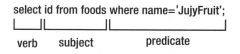

Figure 4-2. *General SQL syntax structure*

As you can see, it reads like a normal sentence. SQL was designed specifically with nontechnical people in mind, and was thus meant to be very simple and easy to understand.

Part of SQL's ease of use comes from its being (for the most part) a *declarative* language, as opposed to an imperative language such as C or Perl. A declarative language is one in which you describe *what* you want whereas an imperative language is one in which you specify *how* to get it. For example, consider the process of ordering a cheeseburger. As a customer, you use a declarative language to articulate your order. That is, you simply declare to the person behind the counter what you want:

Give me a double meat Whataburger with jalapeños and cheese, hold the mayo.

The order is passed back to chef who, on the other hand, fulfills the order using a program written in an imperative language—the recipe. He follows a series of well-defined steps that must be executed in a specific order to create the cheeseburger per your (declarative) specifications:

1. Get ground beef from the third refrigerator on the left.

2. Make a patty.

3. Cook for three minutes.

4. Flip.

5. Cook three more minutes.

6. Repeat steps 1–5 for second patty.

7. Add mustard to top bun.

8. Add patties to bottom bun.

9. Add cheese, lettuce, tomatoes, onions, and jalapeños to burger, but not mayo.

10. Combine top and bottom buns, and wrap in yellow paper.

As you can see, declarative languages tend to be more succinct than imperative ones. In this example, it took the declarative burger language (DBL) one step to materialize the cheeseburger, while it took the imperative chef language (ICL) 10 steps. Declarative languages do more with less. In fact, SQL's ease of use is not far from this example. A suitable SQL equivalent to the DBL statement above might be something along the lines of

```
SELECT burger FROM kitchen WHERE patties=2 AND toppings='jalopenos'
AND condiment != 'mayo' LIMIT 1;
```

Pretty simple. As we've mentioned, SQL was designed to be a user-friendly language. In the early days, SQL was targeted specifically for end users for tasks such as ad hoc queries and report generation (unlike today where it is almost exclusively the domain of developers and database administrators).

Commands

SQL is made up of *commands*. Commands are typically terminated by a semicolon, which marks the end of the command. For example, the following are three distinct commands:

```
SELECT id, name FROM foods;
INSERT INTO foods VALUES (NULL, 'Whataburger');
DELETE FROM foods WHERE id=413;
```

Note The semicolon, or command terminator, is associated primarily with interactive programs designed for letting users execute queries against a database. While the command terminator is commonly a semicolon, it nevertheless varies by both database system and query program. Some systems, for example, use \g or even the word go; SQLite, however, uses the semicolon as its command terminator in its command-line program and in the C API.

Commands, in turn, are composed of a series of *tokens*. Tokens can be literals, keywords, identifiers, expressions, or special characters. Tokens are separated by white space, such as spaces, tabs, and newlines.

Literals

Literals, also called constants, denote explicit values. There are three kinds: string constants, numeric constants, and binary constants. String constants are one or more alphanumeric characters surrounded by single quotes. Examples include

```
'Jerry'
'Newman'
'JujyFruit'
```

String values are delimited by single or double quotes. If single quotes are part of the string value, they must be represented as two successive single quotes. For example, Kenny's chicken would be expressed as:

```
'Kenny''s chicken'
```

Numeric constants are represented in integer, decimal, or scientific notation. Examples include

```
-1
3.142
6.0221415E23
```

Binary values are represented using the notation x'0000', where each digit is a hexadecimal value. Binary values must be expressed in by multiples of 2 hexadecimal values (8 bits). Here are some examples:

```
x'01'
X'0fff'
x'0F0EFF'
X'0f0effab'
```

Keywords and Identifiers

Keywords are words that have a specific meaning in SQL. These include words like SELECT, UPDATE, INSERT, CREATE, DROP, and BEGIN. *Identifiers* refer to specific objects within the database, such as tables or indexes. Keywords are reserved words, and may not be used as identifiers. SQL is case insensitive with respect to keywords and identifiers. The following are equivalent statements:

```
SELECT * from foo;
SeLeCt * FrOm FOO;
```

Throughout this chapter, all SQL keywords are represented in uppercase and all identifiers in lowercase for clarity. By default, SQLite is case sensitive with respect to string values, so the value 'Mike' is not the same as the value 'mike'.

Comments

Comments in SQL are denoted by two consecutive hyphens (--), which comment the remaining line, or by the multiline C-style notation (/* */), which can span multiple lines. For example:

```
-- This is a comment on one line
/* This is a comment spanning
   two lines */
```

Creating a Database

Before you can do anything, you have to understand tables. If you don't have a table, you have nothing to work on. The table is the standard unit of information in a relational database. Everything revolves around tables. Tables are composed of rows and columns. And while that sounds simple, the sad truth is that tables are not simple. Tables bring along with them all kinds of other concepts, concepts that can't be nicely summarized in a few tidy paragraphs. In fact, it takes almost the whole chapter. So what we are going to do here is the 2-minute over-view of tables—just enough for you to create a simple table, and get rid of it if you want to. And once we have that out of the way, all of the other parts of this chapter will have something to build on.

Creating Tables

Like the relational model, SQL is made up of several parts. It has a structural part, for example, which is designed to create and destroy database objects. This part of the language is generally referred to as a *data definition language* (DDL). Similarly, it has a functional part for performing operations on those objects (e.g., retrieving and manipulating data). This part of the language is referred to as a *data manipulation language* (DML). Creating tables falls under DDL, the structural part.

You create a table with the `CREATE TABLE` command, which is defined as follows:

```
CREATE [TEMP] TABLE table_name (column_definitions [, constraints]);
```

The `TEMP` or `TEMPORARY` keyword creates a *temporary table*. This kind of table is, well, temporary— it will only last as long your session. As soon as you disconnect, it will be destroyed (if you haven't already destroyed it manually). The brackets around the `TEMP` denote that it is an optional part of the command. Whenever you see any syntax in brackets, it means that the contents within them are optional. Furthermore, the pipe symbol (|) denotes an alternative (think of the word *or*). Take, for example, the syntax

```
CREATE [TEMP|TEMPORARY] TABLE … ;
```

This means that either the `TEMP` *or* `TEMPORARY` keyword may be optionally used. You could say `CREATE TEMP table foo…`, or `CREATE TEMPORARY TABLE foo…`. In this case, they mean the same thing.

If you don't create a temporary table, then `CREATE TABLE` creates a *base table*. The term base table refers to a table that is a named, persistent table in the database. This is the most common kind of table. There are other kinds of tables, such as *system tables* and *views*, which can exist in the database as well. But they aren't important right now. In general, the term base table is used to differentiate tables created by `CREATE TABLE` from all of the other kinds.

The minimum required information for `CREATE TABLE` is a table name and a column name. The name of the table, given by `table_name`, must be unique among all other identifiers. In the body, `column_definitions` consists of a comma-separated list of column definitions composed of a name, a *domain*, and a comma-separated list of *column constraints*. A domain, sometimes referred to as a *type*, is synonymous with a data type in a programming language. It denotes the type of information that is stored in the column. There are five native types in SQLite: `INTEGER`, `REAL`, `TEXT`, `BLOB`, and `NULL`. All of these domains are covered in the section called "Storage Classes" later in this chapter. *Constraints* are constructs that control what kind of values can be placed in the table or in individual columns. For instance, you can ensure that only unique values are placed in a column by using a `UNIQUE` constraint. Constraints are covered in the section "Data Integrity."

Following that, you can include a list of additional column constraints, denoted by `constraints`. Consider the following example:

```
CREATE TABLE contacts ( id INTEGER PRIMARY KEY,
                        name TEXT NOT NULL COLLATE NOCASE,
                        phone TEXT NOT NULL DEFAULT 'UNKNOWN',
                        UNIQUE (name,phone) );
```

Column `id` is declared to have type `INTEGER` and constraint `PRIMARY KEY`. As it turns out, the combination of this type and constraint has a special meaning in SQLite. `INTEGER PRIMARY KEY` basically turns the column into an autoincrement column (as explained in the section "Primary Key Constraints" later in this chapter). Column `name` is declared to be of type `TEXT` and has two constraints: `NOT NULL` and `COLLATE NOCASE`. Column `phone` is of type `TEXT` and has two constraints defined as well. After that, there is a table-level constraint of `UNIQUE`, which is defined for columns `name` and `phone` together.

This is a lot of information to absorb all at once, but it will all be explained in due course. I warned you that tables bring a lot of baggage with them. The only important thing here, however, is that you understand the general format of the CREATE TABLE statement.

Altering Tables

You can change parts of a table with the ALTER TABLE command. SQLite's version of ALTER TABLE can either rename a table or add columns. The general form of the command is

```
ALTER TABLE table { RENAME TO name | ADD COLUMN column_def }
```

Note that there is some new notation here: {}. Braces enclose a list of options, where one option is required. In this case, we have to use either ALTER TABLE table RENAME... or ALTER TABLE table ADD COLUMN.... That is, you can either rename the table using the RENAME clause, or add a column with the ADD COLUMN clause. To rename a table, you simply provide the new name given by name.

If you add a column, the column definition, denoted by column_def, follows the form in the CREATE TABLE statement. It is a name, followed by an optional domain and list of constraints. For example:

```
sqlite> ALTER TABLE contacts
        ADD COLUMN email TEXT NOT NULL DEFAULT '' COLLATE NOCASE;
sqlite> .schema contacts

CREATE TABLE contacts ( id INTEGER PRIMARY KEY,
                        name TEXT NOT NULL COLLATE NOCASE,
                        phone TEXT NOT NULL DEFAULT 'UNKNOWN',
                        email TEXT NOT NULL DEFAULT '' COLLATE NOCASE,
                        UNIQUE (name,phone) );
```

To view the table definition from with the SQLite command-line program, use the .schema shell command followed by the table name. It will print the current table definition. If you don't provide a table name, then .schema will print the entire database schema.

Tables can also be created from SELECT statements, allowing you to create not only the structure but also the data at the same time. This particular use of the CREATE TABLE statement is covered later in the section "Inserting Records."

Querying the Database

As mentioned previously in the section "Creating a Database," the manipulative component of SQL is called Data Manipulation Language (DML). DML, in turn has two basic parts: data retrieval and data modification. Data retrieval is the domain of the SELECT command. It is the sole command for querying the database. SELECT is by far the largest and most complex command in SQL. SELECT derives many of its operations from relational algebra, and encompasses a large portion of it.

Relational Operations

There are 13 relational operations used in SELECT, which are divided into three categories:

- Fundamental Operations

  - Restriction

  - Projection

  - Cartesian Product

  - Union

  - Difference

  - Rename

- Additional Operations

  - Intersection

  - Natural Join

  - Assign

- Extended Operations

  - Generalized Projection

  - Left Outer Join

  - Right Outer Join

  - Full Outer Join

The fundamental operations are just that: fundamental. They define the basic relational operations, and all of them (with the exception of *rename*) have their basis in set theory. The additional operations are for convenience. They can be expressed (or performed) in terms of the fundamental operations. They simply offer a shorthand way of performing frequently used combinations of the fundamental operations. Finally, the extended operations add features to the fundamental and additional operations. The generalized projection operation adds arithmetic expressions, aggregates, and grouping features to the fundamental projection operations. The outer joins extend the join operations and allow additional information and/or incomplete information to be retrieved from the database.

In ANSI SQL, SELECT can perform every one of these relational operations. These operations in turn make up all of the original relational operators defined by Codd (and then some) with one exception—*divide*. SQLite supports all of the relational operations in ANSI SQL with the exception of right and full outer joins (although these operations can be performed by other indirect means).

All of these operations are defined in terms of relations. They take one or more relations as their inputs, and produce a relation as their output. It means that the fundamental structure of information never changes as a result of the operations performed upon it. Relational operations take only relations and produce only relations. This property is called *closure*. Closure makes possible *relational expressions*. The output of one operation, being a relation, can therefore serve as the input to another operation. Thus, operations can take as their arguments not only relations but also other operations (as they will produce relations). This allows operations to be strung together into relational expressions. Relational expressions can therefore be created to arbitrary complexity. For example, the output of a SELECT operation (a relation) can be fed as the input to another, as follows:

```
SELECT name FROM (SELECT name, type_id FROM (SELECT * FROM foods));
```

Here, the output of the innermost SELECT is fed to the next SELECT, whose output is in turn fed to the outermost SELECT. It is all a single relational expression.

The end result is that relational operations are not only powerful in their own right but can be combined to make even more powerful and elaborate expressions. As it turns out, the additional operators, as mentioned earlier, are in fact relational expressions composed of fundamental operations. For example, the intersection operation is defined in terms of two *difference* operations.

The Operational Pipeline

Syntactically, the SELECT command incorporates many of the relational operations through a series of *clauses*. Each clause corresponds to specific relational operation. Almost all of the clauses are optional, so you can selectively employ only the operations you need to obtain the data you are looking for.

SELECT is a very large command. A very general form of SELECT (without too much distracting syntax) can be represented as follows:

```
SELECT DISTINCT heading FROM tables WHERE predicate
       GROUP BY columns HAVING predicate
       ORDER BY columns LIMIT count,offset;
```

Each keyword—DISTINCT, FROM, WHERE, HAVING—is a separate clause. Each clause is made up of the keyword (represented in uppercase) followed by arguments (represented in italics). The syntax of the particular arguments varies according to the clause. The clauses, their corresponding relational operations, and their various arguments are listed in Table 4-1. The ORDER BY clause does not correspond to a formal relational operation as it only reorders rows—that is the meaning of the double hyphens in the Operation column. From here on out, I will in most cases refer to these clauses simply by name. That is, rather than "the WHERE clause," I will simply use WHERE. While there is both a SELECT command and a SELECT clause, I will refer to the command as the SELECT command, and the clause by the convention.

Table 4-1. *SELECT Clauses*

Order	Clause	Operation	Input
1	FROM	Join	List of tables
2	WHERE	Restriction	Logical predicate
3	ORDER BY	--	List of columns
4	GROUP BY	Restriction	List of columns
5	HAVING	Restriction	Logical predicate
6	SELECT	Projection	List of columns or expressions
7	DISTINCT	Restriction	List of columns
8	LIMIT	Restriction	Integer value
9	OFFSET	Restriction	Integer value

Operationally, the SELECT command is like a pipeline that processes relations. This pipeline has optional processes that you can plug into it as you need them. Regardless of whether you include or exclude a particular operation, the relative operations is always the same. This order is shown in Figure 4-3.

The SELECT command starts with FROM, which takes one or more input relations, combines them into a single composite relation, and passes it through the subsequent chain of operations. Each subsequent operation takes exactly one relation as input and produces exactly one relation as output.

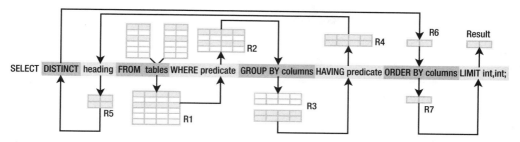

Figure 4-3. *SELECT phases*

All operations are optional with the exception of SELECT. You must always provide at least this clause to make a valid SELECT command. By far the most common invocation of the SELECT command consists of three clauses: SELECT, FROM, and WHERE. This basic syntax and its associated clauses are shown as follows:

```
SELECT heading FROM tables WHERE predicate;
```

The FROM clause is a comma-separated list of one or more tables (represented by the variable tables in Figure 4-3). If more than one table is specified, they will be combined to form a single relation (represented by *R1* in Figure 4-3). This is done by one of the join operations. The resulting relation produced by FROM serves as the initial material. All subsequent operations will either work directly from it or from derivatives of it.

The WHERE clause filters rows in *R1*. In a way, it determines the number of rows (or *cardinality*) of the result. WHERE is a restriction operation, which (somewhat confusingly) is also known as *selection*. Restriction takes a relation and produces a row-wise subset of that relation. The argument of WHERE is a *predicate*, or logical expression, which defines the selection criteria by which rows in *R1* are included in (or excluded from) the result. The selected rows from the WHERE clause form a new relation *R2*, as shown in Figure 4-3. *R2* is a restriction of *R1*.

In this particular example, *R2* passes through the other operations unscathed until it reaches the SELECT clause. The SELECT clause filters the columns in *R2*. Its argument consists of a comma-separated list of columns or expressions that define the result. This is called the *projection list*, or *heading* of the result. The number of columns in the heading is called the *degree* of the result. The SELECT clause is a projection operation, which is the process of producing a column-wise subset of a relation. Figure 4-4 illustrates a projection operation. The input is a relation composed of five columns, including the columns 1, 2, and 3. The projection operation as represented by the arrow produces a new relation by extracting these columns and discarding the others.

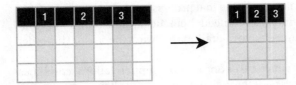

Figure 4-4. *Projection*

Consider the following example:

```
sqlite> SELECT id, name FROM food_types;
id          name
----------  ----------
1           Bakery
2           Cereal
3           Chicken/Fowl
4           Condiments
5           Dairy
6           Dip
7           Drinks
8           Fruit
9           Junkfood
10          Meat
11          Rice/Pasta
12          Sandwiches
13          Seafood
14          Soup
15          Vegetables
```

There is no WHERE clause to filter rows. The SELECT clause specifies all of the columns in food_types, and the FROM clause does not join tables. So there really isn't much taking place. The result is an exact copy of food_types. The input relation and the result relation are the same. If you want to include all possible columns in the result, rather than listing them one by one, you can use a shorthand notation—an asterisk (*)—instead. Thus, the previous example can just as easily be expressed as

```
SELECT * FROM food_types;
```

This is almost the simplest SELECT command. In reality, the simplest SELECT command requires only a SELECT clause, and the SELECT clause requires only a single argument. Therefore, the simplest SELECT command is

```
sqlite> SELECT NULL;

NULL
----
NULL
```

The result is a relation composed of one row and one column, with an unknown value—NULL. NULL is covered later in the section "The Thing Called Null."

Now let's look at an example that actually does something operationally. Consider the following:

```
SELECT name, type_id FROM foods;
```

This performs a projection on foods, selecting two of its three columns—name and type_id. The id column is thrown out, as shown in Figure 4-5.

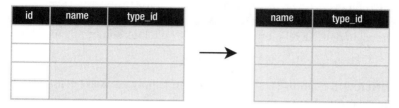

Figure 4-5. *A projection of foods*

Let's summarize: the FROM clause takes the input relations and performs a join, which combines them into a single relation *R1*. The WHERE clause takes *R1* and filters it via restriction, producing a new relation *R2*. The SELECT clause takes *R2* and performs projection, producing the final result. This process is shown in Figure 4-6.

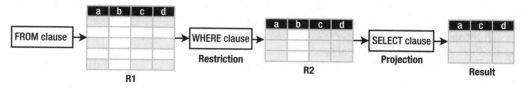

Figure 4-6. *Restriction and projection in SELECT*

With this simple example, you can begin to see how a query language in general and SQL in particular ultimately operates in terms of relational operations. There is real math under the hood.

Filtering

If the SELECT command is the most complex command in SQL, then the WHERE clause is the most complex clause in SELECT. And, just as the SELECT command pulls in aspects of set theory, the WHERE clause also pulls in aspects of formal logic. By and large, the WHERE clause is usually the part of the SELECT command that harbors the most complexity. But it also does most of the work. Having a solid understanding of its mechanics will most likely bring the best overall returns in your day-to-day use of SQL.

The database applies the WHERE clause to each row of the relation produced by the FROM clause (*R1*). As stated earlier, WHERE—a restriction—is a filter. The argument of WHERE is a logical predicate. A predicate, in the simplest sense, is just an assertion about something. Consider the following statement:

The dog (subject) is purple and has a toothy grin (predicate).

The dog is the subject and the predicate consists of the two assertions (color is purple and grin is toothy). This statement may be true or false, depending on the dog the predicate is applied to. In the terminology of formal logic, a statement consisting of a subject and a predicate is called a *proposition*. All propositions are either true or false.

A predicate then says something about a subject. The subject in the WHERE clause is a row. The row is the logical subject. The WHERE clause is the logical predicate. Together (as in a grammatical sentence) they form a logical proposition, which evaluates to true or false. This proposition is formulated and evaluated for every row in *R1*. Each row in which the proposition evaluates to true is included (or selected) as part of the result (*R2*). Each row in which it is false is excluded. So the dog proposition translated into a relational equivalent would look something like this:

```
SELECT * FROM dogs WHERE color='purple' AND grin='toothy';
```

The database will take each row in relation dogs (the subject) and apply the WHERE clause (the predicate) to form the logical proposition:

```
This row has color='purple' AND grin='toothy'.
```

This is either true of the given row, or it is false—nothing more. If it is true, then the row (or dog) is indeed purple and toothy, and it is included in the result. If the proposition is false, then the row may be purple but not toothy, or toothy but not purple, or neither purple nor toothy. In any case, the proposition is false and the row is therefore excluded.

WHERE is a powerful filter. It provides you with a great degree of control over the conditions with which to include (or exclude) rows in (or from) the result. As a logical predicate, it is also a logical expression. A logical expression is an expression that evaluates to exactly one of two possible logical outcomes: *true or false*. A logical predicate then is just a logical expression that is used in a specific way—to qualify a subject and form a proposition.

At their simplest, logical expressions consist of two *values* or *value expressions* compared by *relational operators*. *Value expressions* are built from *values* and *operators*.

A relational operator referred to here is a relational operator in the mathematical sense. It is different from a relational operator in the relational sense, as defined in relational algebra. A relational operator in math is an operator that relates two values and evaluates to true or false (e.g., $x>y$, $x<=y$). A relational operator in relational algebra is an operator that takes two or more relations and produces a new relation. To minimize confusion, the scope of this discussion is limited to one relational operation—restriction—as implemented by the WHERE clause in SQL. The WHERE clause is expressed in terms of logical propositions, which use relational (in the mathematical sense) operators. For the remainder of this section, "relational operator" refers specifically to that in the mathematical sense.

Values

Everything begins with *values*, which represent some kind of data in the real world. Values can be classified by their domain (or type), such as a numerical value (1, 2, 3, etc.) or string value ("Jujy-Fruit"). Values can be expressed as *literal values* (an explicit quantity such as 1, 2, 3 or "JujyFruit"), *variables* (often in the form of column names like foods.name), expressions (3+2/5), or the results of functions (COUNT(foods.name))—which are covered later.

Operators

An operator takes one or more values as input and produces a value as output. An operator is so named because it performs some kind of operation, producing some kind of result. *Binary operators* are operators that take two input values (or operands). *Ternary operators* take three operands, *unary operators* take just one, and so on.

Many operators produce the same kind of information they consume (operators that operate on numbers produce numbers, etc.). Such operators can be strung together, feeding the output of one operator into the input of another (Figure 4-7), forming value expressions.

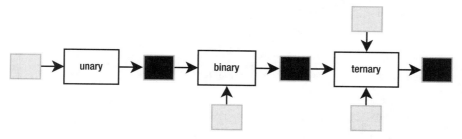

Figure 4-7. *Unary, binary, and ternary operators*

By stringing operators together, you can create value expressions that are expressed in terms of yet other value expressions to arbitrary complexity. For example:

```
x = count(episodes.name)
y = count(foods.name)
z = y/x * 11
```

Binary Operators

Binary operators are by far the most common of all operators in SQL. Table 4-2 lists the binary operators supported in SQLite by *precedence*, from highest to lowest. Operators in each color group have equal precedence. Precedence determines the default order of evaluation in an expression with multiple operators. For example, take the expression 4+3*7. It evaluates to 25. The multiplication operator has higher precedence than addition, and is therefore evaluated first. So the expression is computed (3*7)+4. Precedence can be overridden using parentheses. The expression (4+3)*7 is not 25. Here, the parentheses have declared an explicit order of operation.

Table 4-2. *Binary Operators*

Operator	Type	Action
||	String	Concatenation
*	Arithmetic	Multiply
/	Arithmetic	Divide
%	Arithmetic	Modulus
+	Arithmetic	Add

Table 4-2. *Binary Operators (Continued)*

Operator	Type	Action
–	Arithmetic	Subtract
<<	Bitwise	Right shift
>>	Bitwise	Left shift
&	Logical	And
|	Logical	Or
<	Relational	Less than
<=	Relational	Less than or equal to
>	Relational	Greater than
>=	Relational	Greater than or equal to
=	Relational	Equal to
==	Relational	Equal to
<>	Relational	Not equal to
!=	Relational	Not equal to
IN	Logical	In
AND	Logical	And
OR	Logical	Or
LIKE	Relational	String matching
GLOB	Relational	Filename matching

Arithmetic operators (e.g., addition, subtraction, division) are binary operators that take numeric values and produce a numeric value. *Relational operators* (e.g., >, <, =) are binary operators that compare values and value expressions and return a *logical value* (also called a *truth* value), which is either true or false. Relational operators form *logical expressions*, for example:

```
x > 5
1 < 2
```

A logical expression is any expression that returns a truth value. In SQLite, false is represented by the number 0, while true is represented by anything else. For example:

```
sqlite> SELECT 1 > 2;

1 > 2
----------
0
```

```
sqlite> SELECT 1 < 2;

1 < 2
----------
1

sqlite> SELECT 1 = 2;

1 = 2
----------
0

sqlite> SELECT -1 AND 1;

-1 AND 1
----------
1
```

Logical Operators

Logical operators (AND, OR, NOT, IN) are binary operators that operate on truth values or logical expressions. They produce a specific truth value depending on their inputs. They are used to build more complex logical expressions from simpler expressions, such as

```
(x > 5) AND (x != 3)
(y < 2) OR (y > 4) AND NOT (y = 0)
(color='purple') AND (grin='toothy')
```

The truth value produced by a logical operator for a given pair of arguments depends on the operator. For example, logical AND requires that both input values evaluate to true in order for it to return *true*. Logical OR, on the other hand, only requires that one input value evaluate to *true* in order for it to return *true*. All possible outcomes for a given logical operator are defined in what is known as a *truth table*. The truth tables for AND and OR are shown in Tables 4-3 and 4-4, respectively.

Table 4-3. *Truth Table for Logical And*

Argument 1	Argument 2	Result
True	True	True
True	False	False
False	False	False

Table 4-4. *Truth Table for Logical Or*

Argument 1	Argument 2	Result
True	True	True
True	False	True
False	False	False

This is the stuff the WHERE clause is made of. Using logical operators, you can create a complex logical predicate. The predicate is what defines how WHERE's relational restriction operation restricts. For example:

```
sqlite> SELECT * FROM foods WHERE name='JujyFruit' AND type_id=9;
```

```
id          type_id    name
----------  ----------  ----------
244         9           JujyFruit
```

The restriction here works according to the expression (name='JujyFruit') AND (type_id=9), which consists of two logical expressions joined by logical AND. Both of these conditions must be true for any record in foods to be included in the result.

The LIKE Operator

A particularly useful relational operator is LIKE. LIKE is similar to equals (=), but is used for matching string values against patterns. For example, to select all rows in foods whose names begin with the letter "J," you could do the following:

```
sqlite> SELECT id, name FROM foods WHERE name LIKE 'J%';
```

```
id     name
-----  --------------------
156    Juice box
236    Juicy Fruit Gum
243    Jello with Bananas
244    JujyFruit
245    Junior Mints
370    Jambalaya
```

A percent symbol (%) in the pattern matches any sequence of zero or more characters in the string. An underscore (_) in the pattern matches any single character in the string. The percent symbol is greedy. It will eat everything between two characters except those characters. If it is on the extreme left or right of a pattern, it will consume everything on each respective side. Consider the following examples:

```
sqlite> SELECT id, name FROM foods WHERE name LIKE '%ac%P%';

id      name
-----   --------------------
127     Guacamole Dip
168     Peach Schnapps
198     Mackinaw Peaches
```

Another useful trick is to use NOT to negate a pattern:

```
sqlite> SELECT id, name FROM foods
          WHERE name like '%ac%P%' AND name NOT LIKE '%Sch%'

id      name
-----   --------------------
 38     Pie (Blackberry) Pie
127     Guacamole Dip
198     Mackinaw peaches
```

Limiting and Ordering

You can limit the size and particular range of the result using the LIMIT and OFFSET keywords. LIMIT specifies the maximum number of records to return. OFFSET specifies the number of records to skip. For example, the following statement obtains the Cereal record (the second record in food_types) using LIMIT and OFFSET:

```
SELECT * FROM food_types LIMIT 1 OFFSET 1 ORDER BY id;
```

The OFFSET clause skips one row (the Bakery row) and the LIMIT clause returns a maximum of one row (the Cereal row).

But there is something else here as well: ORDER BY. This clause sorts the result by a column or columns before it is returned. The reason it is important in this example is because the rows returned from SELECT are never guaranteed to be in any specific order—the SQL standard declares this. Thus, the ORDER BY clause is essential if you need to count on the result being in any specific order. The syntax of the ORDER BY clause is similar to the SELECT clause: it is a comma-separated list of columns. Each entry may be qualified with a sort order—ASC (ascending, the default) or DESC (descending). For example:

```
sqlite> SELECT * FROM foods WHERE name LIKE 'B%'
          ORDER BY type_id DESC, name LIMIT 10;

id      type_id   name
-----   --------   --------------------
382     15        Baked Beans
383     15        Baked Potato w/Sour
384     15        Big Salad
385     15        Broccoli
362     14        Bouillabaisse
328     12        BLT
```

327	12	Bacon Club (no turke
326	12	Bologna
329	12	Brisket Sandwich
274	10	Bacon

Typically you only need to order by a second (third, etc.) column when there are duplicate values in the first (second, etc.) ordered column(s). Here, there were many duplicate type_ids. I wanted to group them together, and then arrange the foods alphabetically within these groups.

Note LIMIT and OFFSET are not standard SQL keywords as defined in the ANSI standard. Nevertheless, they are found on several other databases, such as MySQL and PostgreSQL. Oracle, MS SQL, and Firebird also have functional equivalents, although they use different syntax.

If you use both LIMIT and OFFSET together, you can use a comma notation in place of the OFFSET keyword. For example, the following SQL

```
SELECT * FROM foods WHERE name LIKE 'B%'
ORDER BY type_id DESC, name LIMIT 1 OFFSET 2;
```

can be expressed equivalently with

```
sqlite> SELECT * FROM foods WHERE name LIKE 'B%'
        ORDER BY type_id DESC, name LIMIT 1,2;
```

id	type_id	name
384	15	Big Salad

Here, the comma following LIMIT 1 adds the OFFSET of 2 to the clause. Also, note that OFFSET depends on LIMIT. That is, you can use LIMIT without using OFFSET but not the other way around.

Notice that LIMIT and OFFSET are dead last in the operational pipeline. One common misconception of LIMIT/OFFSET is that it speeds up a query by limiting the number of rows that must be collected by the WHERE clause. This is not true. If it were, then ORDER BY would not work properly. For ORDER BY to do its job, it must have the entire result in hand to provide the correct order.

ORDER BY, on the other hand, works after WHERE but before SELECT. How do I know this? The following statement works:

```
SELECT name FROM foods ORDER BY id;
```

I am asking SQLite to order by a column that is not in the result. The only way this could happen is if the ordering takes place before projection (while the id column is still in the set). While this works in SQLite, it is also specified in SQL2003.

Functions and Aggregates

Relational algebra supports the notion of functions and aggregates through the extended operation known as *generalized projection*. The SELECT clause is a generalized projection rather than just a fundamental projection. The fundamental projection operation only accepts column names in the projection list as a means to produce a column-wise subset. Generalized projection accepts this as well as arithmetic expressions, functions, and aggregates in the projection list, in addition to other features such as GROUP BY and HAVING, all of which are covered here and in the subsequent sections.

SQLite comes with various built-in functions and aggregates that can be used within various clauses. Function types range from mathematical functions such as ABS(), which computes the absolute value, to string formatting functions such as UPPER() and LOWER(), which convert text to upper- and lowercase, respectively. For example:

```
sqlite> SELECT UPPER('hello newman'), LENGTH('hello newman'), ABS(-12);

UPPER('hello newman')  LENGTH('hello newman') ABS(-12)
---------------------  ---------------------  ----------
HELLO NEWMAN           12                     12
```

Notice that the function names are case insensitive (i.e., upper() and UPPER() refer to the same function). Functions can accept column values as their arguments:

```
sqlite> SELECT id, UPPER(name), LENGTH(name) FROM foods
        WHERE type_id=1 LIMIT 10;

id     UPPER(name)                  LENGTH(name)
-----  --------------------------   ------------
1      BAGELS                       6
2      BAGELS, RAISIN               14
3      BAVARIAN CREAM PIE           18
4      BEAR CLAWS                   10
5      BLACK AND WHITE COOKIES      23
6      BREAD (WITH NUTS)            17
7      BUTTERFINGERS                13
8      CARROT CAKE                  11
9      CHIPS AHOY COOKIES           18
10     CHOCOLATE BOBKA              15
```

Since functions can be a part of any expression, they can also be used in the WHERE clause:

```
sqlite> SELECT id, UPPER(name), LENGTH(name) FROM foods
        WHERE LENGTH(name) < 5 LIMIT 5;

id     upper(name)           length(name)
-----  --------------------  --------------------
36     PIE                   3
48     BRAN                  4
56     KIX                   3
57     LIFE                  4
80     DUCK                  4
```

Just for reinforcement, let's go through the relational operations performed to carry out the preceding statement:

1. FROM clause (join)

The FROM clause in this case does not join tables; it only produces a relation *R1* containing all the rows in foods.

2. WHERE clause (restriction)

For each row in *R1*:

   a. Apply the predicate LENGTH(name) < 5 to the row. That is, evaluate the proposition "row has LENGTH(name) < 5."

   b. If true, add the row to *R2*.

3. SELECT clause (projection)

For each row in *R2*:

   a. Create a new row *r* in *R3*.

   b. Copy the value of the id field in restriction into the first column of *r*.

   c. Copy the result of the expression UPPER(row.name) to the second column of *r*.

   d. Copy the result of the expression LENGTH(row.name) to the third column or *r*.

4. LIMIT clause (restriction)

Restrict *R3* to just the first five records.

Aggregates are a special class of functions that calculate a composite (or aggregate) value over a group of rows (or relation). According to Webster, an aggregate, by definition, is a value "formed by the collection of units or particles into a body, mass, or amount." The particles here are rows in a table. Standard aggregate functions include SUM(), AVG(), COUNT(), MIN(), and MAX(). For example, to get a count of the number of foods that are baked goods (type_id=1), we can use the COUNT aggregate as follows:

```
sqlite> SELECT COUNT(*) FROM foods WHERE type_id=1;

count
-----
47
```

The COUNT aggregate returns a count of every row in the relation. Whenever you see an aggregate, you should automatically think, "For each row in a table, do something." It is the computed value obtained from doing something with each row in the table. For example, COUNT might be expressed in terms of the following pseudocode:

```
int COUNT():
    count = 0;
    for each row in Relation:
        count = count + 1
    return count;
```

Aggregates can aggregate not only column values, but any expression—including functions. For example, to get the average length of all food names, you can apply the AVG aggregate to the LENGTH(name) expression as follows:

```
sqlite> SELECT AVG(LENGTH(name)) FROM foods;

AVG(LENGTH(name))
-----------------
12.58
```

Aggregates operate within the SELECT clause. They compute their values on the rows selected by the WHERE clause—not from all rows selected by the FROM clause. The SELECT command filters first, then aggregates.

While SQLite comes with a standard set of common SQL functions and aggregates, it is worth noting that the SQLite C API allows you to create custom functions and aggregates as well. See Chapter 7 for more information. For reference, a complete list of the built-in functions and aggregates in SQLite can be found in Appendix A.

Grouping

An essential part of aggregation is grouping. That is, in addition to computing aggregates over an entire result, you can also split that result into groups of rows with like values, and compute aggregates on each group—all in one step. This is the job of the GROUP BY clause. For example:

```
sqlite> SELECT type_id FROM foods GROUP BY type_id;

type_id
----------
1
2
3
.
.
.
15
```

GROUP BY is a bit different than the other parts of SELECT, so you need to use your imagination a little to wrap your head around it. The process is illustrated in Figure 4-8. Operationally, GROUP BY sits in between the WHERE clause and the SELECT clause. GROUP BY takes the output of WHERE and splits it into groups of rows that share a common value (or values) for a specific column (or columns). These groups are then passed to the SELECT clause. In the example, there are 15 different food types (type_id ranges from 1 to 15), and therefore GROUP BY organizes all rows in foods into 15 groups varying by type_id. SELECT takes each group and extracts its common type_id value and puts it into a separate row. Thus, there are 15 rows in the result, one for each group.

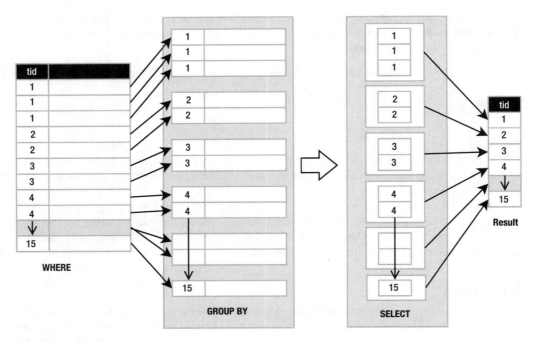

Figure 4-8. *GROUP BY process*

When GROUP BY is used, the SELECT clause applies aggregates to each group separately, rather than the entire result as a whole. Since aggregates produce a single value from a group of values, they collapse these groups of rows into single rows. For example, consider applying the COUNT aggregate to the preceding example to get the number of records in each type_id group:

```
sqlite> SELECT type_id, COUNT(*) FROM foods GROUP BY type_id;
```

type_id	COUNT(*)
1	47
2	15
3	23
4	22
5	17
6	4
7	60
8	23
9	61
10	36
11	16
12	23
13	14
14	19
15	32

Here, COUNT() was applied 15 times—once for each group, as illustrated in Figure 4-9. Note that in the diagram the actual number of records in each group is not represented literally (e.g., it doesn't show 47 records in the group for type_id=1).

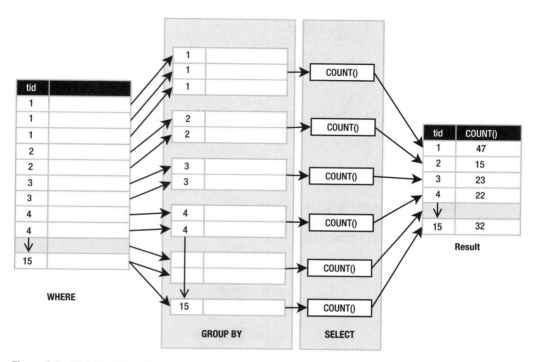

Figure 4-9. *GROUP BY and aggregation*

The number of records with type_id=1 (Baked Goods) is 47. The number with type_id=2 (Cereal) is 15. The number with type_id=3 (Chicken/Fowl) is 23, and so forth. So, to get this information, you could run 15 queries as follows:

```
select count(*) from foods where type_id=1;
select count(*) from foods where type_id=2;
select count(*) from foods where type_id=3;
.
.
.
select count(*) from foods where type_id=15;
```

Or, you get the results using the single SELECT with a GROUP BY as follows:

```
SELECT type_id, COUNT(*) FROM foods GROUP BY type_id;
```

But there is more. Since GROUP BY has to do all this work to create groups with like values, it seems a pity not to let you filter these groups before handing them off to the SELECT clause. That is the purpose of HAVING, a predicate that you apply to the result of GROUP BY. It filters the groups from GROUP BY in the same way that the WHERE clause filters rows from the FROM clause.

The only difference is that the WHERE clause's predicate is expressed in terms of individual row values, and HAVING's predicate is expressed in terms of aggregate values.

Take the previous example, but this time say you are only interested in looking at the food groups that have fewer than 20 foods in them:

```
sqlite> SELECT type_id, COUNT(*) FROM foods
        GROUP BY type_id HAVING COUNT(*) < 20;

type_id     COUNT(*)
----------  ----------
2           15
5           17
6           4
11          16
13          14
14          19
```

Here, HAVING applies the predicate COUNT(*)<20 to all of the groups. Any group that does not satisfy this condition (that has 20 or more foods in it) is not passed on to the SELECT clause. Figure 4-10 illustrates this restriction.

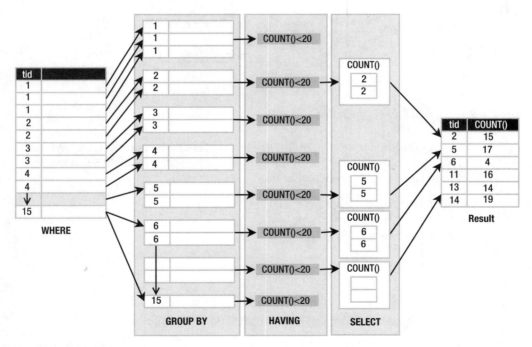

Figure 4-10. *HAVING as group restriction*

The third column in the figure shows groups of rows ordered by type_id. The values shown are the type_id values. The actual number of rows shown in each group is not exact, but figurative. I have only shown two rows in each group to represent the group as a whole.

So GROUP BY and HAVING work as additional restriction phases. GROUP BY takes the restriction produced by the WHERE clause and breaks it into groups of rows that share a common value for a given column. HAVING then applies a filter to each of these groups. The groups that make it through are passed on to the SELECT clause for aggregation and projection.

Removing Duplicates

The next operation in the pipeline is yet another restriction: DISTINCT. DISTINCT takes the result of the SELECT clause and filters out duplicate rows. For example, you'd use this to get all distinct type_id values from foods:

```
sqlite> SELECT DISTINCT type_id FROM foods;

type_id
----------
1
2
3
.
.
.
15
```

This statement works as follows: the WHERE clause returns the entire foods table (all 412 records). The SELECT clause pulls out just the type_id column, and finally DISTINCT removes duplicate rows, reducing the number from 412 rows to 15 rows, all unique. This particular example produces the same result as the GROUP BY example, but it goes about it in a completely different manner. DISTINCT simply compares all columns of all rows listed in the SELECT clause and removes duplicates. There is no grouping on a particular column or columns, nor do you use any predicates. DISTINCT is just a uniqueness filter.

Joining Tables

Your current knowledge of SELECT so far is based entirely on its filtering capabilities: start with something, remove rows, remove columns, aggregate, remove duplicates, and perhaps limit the number of rows even more. The SELECT, WHERE, GROUP BY, HAVING, DISTINCT, and LIMIT clauses are all filters of some sort.

Filtering, however, is only half of the picture. SELECT has two essential parts: collect and refine. Up until now you've only seen the refining, or filtering, part. The source of all this refinement has been only a single table. But SELECT is not limited to filtering just a single table; it can link tables together. SELECT can construct a larger and more detailed picture made of different parts of different tables, and treat that composite as your input table. Then you apply the various filters to whittle it down and isolate the parts you're interested in. This process of linking tables together is called *joining*. Joining is the work of the FROM clause.

Joins are the first operation(s) of the SELECT command. They produce the initial information to be filtered and processed by the remaining parts of the statement. The result of a join is a *composite relation* (or table), which I will refer to as the *input relation*. It is the relation that is provided as the input or starting point for all subsequent (filtering) operations in the SELECT command.

It is perhaps easiest to start with an example. The foods table has a column type_id. As it turns out, the values in this column correspond to values in the id column in the food_types table. A relationship exists between the two tables. Any value in the foods.type_id column must correspond to a value in the food_types.id column, and the id column is the *primary key* (described later) of food_types. The foods.type_id column, by virtue of this relationship, is called a *foreign key*: it contains (or references) values in the primary key of another table. This relationship is called a *foreign key relationship*.

Using this relationship, it is possible to join the foods and food_type tables on these two columns to make a new relation, which provides more detailed information, namely the food_types.name for each food in the foods table. This is done with the following SQL:

```
sqlite> SELECT foods.name, food_types.name
        FROM foods, food_types
        WHERE foods.type_id=food_types.id LIMIT 10;
```

name	name
Bagels	Bakery
Bagels, raisin	Bakery
Bavarian Cream Pie	Bakery
Bear Claws	Bakery
Black and White cookies	Bakery
Bread (with nuts)	Bakery
Butterfingers	Bakery
Carrot Cake	Bakery
Chips Ahoy Cookies	Bakery
Chocolate Bobka	Bakery

You can see the foods.name in the first column of the result, followed by the food_types.name in the second. Each row in the former is linked to its associated row in the latter using the foods.type_id → food_types.id relationship (Figure 4-11).

___

■**Note** I am using a new notation in this example to specify the columns in the SELECT clause. Rather than specifying just the column names, I am using the notation table_name.column_name. The reason is because I have multiple tables in the SELECT statement. The database is smart enough to figure out which table a column belongs to—as long as that column name is unique among all tables. If you use a column whose name is also defined in other tables of the join, the database will not be able to figure out which of the columns you are referring to, and will return an error. In practice, when you are joining tables, it is always a good idea to use the table_name.column_name notation to avoid any possible ambiguity. This is explained in detail in the section "Names and Aliases."

___

To carry out the join, the database finds these matched rows. For each row in the first table, the database finds all rows in the second table that have the same value for the joined columns and includes them in the input relation. So in this example, the FROM clause built a composite relation by joining the rows of two tables.

foods

id	name	type_id
1	Bagels	1
10	Chocolate Bobka	1
49	Cheerios	2
15	Chicken (Kenny's)	8
198	Mackinaw Peaches	8
203	Papaya	8
244	JujyFruit	9
245	Junior Mints	9
412	Wax Beans	15

food_types

id	name
1	Bakery
2	Cereal
3	Chicken/Fowl
8	Fruit
9	Junkfood
15	Vegetables

id	name	type_id	id	name
1	Bagels	1	1	Bakery
10	Chocolate Bobka	1	1	Bakery
49	Cheerios	2	2	Cereal
15	Chicken (Kenny's)	3	3	Chicken/Fowl
198	Mackinaw Peaches	8	8	Fruit
203	Papaya	8	8	Fruit
244	JujyFruit	9	9	Junk Food
245	Junior Mints	9	9	Junk Food
412	Wax Beans	15	1	Vegetable

Figure 4-11. *foods and food_types join*

The subsequent operations (WHERE, GROUP BY, etc.) work exactly the same. It is only the input that has changed through joining tables. However, the predicate in the WHERE clause (foods.type_id=food_types.id) controls what records are returned from the join. This happens in restriction. You might be wondering how this can be if restriction takes place after joining. Well, the short answer is that the database picks up on this by seeing two tables specified in the FROM clause. But this still doesn't explain how anything in the WHERE clause can have any effect on anything in the FROM clause, which is performed before it. You'll find out shortly.

As it turns out, there are six different kinds of joins. The one just described, called an *inner join*, is the most common.

Inner Joins

An inner join is where two tables are joined by a relationship between two columns in the tables, as in this previous example. It is the most common (and perhaps most generally useful) type of join.

An inner join uses another set operation in relational algebra, called an *intersection*. An intersection of two sets produces a set containing elements that exist in both sets. Figure 4-12 illustrates this. The intersection of the set {1, 2, 8, 9} and the set {1, 3, 5, 8} is the set {1, 8}. The intersection operation is represented by a Venn diagram showing the common elements of both sets.

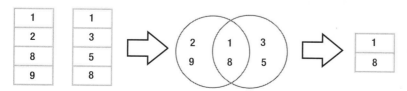

Figure 4-12. *Set intersection*

This is precisely how an inner join works, but the sets in a join are common elements of the related columns. Pretend that the left-hand set in Figure 4-12 represents values in the foods.type_id column and the right-hand set represents values of the food_types.id column. Given the matching columns, an inner join finds the rows from both sides that contain like values and combines them to form the rows of the result (Figure 4-13). Note that this example assumes that the records shown are the only records in foods and food_types.

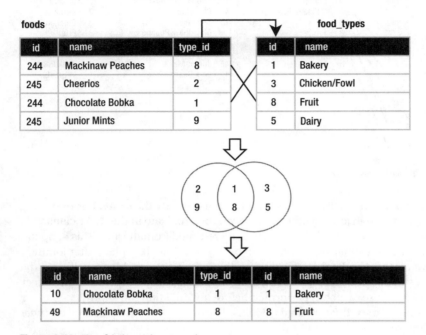

Figure 4-13. *Food join as intersection*

Inner joins only return rows that satisfy the given column relationship, also called the *join condition.* They answer the question, "What rows of *B* match rows in *A* given the following relationship?" Consider the two hypothetical tables shown in Figure 4-14. They both have three columns, with one in common (named a). Table B is shaded just for illustration purposes.

a	b	c
1	4	7
2	5	8
3	6	9

A

a	d	e
1	4	7
2	5	8
4	6	9

B

Figure 4-14. *Two hypothetical tables*

You can see that two rows in B match two rows in A with respect to column a. This is the inner join:

```
SELECT * FROM A, B where A.a=B.a;
```

The result is shown in Figure 4-15.

a	b	c	a	d	e
1	4	7	1	4	7
2	5	8	2	5	8

Figure 4-15. *Inner join of A and B*

Notice that the third row of B does not match any row in A for this condition (and vice versa). Therefore only two rows are included in the result. The join condition (e.g., A.a=B.a) is what makes this an inner join as opposed to another type of join.

Cross Joins

Imagine for a moment that there were no join condition. What would you get? In this case, if the two tables were not related in any way, SELECT would produce a more fundamental kind of join (the *most* fundamental), which is called a *cross join* or *Cartesian join* (if you read Chapter 3, you will know this as the *cross product* or *Cartesian product*). The Cartesian join is one of the fundamental relational operations. It is a brute-force, almost nonsensical join that results in the combination of all rows from the first table with all rows in the second. A cross join of tables A and B can be expressed with the following pseudocode:

```
for each record a in A
    for each record b in B
        make record a + b
```

In SQL, the cross join of A and B is expressed as follows:

```
SELECT * FROM A,B;
```

FROM, in the absence of anything else, produces a cross join. The result is shown in Figure 4-16. Every row in A is combined with every row in B. In a cross join, no relationship exists between the rows; there is no join condition but they are simply jammed together.

This, then, is what the WHERE clause was filtering with the (inner) join condition in the preceding example. It was removing all those rows in the cross join that had no sensible relationship. An inner join is a subset of a cross join. A cross join contains every possible combination of rows in two tables, whereas an inner join contains only those rows that satisfy a specific relationship between columns in the two tables.

a	b	c	a	d	e
1	4	7	1	4	7
1	4	7	2	5	8
1	4	7	4	6	9
2	5	8	1	4	7
2	5	8	2	5	8
2	5	8	4	6	9
3	6	9	1	4	7
3	6	9	2	5	8
3	6	9	4	6	9

Figure 4-16. *Cross join of tables A and B*

From a purely relational sense, a join is composed of the following set operations, in order:

1. **Cross join**: Take the cross product of all tables in the source list.

2. **Restrict**: Apply the join condition (and any other restrictions) to the cross product to narrow it down. An inner join takes the intersection of related columns to select matching rows. Other joins use other criteria.

3. **Project**: Select the desired columns from the restriction.

In this sense, all joins then begin as a cross join of all tables in the FROM clause, producing a set of every combination of rows therein. This is the mathematical process. It is most certainly *not* the process used by relational databases. It would be wasteful, to say the least, for databases to blindly start every join by computing the cross product of all tables listed in the FROM clause. There are many ways databases optimize this process so as to avoid combining rows that will simply be thrown out by the WHERE clause. Thus, the mathematical concept and the database implementation are completely different. However, the end results are logically equivalent.

Outer Joins

Three of the remaining four joins are called *outer joins*. An inner join selects rows across tables according to a given relationship. An outer join selects all of the rows of an inner join plus some rows outside of the relationship. The three outer join types are called *left*, *right*, and *full*. A left join operates with respect to the "left table" in the SQL command. For example, in the command

```
SELECT * FROM A LEFT JOIN B ON A.a=B.a;
```

table A is the left table here. The left join favors it. It is the table of significance in a left join. The left join tries to match every row of A with every row in B per the join condition (A.a=B.a). All such matching rows are included in the result. However, the remaining rows of A that don't match B are still included in the result. In this case, these rows have empty values for the B columns. The result is shown in Figure 4-17.

a	b	c	a	d	e
1	4	7	1	4	7
2	5	8	2	5	8
3	6	9			

Figure 4-17. *Left join of A and B*

Remember that the third row of A has no matching row in B with respect to column a. Despite this, the left join includes all rows of A, matching or not.

The right join works similarly, except the right table is the one whose rows are included, matching or not. Operationally, left and right joins are identical; they do the same thing. They differ only in order and syntax. You could argue that there never is any need to do a right join as the only thing it does is swap the arguments in a left join.

A full outer join is the combination of a left and right outer join. It includes all matching records, followed by unmatched records in the right and left tables. Currently, both right and full outer joins are not supported in SQLite. However, as mentioned earlier, a right join can be replaced with a left join, and a full outer join can be performed using compound queries (see the section "Compound Queries" later in this chapter).

Natural Joins

The last join on the list is called a *natural join*. It is actually an inner join in disguise, but with a little syntax and convention thrown in. A natural join joins two tables by their common column names. Thus, using the natural join you can get the inner join of A and B without having to add the join condition A.a=B.a:

```
sqlite> SELECT * FROM A NATURAL JOIN B;

a          b          c          d          e
---------- ---------- ---------- ---------- ----------
1          4          7          4          7
2          5          8          5          8
```

Here, the natural join automatically detects the common column names in A and B (in this case just column a) and links them together. In practice, it is a good idea to avoid natural joins in your applications if you can. Natural joins will join *all* columns by the same name in both tables. Just the process of adding to or removing a column from a table can drastically change the results of a natural join query. Say a program uses a natural join query on A and B. Then suppose someone comes along and adds a new column e to A. That will cause the natural join (and thus the program) to produce completely different results. It's always better to explicitly define the join conditions of your queries than rely on the semantics of the table schema.

Preferred Syntax

Syntactically, there are various ways of specifying a join. The inner join example of A and B illustrates performing a join implicitly in the WHERE clause:

```
SELECT * FROM A,B WHERE A.a=B.a;
```

When the database sees more than one table listed, it knows there will be a join—at the very least a cross join. The WHERE clause here calls for an inner join.

This implicit form, while rather clean, is actually an older form of syntax that you should avoid. The politically correct way (per SQL92) to express a join in SQL is using the JOIN keyword. The general form is

```
SELECT heading FROM LEFT_TABLE join_type RIGHT_TABLE ON join_condition;
```

This explicit form can be used for all join types. For example:

```
SELECT * FROM A INNER JOIN B ON A.a=B.a;
SELECT * FROM A LEFT JOIN B ON A.a=B.a;
SELECT * FROM A NATURAL JOIN B ON A;
SELECT * FROM A CROSS JOIN B ON A;
```

Finally, when the join condition is based on columns that share the same name, it can be simplified with the USING keyword. USING simply names the common column (or columns) to include in the join condition:

```
SELECT * FROM A INNER JOIN B USING(a);
```

The argument of USING is a comma-separated list of column names within parentheses.

Joins are processed from left to right. Consider the mutliway join shown in Figure 4-18.

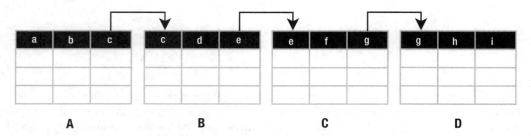

Figure 4-18. *Multiway join*

Using the preferred form, you simply keep tacking on additional tables by adding more join expressions to the end of the statement:

```
SELECT * FROM A JOIN B USING (c) JOIN C USING (e) JOIN D USING (g);
```

The first relation, *R1*, is from A join B on c. The second relation, *R2*, is R1 join C on e. The final relation, *R3*, is R2 join D on g. This is shown in Figure 4-19.

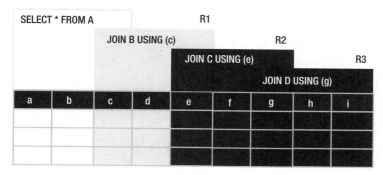

Figure 4-19. *A politically correct multiway join construction*

Names and Aliases

When joining tables, column names can become ambiguous. For example, A and B as defined in Figure 4-14 both have a column a. What if they have another column named name, and you just want to select the name column of B but not A? To help with this type of task, you can qualify column names with their table names to remove any ambiguity. So in this example, you could write

```
SELECT B.name FROM A JOIN B USING (a);
```

Another useful feature is *aliases*. If your table name is particularly long, and you don't want to have to use its name every time you qualify a column, you can use an alias. Aliasing is actually a fundamental relational operation called *rename*. The rename operation simply assigns a new name to a relation. For example, consider the statement:

```
SELECT foods.name, food_types.name FROM foods, food_types
WHERE foods.type_id=food_types.id LIMIT 10;
```

There is a good bit of typing here. You can rename the tables in the source clause by simply including the new name directly after the table name, as in the following example:

```
SELECT f.name, t.name FROM foods f, food_types t
WHERE f.type_id=t.id LIMIT 10;
```

Here, the foods table is assigned the alias f, and the food_types table is assigned the alias t. Now, every other reference to foods or food_types in the statement must use the alias f and t, respectively. Aliases make it possible to do *self-joins*—joining a table with itself. For example, say you want to know what foods in season 4 are mentioned in other seasons. You would first need to get a list of episodes and foods in season 4, which you would obtain by joining episodes and episodes_foods. But then you would need a similar list for foods outside of season 4. Finally, you would combine the two lists based on their common foods. The following query uses self-joins to do the trick:

```
SELECT f.name as food, e1.name, e1.season, e2.name, e2.season
FROM episodes e1, foods_episodes fe1, foods f,
    episodes e2, foods_episodes fe2
```

```
WHERE
    -- Get foods in season 4
    (e1.id = fe1.episode_id AND e1.season = 4) AND fe1.food_id = f.id
    -- Link foods with all other epsisodes
    AND (fe1.food_id = fe2.food_id)
    -- Link with their respective episodes and filter out e1's season
    AND (fe2.episode_id = e2.id AND e2.season != e1.season)
ORDER BY f.name;
```

food	name	season	name	season
Bouillabaisse	The Shoes	4	The Stake Out	1
Decaf Cappuccino	The Pitch	4	The Good Samaritan	3
Decaf Cappuccino	The Ticket	4	The Good Samaritan	3
Egg Salad	The Trip 1	4	Male Unbonding	1
Egg Salad	The Trip 1	4	The Stock Tip	1
Mints	The Trip 1	4	The Cartoon	9
Snapple	The Virgin	4	The Abstinence	8
Tic Tacs	The Trip 1	4	The Merv Griffin Show	9
Tic Tacs	The Contest	4	The Merv Griffin Show	9
Tuna	The Trip 1	4	The Stall	5
Turkey Club	The Bubble Boy	4	The Soup	6
Turkey Club	The Bubble Boy	4	The Wizard	9

I have put comments in the SQL to better explain what is going on. This example uses two self-joins. There are two instances of episodes and foods_episodes, but they are treated as if they are two independent tables. The query joins foods_episodes back on itself to link the two instances of episodes. Furthermore, the two episodes instances are related to each other by an inequality condition to ensure that they are in different seasons.

You can alias column names and expressions in the same way. For example, to get the top ten episodes with the most foods, nicely labeled, you'd use this:

```
sqlite> SELECT e.name AS Episode, COUNT(f.id) AS Foods
        FROM foods f
          JOIN foods_episodes fe on f.id=fe.food_id
          JOIN episodes e on fe.episode_id=e.id
        GROUP BY e.id
        ORDER BY Foods DESC
        LIMIT 10;
```

Episode	Foods
The Soup	23
The Fatigues	14
The Bubble Boy	12
The Finale 1	10
The Merv Griffin Show	9
The Soup Nazi	9

The Wink	9
The Dinner Party	9
The Glasses	9
The Mango	9

Note that the AS keyword is optional. I just use it because it seems more legible that way to me. Column aliases will change the column headers returned in the result set. You may refer to columns or expressions by their aliases elsewhere in the statement if you wish (as in the ORDER BY clause in the preceding example), but you are not required to do so like you are with tables.

Subqueries

Subqueries are SELECTs within SELECTs. They are also called *subselects*. Subqueries are useful in many ways, they work anywhere normal expressions work, and they can therefore be used in a variety of places in a SELECT statement. Subqueries are useful in other commands as well.

Perhaps the most common use of subqueries is in the WHERE clause, specifically using the IN operator. The IN operator is a binary operator that takes an input value and a list of values and returns true if the input value exists in the list, or false otherwise. Here's an example:

```
sqlite> SELECT 1 IN (1,2,3);
1
sqlite> SELECT 2 IN (3,4,5);
0
sqlite> SELECT COUNT(*) FROM foods WHERE type_id IN (1,2);
62
```

Using a subquery, you can rewrite the last statement in terms of names from the food_types:

```
sqlite> SELECT COUNT(*) FROM foods WHERE type_id
        IN (SELECT id FROM food_types WHERE name='Bakery' OR name='Cereal');

62
```

Subqueries in the SELECT clause can be used to add additional data from other tables to the result set. For example, to get the number of episodes each food appears in, the actual count from foods_episodes can be performed in a subquery in the SELECT clause:

```
sqlite> SELECT name,
        (SELECT COUNT(id) FROM foods_episodes WHERE food_id=f.id) count
        FROM foods f ORDER BY count DESC LIMIT 10;
```

name	count
----------	----------
Hot Dog	5
Pizza	4
Ketchup	4
Kasha	4
Shrimp	3
Lobster	3
Turkey Sandwich	3

```
Turkey Club     3
Egg Salad       3
Tic Tacs        3
```

The ORDER BY and LIMIT clauses here serve to create a top ten list, with hot dogs at the top. Notice that the subquery's predicate references a table in the enclosing SELECT command: food_id=f.id. The variable f.id exists in the outer query. The subquery in this example is called a *correlated subquery* because it references, or correlates to, a variable in the outer (enclosing) query.

Subqueries in the SELECT clause are also helpful with computing percentages of aggregates. For example, the following SQL breaks foods down by types and their respective percentages:

```
SELECT (SELECT name FROM food_types WHERE id=f.type_id) Type,
COUNT(type_id) Items,
COUNT(type_id)*100.0/(SELECT COUNT(*) FROM foods) as Percentage
FROM foods f GROUP BY type_id ORDER BY Percentage DESC;
```

Type	Items	Percentage
Junkfood	61	14.76997578692
Drinks	60	14.52784503631
Bakery	48	11.62227602905
Meat	36	8.716707021791
Vegetables	32	7.748184019370
Chicken/Fowl	23	5.569007263922
Fruit	23	5.569007263922
Sandwiches	23	5.569007263922
Condiments	22	5.326876513317
Soup	19	4.600484261501
Dairy	17	4.116222760290
Rice/Pasta	16	3.874092009685
Cereal	15	3.631961259079
Seafood	14	3.389830508474
Dip	4	0.968523002421

Here, a subquery must be used as the divisor rather than COUNT() because the statement uses a GROUP BY. Remember that aggregates in GROUP BY are applied to groups, not the entire result set; therefore the subquery's COUNT() must be used to get the total rows in foods.

Subqueries can be used in the ORDER BY clause as well. The following SQL groups foods by the size of their respective food groups, from greatest to least:

```
SELECT * FROM foods f
ORDER BY (SELECT COUNT(type_id)
FROM foods WHERE type_id=f.type_id) DESC;
```

ORDER BY in this case does not refer to any specific column in the result. How does this work then? The ORDER BY subquery is run for each row, and the result is associated with the given row. You can think of it as an invisible column in the result set, which is used to order rows.

Finally, we have the FROM clause. There may be times when you want to join only part of a table rather than all of it. Yet another job for a subquery:

```
SELECT f.name, types.name FROM foods f
INNER JOIN (SELECT * FROM food_types WHERE id=6) types
ON f.type_id=types.id;
```

name	name
Generic (as a meal)	Dip
Good Dip	Dip
Guacamole Dip	Dip
Hummus	Dip

Notice that the use of a subquery in the FROM clause requires a rename operation. In this case, the subquery was named types. This query could have been written using a full join of food_types, of course, but it may have incurred more overhead as there would have been more records to match.

Another use of subqueries is in reducing the number of rows in an aggregating join. Consider the following query:

```
SELECT e.name name, COUNT(fe.food_id) foods FROM episodes e
INNER JOIN foods_episodes fe ON e.id=fe.episode_id
GROUP BY e.id
ORDER BY foods DESC
LIMIT 10;
```

name	foods
The Soup	23
The Fatigues	14
The Bubble Boy	12
The Finale 1	10
The Mango	9
The Glasses	9
The Dinner Par	9
The Wink	9
The Soup Nazi	9
The Merv Griff	9

This query lists the top ten shows with the most food references. The join here must match 181 rows in episodes with 502 rows in foods_episodes (181/502). Then it has to compute the aggregate. The fewer rows it has to match, the less work it has to do and the more efficient (and faster) the query becomes. Aggregation collapses rows, right? Then a great way to reduce the number of rows the join must match is to aggregate *before* the join. The only way to do this is with a subquery:

```
SELECT e.name, agg.foods FROM episodes e
INNER JOIN
(SELECT fe.episode_id as eid, count(food_id) as foods
   FROM foods_episodes fe
   GROUP BY episode_id ) agg
ON e.id=agg.eid
ORDER BY agg.foods DESC
LIMIT 10;
```

This query moves aggregation into a subquery that is run before the join, the results of which are joined to the episodes table for the final result. The subquery produces one aggregate (the number of foods) per episode. There are 181 episodes. Thus, this query reduces the join size from 181:502 to 181:181. However, since we are only looking for the top ten food-referencing episodes, we can also move the LIMIT 10 clause into the subquery as well and reduce the number still, to 181:10:

```
SELECT e.name, agg.foods FROM episodes e
INNER JOIN
(SELECT fe.episode_id as eid, count(food_id) as foods
   FROM foods_episodes fe
   GROUP BY episode_id
   ORDER BY foods DESC LIMIT 10) agg
ON e.id=agg.eid
ORDER BY agg.foods DESC;
```

This subquery returns only ten rows, which correspond to the top ten food shows. The join disrupts the descending order of the subquery so another ORDER BY is required in the main query to reestablish it.

The thing to remember about subqueries is that they can be used *anywhere* a relational expression can be used. A good way to learn how, where, and when to use them is to just play around with them and see what you can get away with. There is often more than one way to skin a cat in SQL. When you understand the big picture, you can make more informed decisions on when a query might be rewritten to run more efficiently.

Compound Queries

Compound queries are kind of the inverse of subqueries. A compound query is a query that processes the results of multiple queries using three specific relational operations: union, intersection, and difference. In SQL, these are defined using the UNION, INTERSECT, and EXCEPT keywords, respectively.

Compound query operations require a few things of their arguments:

- The relations involved must have the same number of columns (degree).

- There can only be one ORDER BY clause, which is at the end of the compound query, and applies to the combined result.

Furthermore, relations in compound queries are processed from left to right.

The INTERSECT operation takes two relations *A* and *B*, and selects all rows in *A* that also exist in *B*. The following SQL uses INTERSECT to find the all-time top ten foods that appear in seasons 3 through 5:

```
SELECT f.* FROM foods f
INNER JOIN
  (SELECT food_id, count(food_id) as count FROM foods_episodes
    GROUP BY food_id
    ORDER BY count(food_id) DESC LIMIT 10) top_foods
  ON f.id=top_foods.food_id
INTERSECT
SELECT f.* FROM foods f
  INNER JOIN foods_episodes fe ON f.id = fe.food_id
  INNER JOIN episodes e ON fe.episode_id = e.id
  WHERE e.season BETWEEN 3 and 5
ORDER BY f.name;
```

id	type_id	name
4	1	Bear Claws
146	7	Decaf Cappuccino
153	7	Hennigen's
55	2	Kasha
94	4	Ketchup
164	7	Naya Water
317	11	Pizza

To produce the top ten foods, I needed an ORDER BY in the first SELECT statement. Since compound queries only allow one ORDER BY at the end of the statement, I got around this by performing an inner join on a subquery in which I computed the top ten most common foods. Subqueries can have ORDER BY clauses because they run independently of the compound query. The inner join then produces a relation containing the top ten foods. The second query returns a relation containing all foods in episodes 3 through 5. The INTERSECT operation then finds all matching rows.

The EXCEPT operation takes two relations *A* and *B* and finds all rows in *A* that are not in *B*. By changing the INTERSECT to EXCEPT in the previous example, you can find which top ten foods are *not* in seasons 3 through 5:

```
SELECT f.* FROM foods f
INNER JOIN
  (SELECT food_id, count(food_id) AS count FROM foods_episodes
    GROUP BY food_id
    ORDER BY count(food_id) DESC LIMIT 10) top_foods
  ON f.id=top_foods.food_id
```

```
EXCEPT
SELECT f.* FROM foods f
  INNER JOIN foods_episodes fe ON f.id = fe.food_id
  INNER JOIN episodes e ON fe.episode_id = e.id
  WHERE e.season BETWEEN 3 and 5
ORDER BY f.name;
```

id	type_id	name
192	8	Banana
133	7	Bosco
288	10	Hot Dog

As mentioned earlier, what is called the EXCEPT operation in SQL is referred to as the *difference* operation in relational algebra.

The UNION operation takes two relations, *A* and *B*, and combines them into a single relation containing all distinct rows of *A* and *B*. In SQL, UNION combines the results of two SELECT statements. By default, UNION eliminates duplicates. If you want duplicates included in the result, then use UNION ALL. For example, the following SQL finds the single most and single least frequently mentioned foods:

```
SELECT f.*, top_foods.count FROM foods f
INNER JOIN
  (SELECT food_id, count(food_id) AS count FROM foods_episodes
    GROUP BY food_id
    ORDER BY count(food_id) DESC LIMIT 1) top_foods
  ON f.id=top_foods.food_id
UNION
SELECT f.*, bottom_foods.count FROM foods f
INNER JOIN
  (SELECT food_id, count(food_id) AS count FROM foods_episodes
    GROUP BY food_id
    ORDER BY count(food_id) LIMIT 1) bottom_foods
  ON f.id=bottom_foods.food_id
ORDER BY top_foods.count DESC;
```

id	type_id	name	top_foods.count
288	10	Hot Dog	5
1	1	Bagels	1

Both queries return only one row. The only difference in the two is which way they sort their results. The UNION simply combines the two rows into a single relation.

UNION ALL also provides a way to implement a full outer join. You simply perform a left join in the first SELECT, a right join (written in the form of a left join) in the second, and the result is a full outer join.

Compound queries are useful when you need to process similar data sets that are materialized in different ways. Basically, if you cannot express everything you want in a single SELECT statement, you can use a compound query to get part of what you want in one SELECT statement and part in another (and perhaps more), and process the sets accordingly. For example, the INTERSECT example earlier compared two lists of foods that could not be materialized with a single SELECT statement. One list contained the top ten foods, and the second contained all foods that appeared in specific seasons. And I wanted the top ten foods that appeared in the specific seasons. A compound query was the only way to get this information. The same was true in the UNION example. It is not possible to select just the first and last records of a result set. The UNION took two slight variations of a query to get the first and last records and combined the results. Also, as with joins, you can string as many SELECT commands together as you like by using any of these compound operations.

Conditional Results

The CASE expression allows you to handle various conditions within a SELECT statement. There are two forms. The first and simplest form takes a static value and lists various case values linked to return values:

```
CASE value
  WHEN x THEN value_x
  WHEN y THEN value_y
  WHEN z THEN value_z
  ELSE default_value
END
```

Here's a simple example:

```
SELECT name || CASE type_id
                 WHEN 7  THEN ' is a drink'
                 WHEN 8  THEN ' is a fruit'
                 WHEN 9  THEN ' is junkfood'
                 WHEN 13 THEN ' is seafood'
                 ELSE NULL
               END description
FROM foods
WHERE description IS NOT NULL
ORDER BY name
LIMIT 10;
```

```
description
-------------------------------------------
All Day Sucker is junkfood
Almond Joy is junkfood
Apple is a fruit
Apple Cider is a drink
Apple Pie is a fruit
Arabian Mocha Java (beans) is a drink
Avocado is a fruit
Banana is a fruit
Beaujolais is a drink
Beer is a drink
```

The CASE expression in this example handles a few different type_id values, returning a string appropriate for each one. The returned value is called description, as qualified after the END keyword. This string is concatenated to name by the string concatenation operator (||), making a complete sentence. For all type_ids not specified in a WHEN condition, CASE returns NULL. The SELECT statement filters out such NULL values in the WHERE clause, so all that is returned are rows that the CASE expression does handle.

The second form of CASE allows for expressions in the WHEN condition. It has the following form:

```
CASE
   WHEN condition1 THEN value1
   WHEN condition2 THEN value2
   WHEN condition3 THEN value3
   ELSE default_value
END
```

CASE works equally well in subselects comparing aggregates. The following SQL picks out frequently mentioned foods:

```
SELECT name,(SELECT
                CASE
                  WHEN count(*) > 4
                    THEN 'Very High'
                  WHEN count(*) = 4
                    THEN 'High'
                  WHEN count(*) IN (2,3)
                    THEN 'Moderate'
                  ELSE 'Low'
                END
            FROM foods_episodes
            WHERE food_id=f.id) frequency
FROM foods f
WHERE frequency LIKE '%High'
```

name	frequency
Kasha	High
Ketchup	High
Hot Dog	Very High
Pizza	High

This query runs a subquery for each row in foods that classifies the food by the number of episodes it appears in. The result of this subquery is included as a column called frequency. The WHERE predicate filters frequency values that have the word "High" in them.

Only one condition is executed in a CASE expression. If more than one condition is satisfied, only the first of them is executed. If no conditions are satisfied and no ELSE condition is defined, CASE returns NULL.

The Thing Called Null

Most relational databases support a special value called NULL. NULL is a placeholder for missing information. NULL is not a value per se. Rather, NULL is the absence of a value. Better yet, it is a value denoting the absence of a value. Some say it stands for "unknown," "not applicable," or "not known." But truth be told, NULL is still rather vague and mysterious. Try as you may to nail it down, NULL can still play with your mind: NULL is not nothing; NULL is not something; NULL is not true; NULL is not false; NULL is not zero. Simply put, NULL is resolutely what it is: NULL. And not everyone can agree on what that means. To some, NULL is a four-letter word. NULL rides a Harley, sports racy tattoos, and refuses to conform. To others, it is a necessary evil and serves an important role in society. You may love it. You may hate it. But it's here to stay. And if you are going to keep company with NULL, you'd better know what you are getting yourself into.

Based on what you already know, it should come as no surprise to learn that even the SQL standard is not completely clear on how to deal with NULL in all cases. Regardless, the SQLite community came to a consensus by evaluating how a number of other major relational databases handled NULL in particular ways. The result was that there was some but not total consistency in how they all worked. Oracle, PostgreSQL, and DB2 were almost identical with respect to NULL handling, so SQLite's approach was to be compatible with them.

Working with NULL is appreciably different than working with any other kind of value. For example, if you are looking for rows in foods whose name is NULL, the following SQL is useless:

```
SELECT * FROM foods WHERE foods.name=NULL;
```

It won't return any rows, period. The problem here is that the expression *anything*=NULL evaluates to NULL (even the expression NULL=NULL is NULL). And NULL is not true (nor is it false), so the WHERE clause will never evaluate to true, and therefore no rows will be selected by the query in its current form. In order to get it to work as intended, you must recast the query to use the IS operator:

```
SELECT * FROM foods WHERE foods.name IS NULL;
```

The IS operator properly checks for a NULL and returns true if it finds one. If you want values that are not NULL, then use IS NOT NULL.

But this is just the beginning of our NULL fun. NULL has a kind of Midas-like quality in that everything it touches turns to NULL. For example:

```
sqlite> SELECT NULL=NULL;
NULL
sqlite> SELECT NULL OR NULL;
NULL
sqlite> SELECT NULL AND NULL;
NULL
sqlite> SELECT NOT NULL;
NULL
sqlite> SELECT 9E9 - 1E-9*NULL;
NULL
```

Additionally, it is important to note that COUNT(*) and COUNT(column) are distinctly different with respect to how they handle NULL. COUNT(*) counts rows, regardless of any particular column value, so NULL has no effect on it. COUNT(column), on the other hand, only counts the rows with non-NULL values in column, and rows where column is NULL are ignored.

In order to accommodate NULL in logical expressions, SQL uses something called *three-value* (or *tristate*) logic, where NULL is one of the truth values. The truth table for logical AND and logical OR with NULL thrown into the mix is shown in Table 4-5.

Table 4-5. *AND and OR with NULL*

x	y	x AND y	y OR y
True	True	True	True
True	False	False	True
True	NULL	NULL	True
False	False	False	False
False	NULL	False	NULL
NULL	NULL	NULL	NULL

Since a single NULL can nullify an entire expression, it seems that there should be some way to specify a suitable default in case a NULL crops up. To that end, SQLite provides a function for dealing with NULL, called COALESCE, which is part of the SQL99 standard. COALESCE takes a list of values and returns the first non-NULL in the list. Take the following example:

```
SELECT item.price-(SELECT SUM(amount) FROM discounts WHERE id=item.id)
FROM products WHERE …
```

This is a hypothetical example of a query that needs to calculate the price of an item with any discounts applied. But what if the subquery returns NULL? Then the whole calculation and therefore the price becomes NULL. That's not good. COALESCE provides a barrier through which NULL may not pass:

```
SELECT item.price-(SELECT COALESCE(SUM(amount),0)
                   FROM discounts WHERE id=item.id)
FROM products WHERE …
```

In this case if SUM(amount) turns out to be NULL, COALESCE will return 0 instead, taking the teeth out of NULL.

Conversely, the NULLIF function takes two arguments and returns NULL if they have the same values; otherwise, it returns the first argument:

```
sqlite> SELECT NULLIF(1,1);
NULL
sqlite> SELECT NULLIF(1,2);
1
```

If you use NULL, you need to take special care in queries that refer to columns that may contain NULL in their predicates and aggregates. NULL can do quite a number on aggregates if you are not careful. Consider the following example:

```
sqlite> CREATE TABLE sales (product_id int, amount real, discount real);
sqlite> INSERT INTO sales VALUES (1, 10.00, 1.00);
sqlite> INSERT INTO sales VALUES (2, 10000.00, NULL);
sqlite> SELECT * FROM sales;
```

product_id	amount	discount
1	10	1
2	10000	NULL

You have a sales table that contains the products sold throughout the day. It holds the product ID, the price, and the total discounts that were included in the sale. There are two sales in the table: one is a $10 purchase with a $1 discount. Another is a $10,000 purchase with no discount, represented by a NULL, as in "not applicable." At the end of the day you want to tabulate net sales after discounts. You try the following:

```
sqlite> SELECT SUM(amount-discount) FROM sales;

SUM(amount-discount)
--------------------
9.0
```

Where did the $10,000 sale go? Well, 10,000 minus NULL is NULL. NULLs are weeded out by the WHERE clause, and therefore contribute nothing to an aggregate, so it simply disappears. Your calculation is off by 99.9 percent. So, knowing better, you investigate and specifically look for the missing sale using the following SQL:

```
sqlite> SELECT SUM(amount) from sales WHERE amount-discount > 100.00;

NULL
```

What's the problem here? Well, when the database evaluates the WHERE clause for the record of interest, the expression becomes 10,000 – NULL > 100.00. Breaking this down, the predicate evaluates to NULL:

```
(10000 - NULL > 100.00)   →   (NULL > 100.00)   →   NULL
```

Again, NULLs don't pass through WHERE, so the $10,000 row seems invisible.

If you are going to stay in the black, you will need to handle NULL better. If NULLs will be allowed in the discount column, then the queries that use that column have to be NULL-aware:

```
sqlite> SELECT SUM(amount-COALESCE(discount,0)) FROM sales;
10009
```

```
sqlite> SELECT SUM(amount) from sales
        WHERE amount-COALESCE(discount,0) > 100.00;
10000.0
```

So, NULL can be useful, and can indeed have a very specific meaning, but using it without understanding the full implications can lead to unpleasant surprises.

Set Operations

Congratulations, you have learned the SELECT command. Not only have you learned how the command works, but you've covered a large part of relational algebra in the process. SELECT contains 12 out of 14 operations defined in relational algebra. Here is a list of all of these operations, along with the parts of SELECT that employ them:

- **Restriction**: Restriction takes a single relation and produces a row-wise subset of it. Restriction is performed by the WHERE, HAVING, DISTINCT, and LIMIT clauses.

- **Projection**: Projection produces a column-wise subset of its input relation. Projection is performed by the SELECT clause.

- **Cartesian product**: The Cartesian product takes two relations, A and B, and produces a relation whose rows are the composite of the two relations by combining every row of A with every other row in B. SELECT performs the Cartesian product when multiple tables are listed in the FROM clause and no join condition is provided.

- **Union**: The union operation takes two relations, A and B, and creates a new relation containing all distinct rows from both A and B. Both A and B must have the same degree (number of columns). SELECT performs union operations in compound queries, which employ the UNION keyword.

- **Difference**: The difference operation takes two relations, A and B, and produces a relation whose rows consist of the rows in A that are not in B. SELECT performs difference in compound queries that employ the EXCEPT operator.

- **Rename**: The rename operation takes a single relation and assigns it a new name. Rename is used in the FROM clause.

- **Intersection**: The intersection operation takes two relations, A and B, and produces a relation whose rows are contained in both A and B. SELECT performs the intersection operation in compound queries that employ the INTERSECT operator.

- **Natural join**: A natural join takes two relations and performs an inner join on them by equating the commonly named columns as the join condition. SELECT performs a natural join with joins that use the NATURAL JOIN clause.

- **Generalized projection**: The generalized projection operation is an extension of the projection operation, which allows the use of arithmetic expressions, functions, and aggregates in the projection list. Generalized projection is used in the SELECT clause. Associated with aggregates is the concept of grouping, whereby rows with similar column values can be separated into individual groups. This is expressed in the SELECT command using the GROUP BY clause. Furthermore, groups can be filtered using the HAVING clause, which consists of a predicate similar to that of the WHERE clause. The predicate in HAVING is expressed in terms of aggregate values.

- **Left outer join**: The left outer join operation takes two relations, *A* and *B*, and returns the inner join of *A* and *B* along with the unmatched rows of *A*. *A* is the first relation defined in the FROM clause, and is hence the left relation. The left join includes the unmatched rows of the left relation along with the matched columns in the result.

- **Right and full outer join**: The right outer join operation is similar to the left join, only it includes the unmatched rows of the right relation. The full outer join includes unmatched rows from both relations.

Modifying Data

Compared to the SELECT command, the statements used to modify data are quite easy to use and understand. There are three DML statements for modifying data—INSERT, UPDATE, and DELETE—and they do pretty much what their names imply.

Inserting Records

You insert records into a table using the INSERT command. INSERT works on a single table, and can both insert one row at a time or many rows at once using a SELECT command. The general form of the INSERT command is as follows:

```
INSERT INTO table (column_list) VALUES (value_list);
```

The variable table specifies which table—the target table—to insert into. The variable column_list is a comma-separated list of column names, all of which must exist in the target table. The variable value_list is a comma-separated list of values that correspond to the names given in column_list. The order of values in value_list must correspond to the order of columns in column_list. For example, you'd use this to insert a row into foods:

```
sqlite> INSERT INTO foods (name, type_id) VALUES ('Cinnamon Bobka', 1);
```

This statement inserts one row, specifying two column values. 'Cinnamon Bobka'—the first value in the value list—corresponds to the column name—the first column in the column list. Similarly, the value 1 corresponds to type_id, which is listed second. Notice that id was not mentioned. In this case, the database uses the default value. Since id is declared as INTEGER PRIMARY KEY, it will be automatically generated and associated with the record (as explained in the section "Primary Key Constraints"). The inserted record can be verified with a simple SELECT:

```
sqlite> SELECT * FROM foods WHERE name='Cinnamon Bobka';

id          type_id     name
----------  ----------  --------------
413         1           Cinnamon Bobka

sqlite> SELECT MAX(id) from foods;

MAX(id)
----------
413

sqlite> SELECT last_insert_rowid();

last_insert_rowid()
-------------------
413
```

Notice that the value 413 was automatically generated for id, which is the largest value in the column. Thus, SQLite provided a monotonically increasing value. You can confirm this with the built-in SQL function last_insert_rowid(), which returns the last automatically generated key value, as shown in the example.

   If you provide a value for every column of a table in INSERT, then the column list can be omitted. In this case, the database assumes that the order of values provided in the value list correspond to the order of columns as declared in the CREATE TABLE statement. For example:

```
sqlite> INSERT INTO foods VALUES(NULL, 1, 'Blueberry Bobka');
sqlite> SELECT * FROM foods WHERE name LIKE '%Bobka';

id          type_id     name
----------  ----------  ----------------
10          1           Chocolate Bobka
413         1           Cinnamon Bobka
414         1           Blueberry Bobka
```

Notice here the order of arguments. 'Blueberry Bobka' came after 1 in the value list. This is because of the way the table was declared. To view the table's schema, type .schema foods at the shell prompt:

```
sqlite> .schema foods
CREATE TABLE foods(
  id integer primary key,
  type_id integer,
  name text );
CREATE INDEX foods_name_idx on foods (name COLLATE NOCASE);
```

The first column is id, followed by type_id, followed by name. This, therefore, is the order you must list values in INSERT statements on foods. Why did I use a NULL value for id in the preceding INSERT statement? Because SQLite knows that id in foods is an autoincrement column, and specifying a NULL is the equivalent of not providing a value at all. This triggers the automatic key generation. It's just a convenient trick. There is no deeper meaning or theoretical basis behind it. We will look at the subtleties of autoincrement columns later in this chapter.

Subqueries can be used in INSERT statements, both as components of the value list and as a complete replacement of the value list. Here's an example:

```
INSERT INTO foods
VALUES (NULL,
        (SELECT id FROM food_types WHERE name='Bakery'),
        'Blackberry Bobka');
SELECT * FROM foods WHERE name LIKE '%Bobka';
```

id	type_id	name
10	1	Chocolate Bobka
413	1	Cinnamon Bobka
414	1	Blueberry Bobka
415	1	Blackberry Bobka

Here, rather than hard-coding the type_id value, I had SQLite look it up for me. Here's another example:

```
INSERT INTO foods
SELECT last_insert_rowid()+1, type_id, name FROM foods
WHERE name='Chocolate Bobka';
SELECT * FROM foods WHERE name LIKE '%Bobka';
```

id	type_id	name
10	1	Chocolate Bobka
413	1	Cinnamon Bobka
414	1	Blueberry Bobka
415	1	Blackberry Bobks
416	1	Chocolate Bobka

This query completely replaces the value list with a SELECT statement. As long as the number of columns in the SELECT clause matches the number of columns in the table (or the number of columns in the columns list, if provided), INSERT will work just fine. Here, I added another chocolate bobka and used the expression last_insert_rowid()+1 as the id value. I could have just as easily used NULL instead. In fact, I probably should have used NULL rather than last_insert_rowid(), as last_insert_rowid() will return 0 if you have not previously inserted a row in the current session. I could safely assume that this would work properly for these examples, but it would not be a good idea to make this assumption in a program.

There is nothing stopping you from inserting multiple rows at a time using the SELECT form of INSERT. As long as the number of columns matches, INSERT will insert every row in the result. For example:

```
sqlite> CREATE TABLE foods2 (id int, type_id int, name text);
sqlite> INSERT INTO foods2 SELECT * FROM foods;
sqlite> SELECT COUNT(*) FROM foods2;

COUNT(*)
--------------------
418
```

This creates a new table foods2 and inserts into it all of the records from foods.

However, there is an easier way to do this. The CREATE TABLE statement has a special syntax for creating tables from SELECT statements. The previous example could have been performed in one step using this syntax:

```
sqlite> CREATE TABLE foods2 AS SELECT * from foods;
sqlite> SELECT COUNT(*) FROM list;

COUNT(*)
--------
418
```

CREATE TABLE does both steps in one fell swoop. This can be especially useful for creating temporary tables:

```
CREATE TEMP TABLE list AS
SELECT f.name Food, t.name Name,
       (SELECT COUNT(episode_id)
         FROM foods_episodes WHERE food_id=f.id) Episodes
FROM foods f, food_types t
WHERE f.type_id=t.id;
SELECT * FROM list;
```

Food	Name	Episodes
Bagels	Bakery	1
Bagels, raisin	Bakery	2
Bavarian Cream Pie	Bakery	1
Bear Claws	Bakery	3
Black and White cook	Bakery	2
Bread (with nuts)	Bakery	1
Butterfingers	Bakery	1
Carrot Cake	Bakery	1
Chips Ahoy Cookies	Bakery	1
Chocolate Bobka	Bakery	1

When using this form of CREATE TABLE, be aware that any constraints defined in the source table are not created in the new table. Specifically, the autoincrement columns will not be created in the new table, nor will indexes, UNIQUE constraints, and so forth.

It is also worth mentioning here that you have to be aware of UNIQUE constraints when inserting rows. If you add duplicate values on columns that are declared as UNIQUE, SQLite will stop you in your tracks:

```
sqlite> SELECT MAX(id) from foods;

MAX(id)
-------
416

sqlite> INSERT INTO foods VALUES (416, 1, 'Chocolate Bobka');
SQL error: PRIMARY KEY must be unique
```

Updating Records

You update records in a table using the UPDATE command. The UPDATE command modifies one or more columns within one or more rows in a table. UPDATE has the general form

```
UPDATE table SET update_list WHERE predicate;
```

The update_list is a list of one or more column assignments of the form column_name=value. The WHERE clause works exactly as in SELECT. Half of UPDATE is really a SELECT statement. The WHERE clause identifies rows to be modified using a predicate. Those rows then have the update list applied to them. For example:

```
UPDATE foods SET name='CHOCOLATE BOBKA'
WHERE name='Chocolate Bobka';
SELECT * FROM foods WHERE name LIKE 'CHOCOLATE%';
```

id	type_	name
10	1	CHOCOLATE BOBKA
11	1	Chocolate Eclairs
12	1	Chocolate Cream Pie
222	9	Chocolates, box of
223	9	Chocolate Chip Mint
224	9	Chocolate Covered Cherries

UPDATE is a very simple and direct command, and this is pretty much the extent of its use. As in INSERT, you must be aware of any UNIQUE constraints, as they will stop UPDATE every bit as much as INSERT:

```
sqlite> UPDATE foods SET id=11 where name='CHOCOLATE BOBKA';
SQL error: PRIMARY KEY must be unique
```

This is true for any constraint, however.

Deleting Records

You delete records from a table using the DELETE command. The DELETE command deletes rows from a table. DELETE has the general form

```
DELETE FROM table WHERE predicate;
```

Syntactically, DELETE is a watered-down UPDATE statement. Remove the SET clause from UPDATE and you have DELETE. The WHERE clause works exactly as in SELECT, except that it identifies rows to be deleted. For example:

```
DELETE FROM foods WHERE name='CHOCOLATE BOBKA';
```

Data Integrity

Data integrity is concerned with defining and protecting relationships within and between tables. There are four general types: *domain integrity, entity integrity, referential integrity,* and *user-defined integrity.* Domain integrity involves controlling values within columns. Entity integrity involves controlling rows in tables. Referential integrity involves controlling rows between tables—specifically foreign key relationships. And user-defined integrity is a catchall for everything else.

Data integrity is implemented using *constraints.* A constraint is a control measure used to restrict the values that can be stored in a column or columns. Going by just the values in columns, the database can enforce all four types of integrity constraints. In SQLite, constraints also include support for *conflict resolution.* Conflict resolution is covered in detail later in this chapter.

This section is a logical continuation of the "Creating a Database" section at the beginning of this chapter. As such, the examples in this section use the same contacts table defined there. It is listed again here for convenience:

```
CREATE TABLE contacts ( id INTEGER PRIMARY KEY,
                        name TEXT NOT NULL COLLATE NOCASE,
                        phone TEXT NOT NULL DEFAULT 'UNKNOWN',
                        UNIQUE (name,phone) );
```

As you know by now, constraints are a part of a table's definition. They can be associated with a column definition, or defined independently in the body of the table definition. Column-level constraints include NOT NULL, UNIQUE, PRIMARY KEY, CHECK, and COLLATE. Table-level constraints include PRIMARY KEY, UNIQUE, and CHECK. All of these constraints are covered in the following sections according to their respective integrity types.

The reason this material was not addressed earlier is because it requires familiarity with the UPDATE, INSERT, and DELETE commands. Just as these commands operate on data, constraints operate on them, making sure that they work within the guidelines defined in the tables they modify.

Entity Integrity

Entity integrity stems from the *Guaranteed Access Rule,* as explained in Chapter 3. It requires that every field in every table be addressable. That is, every field in the database must be uniquely identifiable and capable of being located. In order for a field to be addressable, its corresponding row must also be addressable. And for that, the row must be unique in some way. This is the job of the primary key.

The primary key consists of least one column, or a group of columns with a UNIQUE constraint. The UNIQUE constraint, as you will soon see, simply requires that every value in a column (or group of columns) be distinct. Therefore, the primary key ensures that each row is somehow distinct from all other rows in a table, ultimately ensuring that every field is also addressable. Entity integrity basically keeps data organized in a table. After all, what good is a field if you can't find it?

UNIQUE Constraints

Since primary keys are based on UNIQUE constraints, we'll start with them. A UNIQUE constraint simply requires that all values in a column or a group of columns are distinct from one another, or unique. If you attempt to insert a duplicate value, or update a value to another value that already exists in the column, the database will issue a constraint violation and abort the operation. UNIQUE constraints can be defined at the column or the table level. When defined at the table level, UNIQUE constraints can be applied across multiple columns. In this case, the combined value of the columns must be unique. In contacts, there is a unique constraint on both name and phone together. See what happens if I attempt to insert another 'Jerry' record with a phone value 'UNKNOWN':

```
sqlite> INSERT INTO contacts (name,phone) VALUES ('Jerry','UNKNOWN');
SQL error: columns name, phone are not unique

sqlite> INSERT INTO contacts (name) VALUES ('Jerry');
SQL error: columns name, phone are not unique

sqlite> INSERT INTO contacts (name,phone) VALUES ('Jerry', '555-1212');
```

In the first case, I explicitly specified name and phone. This matched the values of the existing record and the UNIQUE constraint kicked in and did not let me do it. The third INSERT illustrates that the UNIQUE constraint applies to name and phone combined, not individually. It inserted another row with 'Jerry' as the value for name, which did not cause an error, because name by itself it not unique—only name and phone together.

NULL AND UNIQUE

Pop quiz: Based on what you know about NULL and UNIQUE, how many NULL values can you put in a column that is declared UNIQUE? Answer: It depends on which database you are using. PostgreSQL and Oracle say as many as you want. Informix and Microsoft SQL Server say only one. DB2, SQL Anywhere, and Borland Inter-Base say none at all. SQLite follows Oracle and PostgreSQL—you can put as many NULLs as you want in a unique column. This is another classic case of NULL befuddling everyone. On one side, you can argue that one NULL value is never equal to another NULL value because you don't have enough information about either to know if they are equal. On the other side, you don't really have enough information to prove that they are different either. The consensus in SQLite is to assume that they are all different, so you can have a whole unique column stuffed full of NULLs if you like.

Primary Key Constraints

In SQLite, a primary key column is always defined when you create a table, whether you define one or not. This column is a 64-bit integer value called ROWID. It has two aliases, _ROWID_ and OID, which can be used to refer to it as well. Default values are automatically generated for it in monotonically increasing order.

SQLite provides an autoincrement feature for primary keys, should you want to define your own. If you define a column's type as INTEGER PRIMARY KEY, SQLite will create a DEFAULT value on that column, which will provide a monotonically increasing integer value that is guaranteed to be unique in that column. In reality, however, this column will simply be an alias for ROWID. They will all refer to the same value. Since SQLite uses a 64-bit number for the primary key, the maximum value for this column is 9,223,372,036,854,775,807.

Note You may be wondering where the maximum value of a key value comes from. It is based on the limits of a 64-bit integer. A 64-bit integer has 64 bits of storage that can be used to represent a number. That is, 2^{64} (or 18,446,744,073,709,551,616) possible values can be represented with 64 bits. Think of this as a range of values. An *unsigned* integer basically defines this range starting at 0. The range is therefore exclusively positive values, and therefore needs no sign to designate it—hence "unsigned." The maximum value of an unsigned 64-bit integer is therefore 18,446,744,073,709,551,615 (one less because the range starts at 0, not 1). However, SQLite uses *signed* integers. A signed integer splits the range so that half of it is less than zero and half is greater than zero. The range of a signed 64-bit integer is -9,223,372,036,854,775,808 to +9,223,372,036,854,775,807 (which is a range of 18,446,744,073,709,551,616 values). Key values in SQLite are signed 64-bit integers. Therefore, the maximum value of a key in SQLite is +9,223,372,036,854,775,807.

Even if you manage to reach this limit, SQLite will simply start searching for unique values that are not in the column for subsequent INSERTs. When you delete rows from the table, ROWIDs may be recycled and reused on subsequent INSERTs. As a result, newly created ROWIDs might not always be in strictly ascending order.

In the examples so far I have managed to insert two records into contacts. Not once did I ever specify a value for id. As mentioned before, this is because id is declared as INTEGER PRIMARY KEY. Therefore, SQLite supplied an incremental integer value for each INSERT automatically, as you can see here:

```
sqlite> SELECT * FROM contacts;

id   name   phone
---  -----  --------
1    Jerry  UNKNOWN
2    Jerry  555-1212
```

Notice that the primary key is accessible from all the aforementioned aliases, in addition to id:

```
sqlite> SELECT ROWID, OID,_ROWID_,id, name, phone FROM CONTACTS;
```

```
id  id  id  id  name   phone
--  --  --  --  ----   -----
1   1   1   1   Jerry  UNKNOWN
2   2   2   2   Jerry  555-1212
```

If you include the keyword AUTOINCREMENT after INTEGER PRIMARY KEY, SQLite will use a different key generation algorithm for the column. This algorithm basically prevents ROWIDs from being recycled. It guarantees that only new (not recycled) ROWIDs are provided for every INSERT. When a table is created with a column containing the AUTOINCREMENT constraint, SQLite will keep track of that column's maximum ROWID in a system table called sqlite_sequence. It will only use values greater than that maximum on all subsequent INSERTs. If you ever reach the absolute maximum, then SQLite will return a SQLITE_FULL error on subsequent INSERTs. For example:

```
sqlite> CREATE TABLE maxed_out(id INTEGER PRIMARY KEY AUTOINCREMENT, x text);
sqlite> INSERT INTO maxed_out VALUES (9223372036854775807, 'last one');
sqlite> SELECT * FROM sqlite_sequence;

name        seq
----------  --------------------
maxed_out   9223372036854775807

sqlite> INSERT INTO maxed_out VALUES (NULL, 'wont work');
SQL error: database is full
```

Here, I provided the primary key value. SQLite then stored this value as the maximum for maxed_out.id in sqlite_sequence. I supplied the very last (maximum) 64-bit value before wrap-around. In the next INSERT, I used the generated default value, which must be a monotonically increasing value. This wrapped around to 0, and SQLite issued a SQLITE_FULL error.

While SQLite tracks the maximum value for an AUTOINCREMENT column in the sqlite_sequence table, it does not prevent you from providing your own values for it in the INSERT command. The only requirement is that the value you provide must be unique within the column. For example:

```
sqlite> DROP TABLE maxed_out;
sqlite> CREATE TABLE maxed_out(id INTEGER PRIMARY KEY AUTOINCREMENT, x text);
sqlite> INSERT INTO maxed_out values(10, 'works');
sqlite> SELECT * FROM sqlite_sequence;

name        seq
----------  ----------
maxed_out   10

sqlite> INSERT INTO maxed_out values(9, 'works');
sqlite> SELECT * FROM sqlite_sequence;

name        seq
----------  ----------
maxed_out   10
```

```
sqlite> INSERT INTO maxed_out VALUES (9, 'fails');
SQL error: PRIMARY KEY must be unique

sqlite> INSERT INTO maxed_out VALUES (NULL, 'should be 11');
sqlite> SELECT * FROM maxed_out;

id          x
----------  ------------
9           works
10          works
11          should be 11

sqlite> SELECT * FROM sqlite_sequence;

name        seq
----------  ----------
maxed_out   11
```

Here, I dropped and re-created the maxed_out table, and inserted a record with an explicitly defined ROWID of 10. Then I inserted a record with a ROWID less than 10, which worked. I tried it again with the same value and it failed, due to the UNIQUE constraint. Finally, I inserted another record using the default key value, and SQLite provided the next monotonically increasing value—10+1.

In summary, AUTOINCREMENT prevents SQLite from recycling primary key values (ROWIDs) and stops when the ROWID reaches the maximum (signed) 64-bit integer value. This feature was added for specific applications that required this behavior. Unless you have such a specific need in your application, it is perhaps best to just use INTEGER PRIMARY KEY for autoincrement columns.

Like UNIQUE constraints, PRIMARY KEY constraints can be defined over multiple columns. You don't have to use an integer value for your primary key. If you choose to use another value, SQLite will still maintain the ROWID column internally, but it will also place a UNIQUE constraint on your declared primary key. For example:

```
sqlite> CREATE TABLE pkey(x text, y text, PRIMARY KEY(x,y));
sqlite> INSERT INTO pkey VALUES ('x','y');
sqlite> INSERT INTO pkey VALUES ('x','x');
sqlite> SELECT ROWID, x, y FROM pkey;

rowid       x           y
----------  ----------  ----------
1           x           y
2           x           x

sqlite> INSERT INTO pkey VALUES ('x','x');
SQL error: columns x, y are not unique
```

The primary key here is technically just a UNIQUE constraint across two columns, nothing more. As stated before, the concept of a primary key is more or less just lip service to the relational model—SQLite always provides one whether you do or not. If you do define you own primary key, it is in reality just another UNIQUE constraint, nothing more.

Domain Integrity

The simplest definition of domain integrity is the conformance of a column's values to its assigned domain. That is, every value in a column should exist within that column's defined domain. However, the term *domain* is a little vague. Domains are often compared to types in programming languages, such as strings or floats. And while that is not a bad analogy, domain integrity is actually much broader than that.

Domain constraints make it possible for you to start with a simple type—like an integer—and add additional constraints to create a more restricted set of acceptable values for a column. For example, you can create a column with an integer type and add the constraint that only three such values are allowed: {-1, 0. 1}. In this case, you have modified the range of acceptable values (from the domain of all integers to just three integers), but not the data type itself. You are dealing with two things: a type and a range.

Consider another example: the name column in the contacts table. It is declared as follows:

```
name TEXT NOT NULL COLLATE NOCASE
```

The domain TEXT defines the type and initial range of acceptable values. Everything following it serves to restrict and qualify that range even further. The name column is then the domain of all TEXT values that do not include NULL values where uppercase letters and lowercase letters have equal value. It is still TEXT, and operates as TEXT, but its range of acceptable values is further restricted from that of TEXT.

You might say that a column's domain is not the same thing as its type. Rather, its domain is a combination of two things: a type and a range. The column's type defines the representation and operators of its values—how they are stored and how you can operate on them—sort, search, add, subtract, and so forth. A column's range is its set of acceptable values you can store in it, which is not necessarily the same as its declared type. The type's range represents a maximum range of values. The column's range—as you have seen—can be restricted through constraints. So for all practical purposes, you can think of a column's domain as a type with constraints tacked on.

Similarly, there are essentially two components to domain integrity: type checking and range checking. While SQLite supports many of the standard domain constraints for range checking (NOT NULL, CHECK, etc.), its approach to type checking is where things diverge from other databases. In fact, SQLite's approach to types and type checking is one of its most controversial, misunderstood, and disputed features.

But before we get into how SQLite handles types, let's cover the easy stuff first: default values, NOT NULL constraints, CHECK constraints, and collations.

Default Values

The DEFAULT keyword provides a default value for a column if one is not provided in an INSERT command. DEFAULT is not a constraint, because it doesn't enforce anything. It simply steps in when needed. However, it does fall within domain integrity because it provides a policy for handling NULL values in a column. If a column doesn't have a default value, and you don't provide a value for it in an INSERT statement, then SQLite will insert NULL for that column. For example, contacts.name has a default value of 'UNKNOWN'. With this in mind, consider the following example:

```
sqlite> INSERT INTO contacts (name) VALUES ('Jerry');
sqlite> SELECT * FROM contacts;

id          name        phone
----------  ----------  ----------
1           Jerry       UNKNOWN
```

The INSERT command inserted a row, specifying a value for name but not phone. As you can see from the resulting row, the default value for phone kicked in and provided the string 'UNKNOWN'. If phone did not have a default value, then in this example, the value for phone in this row would have been NULL instead.

DEFAULT also accepts three predefined ANSI/ISO reserved words for generating default dates and times. CURRENT_TIME will generate the current local time in ANSI/ISO time format (HH:MM:SS). CURRENT_DATE will generate the current date (in YYYY-MM-DD format). CURRENT_TIMESTAMP will produce a combination of these two (in YYYY-MM-DD HH:MM:SS format). For example:

```
CREATE TABLE times ( id int,
  time NOT NULL DEFAULT CURRENT_DATE
  time NOT NULL DEFAULT CURRENT_TIME,
  time NOT NULL DEFAULT CURRENT_TIMESTAMP );
INSERT INTO times(1);
INSERT INTO times(2);
SELECT * FROMS times;
```

id	date	time	timestamp
1	2006-03-15	23:30:25	2006-03-15 23:30:25
2	2006-03-15	23:30:40	2006-03-15 23:30:40

These defaults come in quite handy for tables that need to log or timestamp events.

NOT NULL Constraints

If you are one of those people who are not fond of NULL, then the NOT NULL constraint is for you. NOT NULL ensures that values in the column may never be NULL. INSERT commands may not add NULL in the column, and UPDATE commands may not change existing values to NULL. Oftentimes, you will see NOT NULL raise its ugly head in INSERT statements. Specifically, a NOT NULL constraint without a DEFAULT constraint will prevent any unspecified values from being used in the INSERT (because the default values provided in this case are NULL). In the preceding example, the NOT NULL constraint on name requires that an INSERT command always provide a value for that column. For example:

```
sqlite> INSERT INTO contacts (phone) VALUES ('555-1212');
SQL error: contacts.name may not be NULL
```

This INSERT command specified a phone value, but not a name. The NOT NULL constraint on name kicked in and forbade the operation.

The way to shut NOT NULL up is to also include a DEFAULT constraint in a column. This is the case for phone. While phone has a NOT NULL constraint, it has a DEFAULT constraint as well. If an INSERT command does not specify a value for phone, the DEFAULT constraint steps in and provides the value 'UNKNOWN', thus satisfying the NOT NULL constraint. To this end, people often use DEFAULT constraints in conjunction with NOT NULL constraints so that INSERT commands can safely use default values while at the same time keeping NULL out of the column.

CHECK Constraints

CHECK constraints allow you to define expressions to test values whenever they are inserted into or updated within a column. If the values do not meet the criteria set forth in the expression, the database issues a constraint violation. Thus, it allows you to define additional data integrity checks beyond UNIQUE or NOT NULL to suit your specific application. An example of a CHECK constraint might be to ensure that the value of a phone number field is at least seven characters long. To do this, you can either add the constraint to the column definition of phone, or as a standalone constraint in the table definition as follows:

```
CREATE TABLE contacts ( id INTEGER PRIMARY KEY,
                        name TEXT NOT NULL COLLATE NOCASE,
                        phone TEXT NOT NULL DEFAULT 'UNKNOWN',
                        UNIQUE (name,phone),
                        CHECK(LENGTH(phone)>=7) );
```

Here, any attempt to insert or update a value for phone less than seven characters will result in a constraint violation. You can use any expression in a CHECK constraint that you would in a WHERE clause. For example, say you have the table foo defined as follows:

```
CREATE TABLE foo( x integer,
                  y integer CHECK(y>x),
                  z integer CHECK(z>ABS(y)) );
```

In this table, every value of z must always be greater than y, which in turn must be greater than x. To show illustrate this, try the following:

```
INSERT into foo values (-2, -1, 2);
INSERT into foo values (-2, -1, 1);
SQL error: constraint failed

UPDATE foo SET y=-3 WHERE x=-3;
SQL error: constraint failed
```

The CHECK constraints for all columns are evaluated before any modification is made. For the modification to succeed, the expressions for all constraints must evaluate to true.

Functionally, triggers can be used just as effectively as check constraints for data integrity. In fact, triggers can do much more. If you find that you can't quite express what you need in a CHECK constraint, then triggers are a good alternative. Triggers are covered later in this chapter in the section "Triggers."

Collations

Collation is related to domain integrity in that it defines what constitutes unique text values. Collation specifically refers to how text values are compared. Different collations employ different comparison methods. For example, one collation might be case insensitive, so the strings 'JujyFruit' and 'JUJYFRUIT' are considered the same. Another collation might be case sensitive, in which case the strings would be considered different.

SQLite has three built-in collations. The default is BINARY, which compares text values byte by byte using a specific C function called memcmp(). This happens to work nicely for many Western languages such as English. NOCASE is basically a case-insensitive collation for the 26 ASCII characters used in English. Finally there is REVERSE, which is the reverse of the BINARY collation. REVERSE is more for testing (and perhaps illustration) than anything else.

The SQLite C API provides a way to create custom collations. This feature allows developers to support languages and/or locales that are not well served by the BINARY collation. See Chapter 7 for more information.

The COLLATE keyword defines the collation for a column. For example, the collation for contacts.name is defined as NOCASE, which means that it is case insensitive. Thus, if I try to insert another row with a name value of 'JERRY' and a phone value of '555-1212' it should fail:

```
sqlite> INSERT INTO contacts (name,phone) VALUES ('JERRY','555-1212');
SQL error: columns name, phone are not unique
```

According to name's collation, 'JERRY' is the same as 'Jerry', and there is already a row with that value. Therefore, a new row with name='JERRY' would be a duplicate value. By default, collation in SQLite is case sensitive. The previous example would have worked had I not defined NOCASE on name.

Storage Classes

As mentioned earlier, SQLite does not work like other databases when it comes to handling data types. It differs in the types it supports, and in how they are stored, compared, enforced, and assigned. The following sections explore SQLite's radically different but surprisingly flexible approach to data types and its relation to domain integrity.

With respect to types, SQLite's domain integrity is better described as *domain affinity*. In SQLite, it is referred to as *type affinity*. To understand type affinity, however, you must first understand *storage classes* and something called *manifest typing*.

Internally, SQLite has five primitive data types, which are referred to as *storage classes*. The term storage class refers to the format in which a value is stored on disk. Regardless, it is still synonymous with type, or data type. The five storage classes are described in Table 4-6.

Table 4-6. *SQLite Storage Classes*

Name	Description
INTEGER	Integer values are whole numbers (positive and negative). They can vary in size: 1, 2, 3, 4, 6, or 8 bytes. The maximum integer range (8 bytes) is {-9223372036854775808,-1,0,1, -9223372036854775807}. SQLite automatically handles the integer sizes based on the numeric value.
REAL	Real values are real numbers with decimal values. SQLite uses 8-byte floats to store real numbers.
TEXT	Text is character data. SQLite supports various character encodings, which include UTF-8 and UTF-16 (big and little endian). The maximum string value in SQLite is unlimited.
BLOB	Binary large object (BLOB) data is any kind of data. The maximum size for BLOBs in SQLite is unlimited.
NULL	NULL values represent missing information. SQLite has full support for NULL values.

SQLite infers a value's type from its representation. The following inference rules are used to do this:

- A value specified as a literal in SQL statements is assigned class TEXT if it is enclosed by single or double quotes.

- A value is assigned class INTEGER if the literal is specified as an unquoted number with no decimal point or exponent.

- A value is assigned class REAL if the literal is an unquoted number with a decimal point or an exponent.

- A value is assigned class NULL if its value is NULL.

- A value is assigned class BLOB if it is of the format X'ABCD', where ABCD are hexadecimal numbers. The X prefix and values can be either uppercase or lowercase.

The typeof() SQL function returns the storage class of a value based on its representation. Using this function, the following SQL illustrates type inference in action:

```
sqlite> select typeof(3.14), typeof('3.14'),
        typeof(314), typeof(x'3142'), typeof(NULL);

typeof(3.14)  typeof('3.14')  typeof(314)  typeof(x'3142')  typeof(NULL)
------------  --------------  -----------  ---------------  ------------
real          text            integer      blob             null
```

Here are all of the five internal storage classes invoked by specific representations of data. The value 3.14 looks like a REAL, and therefore is a REAL. The value '3.14' looks like TEXT, and therefore is TEXT, and so on.

A single column in SQLite may contain different values *of different storage classes.* Consider the following example:

```
sqlite> DROP TABLE domain;
sqlite> CREATE TABLE domain(x);
sqlite> INSERT INTO domain VALUES (3.142);
sqlite> INSERT INTO domain VALUES ('3.142');
sqlite> INSERT INTO domain VALUES (3142);
sqlite> INSERT INTO domain VALUES (x'3142');
sqlite> INSERT INTO domain VALUES (NULL);
sqlite> SELECT ROWID, x, typeof(x) FROM domain;
```

rowid	x	typeof(x)
1	3.142	real
2	3.142	text
3	3142	integer
4	1B	blob
5	NULL	null

This raises a few questions. How are the values in a column sorted or compared? How do you sort a column with INTEGER, REAL, TEXT, BLOB, and NULL values? How do you compare an INTEGER with a BLOB? Which is greater? Can they ever be equal?

As it turns out, values in a column with different storages classes can be sorted. And they can be sorted because they can be compared. There are well-defined rules to do so. Storage classes are sorted by using their respective *class values*, which are defined as follows:

1. The NULL storage class has the lowest class value. A value with a NULL storage class is considered less than any other value (including another value with storage class NULL). Within NULL values, there is no specific sort order.

2. INTEGER or REAL storage classes have higher value than NULLs, and share equal class value. INTEGER and REAL values are compared numerically.

3. The TEXT storage class has higher value than INTEGER or REAL. A value with an INTEGER or a REAL storage class will always be less than a value with a TEXT storage class no matter its value. When two TEXT values are compared, the comparison is determined by the collation defined for the values.

4. The BLOB storage class has the highest value. Any value that is not of class BLOB will always be less than a value of class BLOB. BLOB values are compared using the C function memcmp().

So when SQLite sorts a column, it first groups values according to storage class—first NULLs, then INTEGERs and REALs, next TEXT, and finally BLOBs. It then sorts the values within each group. NULLs are not ordered at all, INTEGERs and REALs are compared numerically, TEXT is arranged by the appropriate collation, and BLOBs are sorted using memcmp(). Figure 4-20 illustrates a hypothetical column sorted in ascending order.

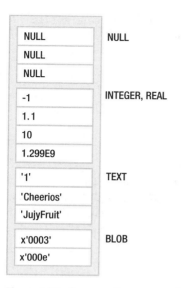

Figure 4-20. *Storage class sort order*

The following SQL illustrates the differences between storage class values:

```
sqlite> SELECT 3 < 3.142, 3.142 < '3.142', '3.142' < x'3000',
                x'3000' < x'3001';


3 < 3.142   3.142 < '3.142' '3.142' < x'3000' x'3000' < x'3001'
---------   --------------- ----------------- ------------------
1           1               1                 1
```

INTEGERs and REALs are compared numerically and are both less than TEXTs, and TEXTs are less than BLOBs.

Manifest Typing

SQLite uses manifest typing. If you do a little research, you will find that the term *manifest typing* is subject to multiple interpretations. In programming languages, manifest typing refers to how the type of a variable or value is defined and/or determined. There are two main interpretations:

> *Manifest typing means that a variable's type must be explicitly declared in the code.* By this definition, languages such as C/C++, Pascal, and Java would be said to use manifest typing. Dynamically typed languages such as Perl, Python, and Ruby, on the other hand, are the direct opposite as they do not require that a variable's type be declared.

> *Manifest typing means that variables don't have types at all. Rather, only values have types.* This seems to be in line with dynamically typed languages. Basically, a variable can hold any value, and the type of that variable at any point in time is determined by its value at that moment. Thus if you set variable x=1, then x at that moment is of type INTEGER. If you then set x='JujyFruit', it is then of type TEXT. That is, if it looks like an INTEGER, and it acts like an INTEGER, it is an INTEGER.

For the sake of brevity, I will refer to the first interpretation as MT 1 and the second as MT 2. At first glance, it may not be readily apparent as to which interpretation best fits SQLite. For example, consider the following table:

```
CREATE TABLE foo( x integer,
                  y text,
                  z real );
```

Say we now insert a record into this table as follows:

```
INSERT INTO foo VALUES ('1', '1', '1');
```

When SQLite creates the record, what type is stored internally for x, y, and z? The answer: INTEGER, TEXT, and REAL. Then it seems that SQLite uses MT 1: variables have declared types. But wait a second; column types in SQLite are optional, so we could have just as easily defined foo as follows:

```
CREATE TABLE foo(x, y, z);
```

Now let's do the same INSERT:

```
INSERT INTO foo VALUES ('1', '1', '1');
```

What type are x, y, and z now? The answer: TEXT, TEXT, and TEXT. Well, maybe SQLite is just setting columns to TEXT by default. If you think that, then consider the following INSERT statement on the same table:

```
INSERT INTO foo VALUES (1, 1.0, x'10');
```

What are x, y, and z in this row? INTEGER, REAL, and BLOB. This looks like MT 2, where the value itself determines its type.

So which one is it? The short answer: neither and both. The long answer is a little more involved. With respect to MT 1, SQLite lets you declare columns to have types if you want to. This looks and feels like what other databases do. But you don't *have to*, thereby violating this interpretation as well. This is because in all situations SQLite can take any value and infer a type from it. It doesn't need the type declared in the column to help it out. With respect to MT 2, SQLite allows the type of the value to "influence" (maybe not completely determine) the type that gets stored in the column. But you can still declare the column with a type and that type will exert some influence, thereby violating this interpretation as well—that types come from values only. What we really have here is the MT 3—the SQLite interpretation. It borrows from both MT 1 and MT 2.

But interestingly enough, manifest typing does not address the whole issue with respect to types. It seems to be concerned with only declaring and resolving types. What about type checking? That is, if you declare a column to be type integer, what exactly does that mean?

First let's consider what most other relational databases do. They enforce *strict type checking* as a standard part of standard domain integrity. First you declare a column's type. Then only values of that type can go in it. End of story. You can use additional domain constraints if you want, but under no conditions can you ever insert values of other types. Consider the following example with Oracle:

```
SQL> create table domain(x int, y varchar(2));
Table created.

SQL> INSERT INTO domain VALUES ('pi', 3.14);
INSERT INTO domain VALUES ('pi', 3.14)
                            *
ERROR at line 1:
ORA-01722: invalid number
```

The value 'pi' is not an integer value. And column x was declared to be of type int. I don't even get to hear about the error in column y because the whole INSERT is aborted due to the integrity violation on x. When I try this in SQLite,

```
sqlite> CREATE TABLE domain (x int, y varchar(2));
sqlite> INSERT INTO domain VALUES ('pi', 3.14);
sqlite> SELECT * FROM domain;

x     y
----  -----
pi    3.14
```

there's no problem. I said one thing and did another, and SQLite didn't stop me. *SQLite's domain integrity does not include strict type checking.* So what is going on? Does a column's declared type count for anything? Yes. Then how is it used? It is all done with something called *type affinity*.

In short, SQLite's manifest typing states that 1) columns can have types and 2) that types can be inferred from values. Type affinity addresses how these two things relate to one another. Type affinity is a delicate balancing act that sits between strict typing and dynamic typing.

Type Affinity

In SQLite, columns don't have types or domains. While a column can have a declared type, internally it only has a type affinity. Declared type and type affinity are two different things. Type affinity determines the storage class SQLite uses to store values within a column. The actual storage class a column uses to store a given value is a function of both the value's storage class and the column's affinity. Before getting into how this is done, however, let's first talk about how a column gets its affinity.

Column Types and Affinities

To begin with, every column has an affinity. There are four different kinds: NUMERIC, INTEGER, TEXT, and NONE. A column's affinity is determined directly from its declared type (or lack thereof). Therefore, when you declare a column in a table, the type you choose to declare it as will ultimately determine that column's affinity. SQLite assigns a column's affinity according to the following rules:

- By default, a column's default affinity is NUMERIC. That is, if a column is not INTEGER, TEXT, or NONE, then it is automatically assigned NUMERIC affinity.

- If a column's declared type contains the string 'INT' (in uppercase or lowercase), then the column is assigned INTEGER affinity.

- If a column's declared type contains any of the strings 'CHAR', 'CLOB', or 'TEXT' (in uppercase or lowercase), then that column is assigned TEXT affinity. Notice that 'VARCHAR' contains the string 'CHAR' and thus will confer TEXT affinity.

- If a column's declared type contains the string 'BLOB' (in uppercase or lowercase), *or if it has no declared type*, then it is assigned NONE affinity.

▓**Note** Pay attention to defaults. If you don't declare a column's type, then its affinity will be NONE, in which case all values will be stored using their given storage class (or inferred from their representation). If you are not sure what you want to put in a column, or want to leave it open to change, this is the best affinity to use. However, be careful of the scenario where you declare a type that does not match any of the rules for NONE, TEXT, or INTEGER. While you might intuitively think the default should be NONE, it is actually NUMERIC. For example, if you declare a column of type JUJYFRUIT, it will *not* have affinity NONE just because SQLite doesn't recognize it. Rather it will have affinity NUMERIC. (Interestingly, the scenario also happens when you declare a column's type to be numeric for the same reason.) Rather than using an unrecognized type that ends up as numeric, you may prefer to leave the column's declared type out altogether, which will ensure it has affinity NONE.

Affinities and Storage

Each affinity influences how values are stored in its associated column. The rules governing storage are as follows:

- A NUMERIC column may contain all five storage classes. A NUMERIC column has a bias toward numeric storage classes (INTEGER and REAL). When a TEXT value is inserted into a NUMERIC column, it will attempt to convert it to an INTEGER storage class. If this fails, it will attempt to convert it to a REAL storage class. Failing that, it stores the value using the TEXT storage class.

- An INTEGER column tries to be as much like a NUMERIC column as it can. An INTEGER column will store a REAL value as REAL. *However*, if a REAL value has *no fractional component*, then it will be stored using an INTEGER storage class. INTEGER column will try to store a TEXT value as REAL if possible. If that fails, they try to store it as INTEGER. Failing that, TEXT values are stored as TEXT.

- A TEXT column will convert all INTEGER or REAL values to TEXT.

- A NONE column does not attempt to convert any values. All values are stored using their given storage class.

- No column will ever try to convert NULL or BLOB values—regardless of affinity. NULL and BLOB values are always stored as is in every column.

These rules may initially appear somewhat complex, but their overall design goal is simple: to make it possible for SQLite to mimic other relational databases if you need it to. That is, if you treat columns like a traditional database, type affinity rules will store values in the way you expect. If you declare a column of type INTEGER, and put integers into it, they will be stored as

INTEGER. If you declare a column to be of type TEXT, CHAR, or VARCHAR and put integers into it, they will be stored as TEXT. However, if you don't follow these conventions, SQLite will still find a way to store the value.

Affinities in Action

Let's look at a few examples to get the hang of how affinity works. Consider the following:

```
sqlite> CREATE TABLE domain(i int, n numeric, t text, b blob);
sqlite> INSERT INTO domain VALUES (3.142,3.142,3.142,3.142);
sqlite> INSERT INTO domain VALUES ('3.142','3.142','3.142','3.142');
sqlite> INSERT INTO domain VALUES (3142,3142,3142,3142);
sqlite> INSERT INTO domain VALUES (x'3142',x'3142',x'3142',x'3142');
sqlite> INSERT INTO domain VALUES (null,null,null,null);
sqlite> SELECT ROWID,typeof(i),typeof(n),typeof(t),typeof(b) FROM domain;
```

rowid	typeof(i)	typeof(n)	typeof(t)	typeof(b)
1	real	real	text	real
2	real	real	text	text
3	integer	integer	text	integer
4	blob	blob	blob	blob
5	null	null	null	null

The first INSERT inserts a REAL value. You can see this both by the format in the INSERT statement and by the resulting type shown in the typeof(b) column returned in the SELECT statement. Remember that BLOB columns have storage class NONE, which does not attempt to convert the storage class of the input value, so column b uses the same storage class that was defined in the INSERT statement. Column i keeps the NUMERIC storage class, because it tries to be NUMERIC when it can. Column n doesn't have to convert anything. Column t converts it to TEXT. Column b stores it exactly as given in the context. In each subsequent INSERT, you can see how the conversion rules are applied in each varying case.

The following SQL illustrates storage class sort order and interclass comparison (which are governed by the same set of rules):

```
sqlite> SELECT ROWID, b, typeof(b) FROM domain ORDER BY b;
```

rowid	b	typeof(b)
5	NULL	null
1	3.142	real
3	3142	integer
2	3.142	text
4	1B	blob

Here, you see that NULLs sort first, followed by INTEGERs and REALs, followed by TEXTs, then BLOBs. The following SQL shows how these values compare with the integer 1,000. The INTEGER and REAL values in b are less than 1,000 because they are numerically compared, while TEXT and BLOB are greater than 1,000 because they are in a higher storage class.

```
sqlite> SELECT ROWID, b, typeof(b), b<1000 FROM domain ORDER BY b;

rowid  b      typeof(b)  b<1000
-----  -----  --------   ----------
5      NULL   null       NULL
1      3.142  real       1
3      3142   integer    1
2      3.142  text       0
4      1B     blob       0
```

The primary difference between type affinity and strict typing is that type affinity will never issue a constraint violation for incompatible data types. SQLite will always find a data type to put any value into any column. The only question is what type it will use to do so. The only role of a column's declared type in SQLite is simply to determine its affinity. Ultimately, it is the column's affinity that has any bearing on how values are stored inside of it. However, SQLite does provide facilities for ensuring that a column may only accept a given type, or range of types. You do this using CHECK constraints, explained in the sidebar "Makeshift Strict Typing," later in this section.

Storage Classes and Type Conversions

Another thing to note about storage classes is that they can sometimes influence how values are compared as well. Specifically, SQLite will sometimes convert values between numeric storage classes (INTEGER and REAL) and TEXT before comparing them. For binary comparisons, it uses the following rules:

- When a column value is compared to the result of an expression, the affinity of the column is applied to the result of the expression before the comparison takes place.

- When two column values are compared, if one column has INTEGER or NUMERIC affinity and the other doesn't, then NUMERIC affinity is applied to TEXT values in the non-NUMERIC column.

- When two expressions are compared, SQLite does not make any conversions. The results are compared as is. If the expressions are of like storage class, then the comparison function associated with that storage class is used to compare values. Otherwise, they are compared on the basis of their storage class.

Note that the term *expression* here refers to any scalar expression or literal *other than a column value*. To illustrate the first rule, consider the following:

```
sqlite> select ROWID,b,typeof(i),i>'2.9' from domain ORDER BY b;

rowid  b      typeof(i  i>'2.9'
-----  -----  --------  ------------
5      NULL   null      NULL
1      3.142  real      1
3      3142   integer   1
2      3.142  real      1
4      1B     blob      1
```

The expression '2.9', while being TEXT, is converted to INTEGER before the comparison. So the column interprets the value in light of what it is. What if '2.9' was a non-numeric string? Then SQLite falls back to comparing storage class, in which INTEGER and NUMERIC types are always less than TEXT:

```
sqlite> SELECT ROWID,b,typeof(i),i>'text' FROM domain ORDER BY b;

rowid  b      typeof(i  i>'text'
-----  -----  --------  ------------
5      NULL   null      NULL
1      3.14   real      0
3      314    integer   0
2      3.14   real      0
4      1B     blob      1
```

The second rule simply states that when comparing a numeric and non-numeric column, where possible SQLite will try to convert the non-numeric column to numeric format:

```
sqlite> CREATE TABLE rule2(a int, b text);
sqlite> insert into rule2 values(2,'1');
sqlite> insert into rule2 values(2,'text');
sqlite> select a, typeof(a),b,typeof(b), a>b from rule2;

a           typeof(a)   b           typeof(b)   a>b
----------  ----------  ----------  ----------  ----------
2           integer     1           text        1
2           integer     text        text        0
```

Column a is an INTEGER, b is TEXT. When evaluating the expression a>b, SQLite tries to coerce b to INTEGER where it can. In the first row, b is '1', which can be coerced to INTEGER. SQLite makes the conversion and compares integers. In the second row, b is 'text' and can't be converted. SQLite then compares storage classes INTEGER and TEXT.

The third rule just reiterates that storage classes established by context are compared at face value. If what looks like a TEXT type is compared with what looks like an INTEGER type, then TEXT is greater.

Additionally, you can manually convert the storage type of a column or an expression using the CAST function. Consider the following example:

```
sqlite> SELECT typeof(3.14), typeof(CAST(3.14 as TEXT));

typeof(3.14)  typeof(CAST(3.14 as TEXT))
------------  --------------------------
real          text
```

MAKESHIFT STRICT TYPING

If you need something stronger than type affinity for domain integrity, then CHECK constraints can help. You can implement pseudo strict typing directly using a single built-in function and a CHECK constraint. As mentioned earlier, SQLite has a function which returns the inferred storage class of a value—typeof(). You can use typeof() in any relational expression to test for a values type. For example:

```
sqlite> select typeof(3.14) = 'text';
0
sqlite> select typeof(3.14) = 'integer';
0
sqlite> select typeof(3.14) = 'real';
1
sqlite> select typeof(3) = 'integer';
1
sqlite> select typeof('3') = 'text';
1
```

Therefore, you can use this function to implement a CHECK constraint that limits the acceptable types allowed in a column:

```
sqlite> create table domain (x integer CHECK(typeof(x)='integer'));
sqlite> INSERT INTO domain VALUES('1');
SQL error: constraint failed

sqlite> INSERT INTO domain VALUES(1.1);
SQL error: constraint failed

sqlite> INSERT INTO domain VALUES(1);
sqlite> select x, typeof(x) from domain;

x    typeof(x)
--   ----------
1    integer
sqlite> update domain set x=1.1;
SQL error: constraint failed
```

The only catch here is that you are limited to checking for SQLite's native storage classes (or what can be implemented using other built-in SQL functions). However, if you are a programmer and either use a language extension that supports SQLite's user-defined functions (e.g., Perl, Python, or Ruby) or use the SQLite C API directly, you can implement even more elaborate functions for type checking, which can be called from within CHECK constraints. Chapter 5 covers this in more detail.

Transactions

Transactions define boundaries around a group of SQL commands such that they either all successfully execute together or not at all. A classic example of the rationale behind transactions is a money transfer. Say a bank program is transferring money from one account to another. The money transfer program can do this in one of two ways: first insert (credit) the funds into account 2 then delete (debit) it from account 1, or first delete it from account 1 and insert it into account 2. Either way, the transfer is a two-step process: an INSERT followed by a DELETE, or a DELETE followed by an INSERT.

Now, say the program is in the process of making a transfer. The first SQL command completes successfully, and then the database server suddenly crashes or the power goes out. Whatever the case, the second operation does not complete. Now the money either exists in both accounts (the first scenario) or has been completely lost altogether (second scenario). Either way, someone's not going to be happy. And the database is in an inconsistent state.

The point here is that these two operations must either happen together or not at all. That is what transactions are for. Now let's replay the example with transactions. In the new scenario, the program first starts a transaction in the database, completes the first SQL operation, and then the lights go out. When they come back on and the database comes back up, it sees an incomplete transaction. It then undoes the changes of the first SQL operation, which brings it back into a consistent state—back where it started before the transfer.

Transaction Scopes

Transactions are issued with three commands: BEGIN, COMMIT, and ROLLBACK. BEGIN starts a transaction. Every operation following a BEGIN can be potentially undone, and will be undone if a COMMIT is not issued before the session terminates. The COMMIT command commits the work performed by all operations since the start of the transaction. Similarly, the ROLLBACK command undoes all of the work performed by all operations since the start of the transaction. A transaction is a scope in which operations are performed together and committed, or completely reversed. Consider the following example:

```
sqlite> BEGIN;
sqlite> DELETE FROM foods;
sqlite> ROLLBACK;
sqlite> SELECT COUNT(*) FROM foods;

COUNT(*)
--------
412
```

I started a transaction, deleted all the rows in foods, changed my mind, and reversed those changes by issuing a ROLLBACK. The SELECT statement shows that nothing was changed.

By default, every SQL command in SQLite is run under its own transaction. That is, if you do not define a transaction scope with BEGIN...COMMIT/ROLLBACK, SQLite will implicitly wrap every individual SQL command with a BEGIN...COMMIT/ROLLBACK. In that case, every command that completes successfully is committed. Likewise, every command that encounters an error is rolled back. This mode of operation (implicit transactions) is referred to as *autocommit mode*:

SQLite automatically runs each command in its own transaction, and if the command does not fail, its changes are automatically committed.

Conflict Resolution

As you've seen in previous examples, constraint violations cause the command that committed the violation to terminate. What exactly happens when a command terminates in the middle of making a bunch of changes to the database? In most databases, all of the changes are undone. That is the way the database is programmed to handle a constraint violation—end of story.

SQLite, however, has a unique feature that allows you to specify different ways to handle (or recover from) constraint violations. It is called *conflict resolution*. Take, for example, the following UPDATE:

```
sqlite> UPDATE foods SET id=800-id;
SQL error: PRIMARY KEY must be unique
```

This results in a UNIQUE constraint violation because once the UPDATE statement reaches the 388th record, it attempts to update its id value to 800-388=412. But a row with an id of 412 already exists, so it aborts the command. But SQLite already updated the first 387 rows before it reached this constraint violation. What happens to them? The default behavior is to terminate the command and reverse all of the changes it made, while leaving the transaction intact.

But what if you wanted these 387 changes to stick despite the constraint violation? Well, believe it or not, you can have it that way too, if you want. You just need to use the appropriate conflict resolution. There are five possible resolutions, or policies, that can be applied to address a conflict (constraint violation): REPLACE, IGNORE, FAIL, ABORT, and ROLLBACK. These five resolutions define a spectrum of error tolerance or sensitivity. On one end of the spectrum is REPLACE, which will effectively allow a statement to plow through almost every possible constraint violation. On the other end is ROLLBACK, which will terminate the entire transaction upon the first violation of any kind. The resolutions are defined as follows in order of their severity:

- REPLACE: When a UNIQUE constraint violation is encountered, SQLite removes the row (or rows) that caused the violation, and replaces it (them) with the new row from the INSERT or UPDATE. The SQL operation continues without error. If a NOT NULL constraint violation occurs, the NULL value is replaced by the default value for that column. If the column has no default value, then SQLite applies the ABORT policy. It is important to note that when this conflict resolution strategy deletes rows in order to satisfy a constraint, it does not invoke delete triggers on those rows. This behavior, however, is subject to change in a future release.

- IGNORE: When a constraint violation is encountered, SQLite allows the command to continue, and leaves the row that triggered the violation unchanged. Other rows before and after the row in question continue to be modified by the command. Thus, all rows in the operation that trigger constraint violations are simply left unchanged, and the command proceeds without error.

- FAIL: When a constraint violation is encountered, SQLite terminates the command but does not restore the changes it made prior to encountering the violation. That is, all changes within the SQL command up to the violation are preserved. For example, if an UPDATE statement encountered a constraint violation on the 100th row it attempts to update, then the changes to the first 99 rows already modified remain intact, but changes to rows 100 and beyond never occur as the command is terminated.

- ABORT: When a constraint violation is encountered, SQLite restores all changes the command made and terminates it. ABORT is the default resolution for all operations in SQLite. It is also the behavior defined in the SQL standard. As a side note, ABORT is also the most expensive conflict resolution policy—requiring extra work even if no conflicts ever occur.

- ROLLBACK: When a constraint violation is encountered, SQLite performs a ROLLBACK— aborting the current command along with the entire transaction. The net result is that all changes made by the current command *and all previous commands* in the transaction are rolled back. This is the most drastic level of conflict resolution where a single violation results in a complete reversal of everything performed in a transaction.

Conflict resolution can be specified within SQL commands as well as within table and index definitions. Specifically, conflict resolution can be specified in INSERT, UPDATE, CREATE TABLE, and CREATE INDEX. Furthermore, it has specific implications within triggers. The syntax for conflict resolution in INSERT and UPDATE is as follows:

```
INSERT OR resolution INTO table (column_list) VALUES (value_list);
UPDATE OR resolution table SET (value_list) WHERE predicate;
```

The conflict resolution policy comes right after the INSERT or UPDATE command and is prefixed with OR. Also, the INSERT OR REPLACE expression can be abbreviated as just REPLACE.

In the preceding UPDATE example, the updates made to the 387 records were rolled back because the default resolution is ABORT. If you wanted the updates to stick, you could use the FAIL resolution. To illustrate this, in the following example I copy foods into a new table test and use it as the guinea pig. I add an additional column to test called modified, the default value of which is 'no'. In the UPDATE, I change this to 'yes' to track which records are updated before the constraint violation occurs. Using the FAIL resolution, these updates will remain unchanged, and I can track afterward how many records were updated.

```
CREATE TABLE test AS SELECT * FROM foods;
CREATE UNIQUE INDEX test_idx on test(id);
ALTER TABLE test ADD COLUMN modified text NOT NULL DEFAULT 'no';
SELECT COUNT(*) FROM test WHERE modified='no';

COUNT(*)
-------------------
412
```

```
UPDATE OR FAIL test SET id=800-id, modified='yes';
SQL error: column id is not unique

SELECT COUNT(*) FROM test WHERE modified='yes';

COUNT(*)
--------------------
387

DROP TABLE test;
```

There is one consideration with FAIL that you need to be aware of. The order that records are updated is nondeterministic. That is, you cannot be certain of the order of the records in the table or the order in which SQLite processes them. You might assume that it follows the order of the ROWID column, but this is not a safe assumption to make: there is nothing in the documentation that says so. The point is, if you are going to use FAIL, in many cases it might be better to use IGNORE. IGNORE will finish the job and modify all records that can be modified rather than bailing out on the first violation.

When defined within tables, conflict resolution is specified for individual columns. For example:

```
sqlite> CREATE TEMP TABLE cast(name text UNIQUE ON CONFLICT ROLLBACK);
sqlite> INSERT INTO cast VALUES ('Jerry');
sqlite> INSERT INTO cast VALUES ('Elaine');
sqlite> INSERT INTO cast VALUES ('Kramer');
```

The cast table has a single column name with a UNIQUE constraint and conflict resolution set to ROLLBACK. Any INSERT or UPDATE that triggers a constraint violation on name will be arbitrated by the ROLLBACK resolution rather than the default ABORT. The result will not only abort the statement but the entire transaction as well:

```
sqlite> BEGIN;
sqlite> INSERT INTO cast VALUES('Jerry');
SQL error: uniqueness constraint failed

sqlite> COMMIT;
SQL error: cannot commit - no transaction is active
```

COMMIT failed here because the name's conflict resolution already aborted the transaction. CREATE INDEX works the same way. Conflict resolution within tables and indices changes the default behavior of the operation from ABORT to that defined for the specific columns when those columns are the source of the constraint violation.

Conflict resolution at statement level (DML) overrides that defined at object level (DDL). Working from the previous example:

```
sqlite> BEGIN;
sqlite> INSERT OR REPLACE INTO cast VALUES('Jerry');
sqlite> COMMIT;
```

The REPLACE resolution in the INSERT overrides the ROLLBACK resolution defined on cast.name.

Database Locks

Locking is closely associated with transactions in SQLite. In order to use transactions effectively, you need to know a little something about how it does locking.

SQLite has coarse-grained locking. When a session is writing to the database, all other sessions are locked out until the writing session completes its transaction. To help with this, SQLite has a locking scheme that helps defer writer locks until the last possible moment in order to maximize concurrency.

SQLite uses a lock escalation policy whereby a connection gradually obtains exclusive access to a database in order to write to it. There are five different locking *states* in SQLite: *unlocked, shared, reserved, pending,* or *exclusive*. Each database session (or connection) can be in only one of these states at any given time. Furthermore, there is a corresponding lock for each state, except for unlocked—there is no lock required to be in the unlocked state.

To begin with, the most basic state is unlocked. In this state, no session is accessing data from the database. When you connect to a database, or even initiate a transaction with `BEGIN`, your connection is in the unlocked state.

The next state beyond unlocked is shared. In order for a session to read from the database (not write), it must first enter the shared state, and must therefore acquire a *shared lock*. Multiple sessions can simultaneously acquire and hold shared locks at any given time. Therefore, multiple sessions can read from a common database at any given time. However, no session can write to the database during this time—while any shared locks are active.

If a session wants to write to the database, it must first acquire a *reserved lock*. Only one reserved lock may be held at one time for a given database. Shared locks can coexist with a reserved lock. A reserved lock is the first phase of writing to a database. It does not block sessions with shared locks from reading, nor does it prevent sessions from acquiring new shared locks.

Once a session has a reserved lock, it can begin the process of making modifications; *however*, these modifications are cached and not actually written to disk. The reader's changes are stored in a memory cache (see the discussion of the `cache_size` pragma in the section "Database Configuration," later in this chapter, for more information).

When the session wants to commit the changes (or transaction) to the database, it begins the process of promoting its reserved lock to an *exclusive lock*. In order to get an exclusive lock, it must first promote its reserved lock to a *pending lock*. A pending lock starts a process of attrition whereby no new shared locks can be obtained. That is, other sessions with existing shared locks are allowed to continue as normal, but other sessions cannot acquire new shared locks. At this point, the session with the pending lock is waiting for the other sessions with shared locks to finish what they are doing and release them.

Once all of shared locks are released, the session with the pending lock can promote it to an exclusive lock. It is then free to make changes to the database. All of the previously cached changes are written to the database file.

Deadlocks

While you may find all of this interesting, you are probably wondering at this point why any of this matters. Why do you need to know this? Because if you don't know what you are doing, you can end up in a deadlock.

Consider the following scenario illustrated in Table 4-7. Two sessions, *A* and *B*—completely oblivious to one another—are working on the same database at the same time. Session A issues the first command, B the second and third, A the fourth, and so on.

Table 4-7. *A Portrait of a Deadlock*

Session A	Session B
sqlite> BEGIN;	
	sqlite> BEGIN;
	sqlite> INSERT INTO foo VALUES ('x');
sqlite> SELECT * FROM foo;	
	sqlite> COMMIT;
	SQL error: database is locked
sqlite> INSERT INTO foo VALUES ('x');	
SQL error: database is locked	

Both sessions wind up in a deadlock. Session *B* was the first to try to write to the database, and therefore has a pending lock. *A* attempts to write, but fails when INSERT tries to promote its shared lock to a reserved lock.

For the sake of argument, let's say that *A* decides to just wait around for the database to become writable. So does *B*. Then at this point, everyone else is effectively locked out too. If you try to open a third session, it won't even be able to read from the database. The reason is that *B* has a pending lock, which prevents any sessions from acquiring shared locks. So not only are *A* and *B* deadlocked, they have locked everyone else out of the database as well. Basically, you have a shared lock and one pending lock that don't want to relinquish control, and until one does, nobody can do anything.

So how do you avoid this? It's not like *A* and *B* can sit down in a meeting and work it out with their lawyers. *A* and *B* don't even know each other *exists*. The answer is to *pick the right transaction type for the job*.

Transaction Types

SQLite has three different transaction types that start transactions in different locking states. Transactions can be started as DEFERRED, IMMEDIATE, or EXCLUSIVE. A transaction's type is specified in the BEGIN command:

```
BEGIN [ DEFERRED | IMMEDIATE | EXCLUSIVE ] TRANSACTION;
```

A *deferred transaction* does not acquire any locks until it has to. Thus with a deferred transaction, the BEGIN statement itself does nothing—it starts in the unlocked state. This is the default. If you simply issue a BEGIN, then your transaction is DEFERRED, and therefore sitting in the unlocked state. Multiple sessions can simultaneously start DEFERRED transactions at the same time without creating any locks. In this case, the first read operation against a database acquires a shared lock and similarly the first write operation *attempts* to acquire a reserved lock.

An *immediate transaction* attempts to obtain a reserved lock as soon as the BEGIN command is executed. If successful, BEGIN IMMEDIATE guarantees that no other session will be able to write to the database. As you know, other sessions can continue to read from the database, but the reserved lock prevents any new sessions from reading. Another consequence of the reserved lock is that no other sessions will be able to successfully issue a BEGIN IMMEDIATE or BEGIN EXCLUSIVE command. SQLite will return a SQLITE_BUSY error. During this time, you can make some modifications to the database, but you may not necessarily be able to commit them. When you call COMMIT, you could get SQLITE_BUSY. This means that there are other readers active, as in the earlier example. Once they are gone, you can commit the transaction.

An *exclusive transaction* obtains an exclusive lock on the database. This works similarly to IMMEDIATE, but when you successfully issue it, EXCLUSIVE guarantees that no other session is active in the database and that you can read or write with impunity.

The crux of the problem in the preceding example is that both sessions ultimately wanted to write to the database but they made no attempt to relinquish their locks. Ultimately, it was the shared lock that caused the problem. If both sessions had started with BEGIN IMMEDIATE, then the deadlock would not have occurred. In this case, only one of the sessions would have been able to enter BEGIN IMMEDIATE at one time, while the other would have to wait. The one that has to wait could keep retrying with the assurance that it would eventually get in. BEGIN IMMEDIATE and BEGIN EXCLUSIVE, if used by all sessions that want to write to the database, provide a synchronization mechanism, thereby preventing deadlocks. For this approach to work, though, everyone has to follow the rules.

The bottom line is this: if you are using a database that no other connections are using, then a simple BEGIN will suffice. If, however, you are using a database that other connections are also writing to, both you and they should use BEGIN IMMEDIATE or BEGIN EXCLUSIVE to initiate transactions. It works out best that way for both of you. Transactions and locks are covered in more detail in Chapter 5.

Database Administration

Database administration is generally concerned with controlling how a database operates. From a SQL perspective, this includes various topics such as views, triggers, and indexes. Additionally, SQLite includes some unique administrative features of its own, such the means to "attach" multiple databases to a single session, as well as database *pragmas*, which can be used for setting various configuration parameters.

Views

Views are virtual tables. They are also known as *derived tables*, as their contents are derived from other tables. While views look and feel like base tables, they aren't. The contents of base tables are persistent whereas the contents of views are dynamically generated when they are used. Specifically, a view is composed of relational expressions that take other tables and produce a new table. The syntax to create a view is as follows:

```
CREATE VIEW name AS sql;
```

The name of the view is given by *name* and its definition by *sql*. The resulting view will look like a base table named name. Imagine you had a query you ran all the time, so much that you get sick of writing it. Views are the cure for this particular sickness. Say your query was as follows:

```
SELECT f.name, ft.name, e.name
FROM foods f
INNER JOIN food_types ft on f.type_id=ft.id
INNER JOIN foods_episodes fe ON f.id=fe.food_id
INNER JOIN episodes e ON fe.episode_id=e.id;
```

This returns the name of every food, its type, and every episode it was in. It is one big table of 504 rows with just about every food fact. Rather than having to write out (or remember) the previous query every time you want these results, you can tidily restate it in the form of a view. Let's name it details:

```
CREATE VIEW details AS
SELECT f.name AS fd, ft.name AS tp, e.name AS ep, e.season as ssn
FROM foods f
INNER JOIN food_types ft on f.type_id=ft.id
INNER JOIN foods_episodes fe ON f.id=fe.food_id
INNER JOIN episodes e ON fe.episode_id=e.id;
```

Now you can query details just as you would a table. For example:

```
sqlite> SELECT fd as Food, ep as Episode
        FROM details WHERE ssn=7 AND tp like 'Drinks';
```

```
Food                     Episode
--------------------     --------------------
Apple Cider              The Bottle Deposit 1
Bosco                    The Secret Code
Cafe Latte               The Postponement
Cafe Latte               The Maestro
Champagne Coolies        The Wig Master
Cider                    The Bottle Deposit 2
Hershey's                The Secret Code
Hot Coffee               The Maestro
Latte                    The Maestro
Mellow Yellow soda       The Bottle Deposit 1
Merlot                   The Rye
Orange Juice             The Wink
Tea                      The Hot Tub
Wild Turkey              The Hot Tub
```

The contents of views are dynamically generated. Thus, every time you use details, its associated SQL will be reexecuted, producing results based on the data in the database at that moment.

Views also have other purposes, such as security, although this particular kind of security does not exist in SQLite. Some databases offer row- and column-level security in which only specific users, groups, or roles can view or modify specific parts of tables. In such databases, views can be defined on tables to exclude sensitive columns, allowing users with less security privileges to access parts of tables that are not secured. For example, say you have a table secure, defined as follows:

```
CREATE TABLE secure (id int, public_data text, restricted_data text);
```

You may want to allow users access to the first two columns but not the third. In other databases, you would limit access to secure to just the users who can access all columns. You would then create a view that contains just the first two columns that everyone else can look at:

```
CREATE VIEW public_secure AS SELECT id, public_data FROM secure;
```

Some of this kind of security is available if you program with SQLite, using its operational control facilities. This is covered in Chapters 5 and 6.

Finally, to drop a view, use the DROP VIEW command:

```
DROP VIEW name;
```

The name of the view to drop is given by name.

Materialized Views

The relational model calls for updatable views, sometimes referred to as *materialized views*. These are views that you can modify. You can run INSERT or UPDATE statements on them, for example, and the respective changes are applied directly to their underlying tables. Materialized views are not supported in SQLite. However, using triggers, you can create something that looks like materialized views. These are covered in the section "Triggers."

Indexes

Indexes are a construct designed to speed up queries under certain conditions. Consider the following query:

```
SELECT * FROM foods WHERE name='JujyFruit';
```

When a database searches for matching rows, the default method it uses to perform this is called a *sequential scan*. That is, it literally searches (or scans) every row in the table to see if its name attribute matches 'JujyFruit'.

However, if this query is used frequently, and foods was very large, there is another method available that can be much faster, called an *index scan*. An index is a special disk-based data structure (called a B-tree), which stores the values for an entire column (or columns) in a highly organized way that is optimized for searching.

The search speed of these two methods can be represented mathematically. The search speed of a sequential scan is proportional to the number of rows in the table: the more rows, the longer the scan. This relationship—bigger table, longer search—is called *linear time*, as in "the search method operates in linear time." It is represented mathematically using what is called the *Big O notation*, which in this case is $O(n)$, where n stands for the number of elements (or rows) in the set. The index scan, on the other hand, has $O(log(n))$ search time, or logarithmic time. This is much faster. If you have a table of 10,000 records, a sequential scan will read all 10,000 rows to find all matches, while an index scan will read 4 rows ($log(10,000)$) to find the first match (and from that point on it would be linear time to find all subsequent matches). This is quite a speed-up.

But there is no such thing as a free lunch. Indexes also increase the size of the database. They literally keep a copy of all columns they index. If you index every column in a table, you effectively double the size of the table. Another consideration is that indexes must be maintained. When you insert, update, or delete records, in addition to modifying the table, the database must modify each and every index on that table as well. So indexes can slow down inserts, updates, and similar operations.

But in moderation, indexes can make a huge performance difference. Whether or not to add an index is more subjective than anything else. Different people have different criteria for what is acceptable. Indexes illustrate one of the great things about SQL: you only need to specify what to get and not how to get it. Because of this, you can often optimize your database (such as by adding or removing indexes) without having to rewrite your code. Just create an index in the right place.

The command to create an index is as follows:

```
CREATE INDEX [UNIQUE] index_name ON table_name (columns)
```

The variable index_name is the name of the index, and must be unique, and table_name is the name of the table containing the column(s) to index. The variable columns is either a single column or a comma-separated list of columns.

If you use the UNIQUE keyword, then the index will have the added constraint that all values in the index must be unique. This applies to both the index, and by extension, to the column or columns it indexes. The UNIQUE constraint covers all columns defined in the index, and it is their combined values (not individual values) that must be unique. For example:

```
sqlite> CREATE TABLE foo(a text, b text);
sqlite> CREATE UNIQUE INDEX foo_idx on foo(a,b);
sqlite> INSERT INTO foo VALUES ('unique', 'value');
sqlite> INSERT INTO foo VALUES ('unique', 'value2');
sqlite> INSERT INTO foo VALUES ('unique', 'value');
SQL error: columns a, b are not unique
```

You can see here that uniqueness is defined by both columns collectively, not individually. Notice that collation plays an important role here as well.

To remove an index, use the DROP INDEX command, which is defined as follows:

```
DROP INDEX index_name;
```

Collation

Each column in the index can have a collation associated with it. For example, to create a case-insensitive index on foods.name, you'd use the following:

```
CREATE INDEX foods_name_idx on foods (name COLLATE NOCASE);
```

This means that values in the name column will sort without respect to case. You can list the indexes for a table in the SQLite command-line program by using the .indices shell command. For example:

```
sqlite> .indices foods
foods_name_idx
For more information, you can use the .schema shell command as well:
sqlite> .schema foods
CREATE TABLE foods(
  id integer primary key,
  type_id integer,
  name text );
CREATE INDEX foods_name_idx on foods (name COLLATE NOCASE);
```

You can also obtain this information by querying the sqlite_master table, described later in this section.

Index Utilization

It is important to understand when indexes are used and when they aren't. There are very specific conditions in which SQLite will decide to use an index. SQLite will use a single column index, if available, for the following expressions in the WHERE clause:

```
column {=|>|>=|<=|<} expression
expression {=|>|>=|<=|<} column
column IN (expression-list)
column IN (subquery)
```

Multicolumn indexes have more specific conditions before they are used. This is perhaps best illustrated by example. Say you have a table defined as follows:

```
CREATE TABLE foo (a,b,c,d);
```

Furthermore, you create a multicolumn index as follows:

```
CREATE INDEX foo_idx on foo (a,b,c,d);
```

The columns of foo_idx can only be used sequentially from left to right. That is, in the query

```
SELECT * FROM foo WHERE a=1 AND b=2 AND d=3
```

only the first and second conditions will use the index. The reason the third condition was excluded is because there was no condition that used c to bridge the gap to d. Basically, when SQLite uses a multicolumn index, it works from left to right column-wise. It starts with the left column and looks for a condition using that column. It moves to the second column, and so on. It continues until either it fails to find a valid condition in the WHERE clause that uses it or there are no more columns in the index to use.

But there is one more requirement. SQLite will use a multicolumn index only if all of the conditions use either the equality (=) or IN operator for all index columns *except for the right-most index column*. For that column, you can specify up to two inequalities to define its upper and lower bounds. Consider, for example:

```
SELECT * FROM foo WHERE a>1 AND b=2 AND c=3 AND d=4
```

SQLite will only do an index scan on column a. The a>1 expression becomes the rightmost index column because it uses the inequality. All columns after it are not eligible to be used as a result. Similarly,

```
SELECT * FROM foo WHERE a=1 AND b>2 AND c=3 AND d=4
```

will use the index columns a and b and stop there as b>2 becomes the rightmost index term by its use of an inequality operator.

An off-the-cuff way to time a query within a SQL statement is to use a subselect in the FROM clause returning the current time, which will be joined to your input relation(s). Then select the current time in the SELECT clause. The time in the FROM clause will be computed at the start of the query. The time in the SELECT clause will be computed as each row is processed. Therefore, the difference between the two times in the last row of the result set will be your relative query time. For example, the following SQL is a triple Cartesian join on food_types. It's quite slow, as it should be. The results display the last five records of the result set.

```
SELECT CAST(strftime('%s','now') as INTEGER)-CAST(time.start as INTEGER) time,
       ft1.id, ft2.id, ft3.id, ft4.id
FROM food_types ft1, food_types ft2, food_types ft3, food_types ft4,
    (SELECT strftime('%s','now') start) time;
```

18	15	15	15	11
18	15	15	15	12
18	15	15	15	13
18	15	15	15	14
18	15	15	15	15

The first column is the elapsed time in seconds. This query took 18 seconds. Although this doesn't represent the actual query time because there is timing overhead, relative query time is all you need to judge an index's worth. If this were an actual slow query that you were trying to optimize, you would now add the index you think might help and rerun the query. Is it significantly faster? If so, then you may have a useful index.

In short, when you create an index, have a reason for creating it. Make sure there is a specific performance gain you are getting before you take on the overhead that comes with it. Well-chosen indexes are a wonderful thing. Indexes that are thoughtlessly scattered here and there in the vain hope of performance are of dubious value.

Triggers

Triggers execute specific SQL commands when specific database events transpire on specific tables. The general syntax for creating a trigger is as follows:

```
CREATE [TEMP|TEMPORARY] TRIGGER name [BEFORE|AFTER]
  [INSERT|DELETE|UPDATE|UPDATE OF columns] ON table
  action
```

A trigger is defined by a name, an action, and a table. The action, or trigger body, consists of a series of SQL commands. Triggers are said to *fire* when such events take place. Furthermore, triggers can be made to fire before or after the event using the BEFORE or AFTER keyword, respectively. Events include DELETE, INSERT, and UPDATE commands issued on the specified table. Triggers can be used to create your own integrity constraints, log changes, update other tables, and many other things. They are limited only by what you can write in SQL.

UPDATE Triggers

UPDATE triggers, unlike INSERT and DELETE triggers, may be defined for specific columns in a table. The general form of this kind of trigger is as follows:

```
CREATE TRIGGER name [BEFORE|AFTER] UPDATE OF column ON table
action
```

The following is a SQL script that shows an UPDATE trigger in action:

```
.h on
.m col
.w 50
.echo on
CREATE TEMP TABLE log(x);

CREATE TEMP TRIGGER foods_update_log UPDATE of name ON foods
BEGIN
  INSERT INTO log VALUES('updated foods: new name=' || NEW.name);
END;

BEGIN;
UPDATE foods set name='JUJYFRUIT' where name='JujyFruit';
SELECT * FROM log;
ROLLBACK;
```

This script creates a temporary table called log, as well as a temporary UPDATE trigger on foods.name that inserts a message into log when it fires. The action takes place inside the transaction that follows. The first step of the transaction updates the name column of the row whose name is 'JUJYFRUIT'. This causes the UPDATE trigger to fire. When it fires, it inserts a record into the log. Next, the transaction reads log, which shows that the trigger did indeed fire. The transaction then rolls back the change, and when the session ends, the log table and the UPDATE trigger are destroyed. Running the script produces the following output:

```
mike@linux tmp # sqlite3 foods.db < trigger.sql
```

```
CREATE TEMP TABLE log(x);

CREATE TEMP TRIGGER foods_update_log AFTER UPDATE of name ON foods
BEGIN
  INSERT INTO log VALUES('updated foods: new name=' || NEW.name);
END;
```

```
BEGIN;
UPDATE foods set name='JUJYFRUIT' where name='JujyFruit';
SELECT * FROM log;
x
--------------------------------------------------
updated foods: new name=JUJYFRUIT
ROLLBACK;
```

SQLite provides access to both the old (original) row and the new (updated) row in UPDATE triggers. The old row is referred to as OLD and the new row as NEW. Notice in the script how the trigger refers to NEW.name. All attributes of both rows are available in OLD and NEW using the dot notation. I could have just as easily recorded NEW.type_id or OLD.id.

Error Handling

Defining a trigger before an event takes place gives you the opportunity to stop the event from happening. BEFORE triggers enable you to implement new integrity constraints. SQLite provides a special SQL function for triggers called RAISE(), which allows them to raise an error within the trigger body. RAISE is defined as follows:

```
RAISE(resolution, error_message);
```

The first argument is a conflict resolution policy (ABORT, FAIL, IGNORE, ROLLBACK, etc.). The second argument is an error message. If you use IGNORE, the remainder of the current trigger along with the SQL statement that caused the trigger to fire, as well as any subsequent triggers that would have been fired, are all terminated. If the SQL statement that caused the trigger to fire is itself part of another trigger, then that trigger resumes execution at the beginning of the next SQL command in the trigger action.

Conflict Resolution

If a conflict resolution policy is defined for a SQL statement that causes a trigger to fire, then that policy supersedes the policy defined within the trigger. If, on the other hand, the SQL statement does not have any conflict resolution policy defined, and the trigger does, then the trigger's policy is used.

Updatable Views

Triggers make it possible to create something like materialized views, as mentioned earlier in this chapter. In reality, they aren't true materialized views but rather more like updatable views. With true materialized views, the view is updatable all by itself—you define the view and it figures out how to map all changes to its underlying base tables. This is not a simple thing. Nor is it supported in SQLite. However, using triggers, we can create the appearance of a materialized view.

The idea here is that you create a view and then create a trigger that handles update events on that view. SQLite supports triggers on views using the INSTEAD OF keywords in the trigger definition. To illustrate this, let's create a view that combines foods with food_types:

```
CREATE VIEW foods_view AS
  SELECT f.id fid, f.name fname, t.id tid, t.name tname
  FROM foods f, food_types t;
```

This view joins the two tables according to their foreign key relationship. Notice that I have created aliases for all column names in the view. This allows me to differentiate the respective id and name columns in each table when I reference them from inside the trigger. Now, let's make the view updatable by creating an UPDATE trigger on it:

```
CREATE TRIGGER on_update_foods_view
INSTEAD OF UPDATE ON foods_view
FOR EACH ROW
BEGIN
  UPDATE foods SET name=NEW.fname WHERE id=NEW.fid;
  UPDATE food_types SET name=NEW.tname WHERE id=NEW.tid;
END;
```

Now if you try to update the foods_view, this trigger gets called. The trigger simply takes the values provided in the UPDATE statement and uses them to update the underlying base tables foods and food_types. Testing it out yields the following:

```
.echo on
-- Update the view within a transaction
BEGIN;
UPDATE foods_view SET fname='Whataburger', tname='Fast Food' WHERE fid=413;
-- Now view the underlying rows in the base tables:
SELECT * FROM foods f, food_types t WHERE f.type_id=t.id AND f.id=413;
-- Roll it back
ROLLBACK;
-- Now look at the original record:
SELECT * FROM foods f, food_types t WHERE f.type_id=t.id AND f.id=413;
```

```
BEGIN;
UPDATE foods_view SET fname='Whataburger', tname='Fast Food' WHERE fid=413;
SELECT * FROM foods f, food_types t WHERE f.type_id=t.id AND f.id=413;
id   type_id name            id   name
---  ------- --------------  ---  ---------
413  1       Whataburger     1    Fast Food

ROLLBACK;

SELECT * FROM foods f, food_types t WHERE f.type_id=t.id AND f.id=413;
id   type_id name            id   name
---  ------- --------------  ---  -------
413  1       Cinnamon Bobka  1    Bakery
```

You can just as easily add INSERT and DELETE triggers and have the rough equivalent of a materialized view.

Foreign Key Constraints Using Triggers

One of the most interesting applications of triggers in SQLite I have seen is the implementation of foreign key constraints, originally posted on the SQLite Wiki (www.sqlite.org/contrib). To further explore triggers, I will use this idea to implement foreign key constraints between foods and food_types.

As mentioned earlier, foods.type_id references food_types.id. Therefore, every value in foods.type_id should correspond to some value in food_types.id. The first step in enforcing this constraint lies in controlling what can be inserted into foods. This is accomplished with the following INSERT trigger:

```
CREATE TRIGGER foods_insert_trg
BEFORE INSERT ON foods
BEGIN
  SELECT CASE
    WHEN (SELECT id FROM food_types WHERE id=NEW.type_id) IS NULL
    THEN RAISE( ABORT,
    'Foreign Key Violation: foods.type_id is not in food_types.id')
  END;
END;
```

This trigger runs a subquery that checks for the value of NEW.type_id in foods_types.id. If no match is found, the subquery returns NULL, which triggers the WHEN condition, calling the RAISE function.

After installing the trigger, the following SQL tries to insert a record with an invalid type_id (the maximum id value in food_types is 15):

```
sqlite> INSERT INTO foods VALUES (NULL, 20, 'Blue Bell Ice Cream');
SQL error: Foreign Key Violation: foods.type_id is not in food_types.id
```

Next is UPDATE. The only thing that matters on UPDATE of foods is the type_id field, so the trigger will be defined on that column alone. Aside from this and the trigger's name, the trigger is identical to INSERT:

```
CREATE TRIGGER foods_update_trg
BEFORE UPDATE OF type_id ON foods
BEGIN
  SELECT CASE
    WHEN (SELECT id FROM food_types WHERE id=NEW.type_id) IS NULL
    THEN RAISE(ABORT,
    'Foreign Key Violation: foods.type_id is not in food_types.id')
  END;
END;
```

Testing this trigger reveals the same results:

```
sqlite> UPDATE foods SET type_id=20 WHERE name='Chocolate Bobka';
SQL error: Foreign Key Violation: foods.type_id is not in food_types.id
```

The final piece of the puzzle is DELETE. Deleting rows in foods doesn't affect the relationship with food_types. Deleting rows in food_types, however, does affect the relationship with foods. If a row is deleted in food_types, then there could potentially be rows in foods that may reference it, in which case the relationship has been compromised. Therefore, we need a DELETE trigger on food_types that does not allow the deletion of a row if there are rows in foods that reference it. To that end, the DELETE trigger is defined as follows:

```
CREATE TRIGGER foods_delete_trg
BEFORE DELETE ON food_types
BEGIN
  SELECT CASE
    WHEN (SELECT COUNT(type_id) FROM foods WHERE type_id=OLD.id) > 0
    THEN RAISE(ABORT,
    'Foreign Key Violation: foods rows reference row to be deleted.')
  END;
END;
```

After installing this trigger, if I try to delete the 'Bakery' row in food_types I get:

```
sqlite> DELETE FROM food_types WHERE name='Bakery';
SQL error: Foreign Key Violation: foods rows reference row to be deleted.
```

To make sure this works under the correct conditions:

```
sqlite> BEGIN;
sqlite> DELETE FROM foods WHERE type_id=1;
sqlite> DELETE FROM food_types WHERE name='Bakery';
sqlite> ROLLBACK;
```

The DELETE trigger allows the delete if there are no rows in foods referencing it.

So there you have it: simple, trigger-based foreign key constraints. As mentioned earlier, while SQLite does support CHECK constraints, triggers can pretty much do everything CHECK constraints can and then some.

Attaching Databases

SQLite allows you to "attach" multiple databases to the current session using the ATTACH command. When you attach a database, all of its contents are accessible in the global scope of the current database file. ATTACH has the following syntax:

```
ATTACH [DATABASE] filename AS database_name;
```

Here, filename refers to the path and name of the SQLite database file, and database_name refers to the logical name with which to reference that database and its objects. The main database is automatically assigned the name main. If you create any temporary objects, then SQLite will create an attached database name temp. (You can see these objects using the database_list pragma, described later.) The logical name may be used to reference objects within the attached database. If there are tables or other database objects that share the same name in both databases, then the logical name is required to reference such objects in the attached database. For example, if both databases have a table called foo, and the logical name of the attached database is db2, then the only way to query foo in db2 is by using the fully qualified name foo.db2, as follows:

```
sqlite> ATTACH DATABASE '/tmp/db' as db2;
sqlite> SELECT * FROM db2.foo;

x
----------
bar
```

If you really want to, you can qualify objects in the main database using the name main:

```
sqlite> SELECT * FROM main.foods LIMIT 2;

id          type_id     name
----------  ----------  ---------------
1           1           Bagels
2           1           Bagels, raisin
```

The same is true with the temporary database:

```
sqlite> CREATE TEMP TABLE foo AS SELECT * FROM food_types LIMIT 3;
sqlite> SELECT * FROM temp.foo;

id   name
---  -------------
1    Bakery
2    Cereal
3    Chicken/Fowl
```

You detach databases with the DETACH DATABASE command, defined as follows:

```
DETACH [DATABASE] database_name;
```

This command takes the logical name of the attached database (given by *database_name*) and detaches the associated database file. You get a list of attached databases using the database_list pragma, explained in the section "Database Configuration."

Cleaning Databases

SQLite has two commands designed for cleaning—REINDEX and VACUUM. REINDEX is used to rebuild indexes. It has two forms:

```
REINDEX collation_name;
REINDEX table_name|index_name;
```

The first form rebuilds all indexes that use the collation name given by collation_name. It is only needed when you change the behavior of a user-defined collating sequence (e.g., multiple sort orders in Chinese). All indexes in a table (or a particular index given its name) can be rebuilt with the second form.

VACUUM cleans out any unused space in the database by rebuilding the database file. VACUUM will not work if there are any open transactions. An alternative to manually running VACUUM statements is autovacuum. This feature is enabled using the auto_vacuum pragma, described in the next section.

Database Configuration

SQLite doesn't have a configuration file. Rather, all of its configuration parameters are implemented using *pragmas*. Pragmas work in different ways. Some are like variables; others are like commands. They cover many aspects of the database, such as runtime information, database schema, versioning, file format, memory use, and debugging. Some pragmas are read and set like variables, while others require arguments and are called like functions. Many pragmas have both temporary and permanent forms. Temporary forms affect only the current session for the duration of its lifetime. The permanent forms are stored in the database and affect every session. The cache size is one such example.

This section covers the most commonly used pragmas. A complete list of all SQLite pragmas can be found in Appendix A.

The Connection Cache Size

The cache size pragmas control how many database pages a session can hold in memory. To set the default cache size for the current session, you use the cache_size pragma:

```
sqlite> PRAGMA cache_size;

cache_size
---------------
2000

sqlite> PRAGMA cache_size=10000;
sqlite> PRAGMA cache_size;

cache_size
---------------
10000
```

You can permanently set the cache size for all sessions using the default_cache_size pragma. This setting is stored in the database. This will only take effect for sessions created after the change, not for currently active sessions.

One of the uses for the cache is in storing pending changes when a session is in a RESERVED state (it has a RESERVED lock), as described earlier in the section "Transactions." If the session fills up the cache, it will not be able to continue further modifications until it gets an EXCLUSIVE lock, which means that it may have to first wait for readers to clear.

If you or your program(s) perform many updates or deletes on a database that is being used by many other sessions, it may help you to increase the cache size. The larger the cache size, the more modifications a session can cache change before it has to get an EXCLUSIVE lock. This not only allows a session to get more work done before having to wait, it also cuts down on the time the exclusive locks needs to be held, as all the work is done up front. In this case, the EXCLUSIVE lock only needs to be held long enough to flush the changes in the cache to disk. Some tips for tuning the cache size are covered in Chapter 5.

Getting Database Information

You can obtain database information using the database schema pragmas, defined as follows:

- database_list: Lists information about all attached databases.

- index_info: Lists information about the columns within an index. It takes an index name as an argument.

- index_list: Lists information about the indexes in a table. It takes a table name as an argument.

- table_info: Lists information about all columns in a table.

The following illustrates some information provided by these pragmas:

```
sqlite> PRAGMA database_list;

seq   name      file
----  -------   --------------------
0     main      /tmp/foods.db
2     db2       /tmp/db

sqlite> CREATE INDEX foods_name_type_idx ON foods(name,type_id);
sqlite> PRAGMA index_info(foods_name_type_idx);

seqn  cid       name
----  -------   --------------------
0     2         name
1     1         type_id

sqlite> PRAGMA index_list(foods);

seq   name                 unique
----- ------------------   ---------------
0     foods_name_type_idx  0

sqlite> PRAGMA table_info(foods);

cid   name             type             notn  dflt  pk
----- ---------------  ---------------  ----  ----  ----------
0     id               integer          0           1
1     type_id          integer          0           0
2     name             text             0           0
```

Synchronous Writes

Normally, SQLite commits all changes to disk at critical moments to ensure transaction durability. However, it is possible to turn this off for performance gains. You do this with the synchronous pragma. There are three settings: FULL, NORMAL, and OFF. They are defined as follows:

- FULL: SQLite will pause at critical moments to make sure that data has actually been written to the disk surface before continuing. This ensures that if the operating system crashes or if there is a power failure, the database will be uncorrupted after rebooting. FULL synchronous is very safe, but it is also slow.

- NORMAL: SQLite will still pause at the most critical moments, but less often than in FULL mode. There is a very small (though non-zero) chance that a power failure at just the wrong time could corrupt the database in NORMAL mode. But in practice, you are more likely to suffer a catastrophic disk failure or some other unrecoverable hardware fault.

- OFF: SQLite continues operation without pausing as soon as it has handed data off to the operating system. This can speed up some operations as much as 50 or more times. If the application running SQLite crashes, the data will be safe. However, if the operating system crashes or the computer loses power, the database may be corrupted.

There is no persistent form of the synchronous pragma. Chapter 5 explains this setting's crucial role in transaction durability and how it works.

Temporary Storage

Temporary storage is where SQLite keeps transient data such as temporary tables, indexes, and other objects. By default, SQLite uses a compiled-in location, which varies between platforms. There are two pragmas that govern temporary storage: temp_store and temp_store_directory. The first pragma determines whether SQLite uses memory or disk for temporary storage. There are actually three possible values: DEFAULT, FILE, or MEMORY. DEFAULT uses the compiled-in default, FILE uses an operating system file, and MEMORY uses RAM. If FILE is set as the storage medium, then the second pragma, temp_store_directory, can be used to set the directory in which the temporary storage file is placed.

Page Size, Encoding, and Autovacuum

The database page size, encoding, and autovacuuming must be set before a database is created. That is, in order to alter the defaults, you must first set these pragmas before creating any database objects in a new database. The defaults are a 1,024-byte page size and UTF-8 encoding. SQLite supports page sizes ranging from 512 to 32,786 bytes, in powers of 2. Supported encodings are UTF-8, UTF-16le (little-endian UTF-16 encoding), and UTF-16be (big-endian UTF-16 encoding).

A database's size can be automatically kept to a minimum using the auto_vacuum pragma. Normally, when a transaction that deletes data from a database is committed, the database file remains the same size. When the auto_vacuum pragma is enabled, the database file shrinks when a transaction that deletes data is committed. To support this functionality, the database stores extra information internally, resulting in slightly larger database files than would otherwise be possible. The VACUUM command has no effect on databases that use auto_vacuum.

Debugging

There are four pragmas for various debugging purposes. The integrity_check pragma looks for out-of-order records, missing pages, malformed records, and corrupted indexes. If any problems are found, then a single string is returned describing the problems. If everything is in order, SQLite returns ok. The other pragmas are used for tracing the parser and virtual database engine and can only be enabled if SQLite is compiled with debugging information. Detailed information on these pragmas can be found in Chapter 9.

The System Catalog

The sqlite_master table is a system table that contains information about all the tables, views, indexes, and triggers in the database. For example, the current contents of the foods database are as follows:

```
sqlite> SELECT type, name, rootpage FROM sqlite_master;
```

type	name	rootpage
table	episodes	2
table	foods	3
table	foods_episodes	4
table	food_types	5
index	foods_name_idx	30
table	sqlite_sequence	50
trigger	foods_update_trg	0
trigger	foods_insert_trg	0
trigger	foods_delete_trg	0

The type column refers to the type of object, name is of course the name of the object, and rootpage refers to the first B-tree page of the object in the database file. This latter column is only relevant for tables and indexes.

The sqlite_master table also contains another column called sql, which stores the DML used to create the object. For example:

```
sqlite> SELECT sql FROM sqlite_master WHERE name='foods_update_trg';

CREATE TRIGGER foods_update_trg
BEFORE UPDATE OF type_id ON foods
BEGIN
  SELECT CASE
    WHEN (SELECT id FROM food_types WHERE id=NEW.type_id) IS NULL
    THEN RAISE( ABORT,
                'Foreign Key Violation: foods.type_id is not in food_types.id')
  END;
END
```

Viewing Query Plans

You can view the way SQLite goes about executing a query by using the EXPLAIN command. EXPLAIN lists the VDBE program that would be used to carry out a SQL command. The VDBE is the virtual machine in SQLite that carries out all of its database operations. Every query in SQLite is executed by first compiling the SQL into VDBE byte code and then running the byte code. For example:

```
sqlite> EXPLAIN SELECT * FROM foods;
```

addr	opcode	p1	p2	p3
0	Goto	0	12	
1	Integer	0	0	
2	OpenRead	0	3	
3	SetNumColumns	0	3	
4	Rewind	0	10	
5	Rowid	0	0	
6	Column	0	1	
7	Column	0	2	
8	Callback	3	0	
9	Next	0	5	
10	Close	0	0	
11	Halt	0	0	
12	Transaction	0	0	
13	VerifyCookie	0	134	
14	Goto	0	1	
15	Noop	0	0	

Studying these query plans is not for the faint of heart. The average person is not going to find a VDBE program very intuitive. However, for those who are willing to try, the VDBE, its op codes, and theory of operation are covered in Chapter 9.

Summary

SQL may be a simple language to use, but there is quite a bit of it. But that shouldn't be too surprising, as it is the sole interface through which to interact with a relational database. Whether you are a casual user, system administrator, or developer, you have to know SQL if you are going to work with a relational database.

SQL is a thin wrapper around the relational model. It is composed of three essential parts: form, function, and integrity. Form relates to how information is represented. In SQL, this is done with the table. The table is the sole unit of information, and is composed of rows and columns. The database is made up of other objects as well, such as views, indexes, and triggers. Views provide a convenient way to represent information in tables in different forms. Indexes work to speed up queries. Triggers enable you to associate programming logic with specific database events as they transpire on tables. All of these objects are created using data definition language (DDL). DDL is the part of SQL reserved for creating and destroying database objects. Furthermore, all objects in a database are listed in the sqlite_master system table.

The functional part of SQL pertains to how information is manipulated. The part of SQL reserved for this is called data manipulation language (DML). DML is composed of the SELECT, UPDATE, INSERT, and DELETE commands. SELECT is the largest and most complicated command in the language. SELECT employs 12 of the 14 operations defined in relational algebra. It arranges those operations in a customizable pipeline. You can use those operations as needed to combine, filter, order, and aggregate information within tables.

The integrity part of SQL controls how data is inserted and modified. It protects information and relationships by ensuring that the values in columns conform to specific rules. It is implemented using constraints, such as UNIQUE, CHECK, and NOT NULL.

SQLite has a unique way of handling data types, unlike most other relational databases. All values have a storage class. SQLite has five storage classes: INTEGER, REAL, TEXT, BLOB, and NULL. These classes specify how values are stored and manipulated in the database. Furthermore, all columns have an affinity, which determines how values are stored within them. SQLite has four kinds of affinity: NUMERIC, INTEGER, TEXT, and NONE. When SQLite stores a value in a column, it uses both the column's affinity and the value's storage class to determine how to store the value. For those who have to have strict type checking on a column, it can be implemented using the typeof() function and a CHECK constraint.

If you are programming with SQLite, then you should be off to a good start on the SQL side of things. Now you need to know a little about how SQLite goes about executing all of these commands. This is where Chapter 5 should prove useful. It will introduce you to the API and show you how it works in relation to the way SQLite functions internally.

CHAPTER 5

■ ■ ■

Design and Concepts

This chapter sets the stage for the next three chapters, which are exclusively devoted to programming with SQLite. It addresses the things that you as a programmer should know about SQLite when using it in your code. Whether you are programming with SQLite in its native C, or in your favorite scripting language, it helps to understand not only its API, but also a little about its architecture and implementation. Armed with this knowledge, you will be better equipped to write code that runs faster and avoids potential pitfalls such as deadlocks or unexpected errors. You will see how SQLite works in relation to your code, and you can be more confident that you are attacking the problem from the right direction.

You don't have to comb through the bowels of the source to understand these things, nor do you have to be a C programmer. SQLite's design and concepts are all very straightforward and easy to understand. And there are only a few things you need to know. This chapter lays them out for you.

Obviously, you need to know how the API works. So this chapter starts with a conceptual introduction to the API, illustrating its major data structures, its general design, as well as its major functions. It also looks at some of the major SQLite subsystems that play important roles in query processing.

Beyond just knowing what functions do what, you also need look above the API, seeing how everything operates in terms of transactions. Everything involving a SQLite database is done within the context of a transaction. Then you need to look beneath the API, to see how transactions work in terms of locks. Locks can cause problems if you don't know how they operate. By understanding locks, not only can you avoid potential concurrency problems, you can also optimize your queries by controlling how your program uses them.

Finally, you have to understand how all of these things apply to writing code. The last part of the chapter brings all three topics—the API, transactions, and locks—together and looks at different examples of good and bad code. It specifically identifies scenarios that could cause problems and provides some insight on how to address them.

With these things in order, you will be well on your way to conquering the C API, or the API of any language extension.

The API

Functionally, the SQLite API can be separated into two general parts: the core API and extension API. The core API consists of all the functions used to perform basic database operations: connecting to the database, processing SQL, and iterating through results. It also includes various utility functions that help with tasks such as string formatting, operational control, debugging, and error handling. The extension API offers different ways to extend SQLite by creating your own user-defined SQL extensions, which you can integrate into SQLite's SQL dialect.

What's New in SQLite Version 3

Before we get started, let's talk about some of the features that have been added to SQLite version 3, as it introduced many major improvements to all major subsystems.

To begin with, SQLite's API has been completely redesigned, and has many new features. It grew from approximately 15 functions in version 2 to 88 functions in version 3. The new API includes native support for UTF-8 and UTF-16 encodings along with many new utility functions. It has a more flexible query model that makes prepared queries easier and supports new parameter binding methods. It also added user-defined collating sequences, CHECK constraints, 64-bit key values, and a new query optimizer.

The backend has dramatically improved concurrency and performance. It has a new locking system that introduces a lock escalation model. This system solves the writer starvation problem in SQLite 2, where new readers can continually prevent writers from getting exclusive access to the database. The new model ensures that writers gain exclusive access on a first-come, first-served basis. Furthermore, writers can even begin performing work before acquiring exclusive access to the database by storing changes in a temporary buffer. The new model has been shown to increase performance for write-intensive applications by as much as 400 percent over version 2.

SQLite 3 includes an improved B-tree module, which now uses B+-trees for tables. B+-trees yield better overall search performance, store larger data fields more efficiently, and omit unused fields from disk. As a result, database files are typically 25–35 percent smaller and offer better overall performance. The B-tree module is covered in more detail in Chapter 9.

SQLite 3 significantly changed its storage model. It went from text-only in version 2 to a new model that supports five native data types, in addition to manifest typing and type affinity as explained in Chapter 4. Each type is optimized for better overall search performance and also uses less storage space. Integer and floating point values, for example, are stored in binary format rather than ASCII and therefore don't have to be converted for evaluation in WHERE clause expressions, as in version 2. Manifest typing gives you the option of declaring a column's types in a meaningful way or not at all. Type affinity determines the format in which a value is stored in a column, based on the value's representation and the column's affinity. Type affinity is directly related to manifest typing—a column's affinity is determined by its declared type, or lack thereof.

In many ways, SQLite version 3 is a completely different database from SQLite version 2 and offers numerous advantages in flexibility, features, and performance.

The Principal Data Structures

As you saw in Chapter 1, there are many components in SQLite—parser, tokenizer, virtual machine, etc. But from a programmer's point of view, the main things to know about are connections, statements, the B-tree, and the pager. Their relationships to one another are shown in Figure 5-1. These objects collectively address the three principal things you must know about SQLite to write good code: the API, transactions, and locks.

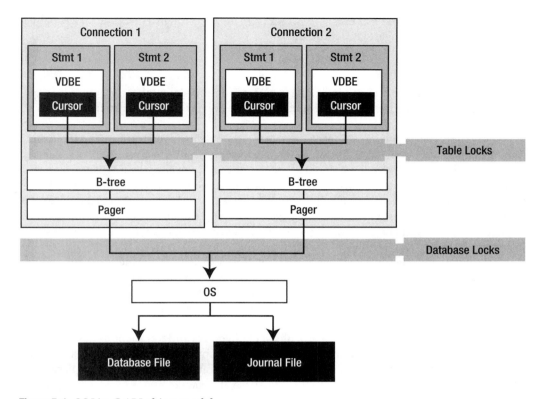

Figure 5-1. *SQLite C API object model*

Technically, the B-tree and pager are not part of the API; they are off limits. But they play a critical role in transactions and locks. We will explore their involvement in these matters here in this section and later in the section "Transactions."

Connections and Statements

The two fundamental data structures in the API associated with query processing are the connection and the statement. In most language extensions you will see both a connection object and a statement object, which are used to execute queries. In the C API, they correspond directly to the sqlite3 and the sqlite3_stmt handles, respectively. Every major operation in the API is done using one of these two structures.

A connection represents a single connection to a database as well as a single transaction context. Statements are derived from connections. That is, every statement has an associated connection object. A statement represents a single compiled SQL statement. Internally, it is expressed in the form of VDBE byte code—a program that when executed will carry out the SQL command. Statements contain everything needed to execute a command. They include resources to hold the state of the VDBE program as it is executed in a stepwise fashion, B-tree cursors that point to records on disk, and other things such as bound parameters, which are addressed later in the section "Parameter Binding." While they contain many different things, you can simply think of them as cursors with which to iterate through a result set, or as opaque handles referencing a single SQL command.

The B-tree and Pager

Each connection can have multiple database objects—one main database followed by any attached databases. Each database object has one B-tree object, which in turn has one pager object.

Statements use their connection's B-tree and pager objects to read and write data to and from the database. Statements that read the database iterate over B-trees using cursors. Cursors iterate over records, and records are stored in pages. As a cursor traverses records, it also traverses pages. For a cursor to access a page, it must first be loaded from disk into memory. This is the pager's job. Whenever the B-tree needs a particular page in the database, it asks the pager to fetch it from disk. The pager then loads the page into its page cache, which is a memory buffer. Once it is in the page cache, the B-tree and its associated cursor can get to the records inside the page.

If the cursor modifies the page, then the pager must also take special measures to preserve the original page in the event of a transaction rollback. Thus, the pager is responsible for reading and writing to and from the database, maintaining a memory cache or pages, as well as managing transactions. In addition to this, it manages locks and crash recovery. All of these responsibilities are covered later in "Transactions."

There are two things you should know about connections and transactions in general. First, when it comes to any operation on the database, a connection *always* operates under a transaction. Second, a connection *never* has more than one transaction open at a time. Basically, whenever a connection does anything with a database, it always operates under exactly one transaction, no more, no less. You can't avoid it.

Therefore, all statements derived from a given connection operate within the same transaction context. So if you allocate two statements from the same connection, and the first issues a `BEGIN` and the second issues a `COMMIT`, then they collectively completed a single transaction. The first statement started it and the second ended it. If you want the two statements to run in separate transactions, then you have to use multiple connections—one connection for each transaction context.

The Core API

As mentioned earlier, the core API is concerned with executing SQL commands. It is made of various functions for performing queries as well as various utility functions for managing other aspects of the database. There are two essential methods for executing SQL commands: prepared queries and wrapped queries. Prepared queries are the way in which SQLite ultimately executes all commands, both in the API and internally. It is a three-phase process consisting of preparation, execution, and finalization. There is a single API function associated with each phase. Associated with the execution phase are functions with which to obtain record and column information from result sets.

In addition to the standard query method, there are two wrapper functions, which wrap the three phases into a single function call. They provide a convenient way to execute a SQL command all at once. These functions are just a few of the many miscellaneous utility functions in the API. We will look at all of the query methods along with their associated utility functions in this section. Before we do however, let's first look at how to connect to a database.

The Connection Lifecycle

Connections are the sole means through which to operate on a database. The connection lifecycle consists of three phases:

1. **Connect to the database**. Connecting involves creating a database connection object of some sort. The connection object manages transactions (through its associated pager), often performs simple one-step queries (using the wrapped query functions), and creates statement objects for prepared queries.

2. **Perform transactions**. As you know, all commands are executed within transactions. By default, a database connection runs in autocommit mode. This means that every SQL command it executes runs under its own independent transaction. The alternative is to manually declare transactions using BEGIN..COMMIT. In this scenario, multiple commands can run together within the same transaction.

3. **Disconnect from the database**. Disconnecting from a database involves closing the database file and the files of any attached databases.

Other activities involved with query processing include handling errors, busy conditions, and schema changes, all of which are done through the utility functions covered in the following sections.

Connecting to a Database

Connecting to a database involves little more than opening a file. Every SQLite database is stored in a single operating system file—one database to one file. The function used to connect, or open, a database in the C API is sqlite3_open(), and is basically just a system call for opening a file. SQLite can also create in-memory databases. In most extensions, if you use :memory: or an empty string as the name for the database, it will create the database in RAM. The database will only be accessible to the connection that created it (it cannot be shared with other connections). Furthermore, the database will only last for the duration of the connection. It is deleted from memory when the connection closes.

When you connect to a database on disk, SQLite opens a file, if it exists. If you try to open a file that doesn't exist, SQLite will assume that you want to create a new database. In this case, SQLite doesn't immediately create a new operating system file. It will only create a new file if you put something into the new database—create a table or view or other database object. If you just open a new database, do nothing, and close it, SQLite does not bother with creating a database file—it would just be an empty file anyway.

There is also another reason for not creating a new file right away. Certain database options, such as encoding, page size, and autovacuum, can only be set before you create a database. By default, SQLite uses a 1,024-byte page size. However, you can use different page sizes ranging from 512 to 32,768 bytes by powers of 2. You might want to use different page sizes for performance reasons. For example, setting the page size to match the operating system's page size can sometimes make I/O more efficient. Sometimes larger page sizes help with applications that deal with a lot of binary data. You set the database page size using the page_size pragma.

Encoding is another permanent database setting. You specify a database's encoding using the encoding pragma, which can be UTF-8, UTF-16, UTF-16le (little endian), and UTF-16be (big endian).

Finally there is autovacuum, which you set with the auto_vacuum pragma. When a transaction deletes data from a database, SQLite's default behavior is to keep the deleted pages around for recycling. The database file remains the same size. To free the pages, you must explicitly issue a VACUUM command to reclaim the unused space. The autovacuum feature causes SQLite to automatically shrink the database file when data is deleted. This feature is often more useful in embedded applications where storage is a premium.

Once you open a database—file or memory—it will be represented internally by an opaque sqlite3 connection handle. This handle represents a single connection to a database. Connection objects in extensions abstract this handle, and sometimes implement methods that correspond to API functions that take the handle as an argument.

Executing Prepared Queries

As stated earlier, the prepared query method is the actual process by which SQLite executes all SQL commands. Executing a SQL command is a three-step process:

- **Preparation**: The parser, tokenizer, and code generator prepare the SQL statement by compiling it into VDBE byte code. In the C API, this is performed by the sqlite3_prepare() function, which talks directly to the compiler. The compiler creates a sqlite3_stmt handle (statement handle) that contains the byte code and all other resources needed to execute the command and iterate over the result set (if the command produces one).

- **Execution**: The VDBE executes the byte code. Execution is a stepwise process. In the C API, each step is initiated by sqlite3_step(), which causes the VDBE to step through the byte code. The first call to sqlite3_step() usually acquires a lock of some kind, which varies according to what the command does (reads or writes). For SELECT statements, each call to sqlite3_step() positions the statement handle's cursor on the next row of the result set. For each row in the set, it returns SQLITE_ROW until it reaches the end, whereupon it returns SQLITE_DONE. For other SQL statements (INSERT, UPDATE, DELETE, etc.), the first call to sqlite3_step() causes the VDBE to process the entire command.

- **Finalization**: The VDBE closes the statement and deallocates resources. In the C API, this is performed by sqlite3_finalize(), which causes the VDBE to terminate the program and close the statement handle. However, if a transaction is manually started, it must be manually committed or rolled back, or sqlite3_finalize() will return an error. When sqlite3_finalize() is successful, all resources associated with the statement object are freed. In autocommit mode, it also releases the associated database lock.

Each step—preparation, execution, finalization—corresponds to a respective statement handle state—prepared, active, or finalized. Prepared means that all necessary resources have been allocated and the statement is ready to be executed, but nothing has been started. No lock has been acquired, nor will a lock be acquired until the first call to sqlite3_step(). The active state starts with the first call to sqlite3_step(). At that point the statement is in the process of being executed and some kind of lock is in play. Finalized means that the statement is closed and all associated resources have been freed. These steps and states are illustrated in Figure 5-2.

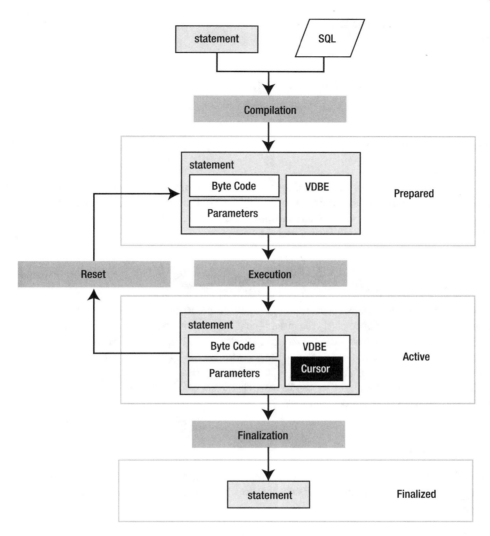

Figure 5-2. *Statement processing*

The following pseudocode illustrates the general process of executing a query in SQLite:

```
# 1. Open the database, create a connection object (db)
db = open('foods.db')

# 2.A. Prepare a statement
stmt = db.prepare('SELECT * FROM episodes')

# 2.B. Execute. Call step() is until cursor reaches end of result set.
while stmt.step() == SQLITE_ROW
  print stmt.column('name')
end
```

```
# 2.C. Finalize. Release read lock.
stmt.finalize()

# 3. Insert a record
stmt = db.prepare('INSERT INTO foods VALUES (…)')
stmt.step()
stmt.finalize()

# 4. Close database connection.
db.close()
```

This pseudocode is an object-oriented analog of the API, similar to what you might find in a scripting language. The methods all correspond to SQLite API functions. For example, prepare() mirrors sqlite3_prepare(), and so on. This example performs a SELECT, iterating over all returned rows, followed by an INSERT, which is processed by a single call to step().

TEMPORARY STORAGE

Temporary storage is an important part of query processing. SQLite occasionally needs to store intermediate results produced in the process of executing commands—for instance, when results need to be sorted for an ORDER BY clause, or rows in one table are joined with rows in another table. This information is often stored in temporary storage. Temporary storage is kept either in RAM or in a file. While SQLite has suitable defaults for all platforms, you may want to control how and where it uses this storage. The temp_store pragma lets you specify whether to use RAM or file-based storage. If you use file-based storage, you can use the temp_store_directory pragma to specify where the storage file is created.

Using Parameterized SQL

SQL statements can contain parameters. Parameters are placeholders in which values may be provided (or "bound") at a later time after compilation. The following statements are examples of parameterized queries:

```
INSERT INTO foods (id, name) VALUES (?,?);
INSERT INTO episodes (id, name) (:id, :name);
```

These statements represent two forms of parameter binding: *positional* and *named*. The first command uses positional parameters and the second command uses named parameters.

Positional parameters are defined by the position of the question mark in the statement. The first question mark has position 1, the second 2, and so on. Named parameters use actual variable names, which are prefixed with a colon. When sqlite3_prepare() compiles a statement with parameters, it allocates placeholders for the parameters in the resulting statement handle. It then expects values to be provided for these parameters before the statement is executed. If you don't bind a value to a parameter, SQLite will use NULL as the default when it executes the statement.

The advantage of parameter binding is that you can execute the same statement multiple times without having to recompile it. You just reset the statement, bind a new set of values, and reexecute. This is where resetting rather than finalizing a statement comes in handy: it avoids the overhead of SQL compilation. By resetting a statement, you are reusing the compiled SQL code. You completely avoid the tokenizing, parsing, and code generation overhead. Resetting a statement is implemented in the API by the `sqlite3_reset()` function.

The other advantage of parameters is that SQLite takes care of escaping the string values you bind to parameters. For example, if you had a parameter value such as `'Kenny's Chicken'`, the parameter binding process will automatically convert it to `'Kenny''s Chicken'`—escaping the single quote for you, helping you avoid syntax errors and possible SQL injection attacks (covered in the section "Formatting SQL Statements"). The following pseudocode illustrates the basic process of using bound parameters:

```
db = open('foods.db')
stmt = db.prepare('INSERT INTO episodes (id, name) VALUES (:id, :name)')

stmt.bind('id', '1')
stmt.bind('name', 'Soup Nazi')
stmt.step()

# Reset and use again
stmt.reset()
stmt.bind('id', '2')
stmt.bind('name', 'The Junior Mint')

# Done
stmt.finalize()

db.close()
```

Here, `reset()` simply deallocates the statement's resources, but leaves its VDBE byte code and parameters intact. The statement is ready to run again without the need for another call to `prepare()`. This can significantly improve performance of repetitive queries such as this because the compiler completely drops out of the equation.

Executing Wrapped Queries

As mentioned earlier, there are two very useful utility functions that wrap the prepared query process, allowing you to execute SQL commands in a single function call. One function—`sqlite3_exec()`—is typically for queries that don't return data. The other—`sqlite3_get_table()`—is typically for queries that do. In many language extensions you will see analogs to both functions. Most extensions refer to the first method simply as `exec()`, and the second as just `get_table()`.

The `exec()` function is a quick and easy way to execute INSERT, UPDATE, and DELETE statements or DDL statements for creating and destroying database objects. It works straight from the database connection, taking a `sqlite3` handle to an open database along with a string containing one or more SQL statements. That's right; `exec()` is capable of processing a string of *multiple* SQL statements delimited by semicolons and running them all together.

Internally, `exec()` parses the SQL string, identifies individual statements, and then processes them one by one. It allocates its own statement handles and prepares, executes, and finalizes each statement. If multiple statements are passed to it and one of them fails, exec() terminates execution on that command, returning the associated error code. Otherwise, it returns a success code. The following pseudocode illustrates conceptually how exec() works in an extension:

```
db = open('foods.db')
db.exec("INSERT INTO episodes (id, name) VALUES (1, 'Soup Nazi')")
db.exec("INSERT INTO episodes (id, name) VALUES (2, 'The Fusilli Jerry')")
db.exec("BEGIN; DELETE from episodes; ROLLBACK")
db.close()
```

While you can also use exec() to process records returned from SELECT, it involves subtle methods for doing so that are generally supported only by the C API.

The second query function, sqlite3_get_table(), is somewhat of a misnomer as it is not restricted to just querying a single table. Rather, its name refers to the tabular results of a SELECT query. You can certainly process joins with it just as well. In many respects, get_table() works in the same way as exec(), but it returns a complete result set in memory. This result set is represented in various ways depending on the extension. The following pseudocode illustrates how it is typically used:

```
db = open('foods.db')
table = db.get_table("SELECT * FROM episodes LIMIT 10")

for i=0; i < table.rows; i++
    for j=0; j < table.cols; j++
        print table[i][j]
    end
end

db.close()
```

The upside of get_table() is that it provides a one-step method to query and get results. The downside is that it stores the results completely in memory. So the larger the result set, the more memory it consumes. Not surprisingly, then, it is not a good idea to use get_table() to retrieve large result sets. The prepared query method, on the other hand, only holds one record (actually its associated database page) in memory at a time, so it is much better suited for traversing large result sets.

Notice that while these functions buy you convenience, you also lose a bit of control simply by not having access to a statement handle. For example, you can't use parameterized SQL statements with either of them. So they are not going to be as efficient for repetitive tasks that could benefit from parameters. Also, the API includes functions that work with statement handles that provide lots of information about columns in a result set—both data and metadata. These are not available with wrapped queries either. Wrapped queries have their uses, to be sure. But prepared queries do as well.

Handling Errors

The previous examples are greatly oversimplified to illustrate the basic parts of query processing. In real life, you always have to consider the possibility of errors. Almost every function you have seen so far can encounter errors of some sort. Common error codes you need to be prepared to handle include SQLITE_ERROR, SQLITE_BUSY, and SQLITE_SCHEMA. The latter two error codes refer to busy conditions that arise when either a connection can't get a lock or the database schema changes between the time a statement is compiled and executed. Busy conditions are addressed in the "Transactions" section while schema errors are covered in detail in Chapter 6.

Many language extensions often handle schema errors differently. Some transparently report them as busy conditions. Others return the actual error code. In any case, when you encounter a schema error, it means that some other connection has changed the database schema and your current statement is no longer valid. You simply have to recompile the statement in order to execute it. Schema errors can only occur between a call to prepare() and the *first* call to step(). If your first call to step() succeeds, then you do not have to worry about schema errors for subsequent calls to step(), as your connection has a lock on the database that prevents other connections from changing the database schema during that time.

With regard to general errors, the API provides the return code of the last called function with the sqlite3_errcode() function. You can get more specific error information using the sqlite3_errmsg() function, which provides a text description of the last error. Most language extensions support this function in some way or another.

With this in mind, each call in the previous example should check for the appropriate errors using something like the following:

```
# Check and report errors
if db.errcode() != SQLITE_SUCCESS
    print db.errmsg(stmt)
end
```

In general, error handling is not difficult. The way you handle any error depends on what exactly you are trying to do. The easiest way to approach error handling is the same as with any other API—read the documentation on the function you are using and code defensively.

Formatting SQL Statements

Another nice convenience function you may see some extensions support is sqlite3_mprintf(). It is a variant of the standard C library sprintf(). It has special substitutions that are specific to SQL that can be very handy. These substitutions are denoted %q and %Q, and escape SQL-specific values. %q works like %s in that it substitutes a null-terminated string from the argument list. But it also doubles every single-quote character as well as every backslash, making your life easier and helping guard against SQL injection attacks (see the sidebar "SQL Injection Attacks"). For example:

```
char* before = "Hey, at least %q no pig-man.";
char* after = sqlite3_mprintf(before, "\he's\");
```

The value after produced here is 'Hey, at least \\he''s\\ no pig-man'. The single quote in *he's* is doubled along with the backslashes around it, making it acceptable as a string literal in a SQL statement. The %Q formatting does everything %q does, but it additionally encloses the resulting string in single quotes. Furthermore, if the argument for %Q is a NULL pointer (in C), it produces the string NULL without single quotes. For more information, see the sqlite3_mprintf() documentation in the C API reference in Appendix B.

SQL INJECTION ATTACKS

If your application relies on any user input with which to construct SQL statements, you could be vulnerable to a SQL injection attack. If you are not careful to filter user input, it could be possible for someone to craft input that could alter the SQL statement, injecting a new SQL statement into the string. For example, say your program uses user input to fill in the value of the following SQL statement:

```
SELECT * FROM foods WHERE name='%s';
```

You replace the %s with whatever the user supplies. If the user has any knowledge of your database, he or she could provide input that can dramatically alter the SQL statement. For example, say the user were to provide the following string value for the name input:

```
nothing' LIMIT 0; SELECT name FROM sqlite_master WHERE name='%
```

After substituting the user's input into your SQL statement, the new statement turns into two statements:

```
SELECT * FROM foods WHERE name='nothing' LIMIT 0; SELECT name FROM
sqlite_master WHERE name='%';
```

The first statement will return nothing and the second will return the names of all objects in your database. Granted, the odds of this happening require quite a bit of knowledge on the attacker's part, but it is nevertheless possible. Some major (commercial) web applications have been known to keep SQL statements embedded in their JavaScript, which can provide plenty of hints about the database being used. In the previous example, all a malicious user has to do now is insert DROP TABLE statements for every table found in sqlite_master and you could find yourself fumbling through backups.

Operational Control

The API includes a variety of commands that allow you to monitor, control, or generally limit what can happen in a database. SQLite implements them in the form of filters, or callback functions that you can register to be called for specific events. There are three "hook" functions: sqlite3_commit_hook(), which monitors transaction commits on a connection; sqlite3_rollback_hook(), which monitors rollbacks; and sqlite3_update_hook(), which monitors changes to rows from INSERT, UPDATE, and DELETE operations. These hooks are called at runtime—while a command is executed. Each hook allows you to register a callback function on a connection-by-connection basis, and lets you provide some kind of application-specific data to be passed to the callback as well. The general use of operational control functions is as follows:

```
def commit_hook(cnx)
  log('Attempted commit on connection %x', cnx)
  return -1
end
db = open('foods.db')
db.set_commit_hook(rollback_hook, cnx)
db.exec("BEGIN; DELETE from episodes; ROLLBACK")
db.close()
```

A hook's return value has the power to alter the event in specific ways, depending on the hook. In this example, because the commit hook returns a non-zero value, the commit will be rolled back.

Additionally, the API provides a very powerful compile time hook called sqlite3_set_authorizer(). This function provides you with fine-grained control over almost everything that happens in the database as well as the ability to limit both access and modification on a database, table, and column basis. This function is covered in detail in Chapter 6.

Using Threads

SQLite has a number of functions for using it in a multithreaded environment. With version 3.3.1, SQLite introduced a unique operational mode called *shared cache mode*, which is designed for multithreaded embedded servers. This model provides a way for a single thread to host multiple connections that share a common page cache, thus lowering the overall memory footprint of the server. It also employs a different concurrency model. Included with this feature are various functions for managing memory and fine-tuning the server. This operational mode is explained further later in the section "Shared Cache Mode," and in full detail in Chapter 6.

The Extension API

The extension API in the SQLite C API offers support for user-defined functions, aggregates, and collations. A user-defined function is a SQL function that maps to some handler function that you implement in C or another language. When using the C API, you implement this handler in C or C++. In language extensions, you implement the handler in the same language as the extension.

User-defined extensions must be registered on a connection-by-connection basis as they are stored in program memory. That is, they are *not* stored in the database, like stored procedures in larger relational database systems. They are stored in your program. When your program or script starts up, it is responsible for registering the desired user-defined extensions for each connection that it intends to use them.

Creating User-Defined Functions

Implementing a user-defined function is a two-step process. First, you write the handler. The handler does something that you want to perform from SQL. Next, you register the handler, providing its SQL name, its number of arguments, and a pointer (or reference) to the handler.

For example, say you wanted to create a special SQL function called hello_newman(), which returns the text 'Hello Jerry'. In the SQLite C API, you would first create a C function to implement this, such as the following:

```
void hello_newman(sqlite3_context* ctx, int nargs, sqlite3_value** values)
{
    /* Create Newman's reply */
    const char *msg = "Hello Jerry";

    /* Set the return value. Have sqlite clean up msg w/ sqlite_free(). */
    sqlite3_result_text(ctx, msg, strlen(msg), sqlite3_free);
}
```

Don't worry if you don't know C or the C API. This handler just returns 'Hello Jerry'. Next, to actually use it, you register this handler using the sqlite3_create_function() (or the equivalent function in your language):

```
sqlite3_create_function(db, "hello_newman", 0, hello_newman);
```

The first argument (db) is the database connection. The second argument is the name of the function as it will appear in SQL, and the third argument means that the function takes 0 arguments. (If you provide -1, then it means that the function accepts a variable number of arguments.) The last argument is a pointer to the hello_newman() C function, which will be called when the SQL function is called.

Once registered, SQLite knows that when it encounters the SQL function hello_newman(), it needs to call the C function hello_newman() to obtain the result. Now, you can execute SELECT hello_newman() within your program and it will return a single row with one column containing the text 'Hello Jerry'.

As mentioned, many language extensions allow you to implement user-defined functions in their respective language. For example, the Java interface provides you with the means to implement hello_newman() in Java, Perl in Perl, and likewise in many other extensions. Different extensions register user-defined functions in different ways, sometimes employing specific features of their respective languages to do so. In Ruby, for example, you implement a user-defined function using a *block*—one of its particular language constructs. Consider the following Ruby program, which creates a user-defined function called bool():

```
db = SQLite3::Database.new(':memory:')

db.create_function('bool', 1) do |func, *args|
  if args[0].to_s.upcase == 'TRUE' or args[0].to_s.upcase == 'FALSE'
    func.result = 1
  else
    func.result = 0
  end
end

def execute(db, sql)
  begin
    db.query(sql)
  rescue Exception
    puts "Statement failed: #{$!}"
  end
end

execute(db, 'create table domain (x CHECK(bool(x)))')
execute(db, "insert into domain values ('true')")
execute(db, "insert into domain values ('JujyFruit')")
```

The bool() function takes a single argument and returns 1 (true) if the argument meets its definition of a Boolean value or 0 (false) if not. The code then uses this function in a CHECK constraint to impose these Boolean values on a column and tests it out. The first INSERT command succeeds, while the second one does not. UPDATE commands will be subject to this CHECK constraint as well. As mentioned in Chapter 5, user-defined functions are a handy way to implement special-ized domain constraints by embedding them in CHECK constraints.

Creating User-Defined Aggregates

Aggregate functions are functions that are applied to all records in a result set and compute some kind of aggregate value from them. SUM(), COUNT(), and AVG() are examples of standard SQL aggregate functions in SQLite.

Implementing user-defined aggregates is a three-step process in which you register the aggregate, implement a step function to be called for each record in the result set, and imple-ment a finalize function to be called after record processing. The finalize function allows you to compute the final aggregate value and do any necessary cleanup.

The following is an example of implementing a simple SUM() aggregate called pysum in one of the SQLite Python extensions:

```
connection=apsw.Connection("foods.db")

def step(context, *args):
    context['value'] += args[0]

def finalize(context):
    return context['value']

def pysum():
    return ({'value' : 0}, step, finalize)

connection.createaggregatefunction("pysum", pysum)

c = connection.cursor()
print c.execute("select pysum(id) from foods").next()[0]
```

The createaggregatefunction() function registers the aggregate, passing in the step function and the finalize function. SQLite passes step() a context, which it uses to store the interme-diate value between calls to step(). In this case, it is the running sum. SQLite calls finalize() after it has processed the last record. Here, finalize() just returns the aggregated sum. SQLite automatically takes care of cleaning up the context.

Creating User-Defined Collations

Collations define how string values are compared. User-defined collations therefore provide a way to create different text comparison and sorting methods. This is done in the API by the sqlite3_create_collation() function. SQLite provides three default collations: BINARY, NOCASE, and REVERSE. BINARY compares string values using the C function memcmp() (which for all intents and purposes is case sensitive). NOCASE is just the opposite—its sorting is case insensitive. REVERSE is just an arbitrary method used for testing, and does the direct opposite of BINARY.

User-defined collations are especially helpful for locales that are not well served by the default BINARY collation, or those that need support for UTF-16. They can also be helpful in specific applications such as sorting date formats that don't lend themselves to both lexicographical and chronological order. Chapter 7 illustrates implementing a user-defined collation to sort Oracle dates natively in SQLite.

Transactions

By now you should have a good picture of how the API is laid out. You've seen different ways to execute SQL commands along with some helpful utility functions. Executing SQL commands, however, involves more than just knowing what's in the API. Transactions and locks are closely intertwined with query processing. Queries are always performed within transactions, transactions involve locks, and locks can cause problems if you don't watch what you are doing. You can control both the type and duration of locks by how you use SQL and the way you write code.

Chapter 4 illustrated a specific scenario where deadlocks can arise just by the way that two connections manage transactions through SQL alone. As a programmer, you will have another variable to juggle—code—which can contain multiple connections in multiple states with multiple statement handles on multiple tables at any given time. All it takes is a single statement handle and your code may be holding an EXCLUSIVE lock without you even realizing it, preventing other connections from getting anything done.

That is why it is critical that you have good grasp of how both transactions and locks work, and how they relate to the various API functions used to perform queries. Ideally, you should be able to look at the code you write and tell what transaction states it will be in, or at least be able to spot potential problems. In this section we will explore the mechanics behind transactions and locks, and in the next section observe them at work in actual code.

Transaction Lifecycles

There are a couple of things to consider with code and transactions. First there is the issue of knowing which objects run under which transactions. Next there is the question of duration—when does a transaction start and when does it end, and at what point does it start to affect other connections? The first question relates directly to the API. The second relates to SQL in general and SQLite's implementation in particular.

As you know, multiple statement handles can be allocated from a single connection. As shown in Figure 5-2, each connection has exactly one B-tree and one pager object associated with it per database. The pager plays a bigger role than the connection in this discussion because it manages transactions, locks, the memory cache, and crash recovery—all of which will be covered in the next few sections. You could just as easily say that the connection object handles all of this, but in reality it is the pager within it, and that is the object I will oftentimes refer to. The important thing to remember is that when you write to the database, you do so with one connection, one transaction at a time. Thus all statement objects run within the single transaction context of the connections they are derived from. This answers the first question.

As for the second question, transaction duration (or the transaction lifecycle) is as short as a single statement, or as long as you like—until you say stop. By default, a connection operates in autocommit mode, which means that every command you issue runs under a separate transaction. Conversely, when you issue a BEGIN, the transaction endures until you call either a COMMIT or a ROLLBACK, or until one of your SQL commands causes a constraint violation that results in a ROLLBACK. The next question is how transactions relate to locks.

Lock States

For the most part, lock duration shadows transaction duration. While the two don't always start together, they do always finish together. When you conclude a transaction, you free its associated lock. A better way of saying this is that a lock is never released until its associated transaction concludes or, in the worse case, the program crashes. And if the program or system crashes, the transaction doesn't conclude in which case there is still an implicit lock on the database that will be resolved by the next connection to access it. This is covered later in the sidebar "Locking and Crash Recovery."

There are five different locks states in SQLite, and a connection is always in one of them no matter what it's doing. SQLite's lock states and transitions are shown in Figure 5-3. This diagram details every possible lock state a connection can be in as well as every path it can take through the life of a transaction. The diagram is represented in terms of lock states, lock transitions, and transaction lifecycles. What you are really looking at in the figure are the lives of transactions in terms of locks.

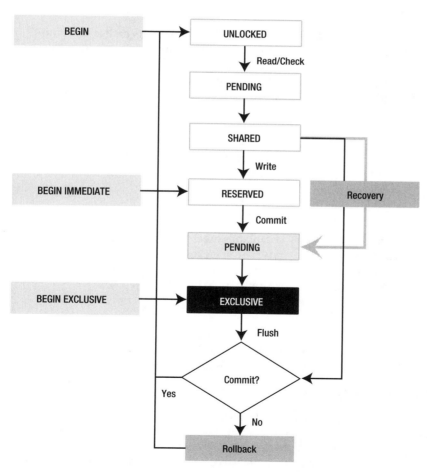

Figure 5-3. *SQLite lock transitions*

Each state has a corresponding lock with the exception of UNLOCKED. So you can say a connection "has a RESERVED lock," or "is in the RESERVED state," or just "is in RESERVED," and it all means the same thing. With the exception of UNLOCKED, for a connection to be in a given state it must first obtain the associated lock.

Every transaction starts at UNLOCKED, RESERVED, or EXCLUSIVE. By default, everything begins in UNLOCKED, as you can see in Figure 5-3. The locks states in white—UNLOCKED, PENDING, SHARED, and RESERVED—can all exist at the same time between connections in a database. Starting with PENDING in gray, however, things become more restrictive. The gray PENDING state represents the lock being held by a single connection—namely a writer that wants to get to EXCLUSIVE. Conversely, the white PENDING state represents a path where connections acquire and release the lock on their way to SHARED. Despite all of these different lock states, every transaction in SQLite boils down to one of two types: transactions that read, and transactions that write. That ultimately is what paints the locking picture: readers versus writers, and how they get along with each other.

Read Transactions

To start with, let's go through the lock process of a SELECT statement. Its path is very simple. A connection that executes a SELECT statement starts a transaction, which goes from UNLOCKED to SHARED and upon COMMIT back to UNLOCKED. End of story.

Now, out of curiosity, what happens when you execute two statements? What is the lock path then? Well, it depends on whether you are running in autocommit or not. Consider the following example:

```
db = open('foods.db')
db.exec('BEGIN')
db.exec('SELECT * FROM episodes')
db.exec('SELECT * FROM episodes')
db.exec('COMMIT')
db.close()
```

Here, with an explicit BEGIN, the two SELECT commands execute within a single transaction and therefore are executed in the same SHARED state. The first exec() runs, leaving the connection in SHARED, and then the second exec() runs. Finally, the manual COMMIT takes the connection from SHARED back to UNLOCKED. The code's lock path would be as follows:

UNLOCKED→PENDING→SHARED→UNLOCKED

Now consider the case where there are no BEGIN and COMMIT lines in the example. Then the two SELECT commands run in autocommit mode. They will therefore go through the entire path independently. The lock path for the code now would be as follows:

UNLOCKED→PENDING→SHARED→UNLOCKED→PENDING→ SHARED→UNLOCKED

Since the code is just reading data, it may not make much of a difference, but it does have to go through twice the file locks in autocommit mode than it does otherwise. And, as you will see, a writer could sneak in between the two SELECT commands and modify the database between exec() calls, so you can't be sure that the two commands will return the same results. With BEGIN..COMMIT, on the other hand, they are guaranteed to be identical in their results.

Write Transactions

Now let's consider a statement that writes to the database, such as an UPDATE. First, the connection has to follow the same path as SELECT and get to SHARED. Every operation—read or write—has to start by going through UNLOCKED→PENDING→SHARED. PENDING, as you will soon see, is a gateway lock.

The Reserved State

The moment the connection tries to write anything to the database, it has to go from SHARED to RESERVED. If it gets the RESERVED lock, then it is ready to start making modifications. Even though the connection cannot actually modify the database at this point, it can store modifications in a localized memory cache inside the pager, called the *page cache*, mentioned earlier. This cache is the same cache you configure with the cache_size pragma, as described in Chapter 4.

When the connection enters RESERVED, the pager initializes the *rollback journal*. This is a file (shown in Figure 5-1) that is used in rollbacks and crash recovery. Specifically, it holds the database pages needed to restore the database to its original state before the transaction. These database pages are put there by the pager when the B-tree modifies a page. In this example, for every record the UPDATE command modifies, the pager takes the database page associated with the *original* record and copies it out to the journal. The journal then holds some of the contents of the database before the transaction. Therefore, all the pager has to do in order to undo any transaction is to simply copy the contents in the journal back into the database file. Then the database is restored to its state before the transaction.

In the RESERVED state there are actually three sets of pages that the pager manages: modified pages, unmodified pages, and journal pages. Modified pages are just that—pages containing records that the B-tree has changed. These are stored in the page cache. Unmodified pages are pages the B-tree read but did not change. These are a product of commands such as SELECT. Finally, there are journal pages, which are the original versions of modified pages. These are not stored in the page cache, but rather written to the journal before the B-tree modifies a page.

Because of the page cache, a writing connection can indeed get real work done in the RESERVED state without interfering with other (reading) connections. Thus, SQLite can effectively have multiple readers and one writer both working on the same database at the same time. The only catch is that the writing connection has to store its modifications in its page cache, not in the database file. Note also that there can only be one connection in RESERVED or EXCLUSIVE for a given database at a given time—multiple readers, but only one writer.

The Pending State

When the connection finishes making changes for the UPDATE, and the time comes to commit the transaction, the pager begins the process of entering the EXCLUSIVE state. You already know how this works from Chapter 4, but I will repeat it for the sake of completeness. From the RESERVED state, the pager tries to get a PENDING lock. Once it does, it holds onto it, preventing any other connections from getting a PENDING lock. Look at Figure 5-3 and see what effect this has. Remember I told you that PENDING was a gateway lock. Now you see why. Since the writer is holding onto the PENDING lock, nobody else can get to SHARED from UNLOCKED anymore. The result is that no new connections can enter the database: no new readers, no new writers. This PENDING state is the attrition phase. The writer is guaranteed that it can wait in line for the database and—as long as everyone behaves properly—get it. Only other sessions that already have

SHARED locks can continue to work as normal. In PENDING, the writer waits for these connections to finish and release their locks. What's involved with waiting for locks is a separate issue, which will be addressed shortly in the section "Waiting for Locks."

When the other connections release their locks, the database then belongs to the writer. Then, the pager moves from PENDING to EXCLUSIVE.

The Exclusive State

During EXCLUSIVE, the main job is to flush the modified pages from the page cache to the database file. This is when things get serious, as the pager is going to actually modify the database. It goes about this with extreme caution.

Before the pager begins writing the modified pages, it first tends to the journal. It checks that the complete contents of the journal have been written to disk. At this point, it is very likely that even though the pager has written pages to the journal file, the operating system has buffered many if not all of them in memory. The pager tells the operating system to literally write all of these pages to the disk. This is where the synchronous pragma comes into play, as described in Chapter 4. The method specified by synchronous determines how careful the pager is to ensure that the operating system commits journal pages to disk. The normal setting is to perform a single "sync" before continuing, telling the operating system to confirm that all buffered journal pages are written to the disk surface. If synchronous is set to FULL, then the pager does two full "syncs" before proceeding. If synchronous is set to NONE, the pager doesn't bother with the journal at all (and while it can be 50 times faster, you can kiss transaction durability goodbye).

The reason that committing the journal to disk is so important is that if the program or system crashes while the pager is writing to the database file, the journal is the only way to restore the database file later on. If the journal's pages weren't completely written to disk before a system crash, then the database cannot be restored fully to its original state, because the journal pages that were in memory were lost in the crash. In this case, you have an inconsistent database at best, and a corrupted one at worse.

■**Caution** Even if you use the most conservative setting for the synchronous pragma, you still may not be guaranteed that the journal is truly committed to disk. This is no fault of SQLite, but rather of certain types of hardware and operating systems. SQLite uses the fsync() system call on Unix and FlushFileBuffers() on Windows to force journal pages to disk. But it has been reported that these functions don't always work, especially with cheap IDE disks. Apparently, some manufacturers of IDE disks use controller chips that tend to bend the truth about actually committing data to disk. In some cases, the chips cache the data in volatile memory while reporting that they wrote it to the drive surface. Also, there have been (unconfirmed) reports that Windows occasionally ignores FlushFileBuffers(). If you have hardware or software that lies to you, your transactions may not be as durable as you might think.

Once the journal is taken care of, the pager then copies all of the modified pages to the database file. What happens next depends on the transaction mode. If, as in this case, the transaction autocommits, then the pager cleans up the journal, clears the page cache, and proceeds from EXCLUSIVE to UNLOCKED. If the transaction does not commit, then the pager continues to hold the EXCLUSIVE lock and the journal stays in play until either a COMMIT or ROLLBACK is issued.

Autocommit and Efficiency

With all this in mind, consider what happens with UPDATEs that run in an explicit transaction versus ones that run in autocommit. In autocommit, every command that modifies the database runs in a separate transaction and travels through the following path:

UNLOCKED→PENDING→SHARED→RESERVED→PENDING→ EXCLUSIVE→UNLOCKED

Additionally, each trip through this path involves creating, committing, and clearing out the rollback journal. This all adds up. Although running multiple SELECTs in autocommit mode is perhaps not that big of a deal performance-wise, you should really rethink autocommit mode for frequent writes. And, as mentioned in the SELECT case, when running multiple commands in autocommit, there is nothing stopping another connection from coming along and modifying the database in between commands. If you have two updates that depend on specific values in the database, you should always run them in the same transaction for this reason.

LOCKING AND CRASH RECOVERY

SQLite's lock implementation is based on standard file locking. SQLite keeps three different file locks on the database file: a reserved byte, a pending byte, and a shared region.

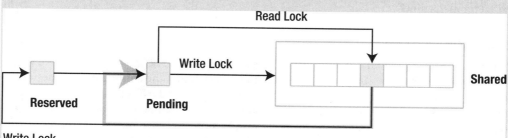

Write Lock

Everything starts at the pending byte. To move from UNLOCKED to SHARED, a connection first attempts to get a read-lock on the pending byte. If successful, it gets a read lock on a random byte in the shared region and releases the read lock on the pending byte. To move from SHARED to RESERVED, a connection attempts to obtain a write lock on the reserved byte. To get from RESERVED to EXCLUSIVE, a connection attempts to get a write lock on the pending byte. If successful, this is what causes the attrition process, as it is no longer possible for other connections to get a read lock on the pending byte to enter SHARED. Finally, to get the EXCLUSIVE lock, the connection attempts to get a write lock on the *entire shared region*. Since the shared region holds read locks by all other active connections, this step guarantees that an EXCLUSIVE lock is only granted after all other SHARED locks are first released.

SQLite's crash recovery mechanism uses the reserved byte to determine when a database needs to be restored. Since the journal file and the RESERVED lock go hand in hand, if the pager sees the former without the latter, then something is wrong. Every time the pager opens a database file or tries to fetch a page from the database, it does a simple consistency check. If it finds a journal file but no RESERVED lock on the database, then the process that created the journal file must have crashed, or the system went down. In this case, the journal is called a *hot journal*, and the database is potentially in an inconsistent state. To make things right, the journal needs to be "played back" to restore the database to its original state before the interrupted transaction.

To start the play back, the pager puts the database into recovery mode. To do this, it goes directly from SHARED to PENDING as shown by the gray line in the illustration (and also in Figure 5-3). This is the only time it ever makes this transition. The reason it skips the reserved lock is twofold. First, by locking the pending byte, it keeps all new connections out of the database. Second, connections that are already in the database (in SHARED) will also see the hot journal the next time they try to access a page. Those connections will attempt to go into recovery mode and replay the journal as well. However, they won't be able to because the first connection already has the PENDING lock. Thus, by going straight from SHARED to PENDING, the first connection ensures that (1) no new connections can enter the database and (2) active connections in SHARED cannot go into recovery mode. Everyone but the restoring connection is temporarily suspended.

Basically, a hot journal is an implicit EXCLUSIVE lock. If a writer crashes, no further activity can transpire in the database until some connection restores it. The next pager to access a page will see the hot journal, lock everyone out, and start recovery. If there are no other active connections, then the first program to connect to the database will detect the hot journal and start recovery.

Tuning the Page Cache

Go back to the beginning of the previous example and say that it started with a BEGIN, followed by the UPDATE, and in the middle of making all those modifications the page cache fills up (runs out of memory). That is, the UPDATE results in more modified pages than will fit in the page cache. What happens now?

Transitioning to Exclusive

The real question is: when exactly does the pager move from RESERVED to EXCLUSIVE and why? There are two scenarios, and you've just seen them both. Either the connection reaches the commit point and deliberately enters EXCLUSIVE, or the page cache fills up and it has no other option. We just looked at the commit point scenario. So what happens when the page cache fills up? Put simply, the pager can no longer store any more modified pages, and therefore can no longer do any work. It is forced to move into EXCLUSIVE in order to continue. In reality, this is not entirely true as there is a soft limit and a hard limit.

The soft limit corresponds to the first time the page cache fills up. At this point, the cache is a mixed bag of modified and unmodified pages. In this case, the pager tries to clean out the page cache. It goes through the cache page by page looking for unmodified pages and clearing them out. Once it does that, it can sputter along with what memory has freed up until the cache fills up again. It repeats the process until the cache is completely made up of modified pages. And that is that hard limit. At this point, the pager has no other recourse but to proceed into EXCLUSIVE.

The RESERVED state, then, is where the cache_size pragma makes a difference. Just as explained in Chapter 4, cache_size controls the size of the page cache. The bigger the page cache, the more modified pages the pager can store, and the more work the connection can do before having to enter EXCLUSIVE. Also, as mentioned, by doing all the database work in RESERVED, you minimize the time in EXCLUSIVE. If you get all your work done in RESERVED, then EXCLUSIVE is only held long enough to flush modified pages to disk—not compile *more* queries and process *more* results and *then* write to disk. Doing the processing in RESERVED can significantly increase overall concurrency. Ideally, if you have a large transaction or a congested database, and you can spare the memory, try to ensure that your cache size is large enough to hold your connection in RESERVED as long as possible.

Sizing the Page Cache

So how do you determine what the cache size should be? It depends on what you are doing. Say that you want to update every record in the episodes table. In this case, you know that every page in the table will be modified. Therefore, you figure out how many pages are in episodes and adjust the cache size accordingly. You can get all the information you need on episodes using sqlite_analyzer. For each table it will dump detailed statistics, including the total page count. For example, if you run it on the foods database, you get the following information about episodes:

```
*** Table EPISODES ***************************************************

Percentage of total database......... 20.0%
Number of entries.................... 181
Bytes of storage consumed............ 5120
Bytes of payload..................... 3229        63.1%
Average payload per entry............ 17.84
Average unused bytes per entry....... 5.79
Average fanout....................... 4.00
Maximum payload per entry............ 38
Entries that use overflow............ 0            0.0%
Index pages used..................... 1
Primary pages used................... 4
Overflow pages used.................. 0
Total pages used..................... 5
Unused bytes on index pages.......... 990          96.7%
Unused bytes on primary pages........ 58           1.4%
Unused bytes on overflow pages....... 0
Unused bytes on all pages............ 1048         20.5%
```

The total page count is 5. But of those, only 4 pages of actual table are used—1 page is an index. Since the default cache size is 2,000 pages, you've got nothing to worry about. There are about 400 records in episodes, which means there are about 100 records per page. You wouldn't have to worry about adjusting the page cache before updating every record unless there were at least 196,000 rows in episodes. And remember, you would only need to do this in environments where there are other connections using the database and concurrency is an issue. If you are the only one using the database, then it really wouldn't matter.

Waiting for Locks

We talked earlier about the pager waiting to go from PENDING to EXCLUSIVE. What exactly is involved with waiting on a lock? First, any call to exec() or step() can involve waiting on a lock. Whenever SQLite encounters a situation where it can't get a lock, the default behavior is to return Delete SQLITE_BUSY to the function that caused it to seek the lock. Regardless of the command you execute, you can potentially encounter SQLITE_BUSY. SELECT commands, as you know by now, can fail to get a SHARED lock if a writer is pending or writing. The simple thing to do when you get SQLITE_BUSY is to just retry the call. However, we will see shortly that this is not always the best course of action.

Using a Busy Handler

Instead of just retrying the call over and over, you can use a *busy handler*. Rather than having the API return SQLITE_BUSY if a connection cannot get a lock, you can get it to call the busy handler instead.

A busy handler is a function you create that kills time, or does whatever else you want it to do—it can send spam to your mother-in-law for all SQLite cares. It's just going to get called when SQLite can't get a lock. The only thing the busy handler *has* to do is provide a return value, telling SQLite what to do next. By convention, if the handler returns true, then SQLite will continue to try for the lock. If it returns false, SQLite will then return SQLITE_BUSY to the function requesting the lock. Consider the following example:

```
counter = 1

def busy()
    counter = counter + 1
    if counter == 2
        return 0
    end

    spam_mother_in_law(100)
    return 1
end

db.busy_handler(busy)
stmt = db.prepare('SELECT * FROM episodes;')
stmt.step()
stmt.finalize()
```

The implementation of spam_mother_in_law() is left as an exercise for the reader.

The step() function has to get a SHARED lock on the database to perform the SELECT. However, say there is a writer active. Normally, step() would return SQLITE_BUSY. However, in this case it doesn't. The pager (which is one that deals with locks) calls the busy() function instead, because it has been registered as the busy handler. busy() increments a counter, forwards your mother-in-law 100 random messages from your spam folder, and returns 1, which the pager interprets as true—keep trying to get the lock. The pager then tries again to get the SHARED lock. Say the database is still locked. The pager calls the busy handler again. Only this time, busy() returns 0, which the pager interprets as false. In this case, rather than retrying the lock, the pager sends SQLITE_BUSY up the stack and that's what step() ends up returning.

If you just want to kill time waiting for a lock, you don't have to write your own busy handler. The SQLite API has one for you. It is a simple busy handler that sleeps for a given period of time waiting for a lock. In the API, the function is called sqlite3_busy_timeout(), and it is supported by some extension libraries. You can essentially say "try sleeping for 10 seconds when you can't get a lock," and the pager will do that for you. If it sleeps for 10 seconds and still can't get the lock, then it will return SQLITE_BUSY.

Using the Right Transaction

Let's consider the previous example again, but this time the command is an UPDATE rather than a SELECT. What does SQLITE_BUSY actually mean now? In SELECT, it just means, "I can't get a SHARED lock." But what does is mean for an UPDATE? The truth is, you don't really know what it means. SQLITE_BUSY could mean that the connection failed to get a SHARED lock because there is a writer pending. It could also mean that it got a SHARED lock but couldn't get to RESERVED. The point is you don't know the state of the database, or the state of your connection for that matter. In autocommit mode, SQLITE_BUSY for a write operation is completely indeterminate. So what do you do next? Should you just keep calling step() over and over until the command goes through?

Here's the thing to think about. Suppose SQLITE_BUSY was the result of you getting a SHARED lock but not RESERVED, and now you are holding up a connection in RESERVED from getting to EXCLUSIVE. Again, *you don't know the state of the database*. And just using a brute-force method to push your transaction through is not necessarily going to work, for you or any other connection. If you just keep calling step(), you are just going to butt heads with the connection that has the RESERVED lock, and if neither of you backs down, you'll deadlock.

■**Note** SQLite tries to help with deadlock prevention in this particular scenario by ignoring the busy handler of the offending connection. The SHARED connection's busy handler will not be invoked if it is preventing a RESERVED connection from proceeding. However, it is up to the code to get the hint. The code can still just repeatedly call step() over and over, in which case there is nothing more SQLite can do to help.

Since you know you want to write to the database, then you need to start by issuing BEGIN IMMEDIATE. If you get a SQLITE_BUSY, then at least you know what state you're in. You know you can safely keep trying without holding up another connection. And once you finally do succeed, you know what state you are in then as well—RESERVED. Now you can use brute force if you have to because you are the one in the right. If you start with a BEGIN EXCLUSIVE, on the other hand, then you are assured that you won't have any busy conditions to deal with at all. Just remember that in this case you are doing your work in EXCLUSIVE, which is not as good for concurrency as doing the work in RESERVED.

LOCKS AND NETWORK FILE SYSTEMS

At this point, you should have a good appreciation for what can go wrong when a database is shared over a network file system. SQLite handles concurrency by placing file locks on the database file. It is very important that these locks be both set and released at the right times. SQLite is completely dependent on the file system to manage locks correctly for concurrent use. SQLite uses the same locking mechanisms regardless of whether it is running on a normal file system or network file system. It uses POSIX advisory locks on Unix and the `LockFile()`, `LockFileEx()`, and `UnlockFile()` system calls on Windows. These calls are standard system calls, and work correctly on normal file systems. It is the network file system's job to emulate a normal file system. And unfortunately, this doesn't always work correctly with some implementations. And even if the network file system works correctly, there still other things to consider.

Take NFS, for example. It's a great network file system. However, many original NFS implementations were known to have buggy or in some cases unimplemented locking. And with a SQLite database, this can cause serious problems. Without locking, two connections can get an `EXCLUSIVE` lock on the same database and write to it at the same time, leading to an almost certain database corruption. Or perhaps locking is implemented and a bug does not release the reserved byte or pending byte in a timely manner, or at all. The problems range from delays to database corruption. This is not a problem with the NFS protocol in general, but with some implementations of it in particular. Eric Kustarz, a Sun engineer who has worked on NFS for five years, says the following on his blog regarding NFS locking:

> *The protocol behind locking (NLM) for NFSv2/v3 is not broken*, but rather some of the implementations were broken—especially early on (people spent time on making the NFS protocol work, but NLM was more complex—an after thought)... Running a Solaris client against a Solaris server will find that NFSv3 + NLM works great, and is not broken. Thankfully, NFSv4 fixed this by integrating locking into the one and only protocol. Now, locking has to work or you don't have a NFSv4 implementation.*

Now consider a footnote on the same page:

> **OK, there are a couple very edge cases in NLM that got sorted out in NFSv4. The easiest example is recovery of a client crash...if the client never comes back up, and another client needs to lock the same file? You need administrative intervention at this point. Since NFSv4's state is lease based, no intervention is necessary—if the client doesn't reclaim its state within the allotted time, the locks are lost.*

NFS can still have issues with locking if one of the clients goes down (taking their database lock with it) and does not come back up. For NFSv3, a locked file would need administrative intervention to clear it. For NFSv4, there would be a timeout period. But how long is the timeout? Thirty seconds? A minute? The real issue is not NFS, but specific applications of it. Network file systems, even if perfectly implemented, are not necessarily going to work exactly like a local file system.

The bottom line is, if you are going to mix concurrency and network file systems, there are many issues to consider, even if you are using the best network file system out there. It's not as simple as running on a local file system. There are new variables introduced when any application runs over a network. The real issue is not that SQLite doesn't work on network file systems. It can. Nor is the real issue that network file systems don't work reliably. Any valid implementation of NFS does. The issue is what your application does, what environment it is running in, what network file system(s) it is using (e.g., Linux client and Solaris server), how many other connections are hitting the database, what the specific performance requirements are... the list goes on.

No one can definitively say, "Yes, this network file system will work for you," or "No, SQLite doesn't work." These are only two of many possible variables in the equation—an equation that only you can solve based on your resources and requirements.

Code

By now, you have a pretty good picture of the API, transactions, and locks. To finish up, let's put all three of these things together in the context of your code, and consider a few scenarios that you might want to watch for.

Using Multiple Connections

If you have written code that uses other relational databases, you may have made some assumptions that might have worked with those databases that will not work with SQLite. Many times I have used multiple connections with other databases that work concurrently in a single block of code. The classic example is having one connection iterate over a table while another connection modifies records in place.

In SQLite, using multiple connections in the same block of code can cause problems. You have to be careful of how you go about it. Consider the following example:

```
c1 = open('foods.db')
c2 = open('foods.db')

stmt = c1.prepare('SELECT * FROM episodes')

while stmt.step()
  print stmt.column('name')
  c2.exec('UPDATE episodes SET …')
end

stmt.finalize()

c1.close()
c2.close()
```

I'll bet you can easily spot the problem here. In the while loop, c2 attempts an UPDATE while c1 has a SHARED lock open. That SHARED lock won't be released until stmt is finalized after the while loop. Therefore, it is impossible to write to the database within the while loop. Either the updates will silently fail, or if you have a busy handler then it will only delay the program. The best thing to do here is to use one connection for the job, and to run it under a single BEGIN IMMEDIATE transaction. The new version might be

```
c1 = open('foods.db')

# Keep trying until we get it
while c1.exec('BEGIN IMMEDIATE') != SQLITE_SUCCESS
end

stmt = c1.prepare('SELECT * FROM episodes')

while stmt.step()
  print stmt.column('name')
  c1.exec('UPDATE episodes SET …')
end

stmt.finalize()
c1.exec('COMMIT')
c1.close()
```

In cases like this, you should use statements from a single connection for reading or writing. Then you won't have to worry about database locks causing problems. However, as it turns out, this particular example still won't work. If you are iterating over a table with one statement and updating it with another, there is an additional locking issue that you need to know about as well, which we'll cover next.

Table Locks

Even if you are using just one connection, there is a special edge case that sometimes trips people up. While you would think that two statements from the same connection could work on the database with impunity, there is one important exception.

When you execute a SELECT command on a table, the resulting statement object creates a B-tree cursor on that table. As long as there is a B-tree cursor active on a table, other statements— even in the same connection—cannot modify it. If they try, they will get SQLITE_BUSY. Consider the following example:

```
c = sqlite.open("foods.db")

stmt1 = c.compile('SELECT * FROM episodes LIMIT 10')

while stmt1.step() do
    # Try to update the row
    row = stm1.row()
    stmt2 = c.compile('UPDATE episodes SET …')
    # Uh oh: ain't gonna happen
    stmt2.step()
end

stmt1.finalize()
stmt2.finalize ()

c.close()
```

We are only using one connection here. Regardless, when `stmt2.step()` is called, it won't work because `stmt1` has a cursor on the `episodes` table. In this case, `stmt2.step()` may actually succeed in promoting the connection's database lock to `EXCLUSIVE`, but it will still return `SQLITE_BUSY`. The cursor on `episodes` prevents it from modifying the table. In order to get around this, you can do one of two things:

- Iterate over the results with one statement, storing the information you need in memory. Then finalize the reading statement, and then do the updates.

- Store the `SELECT` results in a temporary table (as described in a moment) and open the read cursor on it. In this case you can have both a reading statement and a writing statement working at the same time. The reading statement's cursor will be on a different table—the temporary table—and won't block the updates on the main table from the second statement. Then when you are done, simply drop the temporary table.

When a statement is open on a table, its B-tree cursor will be removed from the table when one of two things happens:

- The statement reaches the end of the result set. When this happens, `step()` will automatically close the statement's cursor(s). In VDBE terms, when the end of the results set is reached, the VDBE encounters a `Close` instruction, which causes all associated cursors to be closed.

- The statement is finalized. The program explicitly calls `finalize()`, thereby removing all associated cursors.

In many extensions, the call to `sqlite3_finalize()` is done automatically in the statement object's `close()` function, or something similar.

■**Note** As a matter of interest, there are exceptions to these scenarios where you could theoretically get away with reading and writing to the same table at the same time. In order to do so, you would have to convince the optimizer to use a temporary table, using something like an ORDER BY, for example. When this happens, the optimizer will automatically create a temporary table for the SELECT statement and place the reading statement's cursor on it rather than the actual table itself. In this case, it is technically possible for a writer to then modify the real table because the reader's cursor is on a temporary table. The problem with this approach is that the decision to use temporary tables is made by the optimizer. It is not safe to presume what the optimizer will and will not do. Unless you like to gamble, or are just intimately acquainted with the ins and outs of the optimizer, it is best to just follow the general rule of thumb: don't read and write to the same table at the same time.

Fun with Temporary Tables

Temporary tables let you bend the rules. If you absolutely have to have two connections going in the same block of code, or two statements operating on the same table, you can safely do so if you use temporary tables. When a connection creates or writes to a temporary table, it does not have to get a `RESERVED` lock, because temporary tables are maintained outside of the database file. There are two ways of going about this, depending on how you want to manage concurrency. Consider the following example:

```
c1 = open('foods.db')
c2 = open('foods.db')

c2.exec('CREATE TEMPORARY TABLE temp_epsidodes as SELECT * from episodes')

stmt = c1.prepare('SELECT * FROM episodes')

while stmt.step()
  print stmt.column('name')
  c2.exec('UPDATE temp_episodes SET …')
end

stmt.finalize()

c2.exec('BEGIN IMMEDIATE')
c2.exec('DELETE FROM episodes')
c2.exec('INSERT INTO episodes SELECT * FROM temp_episodes')
c2.exec('COMMIT')

c1.close()
c2.close()
```

This example uses a temporary table based on episodes to make modifications within the while loop. Both connections are actually running in SHARED. Again, this is because temporary tables are maintained outside of the database. Therefore, temp_episodes and all of the operations on it don't require that c2 gets a RESERVED or an EXCLUSIVE lock. Once stmt is finalized, then c1's SHARED lock is gone and c2 can safely write to the database all that it collected in the temporary table.

Notice also that this example uses the original episodes table rather than dropping it and re-creating it from temp_episodes using a CREATE TABLE AS SELECT…. If you did it this way, then you would lose any integrity constraints and indexes defined on the original episodes table.

The advantage of the previous example is that it minimizes the duration of RESERVED and EXCLUSIVE locks on the database. Everything is kept in a temporary table during the iteration, so it does not affect other reading connections. Then everything is copied over in one single transaction. The code could be simplified somewhat, but at the cost of decreased concurrency as follows:

```
c1 = open('foods.db')
c2 = open('foods.db')

c1.exec('CREATE TEMPORARY TABLE temp_episodes as SELECT * from episodes')

stmt = c1.prepare('SELECT * FROM temp_episodes')
```

```
while stmt.step()
  print stmt.column('name')
  c2.exec('UPDATE episodes SET …') # What about SQLITE_BUSY?
end

stmt.finalize()

c1.exec('DROP TABLE temp_episodes')

c1.close()
c2.close()
```

This example stores the result set into the temporary table, iterates over it, and performs the updates to the main table. While this code is a little cleaner, keep in mind that you now have additional concurrency issues to deal with. First, there will now be RESERVED and EXCLUSIVE locks associated with each UPDATE where there weren't any before. Second, you have to guard the updates against SQLITE_BUSY conditions (not shown in the example). Finally, if you run the whole thing under a single transaction, it may have an EXCLUSIVE lock on the database during the entire iteration, depending on how much is updated and the size of the page cache. All in all, the first example, while involving a little more code, may be the better approach in general.

The Importance of Finalizing

A common gotcha in processing SELECT statements is the failure to realize that the SHARED lock is not released until finalize() is called—well, most of the time. Consider the following example:

```
stmt = c1.prepare('SELECT * FROM episodes')

while stmt.step()
  print stmt.column('name')
end

c2.exec('BEGIN IMMEDIATE; UPDATE episodes SET …; COMMIT;')

stmt.finalize()
```

While you should never do this in practice, you might end up doing it anyway by accident simply because you can get away with it. If you write the equivalent of this program in the C API, it will actually work. Even though finalize() has not been called, the second connection can modify the database without any problem. Before I tell you why, consider this next example:

```
c1 = open('foods.db')
c2 = open('foods.db')

stmt = c1.prepare('SELECT * FROM episodes')
```

```
stmt.step()
stmt.step()
stmt.step()

c2.exec('BEGIN IMMEDIATE; UPDATE episodes SET …; COMMIT;')

stmt.finalize()
```

Let's say that episodes has 100 records. And the program only stepped through three of them. What happens here? The second connection will get SQLITE_BUSY.

In the first example, SQLite released the SHARED lock when the statement reached the end of the result set. That is, in the final call to step(), where the API returns SQLITE_DONE, the VDBE encountered the Close instruction and SQLite closed the cursor and dropped the SHARED lock. Thus, c2 was able to push its INSERT through even though c1 had not called finalize().

In the second case, the statement had not reached the end of the set. The next call to step() would have returned SQLITE_RESULT, which means there are more rows in the results set, and that the SHARED lock is still active. Thus, c2 could not get the INSERT through this time because of the SHARED lock from c1.

The moral of the story is don't do this, even though sometimes you can. Always call finalize() before you write with another connection. The other thing to remember is that in autocommit mode step() and finalize() are more or less transaction and lock boundaries. They start and end transactions. They acquire and release locks. You should be very careful about what you do with other connections in between these functions.

Shared Cache Mode

Now that you are clear on the concurrency rules, I will give you something new to confuse you. SQLite offers an alternative concurrency model called *shared cache mode*, which relates to how connections can operate within individual threads.

In shared cache mode, a thread can create multiple connections that share the same page cache. Furthermore, this group of connections can have multiple readers *and a single writer* (in EXCLUSIVE) working on the same database at the same time. The catch is that these connections cannot be shared across threads—they are strictly limited to the thread (running specifically in shared cache mode) that created them. Furthermore, writers and readers have to be prepared to handle a special condition involving table locks.

When readers read tables, SQLite automatically puts table locks on them. This prevents writers from modifying those tables. If a writer tries to modify a read-locked table, it will get SQLITE_LOCKED. The same logic applies to readers trying to read from write-locked tables. However, in this latter case, readers can still go ahead and read tables that are being modified by a writer if they run in *read-uncommitted mode*, which is enabled by the read_uncommitted pragma. In this case, SQLite does not place read locks on the tables read by these readers. As a result, these readers don't interfere with writers at all. However, these readers can get inconsistent query results, as a writer can modify tables as the readers read them.

Shared cache mode is designed for embedded servers that need to conserve memory and have slightly higher concurrency under certain conditions. More information on using it with the C API can be found in Chapter 6.

Summary

The SQLite API is flexible, intuitive, and easy to use. It has two basic parts: the core API and the extension API. The core API revolves around two basic data structures used to execute SQL commands: the connection and the statement. Commands are executed in three steps: compilation, execution, and finalization. SQLite's wrapper functions exec() and get_table() wrap these steps into a single function call, automatically handling the associated statement object for you. Other parts of the core API include support for string handling, operational control, and other miscellaneous utility functions.

The extension API provides you with the means to customize SQLite in three difference ways: user defined functions, user-defined aggregates, and user-defined collations. Both user-defined functions and aggregates can be implemented in different languages and called directly from SQL. User-defined collations allow SQLite to be more usable in different locales.

Because SQLite's concurrency model is somewhat different from other databases, it is important that you understand a bit about how it manages transactions and locks, how they work behind the scenes and within your code. Overall, the concepts are not difficult to understand, and there are just a few simple rules to keep in mind when you write code that uses SQLite.

The next three chapters will draw heavily on what you've have learned here, as these concepts apply not only to the C API, but to language extensions as well as they are built on top of the C API.

CHAPTER 6

■ ■ ■

The Core C API

This chapter covers the part of the SQLite API used to work with databases. You already have a good idea of how the API works from Chapter 5. Now let's concentrate on the specifics.

Starting with a few trivial examples, we will take an in-depth tour through the C API and expand upon the examples, filling in various details with a variety of useful functions. As we go along, you should see the C equivalents of the model all fall into place, with some additional features you may not have seen before—features that primarily exist only in the C API. By the time we reach the end of this chapter, you should have seen every API function related to running commands, managing transactions, fetching records, handling errors, and many other tasks related to general database work.

The SQLite version 3 API consists of approximately 80 functions. Only about eight functions, however, are needed to actually connect, process queries, and disconnect from a database. The remaining functions can be arranged into small groups that specialize in accomplishing specific tasks.

As mentioned in Chapter 5, quite a few things have changed in the API between versions 2 and 3. One of the most notable is the addition of UTF support. All functions that accept character strings as function arguments, or produce them as return values, have both UTF-8 and UTF-16 analogs. For example, `sqlite3_open()`, which is used to open a database, takes a UTF-8 string containing a database filename as an argument. Its counterpart—`sqlite3_open16()`— has the exact same signature, but accepts the same argument in UTF-16 encoding. With the exception of the first section, I refer only to the UTF-8 functions, as the UTF-16 versions differ only slightly by their names.

While it is best to read the chapter straight through, if at any point you want more detailed information on a particular function, you can consult Appendix B, which contains the complete C API documentation.

All examples in this chapter can be found in self-contained example programs, the source files of which are located in the *ch6* folder of the examples zip file, available on the Apress website at `www.apress.com`. For every example presented, I specifically identify the name of the corresponding source file from which the example was taken.

Wrapped Queries

You are already familiar with the way that SQLite executes queries, as well as its various wrapper functions for executing SQL commands in a single function call. We will start with the C API versions of these wrappers because they are simple, self-contained, and easy to use. They are a good starting point, which will let you have some fun and not get too bogged down with details. Along the way, I'll introduce some other handy functions that go hand in hand with query processing. By the end of this section, you will be able connect, disconnect, and query a database using the wrapped queries.

Connecting and Disconnecting

Before you can execute SQL commands, you first have to connect to a database. Connecting to a database is perhaps best described as *opening* a database, as SQLite databases are contained in single operating system files (one file to one database). Similarly, the preferred term for disconnecting would be *closing* the database.

You open a database with the sqlite3_open() or sqlite3_open16() functions, which have the following declaration(s):[1]

```
int sqlite3_open(
  const char *filename,    /* Database filename (UTF-8) */
  sqlite3 **ppDb           /* OUT: SQLite db handle */
);

int sqlite3_open16(
  const void *filename,    /* Database filename (UTF-16) */
  sqlite3 **ppDb           /* OUT: SQLite db handle */
);
```

The filename argument can be the name of an operating system file, the text string ':memory:', or an empty string (NULL pointer). If you use NULL or ':memory:', sqlite3_open() will create an in-memory database in RAM that lasts only for the duration of the session. If filename is not NULL, sqlite3_open() attempts to open the database file by using its value. If no file by that name exists, sqlite3_open() will open a new database file by that name.

■**Note** When SQLite creates a new database, it does not actually write anything to disk until the first database object is created. Therefore, if you specify a new database file but do not create a table, view, trigger, or other database object, when you close the database the database file by that name will still not exist in the file system. Therefore, to actually create a new database, you must first create something in it before you close it. Other important considerations associated with creating new databases are covered in Chapter 5.

Upon completion, sqlite3_open() will initialize the sqlite3 structure passed into it by the ppDb argument. This structure should be considered as an opaque handle representing a single connection to a database. This is more of a connection handle than a database handle since it

---

1. Here I have included both the UTF-8 and UTF-16 declarations for sqlite3_open(). From here on out, I will refer to the UTF-8 declarations only for the sake of brevity. Therefore, please keep in mind that there are many functions in the API that have UTF-16 forms. All of these forms are listed in the API documentation in Appendix B.

is possible to attach multiple databases to a single connection. However, this connection still represents exactly one transaction context regardless of how many databases are attached.

If a connection's transaction context is not explicitly defined using BEGIN, COMMIT, and ROLLBACK, SQLite will by default operate in autocommit mode, where every statement issued to the connection is run under a separate transaction.

You close a connection by using the sqlite3_close() function, which is declared as follows:

```
int sqlite3_close(sqlite3*);
```

In order for sqlite3_close() to complete successfully, all prepared queries associated with the connection must be finalized. If any queries remain that have not been finalized, sqlite3_close() will return SQLITE_BUSY with the error message *Unable to close due to unfinalized statements.*

Note If there is a transaction open on a connection when it is closed by sqlite3_close(), the transaction will automatically be rolled back.

The exec Query

The sqlite3_exec() function provides a quick, easy way to execute SQL commands and is especially handy for commands that modify the database (i.e., don't return any data). This function has the following declaration:

```
int sqlite3_exec(
  sqlite3*,                /* An open database */
  const char *sql,         /* SQL to be executed */
  sqlite_callback,         /* Callback function */
  void *data               /* 1st argument to callback function */
  char **errmsg            /* Error msg written here */
);
```

The SQL provided in the sql argument can consist of more than one SQL command. sqlite3_exec() will parse and execute every command in the sql string until it reaches the end of the string or encounters an error. Listing 6-1 (taken from create.c.) illustrates using sqlite3_exec().

Listing 6-1. *Using sqlite3_exec() for Simple Commands*

```
int main(int argc, char **argv)
{
    sqlite3 *db;
    char *zErr;
    int rc;
    char *sql;
```

```
    rc = sqlite3_open("test.db", &db);

    if(rc) {
        fprintf(stderr, "Can't open database: %s\n", sqlite3_errmsg(db));
        sqlite3_close(db);
        exit(1);
    }

    sql = "create table episodes(id int, name text)";
    rc = sqlite3_exec(db, sql, NULL, NULL, &zErr);

    if(rc != SQLITE_OK) {
        if (zErr != NULL) {
            fprintf(stderr, "SQL error: %s\n", zErr);
            sqlite3_free(zErr);
        }
    }

    sql = "insert into episodes values (10, 'The Dinner Party')";
    rc = sqlite3_exec(db, sql, NULL, NULL, &zErr);

    sqlite3_close(db);
    return 0;
}
```

This example opens a database test.db and creates within it a single table called episodes. After that, it inserts one record. The CREATE TABLE command will physically create the database file if it does not already exist.

Processing Records

As mentioned in Chapter 5, it is actually possible to get records from sqlite3_exec(), although you don't see it implemented much outside of the C API. sqlite3_exec() contains a callback mechanism that provides a way to obtain results from SELECT statements. This mechanism is implemented by the third and fourth arguments of the function. The third argument is a pointer to a callback function. If it's provided, SQLite will call the function for each record processed in each SELECT statement executed within the sql argument. The callback function has the following declaration:

```
typedef int (*sqlite3_callback)(
    void*,    /* Data provided in the 4th argument of sqlite3_exec() */
    int,      /* The number of columns in row                        */
    char**,   /* An array of strings representing fields in the row  */
    char**    /* An array of strings representing column names       */
);
```

The fourth argument to sqlite3_exec() is a void pointer to any application-specific data you want to supply to the callback function. SQLite will pass this data as the first argument of the callback function.

The final argument (errmsg) is a pointer to a string to which an error message can be written should an error occur during processing. Thus, sqlite3_exec() has two sources of error information. The first is the return value. The other is the human-readable string, assigned to errmsg. If you pass in a NULL for errmsg, then SQLite will not provide any error message. Note that if you do provide a pointer for errmsg, the memory used to create the message is allocated on the heap. You should therefore check for a non-NULL value after the call and use sqlite3_free() to free the memory used to hold the errmsg string if an error occurs.

Putting it all together, sqlite3_exec() allows you to issue a batch of commands, and you can collect all of the returned data by using the callback interface. For example, let's insert a record into the episodes table and then select all of its records, all in a single call to sqlite3_exec(). The complete code, shown in Listing 6-2, is taken from exec.c.

Listing 6-2. *Using sqlite3_exec() for Record Processing*

```c
int callback(void* data, int ncols, char** values, char** headers);

int main(int argc, char **argv)
{
    sqlite3 *db;
    int rc;
    char *sql;
    char *zErr;

    rc = sqlite3_open("test.db", &db);

    if(rc) {
        fprintf(stderr, "Can't open database: %s\n", sqlite3_errmsg(db));
        sqlite3_close(db);
        exit(1);
    }

    const char* data = "Callback function called";
    sql = "insert into episodes (cid, name) values (11,'Mackinaw Peaches');"
        "select * from episodes;";
    rc = sqlite3_exec(db, sql, callback, data, &zErr);

    if(rc != SQLITE_OK) {
        if (zErr != NULL) {
            fprintf(stderr, "SQL error: %s\n", zErr);
            sqlite3_free(zErr);
        }
    }

    sqlite3_close(db);
    return 0;
}
```

```
int callback(void* data, int ncols, char** values, char** headers)
{
    int i;
    fprintf(stderr, "%s: ", (const char*)data);
    for(i=0; i < ncols; i++) {
        fprintf(stderr, "%s=%s ", headers[i], values[i]);
    }

    fprintf(stderr, "\n");
    return 0;
}
```

SQLite parses the sql string; runs the first command, which inserts a record; and then runs the second command, consisting of the SELECT statement. For the second command, SQLite calls the callback function for each record returned. Running the program produces the following output:

```
Callback function called: id=10 name=The Dinner Party
Callback function called: id=11 name=Mackinaw Peaches
```

Notice that the callback function returns 0. This return value actually exerts some control over sqlite3_exec(). If the callback function returns a non-zero value, then sqlite3_exec() will abort (in other words, it will terminate all processing of this and subsequent commands in the sql string).

So sqlite3_exec() provides not only an easy way to modify the database but an interface with which to process records as well. Why then should you bother with prepared queries? Well, as you will see in the next section, there are quite a few advantages to using the latter:

- Prepared queries don't require a callback interface, which makes coding simple and more linear.

- Prepared queries have associated functions that provide better column information. You can obtain a column's storage type, declared type, schema name (if it is aliased), table name, and database name. sqlite3_exec()'s callback interface provides just the column names.

- Prepared queries provide a way to obtain field/column values in other data types besides text, in native C data types such as int and double, whereas sqlite3_exec()'s callback interface only provides fields as string values.

- Prepared queries can be rerun, allowing you to reuse the compiled SQL.

- Prepared queries support parameterized SQL statements.

As a matter of history, sqlite3_exec()'s callback interface is reminiscent of the old SQLite 2.x API.[2] In that API, the callback interface was the way you performed all queries

---

2. It is interesting to note that sqlite3_exec() is implemented in a source file called legacy.c.

and retrieved all records. The new approach is a refinement of this interface, which works more like other database client libraries.

EXAMINING CHANGES

If you are performing an UPDATE or a DELETE, you may want to know how many records were affected. You can get this information from sqlite3_changes(). It provides the number of affected records for the last executed UPDATE, INSERT, or DELETE statement. Obviously, if you are running a batch of queries (multiple commands in the sql argument of sqlite3_exec()), this function will only be good for the last command in the batch. There are a few other caveats as well:

- Auxiliary changes caused by triggers are not counted. In order to obtain affected records from triggers, use the sqlite3_total_changes() function.

- When deleting *all* records in a table (delete from xyz), sqlite3_changes() will return 0 records. The reason for this is that SQLite optimizes this statement by dropping and re-creating the table in question rather than deleting individual records. If you need to know the actual number of deleted records, modify your DELETE statement to the form DELETE FROM table_name WHERE 1. This will disable the drop/re-create optimization and return the actual number of deleted records. Of course, you could also perform a SELECT count()... on the table in question before deleting all records to get the number of deleted records.

If you are performing an INSERT on a table with an autoincrement column, odds are you will eventually want to know the primary key value of an inserted record. In such cases, you can use sqlite3_last_insert_rowid() to obtain this value. You can also do this from within SQL as well via the last_insert_rowid() SQL function.

String Handling

As discussed in Chapter 5, SQLite includes functions for string handling. If your program has to deal with user input or parameters, some extremely handy functions to know about are SQLite's formatting functions, which are declared as follows:

```
char *sqlite3_mprintf(const char* sql, arg1, arg2, ...);
char *sqlite3_vmprintf(const char*, va_list);
```

The first function, sqlite3_mprintf(), works like sprintf(), but has features specific to SQL formatting. The handy argument here is %q, which is an enhanced %s. When used, %q will automatically escape SQL-sensitive characters in the substituted string. Consider the following code:

```
char *sql;
char *trouble = "'Here's trouble'";
sql = sqlite3_mprintf("insert into x values('%q')", trouble);
/* do something */
sqlite3_free(sql);
```

The result sql will contain

```
insert into x values('''Here''s trouble''')
```

The %Q format does everything %q does, but it also encloses the resulting string in single quotes. Furthermore, if the argument for the %Q formatting options is a NULL pointer, sqlite3_mprintf() will produce the string NULL without single quotes. Furthermore, the string produced by sqlite3_mprintf() is written into memory obtained from malloc() so that there is never a possibility of a buffer overflow.

You may find sqlite3_mprintf() so handy that you may want to create your own modified version of sqlite3_exec() that takes a variable number of arguments and substitutes them into the SQL string automatically. This is where sqlite3_vmprintf() comes in. It allows you to do that very thing. In fact, this is how the execute() function in the common library included with the examples is implemented (see Listing 6-3).

Listing 6-3. *Using sqlite3_vmprintf()*

```
int execute(sqlite3 *db, const char* sql, ...)
{
    char *err, *tmp;

    va_list ap;
    va_start(ap, sql);
    tmp = sqlite3_vmprintf(sql, ap);
    va_end(ap);

    int rc = sqlite3_exec(db, tmp, NULL, NULL, &err);

    if(rc != SQLITE_OK) {
        if (err != NULL) {
            fprintf(stdout, "execute() : Error %i : %s\n", rc, err);
            sqlite3_free(err);
        }
    }

    sqlite3_free(tmp);

    return rc;
}
```

The execute() function takes an arbitrary number of arguments and substitutes them into the sql argument according to its specification. Using this function, you can put together a properly formatted, parameterized SQL statement without having to do any string processing, as shown in the following example:

```
int cid = 1;
char* sql insert into episodes (cid, name) values (%i,'%q');
execute(db, sql, 1, "Here's trouble");
```

This simple wrapper function provides protection against buffer overflows, performs automatic character escaping, and handles memory management, in addition to all the other useful features of sprintf()—all credit due to sqlite3_vmprintf().

The Get Table Query

The sqlite3_get_table() function returns an entire result set of a command in a single function call. Just as sqlite3_exec() wraps the prepared query API functions, allowing you to run them all at once, sqlite3_get_table() wraps sqlite3_exec() for commands that return data with just as much convenience. Using sqlite3_get_table(), you don't have to bother with the sqlite3_exec() callback function, thus making it easier to fetch records. sqlite3_get_table() has the following declaration:

```
int sqlite3_get_table(
  sqlite3*,              /* An open database */
  const char *sql,       /* SQL to be executed */
  char ***resultp,       /* Result written to a char *[] that this points to */
  int *nrow,             /* Number of result rows written here */
  int *ncolumn,          /* Number of result columns written here */
  char **errmsg          /* Error msg written here */
);
```

This function takes all of the records returned from the SQL statement in sql and stores them in the resultp argument using memory declared on the heap (using malloc()). The memory must be freed using sqlite3_free_table(), which takes the resultp pointer as its sole argument. The first record in resultp is actually not a record, but the names of the columns in the result set. Consider the code in Listing 6-4 (taken from get_table.c).

Listing 6-4. *Using sqlite3_get_table*

```
int main(int argc, char **argv)
{
    /* Connect to database, etc. */

    char *result[];
    sql = "select * from episodes;";
    rc = sqlite3_get_table(db, sql, &result, &nrows, &ncols, &zErr);

    /* Do something with data */

    /* Free memory */
    sqlite3_free_table(result)
}
```

If, for example, the result set returned is of the form

```
name              | id
----------------------
The Junior Mint   | 43
The Smelly Car    | 28
The Fusilli Jerry | 21
```

then the format of the result array will be structured as follows:

```
result [0] = "name";
result [1] = "id";
result [2] = "The Junior Mint";
result [3] = "43";
result [4] = "The Smelly Car";
result [5] = "28";
result [6] = "The Fusilli Jerry";
result [7] = "21";
```

The first two elements contain the column headings of the result set. Therefore, you can think of the result set indexing as 1-based with respect to rows, but 0-based with respect to columns. An example may help clarify this. The code to print out each column of each row in the result set is shown in Listing 6-5.

Listing 6-5. *Iterating Through sqlite3_get_table() Results*

```
rc = sqlite3_get_table(db, sql, &result, &nrows, &ncols, &zErr);

for(i=0; i < nrows; i++) {
    for(j=0; j < ncols; j++) {
        /* the i+1 term skips over the first record,
        which is the column headers */
        fprintf(stdout, "%s", result[(i+1)*ncols + j]);
    }
}
```

Prepared Queries

As you saw in Chapter 5, SQLite's approach to executing SQL commands consists of the prepare, step, and finalize functions. This section covers all aspects of this process, including stepping through result sets, fetching records, and using parameterized queries.

The wrapper functions simply wrap all of these steps into a single function call, making it more convenient in some situations to run specific commands. Each query function provides its own way of getting at rows and columns. As a general rule, the more packaged the method is, the less control you have over execution and results. Therefore, prepared queries offer the most features, the most control, and the most information. Following that is sqlite3_exec(); following that is sqlite3_get_table().

Prepared queries use a special group of functions to access field and column information from a row. You get column values using sqlite3_column_xxx(), where xxx represents the data type of the value to be returned (e.g., int, double, blob). You can retrieve data in whatever format you like. You can also obtain the declared types of columns (as they are defined in the CREATE TABLE statement) and other miscellaneous metadata such as storage format and both associated table and database names. sqlite3_exec(), by comparison, provides only a fraction of this information through its callback function. The same is true with sqlite3_get_table(), which only includes the result set's column headers with the data.

In practice you will find that each query method has its uses. sqlite3_exec() is especially good for running commands that modify the database (CREATE, DROP, INSERT, UPDATE, and DELETE). One function call and it's done. Prepared queries are typically better for SELECT statements because they offer so much more information, more linear coding (no callback functions), and more control by using cursors to iterate over results.

As you'll recall from Chapter 5, prepared queries are performed in three basic steps: compilation, execution, and finalization. This process is illustrated in Figure 6-1.

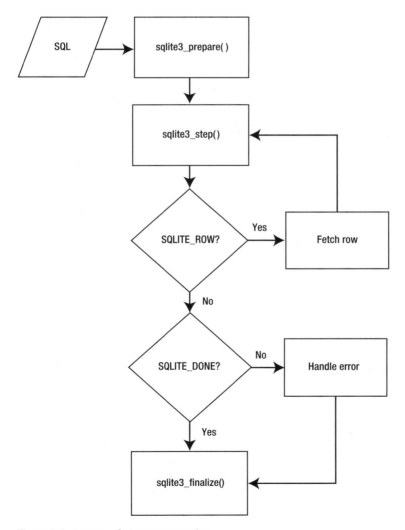

Figure 6-1. *Prepared query processing*

You compile the query with sqlite3_prepare(), execute it step by step using sqlite3_step(), and close it using sqlite3_finalize(), or you can reuse it using sqlite3_reset(). This process and the individual steps are all explained in detail in the following sections.

Compilation

Compilation, or preparation, takes a SQL statement and compiles it into byte code readable by the virtual database engine (VDBE). It is performed by sqlite3_prepare(), which is declared as follows:

```
int sqlite3_prepare(
  sqlite3 *db,           /* Database handle          */
  const char *zSql,      /* SQL text, UTF-8 encoded  */
  int nBytes,            /* Length of zSql in bytes. */
  sqlite3_stmt **ppStmt, /* OUT: Statement handle    */
  const char **pzTail    /* OUT: Pointer to unused portion of zSql */
);
```

sqlite3_prepare() compiles the first SQL statement in the zSQL string (which can contain multiple SQL statements) into VDBE byte code. It allocates all the resources necessary to execute the statement and associates it along with the byte code into a single statement handle (also referred to as simply a statement), designated by the out parameter ppStmt, which is a sqlite3_stmt structure. From the programmer's perspective, this structure is little more than an opaque handle used to execute a SQL statement and obtain its associated records. However, this data structure contains the command's byte code, bound parameters, B-tree cursors, VDBE execution context, and any other data sqlite3_step() needs to manage the state of the query during execution.

sqlite3_prepare() does not affect the connection or database in any way. It does not start a transaction or get a lock. It works directly with the compiler, which simply prepares the query for execution. Statement handles are highly dependent on the database schema they were compiled with. If another connection alters the database schema, between the time you prepare a statement and the time you actually run it, your statement will expire. Your first call to sqlite3_step() with the statement will lead to a SQLITE_SCHEMA error, which is discussed later in the section "Errors and the Unexpected." Then you will have to finalize or reset the statement, recompile, and try again.

Execution

Once you prepare the query, the next step is to execute it using sqlite3_step(), declared as follows:

```
int sqlite3_step(sqlite3_stmt *pStmt);
```

sqlite3_step() takes the statement handle and talks directly to the VDBE. The VDBE reads the statement handle's byte code and steps through its instructions one by one to carry out the SQL statement. On the first call to sqlite3_step(), the VDBE obtains the requisite database lock needed to perform the command. If it can't get the lock, sqlite3_step() will return SQLITE_BUSY, if there is no busy handler installed. If one is installed, it will call that handler instead.

For SQL statements that don't return data, the first call to sqlite3_step() executes the command in its entirety, returning a result code indicating the outcome. For SQL statements that do return data, such as SELECT, the first call to sqlite3_step() positions the statement's B-tree cursor on the first record. Subsequent calls to sqlite3_step() position the cursor on subsequent records in the result set. sqlite3_step() returns SQLITE_ROW for each record in the set until it reaches the end, whereupon it returns SQLITE_DONE, indicating that the cursor has reached the end of the set.

All other API functions related to data access use the statement's cursor to obtain information about the current record. For example, the sqlite3_column_xxx() functions all use the statement handle, specifically its cursor, to fetch the current record's fields.

Finalization and Reset

Once the statement has reached the end of execution, it must be finalized. You can either finalize or reset the statement using one of the following functions:

```
int sqlite3_finalize(sqlite3_stmt *pStmt);
int sqlite3_reset(sqlite3_stmt *pStmt);
```

sqlite3_finalize() will close out the statement. It frees resources and commits or rolls back any implicit transactions (if the connection is in autocommit mode), clearing the journal file and freeing the associated lock.

If you want to reuse the statement, you can do so using sqlite3_reset(). It will keep the compiled SQL statement (and any bound parameters), but commits any changes related to the current statement to the database. It also releases its lock and clears the journal file if auto-commit is enabled. The primary difference between sqlite3_finalize() and sqlite3_reset() is that the latter preserves the resources associated with the statement so that it can be executed again, avoiding the need to call sqlite3_prepare() to compile the SQL command.

A Practical Example

Now that you've seen the whole process, let's go through an example. A simple, complete program using a prepared query is listed in Listing 6-6. It is taken from select.c in the examples.

Listing 6-6. *Using Prepared Queries*

```
int main(int argc, char **argv)
{
    int rc, i, ncols;
    sqlite3 *db;
    sqlite3_stmt *stmt;
    char *sql;
    const char *tail;

    rc = sqlite3_open("foods.db", &db);

    if(rc) {
        fprintf(stderr, "Can't open database: %s\n", sqlite3_errmsg(db));
        sqlite3_close(db);
        exit(1);
    }
```

```
    sql = "select * from episodes;";

    rc = sqlite3_prepare(db, sql, strlen(sql), &stmt, &tail);

    if(rc != SQLITE_OK) {
        fprintf(stderr, "SQL error: %s\n", sqlite3_errmsg(db));
    }

    rc = sqlite3_step(stmt);
    ncols = sqlite3_column_count(stmt);

    while(rc == SQLITE_ROW) {

        for(i=0; i < ncols; i++) {
            fprintf(stderr, "'%s' ", sqlite3_column_text(stmt, i));
        }

        fprintf(stderr, "\n");

        rc = sqlite3_step(stmt);
    }

    sqlite3_finalize(stmt);
    sqlite3_close(db);

    return 0;
}
```

This example connects to the foods.db database, queries the episodes table, and prints out all columns of all records within it. Keep in mind this is a simplified example—there are a few other things we need to check for when calling sqlite3_step(), such as errors and busy conditions, but we will address them later.

Like sqlite3_exec(), sqlite3_prepare() can accept a string containing multiple SQL statements. However, unlike sqlite3_exec(), it will only process the first statement in the string. But it does make it easy for you to process subsequent SQL statements in the string by providing the pzTail out parameter. After you call sqlite3_prepare(), it will point this parameter (if provided) to the starting position of the next statement in the zSQL string. Using pzTail, processing a batch of SQL commands in a given string can be executed in a loop as follows:

```
while(sqlite3_complete(sql) {
    rc = sqlite3_prepare(db, sql, strlen(sql), &stmt, &tail);

    /* Process query results */

    /* Skip to next command in string. */
    sql = tail;
}
```

This example makes use of another API function not yet covered—sqlite3_complete(), which does as its name suggests: it takes a string and returns true (1) if there is at least one complete (but necessarily valid) SQL statement in it, and false otherwise.

Fetching Records

So far, you have seen how to obtain records and columns from sqlite3_exec() and sqlite3_get_table(). Prepared queries, by comparison, offer many more options when it comes to getting information from records in the database.

For a statement that returns records, the number of columns in the result set can be obtained using sqlite3_column_count() and sqlite3_data_count(), which are declared as follows:

```
int sqlite3_column_count(sqlite3_stmt *pStmt);
int sqlite3_data_count(sqlite3_stmt *pStmt);
```

sqlite3_column_count() returns the number of columns associated with a statement handle. You can call it on a statement handle before it is actually executed. If the query in question is not a SELECT statement, sqlite3_column_count() will return 0. Similarly, sqlite3_data_count() returns the number of columns for the current record, after sqlite3_step() returns SQLITE_ROW. This function will only work if the statement handle has an active cursor.

Getting Column Information

You can obtain the name of each column in the current record using sqlite3_column_name(), which is declared as follows:

```
const char *sqlite3_column_name( sqlite3_stmt*, /* statement handle */
                                 int iCol       /* column ordinal   */);
```

Similarly, you can get the associated storage class for each column using sqlite3_column_type(), which is declared as follows:

```
int sqlite3_column_type( sqlite3_stmt*, /* statement handle */
                         int iCol       /* column ordinal   */);
```

This function returns an integer value that corresponds to one of five storage class codes, defined as follows:

```
#define SQLITE_INTEGER  1
#define SQLITE_FLOAT    2
#define SQLITE_TEXT     3
#define SQLITE_BLOB     4
#define SQLITE_NULL     5
```

These are SQLite's native data types, or storage classes as described in Chapter 4. All data stored within a SQLite database is stored in one of these five forms, depending on its initial representation and the affinity of the column. For our purposes, the terms *storage class* and *data type* are synonymous. For more information on storage classes, see the sections "Storage Classes" and "Type Affinity" in Chapter 4.

You can obtain the declared data type of a column as it is defined in the table's schema using the sqlite3_column_decltype() function, which is declared as follows:

```
const char *sqlite3_column_decltype( sqlite3_stmt*, /* statement handle */
                                     int            /* column ordinal  */);
```

If a column in a result set does not correspond to an actual table column (say, for example, the column is the result of a literal value, expression, function, or aggregate), this function will return NULL as the declared type of that column. For example, suppose you have a table in your database defined as

```
CREATE TABLE t1(c1 INTEGER);
```

Then you execute the following query:

```
SELECT c1 + 1, 0 FROM t1;
```

In this case, sqlite3_column_decltype() will return INTEGER for the first column and NULL for the second.

In addition to the declared type, you can obtain other information on a column using the following functions:

```
const char *sqlite3_column_database_name(sqlite3_stmt *pStmt, int iCol);
const char *sqlite3_column_table_name(sqlite3_stmt *pStmt, int iCol);
const char *sqlite3_column_origin_name(sqlite3_stmt *pStmt, int iCol);
```

The first function will return the database associated with a column, the second its table, and the last function returns the column's actual name as defined in the schema. That is, if you assigned the column an alias in the SQL statement, sqlite3_column_origin_name() will return its actual name as defined in the schema. Note that these functions are only available if you compile SQLite with the SQLITE_ENABLE_COLUMN_METADATA preprocessor directive.

COLUMN METADATA

Detailed information about a column can be obtained independently from a query using the sqlite3_table_column_metadata() function, declared as follows:

```
int sqlite3_table_column_metadata(
    sqlite3 *db,                /* Connection handle              */
    const char *zDbName,        /* Database name or NULL          */
    const char *zTableName,     /* Table name                     */
    const char *zColumnName,    /* Column name                    */
    char const **pzDataType,    /* OUTPUT: Declared data type     */
    char const **pzCollSeq,     /* OUTPUT: Collation sequence name */
    int *pNotNull,              /* OUTPUT: True if NOT NULL
                                           constraint exists        */
    int *pPrimaryKey,           /* OUTPUT: True if column part of PK */
    int *pAutoinc               /* OUTPUT: True if colums is
                                           auto-increment           */
);
```

This function is a combination of input and output parameters. It does not work from a statement handle, but rather from a combination of connection handle, database name, table name, and column name.

The optional database name refers to the logical name of an attached database (e.g., "main" or "temp"). If no database name is provided (the argument is NULL), then the function will search all attached databases for matching columns. Both table name and column name are required. The information for the matched column is provided to the memory locations of arguments 5 through 9. The memory for the pzDataType and pzCollSeq out parameters is valid only until the next API call. If no matching column can be found, then sqlite3_table_column_metadata() returns SQLITE_ERROR.

Getting Column Values

You can obtain the values for each column in the current record using the sqlite3_column_*xxx*() functions, which are of the general form

```
xxx sqlite3_column_xxx( sqlite3_stmt*, /* statement handle */
                        int iCol       /* column ordinal  */);
```

Here *xxx* is the data type you want the data represented in (e.g., int, blob, double, etc.). The complete list of the sqlite3_column_*xxx*() functions is as follows:

```
int sqlite3_column_int(sqlite3_stmt*, int iCol);
double sqlite3_column_double(sqlite3_stmt*, int iCol);
long long int sqlite3_column_int64(sqlite3_stmt*, int iCol);
const void *sqlite3_column_blob(sqlite3_stmt*, int iCol);
const unsigned char *sqlite3_column_text(sqlite3_stmt*, int iCol);
const void *sqlite3_column_text16(sqlite3_stmt*, int iCol);
```

For each function, SQLite converts the internal representation (storage class in the column) to the type specified in the function name. There are a number of rules SQLite uses to convert the internal data type representation to that of the requested type. These rules are listed in Table 6-1.

Table 6-1. *Column Type Conversion Rules*

Internal Type	Requested Type	Conversion
NULL	INTEGER	Result is 0.
NULL	FLOAT	Result is 0.0.
NULL	TEXT	Result is a NULL pointer.
NULL	BLOB	Result is a NULL pointer.
INTEGER	FLOAT	Convert from integer to float.
INTEGER	TEXT	Result is the ASCII rendering of the integer.
INTEGER	BLOB	Result is the ASCII rendering of the integer.
FLOAT	INTEGER	Convert from float to integer.

Table 6-1. *Column Type Conversion Rules (Continued)*

Internal Type	Requested Type	Conversion
FLOAT	TEXT	Result is the ASCII rendering of the float.
FLOAT	BLOB	Result is the ASCII rendering of the float.
TEXT	INTEGER	Use atoi().
TEXT	FLOAT	Use atof().
TEXT	BLOB	No change.
BLOB	INTEGER	Convert to TEXT and then use atoi().
BLOB	FLOAT	Convert to TEXT and then use atof().
BLOB	TEXT	Add a \000 terminator if needed.

Like the sqlite3_bind_*xxx*() functions described later, BLOBs require a little more work in that you must specify their length in order to copy them. For BLOB columns, you can get the actual length of the data using sqlite3_column_bytes(), which is declared as follows:

```
int sqlite3_column_bytes( sqlite3_stmt*, /* statement handle   */
                          int            /* column ordinal */);
```

Once you get the length, you can copy the binary data using sqlite3_column_blob(). For example, say the first column in the result set contains binary data. One way to get a copy of that data would be as follows:

```
int len = sqlite3_column_bytes(stmt,0);
void* data = malloc(len);
memcpy(data, len, sqlite3_column_blob(stmt,0));
```

A Practical Example

To help solidify all of these column functions, Listing 6-7 (taken from columns.c) illustrates using the functions we've described to retrieve column information and values for a simple SELECT statement.

Listing 6-7. *Obtaining Column Information*

```
int main(int argc, char **argv)
{
    int rc, i, ncols, id, cid;
    char *name, *sql;
    sqlite3 *db;
    sqlite3_stmt *stmt;

    sql = "select id, name from episodes";
    sqlite3_open("test.db", &db);
```

```
    setup(db);

    sqlite3_prepare(db, sql, strlen(sql), &stmt, NULL);

    ncols = sqlite3_column_count(stmt);
    rc = sqlite3_step(stmt);

    /* Print column information */
    for(i=0; i < ncols; i++) {
        fprintf(stdout, "Column: name=%s, storage class=%i, declared=%s\n",
                        sqlite3_column_name(stmt, i),
                        sqlite3_column_type(stmt, i),
                        sqlite3_column_decltype(stmt, i));
    }

    fprintf(stdout, "\n");

    while(rc == SQLITE_ROW) {
        id = sqlite3_column_int(stmt, 0);
        cid = sqlite3_column_int(stmt, 1);
        name = sqlite3_column_text(stmt, 2);
        if(name != NULL){
            fprintf(stderr, "Row:  id=%i, cid=%i, name='%s'\n", id,cid,name);
        } else {
            /* Field is NULL */
            fprintf(stderr, "Row:  id=%i, cid=%i, name=NULL\n", id,cid);
        }
        rc = sqlite3_step(stmt);
    }

    sqlite3_finalize(stmt);
    sqlite3_close(db);
    return 0;
}
```

This example connects to the database, selects records from the episodes table, and prints the column information and the fields for each row (using their internal storage class). Running the program produces the following output:

```
Column: name=id, storage class=1, declared=integer
Column: name=name, storage class=3, declared=text

Row:  id=1, name='The Dinner Party'
Row:  id=2, name='The Soup Nazi'
Row:  id=3, name='The Fusilli Jerry'
```

FINDING A STATEMENT'S CONNECTION

In practice you may find yourself writing code where some of your functions only have access to the statement handle, not the connection handle. If these functions encounter an error while working with the statement handle, they will not have a way to get error information from sqlite3_errmsg(), as it requires a connection handle to work. This is where sqlite3_db_handle() comes in handy. It is declared as follows:

```
int sqlite3_db_handle(sqlite3_stmt*);
```

Given a statement handle, sqlite3_db_handle() returns the associated connection handle. This way, you don't need to worry about having to pass the connection handle along with the statement handle everywhere you process query results.

Parameterized Queries

The API includes support for designating parameters in a SQL statement, allowing you to provide (or "bind") values for them at a later time. Bound parameters are used in conjunction with sqlite3_prepare(). For example, you could create a SQL statement like the following:

```
insert into foo values (?,?,?);
```

Then you can, for example, bind the integer value 2 to the first parameter (designated by the first ? character), the string value 'pi' to the second parameter, and the double value 3.14 for the third parameter, as illustrated in the following code (taken from parameters.c):

```
const char* sql = "insert into foo values(?,?,?)";
sqlite3_prepare(db, sql, strlen(sql), &stmt, &tail);

sqlite3_bind_int(stmt,    1, 2);
sqlite3_bind_text(stmt,   2, "pi");
sqlite3_bind_double(stmt, 3, 3.14);

sqlite3_step(stmt);
sqlite3_finalize(stmt);
```

This generates and executes the statement

```
insert into foo values (2, 'pi', 3.14)
```

This process is illustrated in Figure 6-2. This particular method of binding uses *positional parameters* (as described in Chapter 5) where each parameter is designated by a question mark (?) character, and later identified by its index or relative position in the SQL statement.

Before delving into the other parameter methods, it is helpful to first understand the process by which parameters are defined, bound, and evaluated. When you write a parameterized statement such as the following, the parameters within it are identified when sqlite3_prepare() compiles the query:

```
insert into episodes (id,name) values (?,?)
```

sqlite3_prepare() recognizes that there are parameters in a SQL statement. Internally, it assigns each parameter a number to uniquely identify it. In the case of positional parameters, it starts with 1 for the first parameter found and uses sequential integer values for subsequent parameters. It stores this information in the resulting statement handle (sqlite3_stmt structure), which will then expect a specific number of values to be bound to the given parameters before execution. If you do notbind a value to a parameter, sqlite3_step() will use NULL for its value by default when the statement is executed.

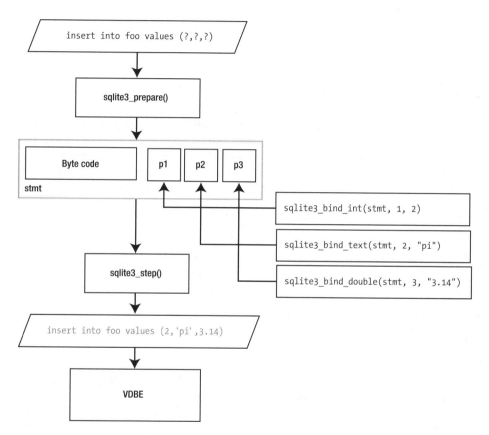

Figure 6-2. *SQL parameter binding*

After you prepare the statement, you then bind values to it. You do this using the sqlite3_bind_*xxx*() functions, which have the general form

```
sqlite3_bind_xxx( sqlite3_stmt*, /* statement handle  */
                  int i,         /* parameter number  */
                  xxx value      /* value to be bound */
                );
```

The *xxx* in the function name represents the data type of the value to bind. For example, to bind a double value to a parameter, you would use sqlite3_bind_double(), which is declared as follows:

```
sqlite3_bind_double(sqlite3_stmt* stmt, int i, double value);
```

The complete list of bind functions is as follows:

```
int sqlite3_bind_int(sqlite3_stmt*, int, int);
int sqlite3_bind_double(sqlite3_stmt*, int, double);
int sqlite3_bind_int64(sqlite3_stmt*, int, long long int);
int sqlite3_bind_null(sqlite3_stmt*, int);

int sqlite3_bind_blob( sqlite3_stmt*, int, const void*,
                       int n, void(*)(void*));
int sqlite3_bind_text( sqlite3_stmt*, int, const char*,
                       int n, void(*)(void*));
int sqlite3_bind_text16( sqlite3_stmt*, int, const void*,
                         int n, void(*)(void*));
```

In general, the bind functions can be divided into two classes, one for scalar values (int, double, int64, and NULL), and the other for arrays (blob, text, and text16). They differ only in that the array bind functions require a length argument and a pointer to a cleanup function. Also, sqlite3_bind_text() automatically escapes quote characters like sqlite3_mprintf(). Using the BLOB variant, the array bind function has the following declaration:

```
int sqlite3_bind_blob( sqlite3_stmt*,    /* statement handle   */
                       int,              /* ordinal            */
                       const void*,      /* pointer to blob data */
                       int n,            /* length (bytes) of data */
                       void(*)(void*)); /* cleanup hander     */
```

There are two predefined values for the cleanup handler provided by the API that have special meanings, defined as follows:

```
#define SQLITE_STATIC      ((void(*)(void *))0)
#define SQLITE_TRANSIENT   ((void(*)(void *))-1)
```

Each value designates a specific cleanup action. SQLITE_STATIC tells the array bind function that the array memory resides in unmanaged space, so SQLite does not attempt to clean it up. SQLITE_TRANSIENT tells the bind function that the array memory is subject to change, so SQLite makes its own private copy of the data, which it automatically cleans up when the statement is finalized. The third option is to provide a pointer to your own cleanup function, which must be of the form

```
void cleanup_fn(void*)
```

If provided, SQLite will call your cleanup function, passing in the array memory when the statement is finalized.

Note Bound parameters remain bound throughout the lifetime of the statement handle. They remain bound even after a call to `sqlite3_reset()` and are only freed when the statement is finalized (by calling `sqlite3_finalize()`).

Once you have bound all of the parameters you want, you can then execute the statement. You do this using the next function in the sequence: `sqlite3_step()`. `sqlite3_step()` will take the bound values, substitute them for the parameters in the SQL statement, and then begin executing the command.

Also, as a matter of convenience, bindings can be transferred from one statement to another using `sqlite3_transfer_bindings()`, which is declared as follows:

```
int sqlite3_transfer_bindings( sqlite3_stmt*,  /* source statement */
                               sqlite3_stmt*); /* dest statement   */
```

This function is useful if you want to prepare the same query using another statement, without having to repeat all of the binding steps. This function is especially useful for dealing with SQLITE_SCHEMA errors, described later.

Now that you understand the binding process, the four parameter-binding methods differ only by

- The way in which parameters are represented in the SQL statement (using a positional parameter, explicitly defined parameter number, or alphanumeric parameter name)

- The way in which parameters are assigned numbers

For positional parameters, `sqlite3_prepare()` assigns numbers using sequential integer values starting with 1 for the first parameter. In the previous example, the first ? parameter is assigned 1, and the second ? parameter is assigned 2. With positional parameters, it is your job to keep track of which number corresponds to which parameter (or question mark) in the SQL statement and correctly specify that number in the bind functions.

Numbered Parameters

Numbered parameters, on the other hand, allow you to specify your own numbers for parameters, rather than use an internal sequence. The syntax for numbered parameters uses a question mark followed by the parameter number. Take, for example, the following piece of code (taken from `parameters.c`):

```
name = "Mackinaw Peaches";
sql  = "insert into episodes (id, cid, name) "
       "values (?100,?100,?101)";

rc = sqlite3_prepare(db, sql, strlen(sql), &stmt, &tail);

if(rc != SQLITE_OK) {
    fprintf(stderr, "sqlite3_prepare() : Error: %s\n", tail);
    return rc;
}
```

```
sqlite3_bind_int(stmt, 100, 10);
sqlite3_bind_text(stmt, 101, name, strlen(name), SQLITE_TRANSIENT);
sqlite3_step(stmt);
sqlite3_finalize(stmt);
```

This example uses 100 and 101 for its parameter numbers. Parameter number 100 has the integer value 10 bound to it. Parameter 101 has the string value 'Mackinaw Peaches' bound to it. Note how numbered parameters come in handy when you need to bind a single value in more than one place in a SQL statement. Consider the values part of the previous SQL statement:

```
insert into episodes (id, cid, name) values (?100,?100,?101)";
```

Parameter 100 is being used twice—once for id and again for cid. Thus, numbered parameters save time when you need to use a bound value in more than one place.

■**Note** When using numbered parameters in a SQL statement, keep in mind that the allowable range consists of the integer values 1–999.

Named Parameters

The third parameter binding method is using named parameters. Whereas you can assign your own numbers using numbered parameters, you can assign alphanumeric names with named parameters. Likewise, as numbered parameters are prefixed with a question mark (?), you identify named parameters by prefixing a colon (:) to the parameter name. Consider the following code snippet (taken from parameters.c):

```
name = "Mackinaw Peaches";
sql = "insert into episodes (id, cid, name) values (:cosmo,:cosmo,:newman)";

rc = sqlite3_prepare(db, sql, strlen(sql), &stmt, &tail);

sqlite3_bind_int( stmt,
                  sqlite3_bind_parameter_index(stmt, ":cosmo"), 10);

sqlite3_bind_text( stmt,
                   sqlite3_bind_parameter_index(stmt, ":newman"),
                   name,
                   strlen(name), SQLITE_TRANSIENT );

sqlite3_step(stmt);
sqlite3_finalize(stmt);
```

This example is identical to the previous example using numbered parameters, except it uses two named parameters called cosmo and newman instead. Like positional parameters, named parameters are automatically assigned numbers by sqlite3_prepare(). While the numbers assigned to each parameter are unknown, you can resolve them using sqlite3_bind_parameter_index(), which takes a parameter name and returns the corresponding parameter number. This is the number you use to bind the value to its parameter. All in all, named parameters mainly help with legibility more than anything else.

PARAMETER INDEXES

While the function `sqlite3_bind_parameter_index()` seems to refer to a parameter number as an *index*, for all intents and purposes the two terms (number and index) are synonymous. I have settled on the term *number* rather than *index* for parameter positions as a result of some discussion on the SQLite mailing list, which has suggested that *number* is perhaps a better description. The term *index* was used when parameter binding was limited only to positional parameters. With the addition of numbered parameters, referring to parameter positions as (sequential) indexes can be somewhat misleading.

Tcl Parameters

The final parameter scheme is called Tcl parameters and is specific more to the Tcl extension than it is to the C API. Basically, it works identically to named parameters except that rather than using alphanumeric values for parameter names, it uses Tcl variable names. In the Tcl extension, when the Tcl equivalent of `sqlite3_prepare()` is called, the Tcl extension automatically searches for Tcl variables with the given parameter names in the active Tcl program environment and binds them to their respective parameters. Despite its current application in the Tcl interface, nothing prohibits this same mechanism from being applied to other language interfaces, which can in turn implement the same feature. In this respect, referring to this parameter method solely as Tcl parameters may be a bit of a misnomer. The Tcl extension just happened to be the first application that utilized this method. Basically, the Tcl parameter syntax does little more than provide an alternate syntax to named parameters—rather than prefixing the parameters with a colon (:), it uses a dollar sign ($).

Errors and the Unexpected

Up to now, we have looked at the API from a rather optimistic viewpoint, as if nothing could ever go wrong. But things do go wrong, and there is a part of the API devoted to that. The three things you always have to guard against in your code are errors, busy conditions, and my personal favorite: schema changes.

Handling Errors

Many of the API functions return integer result codes. That means they can potentially return error codes of some sort. The most common functions to watch are typically the most frequently used, such as `sqlite3_open()`, `sqlite3_prepare()` and friends, as well as `sqlite3_exec()`. You should always program defensively and review every API function (documented in Appendix B) before you use it to ensure that you deal with every possible error condition that can arise. There are about 23 different errors defined in the API. Only a fraction of them will really matter to your application in practice. All of the SQLite return codes are listed in Table 6-2. All of the API functions that can return them are listed as follows:

```
sqlite3_bind_xxx()
sqlite3_close()
sqlite3_create_collation()
sqlite3_collation_needed()
sqlite3_create_function()
sqlite3_prepare()
sqlite3_exec()
sqlite3_finalize()
sqlite3_get_table()
sqlite3_open()
sqlite3_reset()
sqlite3_step()
sqlite3_transfer_bindings()
```

You can get extended information on a given error using sqlite3_errmsg(), which is declared as follows:

```
const char *sqlite3_errmsg(sqlite3*);
```

It takes a connection handle as its only argument and returns the most recent error resulting from an API call on that connection. If no error has been encountered, it returns the string "not an error".

Table 6-2. *SQLite Return Codes*

Code	Description
SQLITE_OK	The operation was successful.
SQLITE_ERROR	General SQL error or missing database. It may be possible to obtain more error information depending on the error condition (SQLITE_SCHEMA, for example).
SQLITE_PERM	Access permission denied. Cannot read or write to the database file.
SQLITE_ABORT	A callback routine requested an abort.
SQLITE_BUSY	The database file is locked.
SQLITE_LOCKED	A table in the database is locked.
SQLITE_NOMEM	A call to malloc() has failed within a database operation.
SQLITE_READONLY	An attempt was made to write to a read-only database.
SQLITE_INTERRUPT	Operation was terminated by sqlite3_interrupt().
SQLITE_IOERR	Some kind of disk I/O error occurred.
SQLITE_CORRUPT	The database disk image is malformed. This will also occur if an attempt is made to open a non-SQLite database file as a SQLite database.
SQLITE_FULL	Insertion failed because the database is full. There is no more space on the file system or the database file cannot be expanded.

Table 6-2. *SQLite Return Codes*

Code	Description
SQLITE_CANTOPEN	SQLite was unable to open the database file.
SQLITE_PROTOCOL	The database is locked or there has been a protocol error.
SQLITE_EMPTY	(Internal only) The database table is empty.
SQLITE_SCHEMA	The database schema has changed.
SQLITE_CONSTRAINT	Abort due to constraint violation. This constant is returned if the SQL statement would have violated a database constraint (such as attempting to insert a value into a unique index that already exists in the index).
SQLITE_MISMATCH	Data type mismatch. An example of this is an attempt to insert non-integer data into a column labeled INTEGER PRIMARY KEY. For most columns, SQLite ignores the data type and allows any kind of data to be stored. But an INTEGER PRIMARY KEY column is only allowed to store integer data.
SQLITE_MISUSE	Library was used incorrectly. This error might occur if one or more of the SQLite API routines is used incorrectly. Examples of incorrect usage include calling sqlite3_exec() after the database has been closed using sqlite3_close() or calling sqlite3_exec() with the same database pointer simultaneously from two separate threads.
SQLITE_NOLFS	Uses OS features not supported on host. This value is returned if the SQLite library was compiled with large file support (LFS) enabled but LFS isn't supported on the host operating system.
SQLITE_AUTH	Authorization denied. This occurs when a callback function installed using sqlite3_set_authorizer() returns SQLITE_DENY.
SQLITE_ROW	sqlite3_step() has another row ready.
SQLITE_DONE	sqlite3_step() has finished executing.

While it is very uncommon outside of embedded systems, one of the most critical errors you can encounter is SQLITE_NOMEM, which means that no memory can be allocated on the heap (e.g., malloc() failed). Normally, after a single malloc() call fails, the SQLite library refuses to function (all major calls can return SQLITE_NOMEM). If the application is able to recover from an out-of-memory condition, it may still be possible to restore the state of the SQLite library using sqlite3_global_recover(), which is declared as follows:

```
int sqlite3_global_recover();
```

This function restores the library state so that it can be used again. You must finalize or reset all active statements (sqlite3_stmt pointers) before calling this function. Otherwise it will return SQLITE_BUSY. This function will also return SQLITE_ERROR if you are using any in-memory databases, either as a main or TEMP. (The TEMP database is where temporary data is stored—see ATTACH DATABASE in Appendix A for details.) In either case, SQLite will not reset the library and it will remain unusable.

■**Caution** sqlite3_global_recover() is not thread safe. Calling it from within a threaded application when threads other than the caller have used SQLite is dangerous and will almost certainly result in malfunctions. SQLite includes memory management functions specifically for threads. These are covered later in the section "Threads and Memory Management."

The sqlite3_global_recover() function is aimed at embedded applications where memory is scarcer than normal applications. It can be omitted from SQLite at compile time by defining the SQLITE_OMIT_GLOBALRECOVER preprocessor directive.

Handling Busy Conditions

Two important functions related to processing queries are sqlite3_busy_handler() and sqlite3_busy_timeout(). If your program uses a database on which there are other active connections, odds are it will eventually have to wait for a lock, and therefore will have to deal with SQLITE_BUSY. Whenever you call an API function that causes SQLite to seek a lock and SQLite is unable to get it, the function will return SQLITE_BUSY. There are three ways to deal with this:

- Handle SQLITE_BUSY yourself, either by rerunning the statement or taking some other action.
- Have SQLite call a busy handler.
- Ask SQLite to wait (block or sleep) for some period of time for the lock to clear.

The last option involves using sqlite3_busy_timeout(). This function tells SQLite how long to wait for a lock to clear before returning SQLITE_BUSY. While it can ultimately result in you still having to handle SQLITE_BUSY, in practice setting this value to a sufficient period of time (say 30 seconds) usually provides enough time for even the most intensive transaction to complete. Nevertheless, you should still have some contingency plan in place to handle SQLITE_BUSY.

User-Defined Busy Handlers

The second option entails using sqlite3_busy_handler(). This function provides a way to call a user-defined function rather than blocking or returning SQLITE_BUSY right away. It's declared as follows:

```
int sqlite3_busy_handler(sqlite3*, int(*)(void*,int), void*);
```

The second argument is a pointer to a function to be called as the busy handler, and the third argument is a pointer to application-specific data to be passed as the first argument to the handler. The second argument to the busy handler is the number of prior calls made to the handler for the same lock.

Such a handler might call sleep() for a period to wait out the lock, or it may send some kind of notification. It may do whatever you like, as it is yours to implement. Be warned, though, that registering a busy handler does not guarantee that it will always be called. As mentioned in Chapter 5, SQLite will forego calling a busy handler for a connection if it perceives a deadlock might result. Specifically, if your connection in SHARED is interfering with another connection in

RESERVED, SQLite will not invoke your busy handler, hoping you will take the hint. In this case, you are trying to write to the database from SHARED (starting the transaction with BEGIN) when you really should be starting from RESERVED (starting the transaction with BEGIN IMMEDIATE).

The only restriction on busy handlers is that they may not close the database. Closing the database from within a busy handler can delete critical data structures out from under the executing query and result in crashing your program.

Advice

All things considered, the best route may be to set the timeout to a reasonable value and then take some precaution if and when you receive a SQLITE_BUSY value. In general, if you are going to write to the database, start in RESERVED. If you don't do this, then the next best thing is to install a busy handler, set the timeout to a known value, and if SQLite returns SQLITE_BUSY, check the response time. If the time is less than the busy handler's delay, then SQLite is telling you that your query (and connection) is preventing a writer from proceeding. If you want to write to the database at this point, you should finalize or reset, then reexecute the statement, this time starting with BEGIN IMMEDIATE.

Handling Schema Changes

Whenever a connection changes the database schema, all other prepared statements that were compiled before the change are invalidated. The result is that the first call to sqlite3_step() for such statements returns SQLITE_ERROR. From a locking standpoint, the schema change occurs between the time a reader calls sqlite3_prepare() to compile a statement and calling sqlite3_step() to execute it.

When this happens, the only course of action for you is to finalize or reset the query and start over. However, you must confirm that the error is in fact due to a schema change. To do so, whenever sqlite3_step() returns SQLITE_ERROR, you should call sqlite3_reset() to see if it returns SQLITE_SCHEMA. Another way to check for this condition is to call sqlite3_expired(), which takes the statement handle as its only argument.

Note It's important that you understand that when a schema change occurs, sqlite3_step() *never* returns SQLITE_SCHEMA directly. It always returns SQLITE_ERROR. You then have to call sqlite3_finalize(), sqlite3_reset(), or sqlite3_expired() to determine if the error was due to SQLITE_SCHEMA. You should always check for this condition whenever you use sqlite3_step().

Several events can cause SQLITE_SCHEMA errors:

- Detaching databases

- Modifying or installing user-defined functions or aggregates

- Modifying or installing user-defined collations

- Modifying or installing authorization functions

- Vacuuming the database

The reason the SQLITE_SCHEMA condition exists ultimately relates to the VDBE. When a connection changes the schema, other compiled queries may have VDBE code that points to database objects that no longer exist, or are in a different location in the database. Rather than running the risk of a bizarre runtime error later, SQLite invalidates all statements that have been compiled but not executed. They must be recompiled.

SQLITE_SCHEMA can only occur on the first call to sqlite3_step(). This is because sqlite3_step(), when successful, always gets a lock on the database. Once you have a lock on the database, it is impossible for any other connection to write to or alter the database. So if the first call is successful, you are guaranteed that all subsequent calls to sqlite3_step() will *not* encounter SQLITE_SCHEMA. One possible way provided by the SQLite FAQ to handle SQLITE_SCHEMA is shown in Listing 6-8.

Listing 6-8. *Handling SQLITE_SCHEMA*

```
int rc;
sqlite3_stmt *pStmt;
char zSql[] = "SELECT .....";

do {
  /* Compile the statement from SQL. Assume success. */
  sqlite3_prepare(pDb, zSql, -1, &pStmt, 0);

  while( SQLITE_ROW==sqlite3_step(pStmt) ) {
      /* Do something with the row of available data */
  }

  /* Finalize the statement. If a SQLITE_SCHEMA error has
  ** occurred, then the above call to sqlite3_step() will have
  ** returned SQLITE_ERROR. sqlite3_finalize() will return
  ** SQLITE_SCHEMA. In this case the loop will execute again.
  */
  rc = sqlite3_finalize(pStmt);
} while( rc==SQLITE_SCHEMA );
```

A possible variation is to take into consideration bound parameters. These parameters can be automatically transferred to the new compiled query using sqlite3_transfer_bindings(), as shown in Listing 6-9.

Listing 6-9. *Handling SQLITE_SCHEMA with sqlite3_transfer_bindings()*

```
int rc, processed, skip;
sqlite3_stmt *pStmt = NULL;
sqlite3_stmt *plastStmt = NULL;
char zSql[] = "SELECT .....";

do {
    sqlite3_prepare(pDb, zSql, -1, &pStmt, 0);
```

```
    /* If there was a lastStmt, transfer bindings from it */
    if(plastStmt != NULL){
            sqlite3_transfer_bindings(plastStmt, pStmt);
    }

    /* Keep track of the current stmt */
    plastStmt = pStmt;

    while( SQLITE_ROW==sqlite3_step(pStmt) ) {
        /* Do something with the row of available data */
        processed++;
    }

    rc = sqlite3_finalize(pStmt);

} while( rc==SQLITE_SCHEMA );
```

Another option for checking for SQLITE_SCHEMA without finalizing (destroying) the query is to call sqlite3_reset() instead of sqlite3_finalize(). This will provide you with the SQLITE_SCHEMA error if it exists. However, if the error is not schema related, you avoid the cost of having to recompile the query since sqlite3_reset() leaves the query in a state where it can still be executed.

TRACING SQL

If you are having a hard time figuring out exactly what your program is doing with the database, you can track what SQL statements it has executed using sqlite3_trace(). Its declaration is as follows:

```
void *sqlite3_trace(sqlite3*, void(*xTrace)(void*,const char*), void*);
```

This function is analogous to putting a wiretap on a connection. You can use it to generate a log file of all SQL executed on a given connection as well provide helpful debugging information. Every SQL statement that is processed is passed to the callback function specified in the second argument. SQLite passes the data provided in the third argument of sqlite3_trace() to the first argument of the callback function.

Operational Control

The API provides several functions you can use to monitor and/or manage SQL commands at compile time and runtime. These functions allow you to install callback functions with which to monitor and control various database events as they happen.

Commit Hooks

The sqlite3_commit_hook() function allows you to monitor when transactions commit on a given connection. It is declared as follows:

```
void *sqlite3_commit_hook( sqlite3 *cnx,                /* database handle   */
                           int(*xCallback)(void *data), /* callback function */
                           void *data);                 /* application data  */
```

This function registers the callback function xCallback, which will be invoked whenever a transaction commits on the connection given by cnx. The third argument (data) is a pointer to application-specific data, which SQLite passes to the callback function. If the callback function returns a non-zero value, then the commit is converted into a rollback.

Passing a NULL value in for the callback function effectively disables the currently registered callback (if any). Also, only one callback can be registered at a time for a given connection. The return value for sqlite3_commit_hook() is NULL unless another callback function was previously registered, in which case the previous data value is returned.

■**Note** The sqlite3_commit_hook() function is currently marked as experimental and is therefore subject to change. However, according SQLite's author, this is extremely unlikely as this function has been in the API for some time now.

Rollback Hooks

Rollback hooks are similar to commit hooks except that they watch for rollbacks for a given connection. Rollback hooks are registered with the following function:

```
void *sqlite3_rollback_hook(sqlite3 *cnx, void(*xCallback)(void *data), void *data);
```

This function registers the callback function xCallback, which will be invoked in the event of a rollback on cnx, whether by an explicit ROLLBACK command or an implicit error or constraint violation. The callback is *not* invoked if a transaction is automatically rolled back due to the database connection being closed. The third argument (data) is a pointer to application-specific data, which SQLite passes to the callback function.

As in sqlite3_commit_hook(), each time you call sqlite3_rollback_hook(), the new callback function you provide will replace any currently registered callback function. If a callback function was previously registered, sqlite3_rollback_hook() returns the previous data argument.

Update Hooks

The sqlite3_update_hook() is used to monitor all UPDATE, INSERT, and DELETE operations on rows for a given database connection. It has the following form:

```
void *sqlite3_update_hook(
  sqlite3 *cnx,
  void(*)(void *, int, char const*, char const*, sqlite_int64),
  void *data);
```

The first argument of the callback function is a pointer to application-specific data, which you provide in the third argument. The callback function has the following form:

```
void callback ( void * data,
                int operation_code,
                char const *db_name,
                char const *table_name,
                sqlite_int64 rowid),
```

The operation_code argument corresponds to SQLITE_INSERT, SQLITE_UPDATE, and SQLITE_DELETE for INSERT, UPDATE, and DELETE operations, respectively. The third and fourth arguments correspond to the database name and table name the operation took place on. The final argument is the ROWID of the affected row. The callback is not invoked for operations on system tables (e.g., sqlite_master and sqlite_sequence). The return value is a pointer to the previously registered callback function's data argument, if it exists.

Authorizer Functions

Perhaps the most powerful event filter is sqlite3_set_authorizer(). It allows you to monitor and control queries as they are compiled. This function is declared as follows:

```
int sqlite3_set_authorizer(
  sqlite3*,
  int (*xAuth)( void*,int,
                const char*, const char*,
                const char*,const char*),
  void *pUserData
);
```

This routine registers a callback function that serves as an authorization function. SQLite will invoke the callback function at statement compile time (not at execution time) for various database events. The intent of the function is to allow applications to safely execute user-supplied SQL. It provides a way to restrict such SQL from certain operations (e.g., anything that changes the database) or to deny access to specific tables or columns within the database.

For clarity, the form of the authorization callback function is as follows:

```
int auth( void*,        /* user data      */
          int,          /* event code     */
          const char*,  /* event specific */
          const char*,  /* event specific */
          const char*,  /* database name  */
          const char*   /* trigger or view name */ );
```

The first argument is a pointer to application-specific data, which is passed in on the fourth argument of sqlite3_set_authorizer(). The second argument to the authorization function will be one of the defined constants listed in Table 6-3. These values signify what kind of operation is to be authorized. The third and fourth arguments to the authorization function are specific to the event code. These arguments are listed with their respective event codes in Table 6-3.

The fifth argument is the name of the database ("main", "temp", etc.) if applicable. The sixth argument is the name of the innermost trigger or view that is responsible for the access attempt or NULL if this access attempt is directly from top-level SQL.

The return value of the authorization function should be one of the constants SQLITE_OK, SQLITE_DENY, or SQLITE_IGNORE. The meaning of the first two values is consistent for all events—permit or deny the SQL statement. SQLITE_DENY will abort the entire SQL statement and generate an error.

The meaning of SQLITE_IGNORE is specific to the event in question. Statements that read or modify records generate SQLITE_READ or SQLITE_UPDATE events for each column the statement attempts to operate on. In this case, if the callback returns SQLITE_IGNORE, the column in question will be excluded from the operation. Specifically, attempts to read data from this column yield only NULL values, and attempts to update it will silently fail.

Table 6-3. *SQLite Authorization Events*

Event Code	Argument 3	Argument 4
SQLITE_CREATE_INDEX	Index name	Table name
SQLITE_CREATE_TABLE	Table name	NULL
SQLITE_CREATE_TEMP_INDEX	Index name	Table name
SQLITE_CREATE_TEMP_TABLE	Table name	NULL
SQLITE_CREATE_TEMP_TRIGGER	Trigger name	Table name
SQLITE_CREATE_TEMP_VIEW	View name	NULL
SQLITE_CREATE_TRIGGER	Trigger name	Table name
SQLITE_CREATE_VIEW	View name	NULL
SQLITE_DELETE	Table name	NULL
SQLITE_DROP_INDEX	Index name	Table name
SQLITE_DROP_TABLE	Table name	NULL
SQLITE_DROP_TEMP_INDEX	Index name	Table name
SQLITE_DROP_TEMP_TABLE	Table name	NULL
SQLITE_DROP_TEMP_TRIGGER	Trigger name	Table name
SQLITE_DROP_TEMP_VIEW	View name	NULL
SQLITE_DROP_TRIGGER	Trigger name	Table name
SQLITE_DROP_VIEW	View name	NULL
SQLITE_INSERT	Table name	NULL
SQLITE_PRAGMA	Pragma name	First argument or NULL
SQLITE_READ	Table name	Column name
SQLITE_SELECT	NULL	NULL
SQLITE_TRANSACTION	NULL	NULL
SQLITE_UPDATE	Table name	Column name
SQLITE_ATTACH	Filename	NULL
SQLITE_DETACH	Database name	NULL

To illustrate this, the following example (the complete source of which is in `authorizer.c`) will create a table `foo`, defined as follows:

```
create table foo(x int, y int, z int)
```

It registers an authorizer function, which will

- Block reads of column z

- Block updates to column x

- Monitor ATTACH and DETACH database events

- Log database events as they happen

This is a rather long example, which uses the authorizer function to filter many different database events, so for clarity I am going to break the code into pieces. The authorizer function has the general form shown in Listing 6-10.

Listing 6-10. *Example Authorizer Function*

```
int auth( void* x, int type,
          const char* a, const char* b,
          const char* c, const char* d )
{
    const char* operation = a;

    printf( "    %s ", event_description(type));

    /* Filter for different database events
    ** from SQLITE_TRANSACTION to SQLITE_INSERT,
    ** UPDATE, DELETE, ATTACH, etc. and either allow or deny
    ** them.
    */

    return SQLITE_OK;
}
```

The first thing the authorizer looks for is a change in transaction state. If it finds a change, it prints a message:

```
    if((a != NULL) && (type == SQLITE_TRANSACTION)) {
        printf(": %s Transaction", operation);
    }
```

Next the authorizer filters events that result in a schema change:

```
    switch(type) {
        case SQLITE_CREATE_INDEX:
        case SQLITE_CREATE_TABLE:
        case SQLITE_CREATE_TRIGGER:
        case SQLITE_CREATE_VIEW:
```

```
case SQLITE_DROP_INDEX:
case SQLITE_DROP_TABLE:
case SQLITE_DROP_TRIGGER:
case SQLITE_DROP_VIEW:
{
    // Schema has been modified somehow.
    printf(": Schema modified");
}
```

The next filter looks for read attempts (which are fired on a column-by-column basis). Here, all read attempts are allowed unless the column name is z, in which case the function returns SQLITE_IGNORE. This will cause SQLite to return NULL for any field in column z, effectively blocking access to its data.

```
if(type == SQLITE_READ) {
    printf(": Read of %s.%s ", a, b);

    /* Block attempts to read column z */
    if(strcmp(b,"z")==0) {
        printf("-> DENIED\n");
        return SQLITE_IGNORE;
    }
}
```

Next come INSERT and UPDATE filters. All INSERT statements are allowed. However, UPDATE statements that attempt to modify column x are denied. This will *not* block the UPDATE statement from executing; rather, it will simply filter out any attempt to update column x.

```
if(type == SQLITE_INSERT) {
    printf(": Insert records into %s ", a);
}

if(type == SQLITE_UPDATE) {
    printf(": Update of %s.%s ", a, b);

    /* Block updates of column x */
    if(strcmp(b,"x")==0) {
        printf("-> DENIED\n");
        return SQLITE_IGNORE;
    }
}
```

Finally, the authorizer filters DELETE, ATTACH, and DETACH statements and simply issues notifications when it encounters them:

```
if(type == SQLITE_DELETE) {
    printf(": Delete from %s ", a);
}
```

```
    if(type == SQLITE_ATTACH) {
        printf(": %s", a);
    }

    if(type == SQLITE_DETACH) {
        printf("-> %s", a);
    }

    printf("\n");
    return SQLITE_OK;
}
```

The (abbreviated) program is implemented as follows. As with the authorizer function, I will break it into pieces. The first part of the program connects to the database and registers the authorization function:

```
int main(int argc, char **argv)
{
    sqlite3 *db, *db2;
    char *zErr, *sql;
    int rc;

    /**  Setup */

    /* Connect to test.db */
    rc = sqlite3_open("test.db", &db);

    /**  Authorize and test

    /* 1. Register the authorizer function */
    sqlite3_set_authorizer(db, auth, NULL);
```

Step 2 illustrates the transaction filter:

```
    /* 2. Test transactions events */

    printf("program : Starting transaction\n");
    sqlite3_exec(db, "BEGIN", NULL, NULL, &zErr);

    printf("program : Committing transaction\n");
    sqlite3_exec(db, "COMMIT", NULL, NULL, &zErr);
```

Step 3 tests schema modifications by creating the test table foo:

```
    /* 3. Test table events */

    printf("program : Creating table\n");
    sqlite3_exec(db, "create table foo(x int, y int, z int)", NULL, NULL, &zErr);
```

Step 4 tests read (SELECT) and write (INSERT / UPDATE) control. It inserts a test record, selects it, updates it, and selects it again to observe the results of the UPDATE.

```
/* 4. Test read/write access */
printf("program : Inserting record\n");
sqlite3_exec(db, "insert into foo values (1,2,3)", NULL, NULL, &zErr);

printf("program : Selecting record (value for z should be NULL)\n");
print_sql_result(db, "select * from foo");

printf("program : Updating record (update of x should be denied)\n");
sqlite3_exec(db, "update foo set x=4, y=5, z=6", NULL, NULL, &zErr);

printf("program : Selecting record (notice x was not updated)\n");
print_sql_result (db, "select * from foo");

printf("program : Deleting record\n");
sqlite3_exec(db, "delete from foo", NULL, NULL, &zErr);

printf("program : Dropping table\n");
sqlite3_exec(db, "drop table foo", NULL, NULL, &zErr);
```

Several things are going on here. The program selects all records in the table, one of which is column z. We should see in the output that column z's value is NULL. All other fields should contain data from the table. Next, the program attempts to update all fields, the most important of which is column x. The update should succeed, but the value in column x should be unchanged, as the authorizer denies it. This is confirmed on the following SELECT statement, which shows that all columns were updated except for column x, which is unchanged. The program then drops the foo table, which should issue a schema change notification from the previous filter.

Step 5 tests the ATTACH and DETACH database commands. The thing to notice here is how the authorizer function is provided with the name of the database and that you can distinguish the operations being performed under the attached database as opposed to the main database.

```
/* 5. Test ATTACH/DETACH */

/* Connect to test2.db */
rc = sqlite3_open("test2.db", &db2);

if(rc) {
    fprintf(stderr, "Can't open database: %s\n", sqlite3_errmsg(db2));
    sqlite3_close(db2);
    exit(1);
 }

sqlite3_exec(db2, "drop table foo2", NULL, NULL, &zErr);
sqlite3_exec(db2, "create table foo2(x int, y int, z int)",
                   NULL, NULL, &zErr);

printf("program : Attaching database test2.db\n");
sqlite3_exec(db, "attach 'test2.db' as test2", NULL, NULL, &zErr);
```

```
    printf("program : Selecting record from attached database test2.db\n");
    sqlite3_exec(db, "select * from foo2", NULL, NULL, &zErr);

    printf("program : Detaching table\n");
    sqlite3_exec(db, "detach test2", NULL, NULL, &zErr);
```

Again for clarity, I will break up the program output into pieces. Upon executing it, the first thing we see is the transaction filter catching changes in transaction state:

```
program : Starting transaction
    SQLITE_TRANSACTION : BEGIN Transaction
program : Committing transaction
    SQLITE_TRANSACTION : COMMIT Transaction
program : Starting transaction
    SQLITE_TRANSACTION : BEGIN Transaction
program : Aborting transaction
    SQLITE_TRANSACTION : ROLLBACK Transaction
```

Next we see a schema change notification as the result of creating the test table foo. The interesting thing to notice here is all the other events that transpire in the sqlite_master table as a result of creating the table:

```
program : Creating table
    SQLITE_INSERT : Insert records into sqlite_master
    SQLITE_CREATE_TABLE : Schema modified
    SQLITE_READ : Read of sqlite_master.name
    SQLITE_READ : Read of sqlite_master.rootpage
    SQLITE_READ : Read of sqlite_master.sql
    SQLITE_UPDATE : Update of sqlite_master.type
    SQLITE_UPDATE : Update of sqlite_master.name
    SQLITE_UPDATE : Update of sqlite_master.tbl_name
    SQLITE_UPDATE : Update of sqlite_master.rootpage
    SQLITE_UPDATE : Update of sqlite_master.sql
    SQLITE_READ : Read of sqlite_master.ROWID
    SQLITE_READ : Read of sqlite_master.name
    SQLITE_READ : Read of sqlite_master.rootpage
    SQLITE_READ : Read of sqlite_master.sql
    SQLITE_READ : Read of sqlite_master.tbl_name
```

Next the program inserts a record, which the authorizer detects:

```
program : Inserting record
    SQLITE_INSERT : Insert records into foo
```

Now here is where things get more interesting. We are going to be able to see the authorizer block access to individual columns. The program selects all records from the foo table. We see the SQLITE_SELECT event take place, followed by the subsequent SQLITE_READ events generated for each attempted access of each column in the SELECT statement. When it comes to column z, the authorizer denies access. Immediately following that, SQLite executes the statement and print_sql_result() prints the column information and rows for the result set:

```
program : Selecting record (value for z should be NULL)
    SQLITE_SELECT
    SQLITE_READ : Read of foo.x
    SQLITE_READ : Read of foo.y
    SQLITE_READ : Read of foo.z -> DENIED
  Column: x (1/int)
  Column: y (1/int)
  Column: z (5/(null))
  Record: '1' '2' '(null)'
```

Look at what goes on with column z. Its value is NULL, which confirms that the authorizer blocked access. But also look at the column information. While SQLite revealed the storage class of column z, it denied access to its declared type in the schema.

Next comes the update. Here we are interested in column x. The UPDATE statement will attempt to change every value in the record. But update of column x will be denied:

```
program : Updating record (update of x should be denied)
    SQLITE_UPDATE : Update of foo.x -> DENIED
    SQLITE_UPDATE : Update of foo.y
    SQLITE_UPDATE : Update of foo.z
```

To confirm this, the program then selects the record to show what happened. The UPDATE did execute, but column x was not changed. Even more interestingly, while z was updated (trust me, it was), the authorizer will not let us see its value:

```
program : Selecting record (notice x was not updated)
    SQLITE_SELECT
    SQLITE_READ : Read of foo.x
    SQLITE_READ : Read of foo.y
    SQLITE_READ : Read of foo.z -> DENIED
  Column: x (1/int)
  Column: y (1/int)
  Column: z (5/(null))
  Record: '1' '5' '(null)'
```

Next the program deletes the record and drops the table. The latter operation generates all sorts of events on the sqlite_master table, just as when the table was created:

```
program : Deleting record
    SQLITE_DELETE : Delete from foo
program : Dropping table
    SQLITE_DELETE : Delete from sqlite_master
    SQLITE_DROP_TABLE : Schema modified
    SQLITE_DELETE : Delete from foo
    SQLITE_DELETE : Delete from sqlite_master
    SQLITE_READ : Read of sqlite_master.tbl_name
    SQLITE_READ : Read of sqlite_master.type
    SQLITE_UPDATE : Update of sqlite_master.rootpage
    SQLITE_READ : Read of sqlite_master.rootpage
```

Finally, the program creates another database on a separate connection and then attaches it on the main connection. The main connection then selects records from a table in the attached database, and we can see how the authorizer reports these operations as happening in the attached database:

```
program : Attaching database test2.db
    SQLITE_ATTACH : test2.db
    SQLITE_READ : Read of sqlite_master.name
    SQLITE_READ : Read of sqlite_master.rootpage
    SQLITE_READ : Read of sqlite_master.sql
program : Selecting record from attached database test2.db
    SQLITE_SELECT
    SQLITE_READ : Read of foo2.x
    SQLITE_READ : Read of foo2.y
    SQLITE_READ : Read of foo2.z -> DENIED
program : Detaching table
    SQLITE_DETACH -> test2
```

As you can see, sqlite3_set_authorizer() and its event-filtering capabilities are quite powerful. It gives you a great deal of control over what the user can and cannot do on a given database. You can monitor events and, if you wish, stop them before they happen. Or, you can allow them to proceed, but impose specific restrictions on them. sqlite3_set_authorizer() can be a helpful tool for dealing with SQLITE_SCHEMA conditions. If you know you don't need any changes to your database schema in your application, you can simply install an authorizer function to deny any operations that attempt to modify the schema in certain ways.

■**Caution** Keep in mind that denying schema changes in an authorizer is by no means a cure-all for SQLITE_SCHEMA events. You need to be careful about all of the implications of denying various changes to the schema. Just blindly blocking all events resulting in a schema change can restrict other seemingly legitimate operations such as VACUUM.

HELP FOR INTERACTIVE PROGRAMS

SQLite provides two functions that make it easier to work with interactive programs. The first is
`sqlite3_interrupt()`, which is declared as follows:

```
void sqlite3_interrupt(sqlite3* /* connection handle */);
```

   `sqlite3_interrupt()` causes any pending database operation on the given connection to abort and
return at its earliest opportunity. This routine is design to be called in response to a user interrupt action such
as clicking a Cancel button in a graphical application or pressing Ctrl+C in a command-line program. It is
intended to make it easier to accommodate cases where the user wants a long query operation to halt immediately. For a command-line program, you might put this function in a signal handler, or an event handler in a
graphical application.
   Another function that can be useful for interactive programs is `sqlite3_progress_handler()`. It is
somewhat related in functionality to the `sqlite3_interrupt()` function, but with a few twists. It is declared
as follows:

```
void sqlite3_progress_handler( sqlite3*,       /* connection handle   */
                               int frq,        /* frequency of callback */
                               int(*)(void*),  /* callback function   */
                               void*);         /* application data    */
```

   This function installs a callback function that will be invoked during calls to `sqlite3_exec()`,
`sqlite3_step()`, and `sqlite3_get_table()`. The intent of this function is to give applications a way to
provide feedback to the user during long-running queries.
   The second argument (`frq`) specifies the frequency of the callback in terms of VDBE instructions. That
is, the progress callback (provided in the third argument) will be called for every `frq` VDBE instruction performed
in query execution. If a call to `sqlite3_exec()`, `sqlite3_step()`, or `sqlite3_get_table()` requires
less than `frq` instructions to be executed, then the progress callback will not be invoked. The fourth argument
is a pointer to application-specific data, which is passed back to the progress handler (as its one and only
argument). If `NULL` is provided for the callback function argument, then the currently installed progress handler
(if any) is disabled.
   If the progress callback returns a non-zero value, the current query will be immediately terminated and
any database changes rolled back. If the query was part of a larger transaction, then the transaction is *not*
rolled back and remains active. The `sqlite3_exec()` call in that case will return `SQLITE_ABORT`.

Threads

There are a few basic rules to follow when using SQLite in a multithreaded environment. The
first thing to be aware of, as mentioned in Chapter 2, is that you have compiled SQLite with
thread support.
   Before SQLite version 3.3.1, the general rule of thumb for using SQLite with threads was
that a connection handle (`sqlite3` structure) can only be created, used, and destroyed within a
given thread. It could not be safely passed around to other threads. This seems to be due mainly
to limitations in specific thread implementations of some operating systems. Starting with
3.3.1, you can pass connections around between threads as long as they are in the UNLOCKED
state at the time of the transfer (the connection has no transaction open).

One other limitation that is somewhat thread-related pertains to the fork() system call on Unix. You should never try to pass a connection across a fork() call to a child process. It will not work correctly.

Shared Cache Mode

Starting with SQLite version 3.3.0, SQLite supports something called *shared cache mode*, which allows multiple connections in a single thread to use a common page cache, as shown in Figure 6-3. This feature is designed for embedded servers where a single thread can efficiently manage multiple database connections on behalf of other threads. The connections in this case share a single page cache as well as a different concurrency model. Because of the shared cache, the server thread can operate with significantly lower memory usage and better concurrency than if each thread were to manage its own connection. Normally, each connection allocates enough memory to hold 2,000 pages in the page cache. Rather than each thread consuming that much memory with its own connection, it shares that memory with other threads using a single page cache.

In this model, threads rely on a server thread to manage their database connections for them. A thread sends SQL statements to the server through some communication mechanism; the server executes them using the thread's assigned connection, and then sends the results back. The thread can still issue commands and control its own transactions; only its actual connection exists in, and is managed by, another thread.

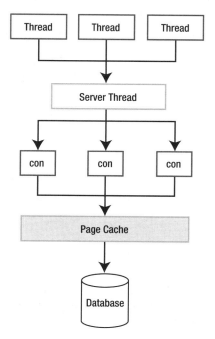

Figure 6-3. *The shared cache model*

Connections in shared cache mode use a different concurrency model and isolation level. Connections in a shared cache are strictly limited to the thread that created them. They cannot be passed around to other threads like normal connections can. Furthermore, connections in a shared cache can see what their kindred connections have changed. That is, there can be both multiple readers and an active writer in the database at the same time. That writer can write to the database—performing complete write transactions—without having to wait for other readers to clear. Therefore, data can change in the database within a reader's transaction. While SQLite normally runs in a serialized isolation level, meaning that readers and writers always see a consistent view of the database, in shared cache mode, readers are subject to the database changing underneath them.

There are some control measures in place to keep connections out of one another's way. By default, shared cache mode uses *table locks* to keep reader connections and writer connections separated. Table locks are not the same as database locks, and exist only within connections of the shared cache. Whenever a connection reads a table, SQLite first tries to get a read lock on it. The same is true for writing to a table. A connection may not write to a table that another connection has a read lock on, and vice versa. Furthermore, table locks are tied to their respective connection and last for the duration of its transaction.

A Practical Example

To make all this clear, let's go through an example. Say we have two threads, Thread A and Thread B. These threads communicate with a server thread, which we will represent as the program thread. Consider the first part of program in Listing 6-11, which represents the server thread starting up.

Listing 6-11. *Shared Cache Mode Example*

```
int main(int argc, char **argv)
{
    int rc, i, ncols;
    sqlite3 *db1;
    sqlite3 *db2;
    sqlite3_stmt *stmt;
    sqlite3_stmt *stmt2;
    char *sql;
    char *zErr;
    const char *tail;

    /* Enable shared cache mode */
    sqlite3_enable_shared_cache(1);
```

It's that simple. This program starts up and goes into shared cache mode by calling sqlite3_enable_shared_cache(). This function takes a single integer argument where 0 turns shared cache mode off for the thread, and any non-zero argument turns it on.

Next it simulates receiving a request from Thread A, which wants to connect to the database, query the episodes table, and put a cursor on the first row. This will get both a SHARED lock on the database and a table lock on episodes. The code for this step is shown in Listing 6-12.

Listing 6-12. *Thread A Initial Request*

```
sqlite3_open("foods.db", &db1);
sqlite3_exec(db1, "BEGIN", NULL, NULL, &zErr);
fprintf(stderr, "Thread A: Connected\n");
fprintf(stderr, "Thread A: BEGIN TRANSACTION\n");

sql = "select * from episodes;";
rc = sqlite3_prepare(db1, sql, strlen(sql), &stmt, &tail);
rc = sqlite3_step(stmt);

/* Send row back to A and wait for further instructions */
fprintf(stderr, "Thread A: SHARED lock on database, table lock on episodes\n");
```

The server thread connects to the database, manually starts a transaction, runs a SELECT on episodes, sits on the first record, and then pretends to send the first row back to Thread A.

Next, Thread B's request comes in. It tries to delete any rows in foods by the name of 'Whataburger'. Next, it tries to insert a row with the name of 'Whataburger'. After that, in order to illustrate table locks, it tries to insert a 'Whataburger' row into episodes, which shouldn't work. It then closes its connection and exits. The code for this step is listed in Listing 6-13.

Listing 6-13. *Thread B Modifying the Database*

```
/* Request comes in from Thread B. Modify the foods table in auto-commit. */
sqlite3_open("foods.db", &db2);
fprintf(stderr, "Thread B: Connected\n");

sql = "delete from foods where name='Whataburger'";
rc = sqlite3_exec(db2, sql, NULL, NULL, &zErr);

if(rc != SQLITE_OK) {
    if (zErr != NULL) {
        fprintf(stderr, "Thread B: SQL error: %s\n", zErr);
        sqlite3_free(zErr);
    }
}
else {
    fprintf(stderr, "Thread B: TRANSACTION: ");
    fprintf(stderr, "Deleted any Whataburger rows from foods\n");
}
```

```
sql = "insert into foods values (NULL, 12, 'Whataburger')";
rc = sqlite3_exec(db2, sql, NULL, NULL, &zErr);

if(rc != SQLITE_OK) {
    if (zErr != NULL) {
        fprintf(stderr, "Thread B: SQL error: %s\n", zErr);
        sqlite3_free(zErr);
    }
}
else {
    fprintf(stderr, "Thread B: TRANSACTION: ");
    fprintf(stderr, "Inserted Whataburger row into foods\n");
}

/* Try to insert a record into episodes.
** This should not work b/c of Thread A's table lock. */
fprintf(stderr, "Thread B: Trying to insert Whataburger row into episodes\n");
sql = "insert into episodes values (NULL, 12, 'Whataburger')";
rc = sqlite3_exec(db2, sql, NULL, NULL, &zErr);

if(rc != SQLITE_OK) {
    if (zErr != NULL) {
        fprintf(stderr, "Thread B: SQL error: %s\n", zErr);
        sqlite3_free(zErr);
    }
}
else {
    fprintf(stderr, "Thread B: Inserted Whataburger row into episodes\n");
}

sqlite3_close(db2);
fprintf(stderr, "Thread B: Disconnected\n");
```

Finally, Thread A finalizes its initial statement and searches for the row that Thread B inserted into foods. The code for this step is shown in Listing 6-14.

Listing 6-14. *Thread A Reading Thread B's Modifications*

```
/* Close the last statement and look for Thread B's row. */
sqlite3_finalize(stmt);

fprintf(stderr, "Thread A: Querying foods for Whataburger record\n");
sql = "select id as foo, type_id, name from foods where name='Whataburger'";
rc = sqlite3_prepare(db1, sql, strlen(sql), &stmt, &tail);
rc = sqlite3_step(stmt);
ncols = sqlite3_column_count(stmt);
```

```
    fprintf(stderr, "Thread A: Results: ");
    for(i=0; i < ncols; i++) {
        fprintf(stderr, "'%s' ", sqlite3_column_origin_name(stmt, i));
        fprintf(stderr, "'%s' ", sqlite3_column_text(stmt, i));
    }
    fprintf(stderr, "\n", ncols);

    sqlite3_finalize(stmt);

    rc = sqlite3_exec(db1, "COMMIT", NULL, NULL, &zErr);
    fprintf(stderr, "Thread A: COMMIT\n");
    sqlite3_close(db1);
    fprintf(stderr, "Thread A: Exiting\n", ncols);
```

Running the program produces the following results:

```
Thread A: Connected
Thread A: BEGIN TRANSACTION
Thread A: SHARED lock on database, table lock on episodes
Thread B: Connected
Thread B: TRANSACTION: Deleted any Whataburger rows from foods
Thread B: TRANSACTION: Inserted Whataburger row into foods
Thread B: Trying to insert Whataburger row into episodes
Thread B: SQL error: database table is locked: episodes
Thread B: Disconnected
Thread A: Querying foods for Whataburger record
Thread A: Results: 'id' '413' 'type_id' '12' 'name' 'Whataburger'
Thread A: COMMIT
Thread A: Exiting
```

So what happened? In shared cache mode, both threads worked concurrently in the same database. Thread A got a table lock on episodes, and a SHARED lock on the database. Thread B came along and modified foods. It did two full write transactions—DELETE and INSERT—on foods in autocommit mode, each of which went all the way from UNLOCKED to EXCLUSIVE and back to UNLOCKED. When each transaction completed, its associated table lock on foods was released. Thread B couldn't modify episodes, however, because of Thread A's table lock. After Thread B exited, Thread A could read from foods and see Thread B's changes from within the same transaction.

Read Uncommitted Isolation Level

While table locks help keep connections in shared cache mode out of one another's way, it is possible for connections to elect not to be in the way at all. That is, a connection can choose to have a *read-uncommitted* isolation level by using the read_uncommitted pragma. If it is set to true, then the connection will not put read locks on the tables it reads. Therefore, another writer can actually change a table as the connection reads it. While this can lead to inconsistent query results, it also means that a connection in read-uncommitted mode can neither block nor be blocked by any other connections.

It would be easy to modify the previous example to illustrate this kind of behavior. I will simply paraphrase it; you can code it if you want to. In this case, Thread A would go into read-committed isolation level, do a SELECT..ORDER BY id, and hold a cursor on the first row of the result set. Then Thread B would delete the second row of episodes (id=2). Then you have Thread A position its cursor to the next row and see that it is in fact is the third row in episodes and not the second.

SCHEMA CHANGES IN SHARED CACHE MODE

There are additional things to consider in shared cache mode when a thread wants to modify the database schema. As it turns out, before SQLite issues a table lock, it first gets a read table lock on the sqlite_master table. In order for a thread to alter the schema, it must first get a write table lock on sqlite_master. It can only do this if there are no read locks on it from other tables. When a thread does get a write lock on sqlite_master, then no other threads are allowed to compile SQL statements during that time. They will get SQLITE_SCHEMA errors.

Threads and Memory Management

Since shared cache mode is about conserving memory, SQLite has several functions associated with threads and memory management. They allow you to specify an advisory heap limit—a soft heap limit—as well as manually initiate memory cleanups. These functions are as follows:

```
void sqlite3_soft_heap_limit(int N);
int sqlite3_release_memory(int N);
void sqlite3_thread_cleanup(void);
```

The sqlite3_soft_heap_limit() function sets the current soft heap limit of the calling thread to N bytes. If the thread's heap usage exceeds N, then SQLite automatically calls sqlite3_release_memory(), which attempts to free at least N bytes of memory from the caches of all database connections associated with the calling thread. The return value of sqlite3_release_memory() is the number of bytes actually freed.

If you use it, you must also set sqlite3_soft_heap_limit() back to zero (the default) prior to shutting down a thread or else it will leak memory. Alternatively, you can use sqlite3_thread_cleanup(), which ensures that a thread has released any thread-local storage it may have allocated. When the API is used properly, thread-local storage should be managed automatically, and you shouldn't need to call sqlite3_thread_cleanup(). However, it is provided as a precaution and a potential work-around for future thread-related memory leaks.

These routines are only available if you have enabled memory management by compiling SQLite with the SQLITE_ENABLE_MEMORY_MANAGEMENT preprocessor directive.

Summary

The core C API contains everything you need to process SQL commands and then some. It contains a variety of convenient query methods that are useful in different ways. These include `sqlite3_exec()` and `sqlite3_get_table()`, which allow you to execute commands in a single function call. The API includes many utility functions as well, allowing you to determine the number of affected records in a query, get the last inserted `ROWID` of an `INSERT` statement, trace SQL commands run on a connection, and conveniently format strings for SQL statements.

The `sqlite3_prepare()`, `sqlite3_step()`, and `sqlite3_finalize()` methods provide you with a lot of flexibility and control over statement execution through the use of statement handles. Statement handles provide more detailed row and column information, the convenience of bound parameters, as well as the ability to reuse prepared statements, avoiding the overhead of query compilation.

SQLite provides a variety of ways to manage runtime events through the use of event filters. Its commit, rollback, and update hooks allow you to monitor and control specific changes in database state. You can watch changes to rows and columns as they happen, and use an authorizer function to monitor and restrict what queries can do as they are compiled.

SQLite has support for threads as well, and offers a higher concurrency model for multi-threaded environments through the use of shared cache mode. This mode enables connections created by a single thread to share a common page cache, allowing the program to be more memory efficient. Furthermore, it is possible for multiple readers and one writer to work in the same database at the same time.

And believe it or not, you've only seen half of the API! Actually, you've seen more like three-quarters, but you are likely to find that what is in the next chapter—user-defined functions, aggregates, and collations—is every bit as useful and interesting as what is in this one.

CHAPTER 7

■ ■ ■

The Extension C API

This chapter is about teaching SQLite new tricks. The previous chapter dealt with generic database work; this chapter is about being creative. The latter half of the API—the Extension API—offers three basic ways to extend (or customize) SQLite, through the creation of user-defined *functions*, *aggregates*, and *collation sequences*.

User-defined functions are SQL functions that map to some implementation that you write. They are callable from within SQL. For example, you could create a function `hello_newman()` that returns the string `'Hello Jerry'` and, once it is registered, call it from SQL as follows:

```
sqlite > select hello_newman() as reply;
reply
------------------
'Hello Jerry'
```

This is a special version of the SQLite command-line program I customized myself that includes `hello_newman()`. When I get bored, I call it occasionally.

Aggregates are a special form of function and work in much the same way except that they operate on sets of records and return aggregated values or expressions computed over a particular column in the set. Or they may be computed from multiple columns. Standard aggregates that are built into SQLite include `SUM()`, `COUNT()`, and `AVG()`, for example.

Collations are methods of comparing and sorting text. That is, given two strings, a Collation would decide which one is greater, or whether the two are equal. The default Collation in SQLite is `BINARY`—it compares strings byte by byte using `memcmp()`. While this collation happens to work well for words in the English language (and other languages that use UTF-8 encoding), it doesn't necessarily work so well for other languages that use different encodings. This is why SQLite version 3 introduced user-defined collations.

This chapter covers each of these three user-defined extension facilities and their associated API functions. As you will see, when combined with other facilities such as triggers and conflict resolution, the user-defined extensions API can prove to be a powerful tool for creating nontrivial features that extend SQLite.

All of the code in this chapter is included in examples that you can obtain online from the Apress website (`www.apress.com`). The examples for this particular chapter are located in the *ch7* subdirectory of the examples folder. I will specifically point out all the source files corresponding to the examples as they are introduced in the text. Some of the error-checking code in the figures has been taken out for the sake of clarity.

Also, many examples in this chapter use simple convenience functions from a common library I wrote that helps simplify the examples. I will point out these functions and explain what they do as they are introduced in the text. The common code is located in the *common* subdirectory of the examples folder, and must first be built before the examples are built. Please refer to the README file in the examples folder for details on building the common library.

Finally, to clear up any confusion, the terms *storage class* and *data type* are interchangeable. You know that SQLite stores data internally using five different data types, or storage classes. These classes are INTEGER, FLOAT, TEXT, BLOB, and NULL, as described in Chapter 4. Throughout the chapter, I try to use the term that best fits the context. When speaking generally, I use the term *data type*, as it seems the most appropriate. When speaking about how SQLite handles a specific value internally, I find that the term *storage class* seems to work better. In either case, you can equate either term as describing a specific form or representation of data.

The API

The basic method for implementing functions, aggregates, and collations consists of implementing a callback function and then registering it in your program. Once registered, they can be used from SQL. Functions and aggregates use the same registration function and similar callback functions. Collation sequences, while using a separate registration function, are almost identical and can be thought of as a particular class of user-defined function.

The lifetime of user-defined aggregates, functions, and collations is transient. They are registered on a connection-by-connection basis; they are *not* stored in the database. It is up to you to ensure that your application loads your custom extensions and registers them on each connection. Sometimes you may find yourself thinking of your extensions in terms of stored procedures and completely forget about the fact that they don't actually reside in the database. Extensions exist in libraries, not in databases, and are restricted to the life of your program. If you don't grasp this concept, you may do something like try to create a trigger (which is stored in the database) that references your extensions (which aren't stored in the database) and then turn around and try to call it from the SQLite shell or from an application that knows nothing of your extensions. In this case, you will find that either it triggers an error or nothing happens. Extensions require your program to register them on *each* and *every* connection; otherwise, that connection's SQL syntax will know nothing about them.

Registering Functions

That said, you can register functions and aggregates on a connection using the sqlite3_create_function(), which is declared as follows:

```
int sqlite3_create_function(
    sqlite3 *cnx,                 /* connection handle                    */
    const char *zFunctionName,    /* function/aggregate name in SQL       */
    int nArg,                     /* number of arguments. -1 = unlimited. */
    int eTextRep,                 /* encoding (UTF8, 16, etc.)            */
    void *pUserData,              /* application data, passed to callback */
    void (*xFunc)(sqlite3_context*,int,sqlite3_value**),
    void (*xStep)(sqlite3_context*,int,sqlite3_value**),
    void (*xFinal)(sqlite3_context*)
);
```

```
int sqlite3_create_function16(
  sqlite3 *cnx,
  const void *zFunctionName,
  int nArg,
  int eTextRep,
  void *pUserData,
  void (*xFunc)(sqlite3_context*, int args, sqlite3_value**),
  void (*xStep)(sqlite3_context*, int args, sqlite3_value**),
  void (*xFinal)(sqlite3_context*)
);
```

As in the previous chapter, I have included both the UTF-8 and UTF-16 versions of this function to underscore the fact that the SQLite API has functions that support both encodings. However, from now on, I will only refer to the UTF-8 versions for the sake of brevity.

The arguments for sqlite3_create_function() are defined as follows:

- cnx: The connection handle. Functions and aggregates are connection specific. They must be registered on the connection as it is opened in order to be used.

- zFunctionName: The function name as it will be called in SQL.

- nArg: The number of arguments required by the function. SQLite will enforce this as the exact number of arguments that must be provided to the function. However, if you specify -1 for this value, SQLite will allow a variable number of arguments.

- eTextRep: The encoding. Allowable values are SQLITE_UTF8, SQLITE_UTF16, SQLITE_UTF16BE, SQLITE_UTF16LE, and SQLITE_ANY. SQLITE_ANY is for a single function implementation that can negotiate any kind of text representation provided.

- pUserData: Application-specific data. This data is made available through the callback functions specified in xFunc, xStep, and xFinal. Unlike other functions, which receive the data as a void pointer in the argument list, these functions must use a special API function to obtain this data

- xFunc: The function callback. This is the actual implementation of the SQL function. Functions only provide this callback and leave the xStep and xFinal function pointers NULL. These latter two callbacks are exclusively for aggregate implementations.

- xStep: The aggregate step function. Each time SQLite processes a row in an aggregated result set, it calls xStep to allow the aggregate to process the relevant field value(s) of that row and include the result in its aggregate computation.

- xFinal: The aggregate finalize function. When all rows have been processed, SQLite calls this function to allow the aggregate to conclude its processing, which usually consists of computing the final value and optionally cleaning up.

With regard to encoding, you can register multiple versions of the same function differing only in the encoding (eTextRep argument) and SQLite will automatically select the best version of the function for the case in hand.

The Step Function

The function and aggregate step functions are identical, and are declared as

```
void fn(sqlite3_context* ctx, int nargs, sqlite3_value** values)
```

The `ctx` argument is the function/aggregate context. It holds state for a particular function call instance and is the means through which you obtain the application data (`pUserData`) argument provided in `sqlite3_create_function()`. The user data is obtained from the context using `sqlite3_user_data()`, which is declared as follows:

```
void *sqlite3_user_data(sqlite3_context*);
```

For functions, this data is shared among all calls to like functions, so it is not really unique to a particular instance of function call. That is, the same `pUserData` is passed or shared among all instances of a given function. Aggregates, however, can allocate their own state for each particular instance using `sqlite3_aggregate_context()`, declared as follows:

```
void *sqlite3_aggregate_context(sqlite3_context*, int nBytes);
```

The first time this routine is called for a particular aggregate, a chunk of memory of size `nBytes` is allocated, zeroed, and associated with that context. On subsequent calls with the same context (for the same aggregate instance), this allocated memory is returned. Using this, aggregates have a way to store state in between calls in order to accumulate data. When the aggregate completes the `final()` callback, the memory is automatically freed by SQLite.

■**Note** One of the things you will see throughout the API is the use of user data in void pointers. Since many parts of the API involve callback functions, these simply serve as a convenience to help you maintain state when implementing said callback functions.

The `nargs` argument of the callback function contains the number of arguments passed to the function.

Return Values

The `values` argument is an array of SQLite value structures that are handles to the actual argument values. The actual data for these values is obtained using the family of `sqlite3_value_xxx()` functions, which have the following form:

```
xxx sqlite3_value_xxx(sqlite3_value* value);
```

where *xxx* is the C data type to be returned from the `value` argument. If you read Chapter 6, you may be thinking that these functions have a striking resemblance to the `sqlite3_column_xxx()` family of functions—and you'd be right. They work in exactly the same way, even down to the difference between the way scalar and array values are obtained. The functions for obtaining scalar values are as follows:

```
int sqlite3_value_int(sqlite3_value*);
long long int sqlite3_value_int64(sqlite3_value*);
double sqlite3_value_double(sqlite3_value*);
```

The functions used to obtain array values are as follows:

```
int sqlite3_value_bytes(sqlite3_value*);
const void *sqlite3_value_blob(sqlite3_value*);
const unsigned char *sqlite3_value_text(sqlite3_value*);
```

The sqlite3_value_bytes() function returns the amount of data in the value buffer for a BLOB. The sqlite3_value_blob() function returns a pointer to that data. Using the size and the pointer, you can then copy out the data. For example, if the first argument in your function was a BLOB, and you wanted to make a copy, you would do something like this:

```
int len;
void* data;

len = sqlite3_value_bytes(values[0]);
data = malloc(len);
memcpy(data, sqlite3_value_blob(values[0]), len);
```

Just as the sqlite3_column_xxx() functions have sqlite_column_type() to provide the column types, the sqlite3_value_xxx() functions likewise have sqlite3_value_type(), which works in the same way. It is declared as follows:

```
int sqlite3_value_type(sqlite3_value*);
```

This function returns one of the following values, which correspond to SQLite's internal, storage classes (data types), defined as

```
#define SQLITE_INTEGER   1
#define SQLITE_FLOAT     2
#define SQLITE_TEXT      3
#define SQLITE_BLOB      4
#define SQLITE_NULL      5
```

This covers the basic workings of the function/aggregate interface. We can now dive into some examples and even a few practical applications. The Collation interface is so similar that rather than previewing it here, we will just address it in full after we cover functions and aggregates.

Functions

Let's start with a trivial example, one that is very easy to follow. Let's implement hello_newman(), but with a slight twist. I want to include using function arguments in the example, so hello_newman() will take one argument: the name of the person addressing him. It will thus work as follows:

```
sqlite > select hello_newman('Jerry') as reply;
reply
-----------------
Hello Jerry

sqlite > select hello_newman('Kramer') as reply;
reply
-----------------
Hello Kramer

sqlite > select hello_newman('George') as reply;
reply
-----------------
Hello George
```

The basic program (taken from hello_newman.c) is shown in Listing 7-1. Some of the error-checking code has been removed for clarity.

Listing 7-1. *The hello_newman() Test Program*

```c
int main(int argc, char **argv)
{
    int rc; sqlite3 *db;

    sqlite3_open("test.db", &db);
    sqlite3_create_function( db, "hello_newman", 1, SQLITE_UTF8, NULL,
                             hello_newman, NULL, NULL);

    /* Log SQL as it is executed. */
    log_sql(db,1);

    /* Call function with one text argument. */
    fprintf(stdout, "Calling with one argument.\n");
    print_sql_result(db, "select hello_newman('Jerry')");

    /* Call function with two arguments. This will fail as we registered the
    ** function as taking only one argument. */
    fprintf(stdout, "\nCalling with two arguments.\n");
    print_sql_result(db, "select hello_newman ('Jerry', 'Elaine')");

    /* Call function with no arguments. This will fail too */
    fprintf(stdout, "\nCalling with no arguments.\n");
    print_sql_result(db, "select hello_newman()");

    /* Done */
    sqlite3_close(db);

    return 0;
}
```

This program connects to the database, registers the function, and then calls it three times. The callback function is implemented as follows:

```
void hello_newman(sqlite3_context* ctx, int nargs, sqlite3_value** values)
{
    const char *msg;

    /* Generate Newman's reply */
    msg = sqlite3_mprintf("Hello %s", sqlite3_value_text(values[0]));

    /* Set the return value. Have sqlite clean up msg w/ sqlite_free(). */
    sqlite3_result_text(ctx, msg, strlen(msg), sqlite3_free);
}
```

Running the program yields the following output:

```
Calling with one argument.
  TRACE: select hello_newman('Jerry')
hello_newman('Jerry')
---------------------
Hello Jerry

Calling with two arguments.
execute() Error: wrong number of arguments to function hello_newman()

Calling with no arguments.
execute() Error: wrong number of arguments to function hello_newman()
```

The first call consists of just one argument. Since the example registered the function as taking exactly one argument, it succeeds. The second call attempts to use two arguments, which fails. The third call uses no arguments, and also fails.

And there you have it: a SQLite extension function. This does bring up a few new functions that I have not addressed yet. The first few functions are specific to the common code. The function log_sql() simply calls sqlite3_trace(), passing in a tracing function that prefixes the traced SQL with the word *TRACE*. I use this so you can see what is happening in the example as the SQL is executed. The second function is print_sql_result(), which has the following declaration:

```
int print_sql_result(sqlite3 *db, const char* sql, ...)
```

This is a simple wrapper around sqlite3_prepare() and friends that executes a SQL statement and prints the results.

Return Values

This example introduces a new SQLite function: sqlite3_result_text().This function is just one of a family of sqlite_result_xxx() functions used to set return values for user-defined functions and aggregates. The scalar functions are as follows:

```
void sqlite3_result_double(sqlite3_context*, double);
void sqlite3_result_int(sqlite3_context*, int);
void sqlite3_result_int64(sqlite3_context*, long long int);
void sqlite3_result_null(sqlite3_context*);
```

These functions simply take a (second) argument of the type specified in the function name and set it as the return value of the function. The array functions are

```
void sqlite3_result_text(sqlite3_context*, const char*, int n, void(*)(void*));
void sqlite3_result_blob(sqlite3_context*, const void*, int n, void(*)(void*));
```

These functions take array data and set that data as the return value for the function. They have the general form

```
void sqlite3_result_xxx(
    sqlite3_context *ctx,    /* function context */
    const xxx* value,        /* array value */
    int len,                 /* array length */
    void(*free)(void*));     /* array cleanup function */
```

Here *xxx* is the particular array type—void for BLOBs or char for TEXT. Again, if you read Chapter 6, you may find these functions suspiciously similar to the sqlite3_bind_xxx() functions, which they are. Setting a return value for a function is, for all intents and purposes, identical to binding a value to a parameterized SQL statement. You could even perhaps refer to it as "binding a return value."

Arrays and Cleanup Handlers

Just as in binding array values to SQL statements, these functions work in the same way as sqlite3_bind_xxx(). They require a pointer to the array, the length (or size) of the array, and a function pointer to a cleanup function. This cleanup function pointer can be assigned the same predefined meanings as in sqlite3_bind_xxx():

```
#define SQLITE_STATIC      ((void(*)(void *))0)
#define SQLITE_TRANSIENT   ((void(*)(void *))-1)
```

SQLITE_STATIC means that the array memory resides in unmanaged space, and therefore SQLite should not attempt to clean it up. SQLITE_TRANSIENT tells SQLite that the array data is subject to change, and therefore SQLite needs to make its own copy. In this case, SQLite will copy the data and free it after the function returns. The third option is to pass in an actual function pointer to a cleanup function of the form

```
void cleanup(void*);
```

In this case, SQLite will call the cleanup function after the user-defined function completes. This is the method used in the previous example: I used `sqlite3_mprintf()` to generate Newman's reply, which allocated a string on the heap. I then passed in `sqlite3_free()` as the cleanup function to `sqlite3_result_text()`, which could free the string memory when the extension function completed.

Error Conditions

Sometimes functions encounter errors, in which case the return value should be set appropriately. This is what `sqlite3_result_error()` is for. It is declared as follows:

```
void sqlite3_result_error(
    sqlite3_context *ctx, /* the function context */
    const char *msg,      /* the error message */
    int len);             /* length of the error message */
```

This tells SQLite that there was an error, the details of which are contained in `msg`. SQLite will abort the command that called the function and set the error message to the value contained in `msg`.

Returning Input Values

Sometimes, you may want to pass back an argument as the return value in the exact same form. Rather than your having to determine the argument's type, extract its value with the corresponding `sqlite3_column_xxx()` function, and then turn right around and set the return value with the appropriate `sqlite3_result_xxx()` function, the API offers `sqlite3_result_value()` so you can do all of this in one fell swoop. It is declared as follows:

```
void sqlite3_result_value(
    sqlite3_context *ctx,   /* the function context */
    sqlite3_value* value);  /* the argument value   */
```

For example, say you wanted to create a function `echo()` that spits back its first argument. The implementation is as follows:

```
void echo(sqlite3_context* ctx, int nargs, sqlite3_value** values)
{
    sqlite3_result_value(ctx, values[0]);
}
```

It would work from SQL as follows:

```
sqlite > select echo('Hello Jerry') as reply;
reply
------------------
Hello Jerry
```

Even better, `echo()` works equally well with arguments of any storage class, and returns them accordingly:

```
sqlite> select echo(3.14) as reply, typeof(echo(3.14)) as type;
reply      type
---------- ----------
3.14       real
sqlite> select echo(X'0128') as reply, typeof(echo(X'0128')) as type;
reply      type
---------- ----------
(?         blob
sqlite> select echo(NULL) as reply, typeof(echo(NULL)) as type;
reply      type
---------- ----------
           null
```

A Complete Example

Let's move on to a complete example that uses most of the API functions described earlier. This will give you a better feel for all that is available to you in one place. We will implement a function called function(), which takes a variable number of arguments. It will print the argument types and return an integer value. If, however, the first argument is the string value 'fail', it will call the error handler, returning an error message.

The main function, shown in Listing 7-2, is much the same as the previous example (the complete example is located in func.c). Again, some of the error handling has been excised for clarity.

Listing 7-2. *The main Function*

```
int main(int argc, char **argv)
{
    int rc;
    sqlite3 *db;
    const char* sql;

    sqlite3_open("test.db", &db);
    sqlite3_create_function( db, "function", -1, SQLITE_UTF8, NULL,
                             function, NULL, NULL);

    /* Turn on SQL logging */
    log_sql(db, 1);

    /* Call function with one text argument. */
    execute(db, "select function(1)");

    /* Call function with several arguments of various types. */
    execute(db, "select function(1, 2.71828)");
```

```
    /* Call function with variable arguments, the first argument's value
    ** being 'fail'. This will trigger the function to call
    ** sqlite3_result_error(). */
    execute(db, "select function('fail', 1, 2.71828, 'three', X'0004', NULL)");

    /* Done */
    sqlite3_close(db);

    return 0;
}
```

Note the -1 value for the nArg argument in sqlite3_create_function(). This corresponds to the number of required arguments that must be provided to the function. Using -1 tells SQLite that the function accepts a variable number of arguments. Note that there is a new convenience function here called execute(). This is just a thin wrapper around sqlite3_exec() that executes a SQL command and reports any errors to standard error, if any. It was listed in Chapter 6 and is part of the common library. The function's implementation is shown in Listing 7-3.

Listing 7-3. *A Vanilla User-Defined Function*

```
void function(sqlite3_context* ctx, int nargs, sqlite3_value** values)
{
    int i; const char *msg;

    fprintf(stdout, "function() : Called with %i arguments\n", nargs);

    for(i=0; i < nargs; i++) {
        fprintf( stdout, "    arg %i: value=%-7s type=%i\n", i,
                sqlite3_value_text(values[i]),
                sqlite3_value_type(values[i]));
    }

    if(strcmp(sqlite3_value_text(values[0]), "fail") == 0) {
        msg = "function() : Failing because you told me to.";
        sqlite3_result_error(ctx, msg, strlen(msg));
        fprintf(stdout, "\n");
        return;
    }

    fprintf(stdout, "\n");
    sqlite3_result_int(ctx, 0);
}
```

Running the program produces the following output:

```
  TRACE: select function(1)
function() : Called with 1 arguments
    arg 0: value=1        type=1

  TRACE: select function(1, 2.71828)
function() : Called with 2 arguments
    arg 0: value=1        type=1
    arg 1: value=2.71828 type=2

  TRACE: select function('fail', 1, 2.71828, 'three', X'0004', NULL)
function() : Called with 6 arguments
    arg 0: value=fail     type=3
    arg 1: value=1        type=1
    arg 2: value=2.71828 type=2
    arg 3: value=three    type=3
    arg 4: value=         type=4
    arg 5: value=(null)   type=5
execute() Error: function() : Failing because you told me to.
```

First, we can see that SQLite classifies the values provided as arguments into five possible data types or storage classes. These possible types correspond to SQLite's five internal data types, which, again, are defined as

```
#define SQLITE_INTEGER   1
#define SQLITE_FLOAT     2
#define SQLITE_TEXT      3
#define SQLITE_BLOB      4
#define SQLITE_NULL      5
```

Each call passes in an increasing number of arguments and types to illustrate this. In the final call to function(), one of each storage class is passed in as an argument, and the function's output confirms that SQLite has typed them accordingly. Note that the X'0004' is an example of SQLite's string representation for binary data. The X (which is case insensitive) followed by hexadecimal values delimited by single quotes denotes binary data (a BLOB representation).

The first thing to notice in this example is that the function API provides a way to determine the number of arguments passed to a function, their respective storage classes, and their values.

Second, the function API provides a way to fetch argument values according to their storage class, if so desired. Since all storages classes have respective text representations—even binary data—you can always count on being able to get function arguments in text form, regardless of their internal representation.

Finally, just as you can receive values in their native storage class, you can also return them that way. One special case of return value is the error return value, which is always in text form, and causes the SQL command calling it to fail.

A Practical Application

Now let's move on to a real application of user-defined functions. In the introduction I made the claim that when combined with other SQLite features such as triggers, user-defined extensions can be quite a powerful tool. By design, SQLite uses manifest typing, which in many cases is very useful and convenient. But what if there are some critical columns in a table for which you just have to have strict typing? You might have an integer column that must always hold only integer values. No inserts or updates should be allowed to put any other kind of data type into this column.

In this example (strict_typing.c), we will combine user-defined functions with triggers to implement strict typing in SQLite. Furthermore, we will be able to apply this strict typing to entire tables, if so desired, and for an unlimited number of data types (that is, even for data types that SQLite knows nothing about). All that is required is that we implement validation functions for each respective data type that is to be enforced under the strict typing policy.

To start with, say we have a table episodes, defined as follows:

```
create table episodes (
    id integer primary key,
    cid integer not null default 0, -- main character id
    name text,                      -- episode name
    rating float not null default 0 -- scale 1-10 );
```

The cid column is the main character ID, which corresponds to the id column in the character table, which is defined as follows:

```
create table characters (
    id integer primary key, -- character id
    name text               -- character name );
```

We can infer from these tables that the episodes.cid column should always be an integer. Furthermore, we want to enforce this in our application. We know that in order to do this, we have to be able to control INSERT and UPDATE operations that target this column.

Validation Triggers

This is where triggers come in. We will define two triggers to do this, shown in Listing 7-4.

Listing 7-4. *Validation Triggers*

```
/-- INSERT trigger
CREATE TRIGGER episodes_insert_cid_typecheck_tr
BEFORE INSERT ON episodes
BEGIN
    SELECT CASE
        WHEN(SELECT validate_int(new.cid) != 1)
        THEN RAISE(ABORT, 'invalid int value for episodes.cid ')
    END;
END;
```

```
CREATE TRIGGER episodes_update_cid_typecheck_tr
BEFORE UPDATE OF cid ON episodes
FOR EACH ROW BEGIN
  SELECT CASE
    WHEN(SELECT validate_int(new.cid) != 1)
    THEN RAISE(ABORT, 'invalid int value for episodes.cid ')
  END;
END;
```

Thus, each UPDATE and INSERT on the episodes table will fire a *before* trigger, which will take the proposed cid value being submitted and call validate_int()—a user-defined function that simply tests whether a value (provided as the single argument) is in fact an integer. If the value is an integer, validate_int() returns true (1); otherwise, it returns false (0). The trigger evaluates the returned value in the WHEN clause and if it is not true, the trigger raises an abort. Therefore, only integer values can pass through the trigger and therefore all INSERTs and UPDATEs are only allowed to provide integer values to episodes.cid, giving us strict typing for this column.

Note This implementation makes an assumption you should be aware of. It assumes that INSERT statements always provide a value for the column to be validated. In this example, it assumes that all INSERT statements will always provide a value for cid. If one is not provided, the trigger will fail. To get around this, simply provide a default value for the column in the table definition so that a suitable value will be provided for INSERT statements that don't provide a cid value. If you notice, the definition for cid in this example is cid integer not null default 0. Another thing to remember is that while INSERT triggers can only be defined for entire records, UPDATE triggers can be defined for specific columns, so they do not have this problem.

The Validation Function

The validate_int() function is quite simple. It is shown in Listing 7-5.

Listing 7-5. *The validate_int() Validation Function*

```
void validate_int_udf(sqlite3_context* ctx, int nargs, sqlite3_value** values)
{
    sqlite3 *db;
    const char *value;
    char *tmp;

    db    = (sqlite3*)sqlite3_user_data(ctx);
    value = sqlite3_value_text(values[0]);

    /* Assume NULL values for type-checked columns are not allowed */
    if(value == NULL) {
        sqlite3_result_int(ctx, 0);
        return;
    }
```

```
    /* Validate */
    tmp = NULL;
    strtol(value, &tmp, 0);

    if(*tmp != '\0') {
        /* Value does not conform to type */
        sqlite3_result_int(ctx, 0);
        return;
    }

    /* If we got this far, the value is valid. */
    sqlite3_result_int(ctx, 1);
}
```

It just uses strtol() to look for errors in the conversion. The actual implementation is arbitrary. You can create whatever criteria you want to validate an integer value. Using this function as a template, you can create user-defined functions for any data type—float, double, varchar, date, timestamp, whatever you like. They only differ in how they test the input value for validity. This example uses three general data type tests for integer, float, and text values. It then registers them under various SQL function names:

```
/* Type Validation: Called to validate text. */
sqlite3_create_function( db, "validate_text", 1, SQLITE_UTF8, db,
                         validate_text_udf, NULL, NULL);

/* Type Validation: Called to validate integer. */
sqlite3_create_function( db, "validate_int", 1, SQLITE_UTF8, db,
                         validate_int_udf, NULL, NULL);

/* Type Validation: Called to validate long integer. Same UDF as above,
 * different SQL function name. */
sqlite3_create_function( db, "validate_long", 1, SQLITE_UTF8, db,
                         validate_int_udf, NULL, NULL);

/* Type Validation: Called to validate double. */
sqlite3_create_function( db, "validate_double", 1, SQLITE_UTF8, db,
                         validate_double_udf, NULL, NULL);

/* Type Validation: Called to validate float. Same UDF as above,
 * different SQL function name. */
sqlite3_create_function( db, "validate_float", 1, SQLITE_UTF8, db,
                         validate_double_udf, NULL,
```

Both the validate_int() and validate_long() SQL functions map to the same validate_int_udf() callback function. Their validity test is the same, so why write two callback functions to do the same thing? Likewise, the validate_float() and validate_double() SQL functions call the same validate_double_udf() callback function to validate their respective values.

Installation Functions

So far, so good. Before creating a test program, let's take the example a step further. Instead of having to write and maintain our own triggers for each column we want to control, let's write another user-defined function to do it for us. Actually, we need two such functions: one to create the triggers and one to remove them (in case we don't want type checking any more on a given column). The callback function to add the triggers is called add_strict_type_check_udf(). Its corresponding SQL function is called add_strict_type_check(). The callback function is implemented as shown in Listing 7-6.

Listing 7-6. *The strict_type_check() User-Defined Function*

```
void add_strict_type_check_udf( sqlite3_context* ctx, int nargs,
                                sqlite3_value** values )
{
    sqlite3 *db; sqlite3_stmt *stmt;
    int rc;
    const char *table, *column, *sql, *tmp, *tail, *err;

    db=(sqlite3*)sqlite3_user_data(ctx);

    table  = sqlite3_value_text(values[0]);
    column = sqlite3_value_text(values[1]);

    /* If the column name is an asterisk */
    if(strncmp(column,"*",1) == 0) {

        /* Install type checking on all columns */

        sql = "pragma table_info(%s)";
        tmp = sqlite3_mprintf(sql, table);

        rc = sqlite3_prepare(db, tmp, strlen(tmp), &stmt, &tail);
        sqlite3_free((void*)tmp);

        if(rc != SQLITE_OK) {
            err = sqlite3_errmsg(db);
            sqlite3_result_error(ctx, err, strlen(err));
        }

        rc = sqlite3_step(stmt);

        while(rc == SQLITE_ROW) {
            /* If not primary key */
            if(sqlite3_column_int(stmt, 5) != 1) {
                column = sqlite3_column_text(stmt, 1);
                install_type_trigger(db, ctx, table, column);
            }
        }
```

```
        rc = sqlite3_step(stmt);
    }

    sqlite3_finalize(stmt);
}
else {

    /* Column name specified, just install on that one column. */
    if(install_type_trigger(db, ctx, table, column) != 0) {
        return;
    }
}

sqlite3_result_int(ctx, 0);
}
```

This function installs triggers on either all columns or on a single column specified by column. If the value passed in column is an asterisk (*), it installs the triggers on all columns in the table (with the exception of the primary key column), using PRAGMA table_info() to obtain column information. Whether one or many columns, the real work is ultimately passed on to a helper function install_type_trigger(), which does the trigger installation. It is shown in Listing 7-7.

Listing 7-7. *The Trigger Installation Helper Function*

```
int install_type_trigger( sqlite3* db, sqlite3_context* ctx,
                          const char* table, const char* column )
{
    int rc;
    char buf[256];
    char *tmp;
    const char *type, *sql, *emsg;
    char* err;

    /* Get the column's declared type */
    type = column_type(db, table, column);

    /* Check to see if corresponding validation function exists */

    sql = "select validate_%s(null)";
    tmp = sqlite3_mprintf(sql, type);
    rc = sqlite3_exec(db, tmp, NULL, NULL, &err);
    sqlite3_free(tmp);

    if(rc != SQLITE_OK && err != NULL) {
        emsg = "No validator exists for column type";
        sqlite3_result_error(ctx, emsg, strlen(emsg));
        sqlite3_free((void*)type);
```

```
        sqlite3_free(err);
        return 1;
    }

    /* Create INSERT trigger */
    sql = "CREATE TRIGGER %s_insert_%s_typecheck_tr \n"
        "BEFORE INSERT ON %s \n"
        "BEGIN \n"
        "  SELECT CASE \n"
        "    WHEN(SELECT validate_%s(new.%s) != 1) \n"
        "    THEN RAISE(ABORT, 'invalid %s value for %s.%s') \n"
        "  END; \n"
        "END;";

    tmp = sqlite3_mprintf(sql, table, column, table, type,
                          column, type, table, column);

    rc = sqlite3_exec(db, tmp, NULL, NULL, &err);
    sqlite3_free(tmp);

    if(rc != SQLITE_OK && err != NULL) {
        strncpy(&buf[0], err, 255);
        buf[256] = '\0';
        sqlite3_result_error(ctx, &buf[0], strlen(&buf[0]));
        sqlite3_free((void*)type);

        return 1;
    }

    /* Create UPDATE trigger */

    sql = "CREATE TRIGGER %s_update_%s_typecheck_tr \n"
        "BEFORE UPDATE OF %s ON %s \n"
        "FOR EACH ROW BEGIN \n"
        "  SELECT CASE \n"
        "    WHEN(SELECT validate_%s(new.%s) != 1) \n"
        "    THEN RAISE(ABORT, 'invalid %s value for %s.%s') \n"
        "  END; \n"
        "END;";

    tmp = sqlite3_mprintf(sql, table, column, column, table,
                          type, column, type, table, column);

    rc = sqlite3_exec(db, tmp, NULL, NULL, &err);
    sqlite3_free(tmp);
    sqlite3_free((void*)type);
```

```
    if(rc != SQLITE_OK && err != NULL) {
        strncpy(&buf[0], err, 255);
        buf[256] = '\0';
        sqlite3_result_error(ctx, &buf[0], strlen(&buf[0]));
        sqlite3_free(err);

        return 1;
    }

    return 0;
}
```

As stated, this function does all the real work. First, it gets the column's declared type through another user-defined function column_type(), which in turn just prepares a query with the given column and uses sqlite3_column_decltype() to fetch its declared type. With the type, install_type_trigger() assumes that all validation functions will follow the naming convention validate_xxx(), where *xxx* is the data type to be validated. If, for example, the column's declared type is int, install_type_trigger() tests for the existence of the respective validation function by executing the query

```
select validate_int(1);
```

Exactly one of two things can happen here: the query will fail or succeed. It can only fail if the function does not exist. It doesn't matter if the argument 1 is of the correct type; even if the validate_int() function exists, it will return false (0) and the query will still succeed as the query constitutes as a valid SQL statement. That is, sqlite3_exec() will return SQLITE_OK if validate_int() exists. Otherwise, it will return an error. That is all it needs—a test for existence that answers the question: has a validate_xxx() user-defined function been registered? Yes or no? If the validation function exists, install_type_trigger() proceeds to build the trigger statements (as illustrated earlier) and runs them.

Likewise, the user-defined function to remove the triggers is called drop_strict_type_check_udf(), and works in exactly the same way, except that it executes SQL to drop the triggers. It too uses a helper function to do most of the work.

The Test Program

Putting it all together, strict typing can now be applied to a column using something like

```
select add_strict_type_check('episodes', 'cid');
```

It can be imposed on the entire table using an asterisk for the column argument:

```
select add_strict_type_check('episodes', '*');
```

Similarly, it can be removed with either of the following:

```
select remove_strict_type_check('episodes', 'cid');
select remove_strict_type_check('characters', '*');
```

As a part of the implementation, there is also a handy function with which to get a column's declared type:

```
select column_type('episodes', 'rating') as type;
```

It returns the declared type for the column as defined in the CREATE TABLE definition. The example in strict_typing.c includes all of this code and presents a working model. The complete test program is implemented in Listing 7-8.

Listing 7-8. *The strict_typing Program*

```c
int main(int argc, char **argv)
{
    int rc; sqlite3 *db; char *sql;

    rc = sqlite3_open("test.db", &db);

    /* I. Register SQL functions ---------------------------------------------*/

    /* Generates and installs validation triggers. */
    rc = sqlite3_create_function( db, "add_strict_type_check", 2, SQLITE_UTF8, db,
                                  add_strict_type_check_udf, NULL, NULL);

    /* Removes validation triggers. */
    sqlite3_create_function( db, "drop_strict_type_check", 2, SQLITE_UTF8, db,
                             drop_strict_type_check_udf, NULL, NULL);

    /* Convenience function for pulling a column's type from sqlite_master.
     * It is a fine-grained 'PRAGMA table_info()'.*/
    sqlite3_create_function( db, "column_type", 2, SQLITE_UTF8, db,
                             column_type_udf, NULL, NULL);

    /* Type Validation: Called to validate text values. */
    sqlite3_create_function( db, "validate_text", 1, SQLITE_UTF8, db,
                             validate_text_udf, NULL, NULL);

    /* Type Validation: Called to validate integer values. */
    sqlite3_create_function( db, "validate_int", 1, SQLITE_UTF8, db,
                             validate_int_udf, NULL, NULL);

    /* Type Validation: Called to validate long integer values. It uses
    ** the same C UDF as above, only a different SQL function name. */
    sqlite3_create_function( db, "validate_long", 1, SQLITE_UTF8, db,
                             validate_int_udf, NULL, NULL);

    /* Type Validation: Called to validate double values. */
    sqlite3_create_function( db, "validate_double", 1, SQLITE_UTF8, db,
                             validate_double_udf, NULL, NULL);
```

```
    /* Type Validation: Called to validate float values. It uses the
    ** same as above, and has only a different SQL function name.  */
    sqlite3_create_function( db, "validate_float", 1, SQLITE_UTF8, db,
                             validate_double_udf, NULL, NULL);

/* II. Test SQL functions ----------------------------------------------*/

    /* Turn on SQL tracing */
    log_sql(db, 1);

    /* Add strict type checks to all columns in table episodes */
    printf("1. Add strict typing:\n");
    execute(db, "select add_strict_type_check('episodes', '*')");
    printf("\n");

    /* Insert a record with valid values */
    printf("2. Insert valid values -- should succeed:\n");
    execute(db, "insert into episodes (name,cid,rating) "
                "values ('Fusilli Jerry', 1, 9.5)");
    printf("\n");

    /* Update with invalid values */
    printf("3. Update with invalid values -- should fail:\n");
    execute(db, "update episodes set cid = 'text'");
    execute(db, "update episodes set rating = 'text'");
    printf("\n");

    /* Remove static type checks for table episodes */
    printf("4. Remove strict type checks on table episodes\n");
    execute(db, "select drop_strict_type_check('episodes', '*')");
    printf("\n");

    /* Insert a record with invalid values */
    printf("5. Update rating with non-float value -- should succeed:\n");
    execute(db, "update episodes set rating = 'Two thumbs up'");
    printf("\n");

    printf("6. Select records, show update results:\n");
    print_sql_result(db, "select * from episodes");
    printf("\n");

    /* Test column_type() function:*/
    printf("7. Test column_type() UDF\n");
    sql = "select column_type('episodes', 'id') as 'id',\n"
          "       column_type('episodes', 'name')  as 'name',\n"
          "       column_type('episodes', 'cid')  as 'cid',\n"
          "       column_type('episodes', 'rating') as 'rating'";
```

```
    print_sql_result(db, sql);
    printf("\n");

    sqlite3_close(db);

    return 0;
}
```

Results

This program produces the following output:

```
1. Add strict typing:
  TRACE: select add_strict_type_check('episodes', '*')
  TRACE: pragma table_info(episodes)
  TRACE: select validate_int(null)
  TRACE: CREATE TRIGGER episodes_insert_cid_typecheck_tr
BEFORE INSERT ON episodes
BEGIN
   SELECT CASE
     WHEN(SELECT validate_int(new.cid) != 1)
     THEN RAISE(ABORT, 'invalid int value for episodes.cid')
   END;
END;
  TRACE: CREATE TRIGGER episodes_update_cid_typecheck_tr
BEFORE UPDATE OF cid ON episodes
FOR EACH ROW BEGIN
   SELECT CASE
     WHEN(SELECT validate_int(new.cid) != 1)
     THEN RAISE(ABORT, 'invalid int value for episodes.cid')
   END;
END;
  TRACE: select validate_text(null)
  TRACE: CREATE TRIGGER episodes_insert_name_typecheck_tr
BEFORE INSERT ON episodes
BEGIN
   SELECT CASE
     WHEN(SELECT validate_text(new.name) != 1)
     THEN RAISE(ABORT, 'invalid text value for episodes.name')
   END;
END;
  TRACE: CREATE TRIGGER episodes_update_name_typecheck_tr
BEFORE UPDATE OF name ON episodes
```

```
FOR EACH ROW BEGIN
  SELECT CASE
    WHEN(SELECT validate_text(new.name) != 1)
    THEN RAISE(ABORT, 'invalid text value for episodes.name')
  END;
END;
  TRACE: select validate_float(null)
  TRACE: CREATE TRIGGER episodes_insert_rating_typecheck_tr
BEFORE INSERT ON episodes
BEGIN
  SELECT CASE
    WHEN(SELECT validate_float(new.rating) != 1)
    THEN RAISE(ABORT, 'invalid float value for episodes.rating')
  END;
END;
  TRACE: CREATE TRIGGER episodes_update_rating_typecheck_tr
BEFORE UPDATE OF rating ON episodes
FOR EACH ROW BEGIN
  SELECT CASE
    WHEN(SELECT validate_float(new.rating) != 1)
    THEN RAISE(ABORT, 'invalid float value for episodes.rating')
  END;
END;

2. Insert valid values -- should succeed:
  TRACE: insert into episodes (name,cid,rating) values ('Fusilli Jerry', 1, 9.5)

3. Update with invalid values -- should fail:
  TRACE: update episodes set cid = 'text'
execute() : Error 19 : invalid int value for episodes.cid
  TRACE: update episodes set rating = 'text'
execute() : Error 19 : invalid float value for episodes.rating

4. Remove strict type checks on table episodes
  TRACE: select drop_strict_type_check('episodes', '*')
  TRACE: pragma table_info(episodes)
  TRACE: DROP TRIGGER episodes_insert_cid_typecheck_tr
  TRACE: DROP TRIGGER episodes_update_cid_typecheck_tr
  TRACE: DROP TRIGGER episodes_insert_name_typecheck_tr
  TRACE: DROP TRIGGER episodes_update_name_typecheck_tr
  TRACE: DROP TRIGGER episodes_insert_rating_typecheck_tr
  TRACE: DROP TRIGGER episodes_update_rating_typecheck_tr

5. Update rating with non-float value -- should succeed:
  TRACE: update episodes set rating = 'Two thumbs up'
```

6. Select records, show update results:
  TRACE: select * from episodes
```
id cid name              rating
-- --- ---------------- -------------
1  1   Chocolate Babka  Two thumbs up
2  2   Mackinaw Peaches Two thumbs up
3  3   Soup Nazi        Two thumbs up
4  4   Pig Man          Two thumbs up
5  1   Fusilli Jerry    Two thumbs up
```

7. Test column_type() UDF
  TRACE: select column_type('episodes', 'id') as 'id',
         column_type('episodes', 'name') as 'name',
         column_type('episodes', 'cid') as 'cid',
         column_type('episodes', 'rating') as 'rating'
```
id      name cid rating
------- ---- --- ------
integer text int float
```

Step 1 adds static typing constraints on the table, at which point we see a barrage of CREATE TRIGGER statements in which there is one INSERT and one UPDATE trigger for each column. Step 2 simply inserts a valid record. The absence of an error confirms that this operation completed successfully. Step 3 attempts to update with invalid values by providing text values for the integer cid and float rating columns in two consecutive updates. It is rebuffed both times. Steps 2 and 3 indicate that both of the triggers (INSERT and UPDATE) and their respective validation functions (float, text, and int) are working as intended. Step 4 removes the strict typing constraints on all columns, whereupon we see a parade of DROP TRIGGER statements. Step 5 then attempts what step 3 couldn't manage—sticking text values in a non-text column—and succeeds. Step 6 shows off step 5's handiwork. And finally, step 7 demonstrates the utility function column_type() for good measure.

To sum up, there are certainly other ways to go about implementing strict typing. This example is simplistic at best. But it does illustrate the mileage you can get out of SQLite's user-defined functions. At first glance, I never suspected that I could do something like strict typing until I sat down and started working with the version 3 API. Better yet, I've seen a number of clever ideas on various blogs and on the SQLite mailing list on how to use similar techniques and other useful features.

Aggregates

After the function workout, you should be pretty well versed on the extension process in general. Aggregates and collation sequences work so similarly to functions that you will have no trouble with the remaining parts of this chapter. You are nearing the end of the C API.

Aggregates are only slightly more involved than functions. Whereas you only had to implement one callback function to do the work in user-defined functions, you have to implement both a step function to compute the ongoing value as well as a finalizing function to finish everything off and clean up. The general process is shown in Figure 7-1. It still isn't hard, though. Like functions, one good example will be all you need to get the gist of it.

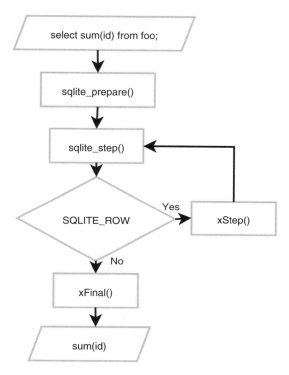

Figure 7-1. *Query processing with aggregates*

Registration Function

As mentioned before, aggregates and functions use the same registration function, sqlite3_create_function(), which is listed here again for convenience:

```
int sqlite3_create_function(
    sqlite3 cnx*,               /* connection handle                      */
    const char *zFunctionName,  /* function/aggregate name in SQL         */
    int nArg,                   /* number of arguments. -1 = unlimited.   */
    int eTextRep,               /* encoding (UTF8, 16, etc.)              */
    void *pUserData,            /* application data, passed to callback   */
    void (*xFunc)(sqlite3_context*,int,sqlite3_value**),
    void (*xStep)(sqlite3_context*,int,sqlite3_value**),
    void (*xFinal)(sqlite3_context*)
);
```

You do exactly the same thing here as you do with functions, but rather than proving a callback for xFunc, you leave it NULL and provide functions for xStep and xFinal.

A Practical Example

The best way to illustrate implementing aggregates is by example. Here we will implement the aggregate SUM(). Yes, SQLite already has this aggregate built in, but SUM() is simple and to the point. To avoid collision, ours will be called sum_int(). Also, this example is a little watered down as it sums only integers. But there is little value in getting caught up in *what* we are aggregating— you can do that later. The goal here is *how* to aggregate. The example program looks almost identical to that of the func.c example, and is shown in Listing 7-9 (taken from aggregate.c).

Listing 7-9. *The sum_int() Test Program*

```c
int main(int argc, char **argv)
{
    int rc; sqlite3 *db; char *sql;

    sqlite3_open("test.db", &db);

    /* Register aggregate. */
    fprintf(stdout, "Registering aggregate sum_int()\n");

    /* Turn SQL tracing on. */
    log_sql(db, 1);

    /* Register aggregate. */
    sqlite3_create_function( db, "sum_int", 1, SQLITE_UTF8, db,
                             NULL, step, finalize);

    /* Test. */
    fprintf(stdout, "\nRunning query: \n");
    sql = "select sum_int(id) from aggregate";
    print_sql_result(db, sql);

    sqlite3_close(db);

    return 0;
}
```

Things to note here are that our step function is called step(), and our finalizing function is called finalize(). Also, this aggregate is registered as taking only one argument.

The Step Function

The step() function is shown in Listing 7-10.

Listing 7-10. *The sum_int() Step Function*

```
void step(sqlite3_context* ctx, int ncols, sqlite3_value** values)
{
    sum* s;
    int x;

    s = (sum*)sqlite3_aggregate_context(ctx, sizeof(sum));

    if(sqlite3_aggregate_count(ctx) == 1) {
        s->x = 0;
    }

    x = sqlite3_value_int(values[0]);
    s->x += x;

    fprintf(stdout, "step()    : value=%i, total=%i\n", x, s->x);
}
```

The value sum is a struct that is specific to this example and is defined as follows:

```
typedef struct {
    int x;
} sum;
```

It's just a glorified integer. This structure serves as our state between aggregate iterations (calls to the step function).

The Aggregate Context

The first order of business is to retrieve the structure for the given aggregate instance. This is done using sqlite3_aggregate_context(). As mentioned earlier, the first call to this function allocates the data for the given context and subsequent calls retrieve it. The structure memory is automatically freed when the aggregate completes (after finalize() is called). In the step() function, the value to be aggregated is retrieved from the first argument using sqlite3_value_int(). This value is then added to the x member of the sum struct, which stores the intermediate summation.

The Finalize Function

Each record in the materialized result set triggers a call to step(). After the last record is processed, SQLite calls finalize(), which is implemented as shown in Listing 7-11.

Listing 7-11. *The sum_int() Finalize Function*

```
void finalize(sqlite3_context* ctx)
{
    sum* s;
    s = (sum*)sqlite3_aggregate_context(ctx, sizeof(sum));
    sqlite3_result_int(ctx, s->x);
```

```
        fprintf(stdout, "finalize() : total=%i\n\n", s->x);
}
```

This function retrieves the sum struct and sets the aggregate's return value to the value stored in the struct's x member using sqlite3_result_int(). The finalize() function basically works just like a user-defined function callback.

Results

The program produces the following output:

```
Dropping table aggregate, if exists.
  TRACE: select count(*) from sqlite_master where name='aggregate'
  TRACE: drop table aggregate
Creating table aggregate.
  TRACE: create table aggregate(id integer)
Populating table aggregate.
  TRACE: insert into aggregate values (1)
  TRACE: insert into aggregate values (2)
  TRACE: insert into aggregate values (3)

Registering aggregate sum_int()

Running query:
  TRACE: select sum_int(id) from aggregate
step()    : value=1, total=1
step()    : value=2, total=3
step()    : value=3, total=6
finalize() : total=6

sum_int(id)
-----------
6
```

I included some output from the setup code in this example (which creates and populates the aggregate table) to better illustrate how this example works. As you can see, the SELECT statement pulls back a total of three records, which results in three calls to step(). After the last step function comes finalize(), which provides the value returned by sum_int(). In this case the value is 6.

And that is the concept of aggregates in a nutshell. They are so similar to functions that there isn't much to talk about once you are familiar with functions.

Collations

As stated before, the purpose of Collations is to sort strings. But before starting down that path, it is important to recall that SQLite's manifest typing scheme allows varying data types to coexist in the same column. For example, consider the following SQL (located in `collate1.sql`):

```
.headers on
.m col
create table foo(x);
insert into foo values (1);
insert into foo values (2.71828);
insert into foo values ('three');
insert into foo values (X'0004');
insert into foo values (null);

select quote(x), typeof(x) from foo;
```

Feeding it to the SQLite CLP will produce the following:

```
C:\temp\examples\ch7> sqlite3 < collate.sql
quote(x)    typeof(x)
----------  ----------
1           integer
2.71828     real
'three'     text
X'0004'     blob
NULL        null
```

You've got every one of SQLite's native storage classes sitting in column x. Naturally, the question arises as to what happens when you try to sort this column. That is, before we can talk about how to sort strings, we need to review how different data types are sorted first.

When SQLite sorts a column in a result set (when it uses a comparison operator like < or >= on the values within that column), the first thing it does is arrange the column's values according to storage class. Then within each storage class, it sorts the values according to methods specific to that class. Storages classes are sorted in the following order, from first to last:

1. NULL values

2. INTEGER and REAL values

3. TEXT values

4. BLOB values

Now let's modify the SELECT statement in the preceding example to include an ORDER BY clause such that the SQL is as follows:

```
select quote(x), typeof(x) from foo order by x;
```

Rerunning the query (located in collate2.sql) confirms this ordering:

```
C:\temp\examples\ch7> sqlite3 < collate.sql
quote(x)    typeof(x)
----------  ----------
NULL        null
1           integer
2.71828     real
'three'     text
X'0004'     blob
```

NULLs are first, INTEGER and REAL next (in numerical order), followed by TEXT, and then BLOBs last.

SQLite employs specific sorting methods for each storage class. NULLs are obvious—there is no sort order. Numeric values are sorted numerically—integers and floats alike are compared based on their respective quantitative values. BLOBs are sorted by binary value. Text, finally, is where Collations come in.

Collation Defined

Collation is the method by which strings are compared. According to Wikipedia,[1] collation is defined as

> In library and information science and computer science, collation is the assembly of written information into a standard order. In common usage, this is called alphabetization, though collation is not limited to ordering letters of the alphabet. Collating lists of words or names into alphabetical order is the basis of most office filing systems, library catalogues, and books of reference.

According to IBM's glossary of Unicode terms, collation is defined as

> Text comparison using language-sensitive rules as opposed to bitwise comparison of numeric character codes.

In general, collation has to do with the arranging of strings and the arranging of characters. Collation methods usually employ *collation sequences*. A collation sequence is just a list of characters, each of which is assigned some numerical value to denote its position in the list. The list in turn is used to dictate how characters are ordered. Given any two characters, the Collation (list) can resolve which would come first, or if they are the same.

How Collation Works

Normally, a collation method compares two strings by breaking them down and comparing their respective characters using a Collation. They do this by lining the strings up and comparing characters from left to right (Figure 7-2). For example, the strings 'jerry' and 'jello' would be compared by first comparing the first letter in each string (both *j* in this case). If one letter's

---

1. See http://en.wikipedia.org/wiki/Collation.

numerical value according to the collation sequence is larger than the other, the comparison is over: the string with the larger letter is deemed greater and no further comparison is required. If, on the other hand, the letters have the same value, then the process continues on to the second letter in each string, and to the third, and so on until some difference is found (or no difference is found, in which case the strings are considered equal). If one string runs out of letters before the other, then it is up to the collation method to determine what this means.

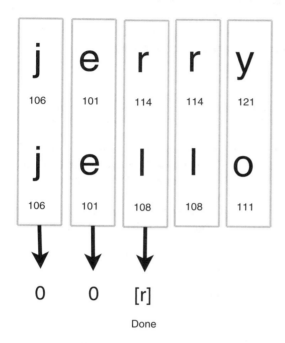

Figure 7-2. *Binary collation*

In this example, the Collation is the ASCII character set. Each character's numeric ASCII value in the figure is displayed underneath it. Using the collation method just described, string comparison continues to the third character, whereupon 'jerry' wins out, as it has an r with the value 114 whereas 'jello' has the inferior 'l' with the value 108. According to this collation method using the ASCII Collation, 'jerry' > 'jello'.

Had 'jerry' been 'Jerry', then 'jello' would have won out, as big J's little 74 pales to little j's big 106, so the comparison would have been resolved on the first character—the prize going to 'jello'. In short, 'jello' > 'Jerry'.

However, to continue the example, we could use a different Collation wherein uppercase values are assigned the same numbers as their lowercase counterparts (a case-insensitive collation sequence). Then the comparison between 'Jerry' and 'jello' would go back to 'Jerry' as in this new Collation J and j are the same, pulling the rug out from under 'jello''s lowercase j superiority.

But enough about Collations. You get the picture. A sequence is a sequence. Ultimately, it's not the collation sequence that matters, but the collation method. Collation methods don't have to use sequences. They can do whatever they want. A collation method is called a method for a reason; it can do whatever it wants, even if its chosen method may be madness.

Odds are that you are really confused by now and are just ready for a summary. So here it is. Think of collation methods as the way that strings are compared. Think of collation sequences as the way characters are compared. Ultimately, all that matters in SQLite is how strings are compared, and the two terms refer to just that. Therefore, the two terms *collation method* and *collation sequence* should just be thought of as string comparison. If you read *collation*, think string comparison. If you read *Collation*, think string comparison. All in all, just think string comparison. That is the way the API is geared. When you create a custom Collation, SQLite hands it two strings, *a* and *b*, and the Collation returns whether string *a* is less than, equal to, or greater than string *b*. That's it, plain and simple.

Standard Collation Types

SQLite comes with a single built-in Collation named BINARY, which is implemented applying the memcmp() routine from the standard C library to the two strings to be compared. The BINARY collation happens to work well for English text. For other languages or locales, alternate Collation may be preferred. SQLite also offers an alternate collation called NOCASE, which does not distinguish between cases, and another called REVERSE, which as you may have guessed compares everything backwards (according to binary value).

Collations are applied by associating them with columns in a table or an index definition, or by specifying them in a query. For example, to create a case-insensitive column bar in foo, you would define foo as follows:

```
create table foo (bar text COLLATE NOCASE, baz text);
```

To create a REVERSE index on baz, you would do something like this:

```
create index bar_rev_idx on foo (baz) COLLATE REVERSE;
```

From that point on, whenever SQLite deals with a bar it will use the NOCASE collation. When it uses an index for baz, it will follow the REVERSE collation.

If you prefer not to attach a Collation to a database object, but would rather specify it as needed on a query-by-query basis, you can specify them directly in queries, as in the following:

```
select * from foo order by bar COLLATE NOCASE;
```

At the time of this writing, there are plans under way to include standard CAST() syntax to allow the collation of an expression to be defined.

A Simple Example

To jump into collations, let's begin with a simple example to get the big picture. Let's implement a collation called POLITICAL. POLITICAL will take two strings and decide which one is greater depending on the day. One Mondays, 'Jello' might be greater than 'jerry'. On Tuesdays, it may be a different story entirely.

Collations are registered with SQLite through the sqlite3_create_collation() function, which is declared as follows:

```
int sqlite3_create_collation(
  sqlite3* db,          /* database handle */
  const char *zName,    /* collation name in SQL */
  int pref16,           /* encoding         */
  void* pUserData,      /* application data */
  int(*xCompare)(void*,int,const void*,int,const void*)
);
```

It looks pretty similar to `sqlite3_create_function()`. There is the standard database handle, the collation name as it will be addressed in SQL (similar to the function/aggregate name), and the encoding, which pertains to the format of the comparison strings when passed to the comparison function.

■**Note** Just as in aggregates and functions, separate collation comparison functions can be registered under the same collation name for each of the UTF-8, UTF-16LE, and UTF-16BE encodings. SQLite will automatically select the best comparison function for the given collation based on the strings to be compared.

Finally, the application data pointer is another API mainstay. The pointer provided there is passed on to the callback function. Basically, `sqlite3_create_collation()` is a stripped-down version of `sqlite3_create_function()`, which takes exactly two arguments (both of which are text) and returns an integer value. It also has the aggregate callback function pointers stripped out.

The Compare Function

The `xCompare` argument is really the only new thing here. It points to the actual comparison function that will resolve the text values. The comparison function must have the form

```
int compare( void* data,       /* application data */
             int len1,         /* length of string 1 */
             const void* str1, /* string 1 */
             int len2,         /* length of string 2 */
             const void* str2) /* string 2 */
```

The function should return negative, zero, or positive if the first string is less than, equal to, or greater than the second string, respectively.

As stated, the political collation is a bit wishy-washy. Its implementation is shown in Listing 7-12.

Listing 7-12. *The Political Collation Function*

```
int political_collation( void* data, int l1, const void* s1,
                                     int l2, const void* s2 )
{
    int result, opinion; struct tm* t; time_t rt;
```

```
        /* Get the unpolitical comparison result */
        result = strcmp(s1,s2);

        /* Get the date and time */
        time(&rt);
        t = localtime(&rt);

        /* Form an opinion: is s1 really < or = to s2 ? */
        switch(t->tm_wday) {
            case 0: /* Monday yes      */
                opinion = result;
                break;
            case 1: /* Tuesday no      */
                opinion = -result;
                break;
            case 2: /* Wednesday bigger is better */
                opinion = l1 >= l2 ? -1:1;
                break;
            case 3: /* Thursday strongly no    */
                opinion = -100;
                break;
            case 4: /* Friday strongly yes     */
                opinion = 100;
                break;
            case 5: /* Saturday golf, everything's the same */
                opinion = 0;
                break;
            default: /* Sunday - Meet the Press, opinion changes
                        every minute */
                opinion = 2*sin(t->tm_min*180);
        }

        /* Now change it on a whim */
        opinion = rand()-(RAND_MAX/2) > 0 ? -1:1;

        return opinion;
}
```

The Test Program

All that remains is to illustrate it in a program. The example program (political.c) implementation is shown in Listing 7-13.

Listing 7-13. *The Political Collation Test Program*

```c
int main(int argc, char **argv)
{
    char *sql; sqlite3 *db; int rc;

    /* For forming more consistent political opinions. */
    srand((unsigned)time(NULL));

    sqlite3_open("test.db", &db);

    /* Create issues table, add records. */
    setup(db);

    /* Register Collation. */
    fprintf(stdout, "1. Register political Collation\n\n");
    sqlite3_create_collation( db, "POLITICAL",
                              SQLITE_UTF8, db,
                              political_collation );

    /* Turn SQL logging on. */
    log_sql(db, 1);

    /* Test default collation. */
    fprintf(stdout, "2. Select records using default collation.\n");
    sql = "select * from issues order by issue";
    print_sql_result(db, sql);

    /* Test Political collation. */
    fprintf(stdout, "\nSelect records using political collation. \n");
    sql = "select * from issues order by issue collate POLITICAL";
    print_sql_result(db, sql);

    fprintf(stdout, "\nSelect again using political collation. \n");
    print_sql_result(db, sql);

    /* Done. */
    sqlite3_close(db);

    return 0;
}
```

Results

Running the program yields the following results:

```
1. Register political Collation

2. Select records using default collation.
   TRACE: select * from issues order by issue
issue
-----------------
Defense
Deficit
Economy
Education
Environment
Foreign Policy
Health Care
National Security
Social Security
Unemployment

Select records using political collation.
   TRACE: select * from issues order by issue collate POLITICAL
issue
-----------------
Health Care
Foreign Policy
National Security
Economy
Social Security
Unemployment
Environment
Defense
Education
Deficit

Select again using political collation.
   TRACE: select * from issues order by issue collate POLITICAL
issue
-----------------
National Security
Defense
Unemployment
Deficit
Foreign Policy
Education
Social Security
```

```
Health Care
Environment
Economy
```

Step 1 registers the political collation sequence. Step 2 selects records using SQLite's default binary collation, which returns records in alphabetical order. Step 3 selects records twice using the political Collation, obtaining different results each time. As the results indicate, we are right on the mark. In fact, the more times you select using the POLITICAL collation, the more you are apt to find that the results continually change. Politics can be very complicated.

Collation on Demand

SQLite provides a way to defer collation registration until it is actually needed. So if you are not sure your application is going to need something like the POLITICAL collation, you can use the sqlite3_collation_needed() function to defer its registration to the last possible moment (which incidentally seems befitting of this particular collation). You simply provide sqlite3_collation_needed() with a callback function, which SQLite can rely on to register unknown collation sequences as needed, given their name. It is a callback for a callback, so to speak. Better yet, it's like saying to SQLite, "Here, if you are ever asked to use a Collation that you don't recognize, call this function, and it will register the unknown sequence, then you can continue your work."

The sqlite3_collation_needed() function is declared as follows:

```
int sqlite3_collation_needed(
  sqlite3* db,      /* connection handle  */
  void* data,       /* application data   */
  void(*crf)(void*,sqlite3*,int eTextRep,const char*)
);
```

The crf argument (the collation registration function as I call it) points to the function that will register the unknown Collation. For clarity, it is defined as follows:

```
void crf( void* data,     /* application data */
          sqlite3* db,     /* database handle */
          int eTextRep,    /* encoding */
          const char*)     /* collation name */
```

The db and data arguments of crf() are the values passed into the first and second arguments of sqlite3_collation_needed(), respectively. To make it all clear, say we want to defer all collation registration. A possible implementation that anticipates the POLITCAL Collation and uses some default binary comparison function for all other unknown Collations would be implemented as shown in Listing 7-14.

Listing 7-14. *Collation Registration Function*

```
void crf( void* data, sqlite3* db,
          int eTextRep, const char* cname)
{
    if(strcmp(collation_name, "POLITICAL") == 0) {
        /* Political collation has not been registered and is now needed */
        sqlite3_create_collation( db, "POLITICAL",
                                  SQLITE_UTF8, db,
                                  political_collation );
    } else {
        /* Punt: Use some default comparison function this collation. */
        sqlite3_create_collation( db, collation_name,
                                  SQLITE_UTF8, db,
                                   default_collation );
    }
}
```

Thus POLITCAL will get registered only if it is ever referenced. Likewise, if SQLite encounters something like

```
select * from issues order by issue COLLATE EMOTIONAL;
```

our crf() handler will just install a generic comparison function default_collation() (which I just made up) as the comparison function for EMOTIONAL collations. Bottom line: the sqlite3_collation_needed() handler's job is to take a Collation name and register a Collation to associate with it.

A Practical Application

We will conclude this chapter with an application of Collations that may prove a little more useful than the previous example (if not more consistent). We will combine what we've learned from functions to create a collation that helps out with date formats. Now, it turns out that ISO dates by virtue of their format happen to sort both lexicographically and chronologically. That is, if you sort a set of ISO dates alphabetically, they will end up in the correct chronological order. As a result, ISO dates tend to work just fine in SQLite.

Let's say you that have some data that you want to pass back and forth between SQLite and an Oracle database. And in your data you have to deal with Oracle style dates. Oracle dates, of the form DD-MONTH-YY, don't simultaneously sort lexicographically and chronologically. It's one or the other, but not both.

And while it's possible to get Oracle to use ISO or ANSI dates, rather than bumbling with converting back and forth, you would rather just have SQLite be able to sort Oracle dates as well as it does ISO dates. This is a perfect job for a user-defined Collation.

The Comparison Function

Rather than using a string compare, we parse the date format, breaking it down into its individual parts, and sort them numerically. The comparison function is simple, as you can see in Listing 7-15.

Listing 7-15. *Oracle Date Collation Function*

```c
int oracle_date_collation( void* data,
                           int len1, const void* arg1,
                           int len2, const void* arg2 )
{
    int len;
    date d1;
    date d2;

    strncpy(&zDate2[0], arg2, len);
    zDate2[len] = '\0';

    /* Convert dates to date struct */
    oracle_date_str_to_struct(arg1, &d1);
    oracle_date_str_to_struct(arg2, &d2);

    fprintf(stdout, "collate_fn() : date1=%s, date2=%s\n", zDate1, zDate2);

    /* Compare structs */

    if(d1.year < d2.year) {
        return -1;
    }
    else if(d1.year > d2.year) {
        return 1;
    }

    /* If this far, years are equal. */

    if(d1.month < d2.month) {
        return -1;
    }
    else if(d1.month > d2.month) {
        return 1;
    }

    /* If this far, months are equal. */

    if(d1.day < d2.day) {
        return -1;
    }
    else if(d1.day > d2.day) {
        return 1;
    }
```

```
    /* If this far, dates are equal. */

    return 0;
}
```

Date Parsing

This function uses another function, called oracle_date_str_to_struct(), to parse the dates
and populate a generic date struct. This function is implemented as shown in Listing 7-16.

Listing 7-16. *The Oracle Date Parsing Function*

```
int oracle_date_str_to_struct(const char* value, date* d)
{
    const char* date, *tmp;
    char *start, *end, zDay[3], zMonth[4], zYear[3];

    date = get_date(value);

    if(date == NULL) {
        fprintf(stderr, "Invalid date\n");
        return -1;
    }

    /* Find first '-' */
    start = strchr(date,'-');

    /* Find last '-' */
    end   = strchr(start+1,'-');

    /* Extract day part, convert to int*/
    strncpy(zDay, date,2);
    zDay[2] = '\0';
    d->day = atoi(zDay);

    /* Extract month part, convert to int*/
    strncpy(zMonth, start+1,3);
    zMonth[3] = 0;
    tmp = uppercase(zMonth);
    d->month = month_num(tmp);
    free((void*)tmp);

    /* Extract year part, convert to int*/
    strncpy(zYear, end+1,2);
    zYear[2] = '\0';
    d->year = atoi(zYear);
```

```
    free((void*)date);

    return 0;
}
```

This function uses another function, get_date(), to extract the minimum part of the string, which makes up a complete Oracle date format. It uses Perl Compatible Regular Expressions to do this. Using a regular expression to define the date format makes it easier to tweak without having to do any additional coding. Using get_date() to extract a date value from a string along with a flexible regex allows us some flexibility to deal with sloppy dates, if needed. The get_date() function is defined in Listing 7-17.

Listing 7-17. *The get_date() Function*

```c
#define ORACLE_DATE_REGEX "[0-9]{1,2}-[a-zA-Z]{3,3}-[0-9]{2,2}";

const char* get_date(const char* value)
{
    pcre *re;
    const char *error, *pattern;
    int erroffset;
    int ovector[3];
    int value_length;
    int rc, substring_length;
    char* result, *substring_start;

    pattern = ORACLE_DATE_REGEX;

    re = pcre_compile(
        pattern,                /* the pattern */
        0,                      /* default options */
        &error,                 /* for error message */
        &erroffset,             /* for error offset */
        NULL);                  /* use default character tables */

    /* Compilation failed */
    if (re == NULL) {
        return NULL;
    }

    value_length = (int)strlen(value);

    rc = pcre_exec(
        re,            /* the compiled pattern */
        NULL,          /* no extra data - we didn't study the pattern */
        value,         /* the value string */
        value_length,  /* the length of the value */
        0,             /* start at offset 0 in the value */
```

```
        0,              /* default options */
        ovector,        /* output vector for substring information */
        3);             /* number of elements in the output vector */

    if (rc < 0) {
        /* Match error */
        return NULL;
    }

    substring_start = (char*)value + ovector[0];
    substring_length = ovector[1] - ovector[0];
    result = malloc(substring_length);
    strncpy(result, substring_start, substring_length);
    result[substring_length] = '\0';

    return result;
}
```

The Test Program

All three of the above functions work together to collate Oracle dates in chronological order.
Our example program is shown in Listing 7-18.

Listing 7-18. *The Oracle Collation Test Program*

```
int main(int argc, char **argv)
{
    int rc;
    sqlite3 *db;
    char *sql;

    sqlite3_open("test.db", &db);

    /* Install oracle related date functions. */
    install_date_functions(db);

    /* Register Collation. */
    fprintf(stdout, "Registering collation sequence oracle_date\n");
    sqlite3_create_collation( db, "oracle_date",
                         SQLITE_UTF8, db,
                         oracle_date_collation );

    /* Create dates table, add records. */
    setup(db);

    /* Turn SQL logging on. */
    log_sql(db, 1);
```

```
    /* Test default collation. */
    fprintf(stdout, "Select records. Use default collation.\n");
    sql = "select * from dates order by date";
    print_sql_result(db, sql);

    /* Test Oracle collation. */
    fprintf(stdout, "\nSelect records. Use Oracle data collation. \n");
    sql = "select * from dates order by date collate oracle_date";
    print_sql_result(db, sql);

    /* Done. */
    sqlite3_close(db);

    return 0;
}
```

Results

Running the program yields the following output:

```
Registering collation sequence oracle_date
Select records. Use default collation.
  TRACE: select * from dates order by date
id date
-- ----------
4  1-APR-05
8  1-AUG-05
12 1-DEC-05
2  1-FEB-05
1  1-JAN-05
7  1-JUL-05
6  1-JUN-05
3  1-MAR-05
5  1-MAY-05
11 1-NOV-05
10 1-OCT-05
9  1-SEP-05

Select records. Use Oracle data collation.
  TRACE: select * from dates order by date collate oracle_date
collate_fn() : date1=1-DEC-05, date2=1-NOV-05
collate_fn() : date1=1-OCT-05, date2=1-SEP-05
collate_fn() : date1=1-NOV-05, date2=1-SEP-05
collate_fn() : date1=1-NOV-05, date2=1-OCT-05
collate_fn() : date1=1-AUG-05, date2=1-JUL-05
collate_fn() : date1=1-JUN-05, date2=1-MAY-05
collate_fn() : date1=1-JUL-05, date2=1-MAY-05
```

```
collate_fn() : date1=1-JUL-05, date2=1-JUN-05
collate_fn() : date1=1-SEP-05, date2=1-MAY-05
collate_fn() : date1=1-SEP-05, date2=1-JUN-05
collate_fn() : date1=1-SEP-05, date2=1-JUL-05
collate_fn() : date1=1-SEP-05, date2=1-AUG-05
collate_fn() : date1=1-APR-05, date2=1-MAR-05
collate_fn() : date1=1-FEB-05, date2=1-JAN-05
collate_fn() : date1=1-MAR-05, date2=1-JAN-05
collate_fn() : date1=1-MAR-05, date2=1-FEB-05
collate_fn() : date1=1-MAY-05, date2=1-JAN-05
collate_fn() : date1=1-MAY-05, date2=1-FEB-05
collate_fn() : date1=1-MAY-05, date2=1-MAR-05
collate_fn() : date1=1-MAY-05, date2=1-APR-05
id date
-- ----------
1  1-JAN-05
2  1-FEB-05
3  1-MAR-05
4  1-APR-05
5  1-MAY-05
6  1-JUN-05
7  1-JUL-05
8  1-AUG-05
9  1-SEP-05
10 1-OCT-05
11 1-NOV-05
12 1-DEC-05
```

So there you have it. If I were really serious about all this, I would implement strict type checking for columns that had Oracle-style dates. I would implement a validate_oradate() SQL function that calls get_date() to determine if the date is legitimate. I would then declare all related columns in my tables as oradate. Included in their declaration would be the oracle_date collation. For example:

```
create table log ( id autoincrement,
                   date oradate COLLATE oracle_date CHECK(get_date(date)),
                   entry text );
```

Notice that I use a CHECK constraint for strict typing in this case. It works just as easily (if not more easily) than the trigger functions used earlier for checking a single column (while the trigger approach can be easier for checking all columns in an entire table). Working together, these user-defined functions ensure that the oracle_date collation is always presented with properly formatted dates to compare.

Summary

As I hope some of the examples in this chapter demonstrate, user-defined functions, aggregates, and Collations can be surprisingly useful. And while it certainly helps that SQLite is an open source library, meaning that you are free to dig in and modify it to your heart's content, the extensions part of the C API goes a long way in providing a friendly, easy-to-user interface that makes it possible to implement a wide range of powerful extensions and customizations, especially when combined with other features already present in SQLite.

In the next chapter, you will see how many extension languages take advantage of this. They use the C API to make it possible to implement user-defined functions, aggregates, and collations in different languages.

CHAPTER 8

■■■■

Language Extensions

SQLite's native language is C. It is written in C and has its own C API. The open source community, however, has provided many extensions for SQLite that make it accessible to many programming languages and libraries such as Perl, Python, Ruby, Java, Qt, and ODBC. In many cases there are multiple extensions to choose from for a given language, developed by different people to meet different needs.

Many extensions conform to various API standards. One of the SQLite Perl extensions, for example, follows the Perl DBI—Perl's standard interface for database access. Similarly, one of the Python extensions conforms to Python's DB API specification, as does at least one of the Java extensions to JDBC. Regardless of their particular APIs, internally all extensions work on top of the same SQLite C API, which has its own unique features and design. And to some degree, all extensions reflect this design. Some extensions provide both a standard interface that conforms to their particular API standard as well as an alternative interface that better reflects the design of the SQLite API. Therefore, in such cases you can choose which interface works best for you based on your requirements.

In general, all extensions have the same comparative anatomy regardless of their particular API. They follow a similar pattern. Once you understand this pattern, every interface will start to look similar in many respects. There is some kind of connection object representing a single connection to the database, and some kind of cursor object representing a SQL query from which you can both execute commands and iterate over results. Conceptually, it is quite simple. Internally, you are looking at a `sqlite3` structure and a `sqlite3_stmt` structure, and from reading Chapter 5 you should have a good feel for how these work. The same rules apply for language extensions as for the C API.

This chapter covers language extensions for six popular languages: Perl, Python, Ruby, Java, Tcl, and PHP. The intent is to provide you with a convenient introduction with which to quickly get started using SQLite in a variety of different languages. Coverage for each language follows a common outline composed of four topics that pertain to both general database work and specific SQLite features:

- Connecting to databases

- Executing queries

- Using bound parameters

- Implementing user-defined functions and aggregates

Together these topics constitute the vast majority of what you will ever use in any particular SQLite extension. Not every extension supports all of these topics. For instance, some don't offer bound parameters. Conversely, some extensions offer unique features that are outside of the topics covered here. The aim here is to provide a consistent, straightforward process with which to easily get started using SQLite in a wide variety of languages. Once you get started with any extension, it is usually easy to pick up any special features available in that extension.

Where appropriate, this chapter addresses how different extensions use various parts of the C API in order to help you understand what is going on under the hood. If you have not read Chapter 5, I strongly recommend that you do so. No matter what language you program in, it will almost always be helpful to understand how SQLite works in order to make the most of it and thus write good code. It will help you select the most suitable query methods, understand the scope of transactions, and know how to anticipate, deal with, or avoid locks, among other things.

This chapter is not a language reference. I assume that you know how to program and are familiar with your particular language of interest. SQLite is first and foremost a programmer's database, and that is the assumption I've made here—you are a programmer and I need not cover what you already know.

Selecting an Extension

In some cases multiple interfaces are available for some languages. In such cases (with the exception of Python), I cover the interface that best fits the following criteria:

- Support for SQLite 3

- Good documentation

- Stability

- Portability

Despite these criteria, there were multiple candidates in some cases that met all the qualifications. In such cases the tiebreaker was more a matter of personal preference than anything else. But the purpose here is not to favor a particular extension. It is to teach concepts so that you can easily pick any extension in any language and quickly put it and SQLite to good use.

And the reasons I chose a particular extension may not be the reasons you would. There are quite a few things to consider when you select a particular extension. You will have requirements that must be satisfied when choosing an extension. Some of the things you might want to take into consideration include the following:

- **License compatibility**: The extension's license can directly affect how you can use it. If you are writing code for a commercial product, you definitely need to take this into consideration.

- **Data type mapping**: Another important point is how the extension maps SQLite's storage classes to the language's native types. Are all values returned as text? If not, is there an easy way to determine the mappings? Do you have any control over how the mapping is done?

- **Query methods**: Three different query methods are supported in the C API. Which one does the extension use? Ideally it supports all three. You are already familiar with the pros and cons of each approach, and it's nice to have all three methods in different situations.

- **API coverage**: How well does the extension cover other areas that don't easily map to many standard database interfaces? For example, does it allow you to call the SQL trace function, or operational security functions? Are these something you need?

- **Linkage and distribution**: How easy is it to use the extension with a particular version of SQLite? Does it include a version of SQLite in the distribution? Does it use a shared library or is it statically linked to a particular version? What if you need to upgrade SQLite; how easily can you do this with the extension?

There are other considerations as well, such as community support, mailing list activity, maintainer support and responsiveness, regression testing, code quality... the list goes on. All of these things may play an important role in your decision to use a particular extension. Only you can answer these questions for yourself.

The SQLite Wiki has a page that provides an exhaustive list of language interfaces, located at `www.sqlite.org/cvstrac/wiki?p=SqliteWrappers`. All of the interfaces covered here were taken from this list. The source code for all of the examples in this chapter is located in the *ch8* directory of the examples zip file, available at the Apress website.

Perl

There are two SQLite extensions for Perl. The one covered here is written by Matt Sergeant, and can be found on CPAN (`http://search.cpan.org/~msergeant/`). This extension follows very closely the Perl DBI standard; therefore, if you understand DBI, you will have no trouble using the extension. The full documentation for Perl DBI can be obtained by typing `man DBI` on POSIX systems, or online at `http://search.cpan.org/search?module=DBI`.

Installation

The current version supporting SQLite 3 at the time of this writing is `DBD-SQLite-1.11`. You can install it by using CPAN or by manually building the package from source. The prerequisites for the SQLite DBD module are of course Perl, a C compiler, as well as the DBI module. To install `DBD::SQLite` using CPAN, invoke the CPAN shell from the command line as follows:

```
mike@linux # cpan
cpan> install DBD::SQLite
```

To install from source in Linux/Unix, change to a temporary directory and do the following:

```
mike@linux # wget http://search.cpan.org/CPAN/authors/id/M/MS/MSERGEANT/
DBD-SQLite-1.11.tar.gz

... lots of wget gibberish ...
```

```
mike@linux # tar xzvf DBD-SQLite-1.11.tar.gz

... lots of tar gibberish ...

mike@linux # cd DBD-SQLite-1.11
mike@linux DBD-SQLite-1.11 # perl Makefile.PL

... lots of perl gibberish ...

Checking installed SQLite version...
Looks good
mike@linux DBD-SQLite-1.11 # make install

... more perl gibberish ...
```

The SQLite Perl extension includes its own copy of the SQLite 3, so there is no need to compile and install SQLite beforehand. SQLite is embedded in the extension.

Connecting

To ensure that you have the SQLite driver installed, you can use the DBI available_drivers() within Perl:

```
print "Drivers: " . join(", ", DBI->available_drivers()), "\n";
```

You connect to a database using the standard DBI::connect function, as follows:

```
use DBI;
my $dbh = DBI->connect( "dbi:SQLite:dbname=foods.db", "", "",
                        { RaiseError => 1 });
$dbh->disconnect;
```

The second and third arguments correspond to the driver name and database name. The third and fourth correspond to username and password, which are not applicable to SQLite.

The function returns a database handle object representing the database connection. Internally, this corresponds to a single sqlite3 structure. You can create in-memory databases by passing :memory: for the name of the database. In this case, all tables and database objects will then reside in memory for the duration of the session, and will be destroyed when the connection is closed. You close the database using the database handle's disconnect method.

Query Processing

Queries are performed using the standard DBI interface as well. You can use the prepare(), execute(), fetch(), or selectrow() functions of the database connection handle. All of these are fully documented in the DBI man page. An example of using queries is shown in Listing 8-1.

Listing 8-1. *Executing Queries in Perl*

```perl
use DBI;
# Connect to database
my $dbh = DBI->connect( "dbi:SQLite:dbname=foods.db", "", "",
                          { RaiseError => 1 });

# Prepare the statment
my $sth = $dbh->prepare("SELECT name FROM foods LIMIT 3");

# Execute
print "\nArray:\n\n";
$sth->execute;

# Iterate over results and print
while($row = $sth->fetchrow_arrayref) {
    print @$row[0] . "\n";
}

# Do the same thing, this time using hashref
print "\nHash:\n\n";
$sth->execute;
while($row = $sth->fetchrow_hashref) {
    print @$row{'name'} . "\n";
}

# Finalize the statement
$sth->finish;

#Disconnect

$dbh->disconnect;
```

Internally, the prepare() method corresponds to the sqlite3_prepare() method. Similarly, execute() calls the first sqlite3_step() method. It automatically figures out if there is data to be returned. If there is no data (e.g., non-SELECT statements), it automatically finalizes the query. The fetchrow_array(), fetchrow_hashref(), and fetch() methods call sqlite3_step() as well, returning a single row in the result set, if one is available.

Additionally, you can run non-SELECT statements in one step using the database object's do() method. Listing 8-2 illustrates this using an in-memory database.

Listing 8-2. *The do() Method*

```perl
use DBI;
my $dbh = DBI->connect("dbi:SQLite:dbname=:memory:", "", "", { RaiseError => 1 });
$dbh->do("CREATE TABLE cast (name)");
$dbh->do("INSERT INTO cast VALUES ('Elaine')");
$dbh->do("INSERT INTO cast VALUES ('Jerry')");
$dbh->do("INSERT INTO cast VALUES ('Kramer')");
```

```
$dbh->do("INSERT INTO cast VALUES ('George')");
$dbh->do("INSERT INTO cast VALUES ('Newman')");

my $sth = $dbh->prepare("SELECT * FROM cast");
$sth->execute;

while($row = $sth->fetch) {
    print join(", ", @$row), "\n";
}
$sth->finish;
$dbh->disconnect;
```

The statement handle object's finish() method will call sqlite3_finalize() on the query object, if it has not already done so. This program produces the following output:

```
Elaine
Jerry
Kramer
George
Newman
```

Parameter Binding

Parameter binding follows the method defined in the DBI specification. While SQLite supports both positional and named parameters, the Perl interface uses only positional parameters, as illustrated in Listing 8-3.

Listing 8-3. *Parameter Binding in Perl*

```
use DBI;

my $dbh = DBI->connect( "dbi:SQLite:dbname=foods.db", "", "",
                        { RaiseError => 1 });

my $sth = $dbh->prepare("SELECT * FROM foods where name like :1");
$sth->execute('C%');

while($row = $sth->fetchrow_hashref) {
    print @$row{'name'} . "\n";
}

$sth->finish;
$dbh->disconnect;
```

The execute() method takes the parameter values defined in prepare().

User-Defined Functions and Aggregates

User-defined functions and aggregates are implemented using private methods of the driver. They follow closely to their counterparts in the SQLite C API. Functions are registered using the following private method:

```
$dbh->func( $name, $argc, $func_ref, "create_function" )
```

Here $name specifies the SQL function name, $argc the number of arguments, and $func_ref a reference to the Perl function that provides the implementation. Listing 8-4 illustrates an implementation of hello_newman() in Perl.

Listing 8-4. *hello_newman() in Perl*

```
use DBI;

sub hello_newman {
    return "Hello Jerry";
}

# Connect
my $dbh = DBI->connect( "dbi:SQLite:dbname=foods.db", "", "",
                        { RaiseError => 1 });

# Register function
$dbh->func('hello_newman', 0, \&hello_newman, 'create_function');

# Call it
print $dbh->selectrow_arrayref("SELECT hello_newman()")->[0] . "\n";

$dbh->disconnect;
```

If you provide -1 as the number of arguments, then the function will accept a variable number of arguments. Listing 8-5 has Newman replying to each of the names supplied as arguments. If no arguments are provided, he simply replies "Hello Jerry."

Listing 8-5. *hello_newman() in Perl with Variable Arguments*

```
use DBI;

sub hello_newman {
    if (@_ == 0) {
        return "Hello Jerry";
    }

    return "Hello " . join ", ", @_;
}
```

```
# Connect
my $dbh = DBI->connect( "dbi:SQLite:dbname=foods.db", "", "",
                        { RaiseError => 1 });

# Register function
$dbh->func('hello_newman', -1, \&hello_newman, 'create_function');

# Call it
print $dbh->selectrow_arrayref("SELECT hello_newman()")->[0] . "\n";
print $dbh->selectrow_arrayref(
   "SELECT hello_newman('Elaine', 'Jerry')")->[0] . "\n";
print $dbh->selectrow_arrayref(
   "SELECT hello_newman('Elaine', 'Jerry', 'George')")->[0] . "\n";

$dbh->disconnect;
```

The hello_newman() function is passed all the arguments provided in the SQL statement in the @_ variable. This example produces the following output:

```
Hello Jerry
Hello Elaine
Hello Elaine, Jerry
Hello Elaine, Jerry, George
```

Aggregates

User-defined aggregates are implemented as packages. Each package implements a step function and a finalize function. The step function is called for each row that is selected. The first value supplied to the function is the context, which is a persistent value maintained between calls to the function. The remaining values are the arguments to the aggregate function supplied in the SQL statement. The finalize function is provided the same context as the step function. The following example implements a simple SUM aggregate called perlsum. The aggregate is implemented in a package called perlsum.pm, shown in Listing 8-6.

Listing 8-6. *The perlsum() Aggregate*

```
package perlsum;

sub new { bless [], shift; }

sub step {
    my ( $self, $value ) = @_;
    @$self[0] += $value;
}
```

```
sub finalize {
    my $self = $_[0];
    return @$self[0];
}

sub init {
    $dbh = shift;
    $dbh->func( "perlsum", 1, "perlsum", "create_aggregate" );
}

1;
```

The init function is used to register the aggregate in the database connection. Listing 8-7 is a simple program illustrating its use.

Listing 8-7. *A perlsum() Test Program*

```
use DBI;
use perlsum;

# Connect
my $dbh = DBI->connect( "dbi:SQLite:dbname=foods.db", "", "",
                        { RaiseError => 1 });

perlsum::init($dbh);

# Call it
print $dbh->selectrow_arrayref("SELECT perlsum(id) from foods")->[0] . "\n";

$dbh->disconnect;
```

There are two other private methods in the driver. One is last_insert_rowid(), used for obtaining the last primary key value generated by an autoincrement key in an INSERT statement, and the other is for setting the busy timeout. These are demonstrated in Listing 8-8.

Listing 8-8. *The last_insert_rowid() and busy_timeout() Methods*

```
use DBI;
use perlsum;

# Connect
my $dbh = DBI->connect( "dbi:SQLite:dbname=foods.db", "", "",
                        { RaiseError => 1 });

# Set timeout to 5 seconds
print $dbh->func(5, 'busy_timeout') . "\n";
print $dbh->func('busy_timeout') . "\n";
```

```
$dbh->do("INSERT INTO foods (type_id, name) values (9, 'Junior Mints')");

# Print the last generated autoincrement key value
print $dbh->func('last_insert_rowid') . "\n";

$dbh->disconnect;
```

Python

There are two SQLite wrappers for Python: PySQLite and APSW. PySQLite was one of the first SQLite extensions for Python. Currently, it is a Python DB API 2–compliant extension that supports both SQLite version 2 and version 3 databases. It follows the Python database API specification very closely and includes many additional features as well.

APSW, short for "Another Python SQLite Wrapper," was built specifically to take advantage of Python's newer language features such as iterators, which weren't around when the Python Database API specification was drafted. It uses these language features to provide a simpler way to work with SQLite, often resulting in cleaner, more concise code. Unlike PySQLite, APSW only supports SQLite 3 databases and does not conform to the Python DB API specification, nor does it have any intention of ever doing so.

The reason I cover both extensions is because APSW capitalizes on new language features (iterators and generators) that make for a simpler and more powerful database interface. To be fair, PySQLite version 2, written after APSW, supports these language features as well. One of the other arguments for APSW is its small footprint and simplicity. Which extension you choose depends on your requirements and/or personal preference. Both extensions compile and run on Windows and POSIX systems alike.

PySQLite

I wrote the original version of PySQLite and started the project in 2002, which then was written using the SQLite 2.x API. Gerhard Häring has since taken over the project and completely rewritten it for PySQLite version 2, which supports SQLite version 3. Project information for PySQLite can be found at http://pysqlite.org. Both the source code and native Windows binaries are available for download.

Installation

Windows users are encouraged to use the provided binaries rather than building them by hand. On POSIX systems, you build and install PySQLite using Python's distutils package. The prerequisites are a C compiler, Python 2.3 or later, and SQLite 3.1 or later. After unpacking the source code, compile the code with the following command:

```
python setup.py build
```

distutils will normally be able to figure out where everything is on your system. If not, you will get an error, in which case you need to edit the setup.cfg file in the main directory to point out where things are. If everything goes well, you should see "Creating library..." in the output, indicating a successful build. Next install the library:

```
python setup.py install
```

To test the install, change to another directory and do the following:

```
mike@linux # python
>>> from pysqlite2 import test
>>> test.test()
...................................................................................
............
----------------------------------------------------------------------
Ran 101 tests in 0.182s
```

You should not see any errors. If you do, report them to the PySQLite bug tracker at http://initd.org/tracker/pysqlite.

For Windows systems, simply download the binary distribution and run the installer. The only prerequisite in this case is that SQLite 3.2 or higher be installed on your system.

Connecting

The PySQLite package is in pysqlite2. The DB API module is located in dbapi2. You connect to a database using the module's connect() function, passing in the relative name or complete file path of the database file you wish to open, as follows:

```
from pysqlite2 import dbapi2 as sqlite

db = sqlite.connect("foods.db")
```

The usual rules apply: you can use in-memory databases by passing in the name :memory: as the database name; new databases are created for new files; and so forth.

Query Processing

Query execution is done according to the Python DB API Specification 2. You create a cursor object with which to run the query and obtain results. Internally, a cursor object holds a sqlite3_stmt handle. Listing 8-9 illustrates executing a basic query.

Listing 8-9. *A Basic Query in PySQLite*

```
from pysqlite2 import dbapi2 as sqlite

# Connect
con = sqlite.connect("foods.db")

# Prepare a statement and execute. This calls sqlite3_prepare() and sqlite3_step()
cur = con.cursor()
cur.execute('SELECT * FROM foods LIMIT 10')
```

```
# Iterate over results, print the name field (row[2])
row = cur.fetchone()
while row:
    print row[2]
    # Get next row
    row = cur.fetchone()

cur.close()
con.close()
```

Running this code produces the following output:

```
Bagels
Bagels, raisin
Bavarian Cream Pie
Bear Claws
Black and White cookies
Bread (with nuts)
Butterfingers
Carrot Cake
Chips Ahoy Cookies
Chocolate Bobka
```

Query compilation and the first step of execution are performed together in Cursor.execute().
It calls sqlite3_prepare() followed by sqlite3_step(). For modifying queries, this completes
the query (short of finalizing the statement handle). For SELECT statements, it fetches the first
row of the result. The close() method finalizes the statement handle.

PySQLite 2 supports iterator-style result sets, similar to APSW. For example, Listing 8-9
could be rewritten as shown in Listing 8-10.

Listing 8-10. *An Iterator-Style Query*

```
from pysqlite2 import dbapi2 as sqlite

con = sqlite.connect("foods.db")
cur = con.cursor()
cur.execute('SELECT * FROM foods LIMIT 10')

for row in cur:
    print row[2]
```

Parameter Binding

PySQLite supports parameter binding by both position and name. You do this by using
Cursor.execute(). Compilation, binding, and the first step of execution are performed in the one
call to execute(). You specify positional parameters by passing a tuple as the second argument

to execute(). You specify named parameters by passing a dictionary rather than a tuple. Listing 8-11 illustrates both forms of parameter binding.

Listing 8-11. *Parameter Binding in PySQLite*

```
from pysqlite2 import dbapi2 as sqlite

con = sqlite.connect("foods.db")
cur = con.cursor()
cur.execute('INSERT INTO episodes (name) VALUES (?)', ('Soup Nazi'))
cur.close()

cur = con.cursor()
cur.execute('INSERT INTO episodes (name) VALUES (:name)', {'name':'Soup Nazi'})
cur.close()
```

This model does not support reuse of compiled queries (sqlite3_reset()). To do this, use Cursor.executemany(). While the DB API specifies that executemany should take a list of parameters, PySQLite extends it to accommodate iterators and generators as well. For example, the canonical form is shown in Listing 8-12.

Listing 8-12. *The executemany() Method*

```
from pysqlite2 import dbapi2 as sqlite

con = sqlite.connect("foods.db")
cur = con.cursor()

episodes = ['Soup Nazi', 'The Fusilli Jerry']
cur.executemany('INSERT INTO episodes (name) VALUES (?)', episodes)
cur.close()
con.commit()
```

But you could just as easily use a generator, as shown in Listing 8-13.

Listing 8-13. *The executemany() Method with a Generator*

```
from pysqlite2 import dbapi2 as sqlite

con = sqlite.connect("foods.db")
cur = con.cursor()

def episode_generator():
    episodes = ['Soup Nazi', 'The Fusilli Jerry']
    for episode in episodes:
        yield (episode,)

cur.executemany('INSERT INTO episodes (name) VALUES (?)', episode_generator())
cur.close()
con.commit()
```

In both Listing 8-12 and Listing 8-13, the query is compiled only once and reused for each item in the sequence or iterator. This improves overall performance when you are running a large batch of identical queries.

TRANSACTION HANDLING IN PYSQLITE

It is important to notice the `con.commit()` lines in the previous examples. Don't forget them if you use PySQLite. If you don't include them, then all transactions in the examples will be rolled back. This behavior differs from both the SQLite C API and other extensions, and it might surprise you. By default, SQLite runs in autocommit mode. This means that if you don't explicitly start a transaction, then every statement is automatically run in its own transaction. Thus, if you execute a successful `INSERT`, the record is inserted, end of story. PySQLite, however, starts and finishes transactions behind the scenes, using its own logic to determine when to start and commit transactions based on what kind of SQL you execute. Before passing your SQL statement to SQLite, PySQLite analyzes it. If you issue an `INSERT`, `UPDATE`, `DELETE`, or `REPLACE`, PySQLite will implicitly start a transaction (issue a `BEGIN`). Then, if you issue any other kind of command following it, PySQLite will automatically issue a `COMMIT` before executing that command. Therefore, if you issue an `INSERT` statement, and then close the connection, your `INSERT` will never make it to the database unless you manually commit it, or strangely enough—run a `SELECT` statement after it. Furthermore, this transaction logic places an additional constraint on your code in that you cannot use `ON CONFLICT ROLLBACK`; otherwise it interferes with PySQLite's monitoring of your transactions.

However, it is possible to turn off this behavior and restore the default SQLite behavior. To do so, you must explicitly turn autocommit mode back on by setting `isolation_level` of the database connection to None, as follows:

```
from pysqlite2 import dbapi2 as sqlite

# Turn on autocommit mode
con = sqlite.connect("foods.db", isolation_level=None)
```

User-Defined Functions and Aggregates

You register user-defined functions using `create_function()`, defined as follows:

```
con.create_function(name, args, pyfunc)
```

Here name is the SQL name of the function, args the number of arguments accepted by the function, and pyfync the Python function that implements the SQL function. Listing 8-14 shows a Python implementation of `hello_newman()` using PySQLite.

Listing 8-14. *hello_newman() in PySQLite*

```
from pysqlite2 import dbapi2 as sqlite

def hello_newman():
    return 'Hello Jerry'
```

```
con = sqlite.connect(":memory:")
con.create_function("hello_newman", 0, hello_newman)
cur = con.cursor()

cur.execute("select hello_newman()")
print cur.fetchone()[0]
```

If you use -1 as the number of arguments, then the function will accept a variable number of arguments. A rendition accepting multiple arguments is illustrated in Listing 8-15.

Listing 8-15. *hello_newman() in PySQLite with Variable Arguments*

```
import string
from pysqlite2 import dbapi2 as sqlite

def hello_newman(*args):
    if len(args) > 0:
        return 'Hello %s' % string.join(args, ', ')
    return 'Hello Jerry'

con = sqlite.connect(":memory:")
con.create_function("hello_newman", -1, hello_newman)
cur = con.cursor()

cur.execute("select hello_newman()")
print cur.fetchone()[0]

cur.execute("select hello_newman('Elaine')")
print cur.fetchone()[0]

cur.execute("select hello_newman('Elaine', 'Jerry')")
print cur.fetchone()[0]

cur.execute("select hello_newman('Elaine', 'Jerry', 'George')")
print cur.fetchone()[0]
```

This produces the following output:

```
Hello Jerry
Hello Elaine
Hello Elaine, Jerry
Hello Elaine, Jerry, George
```

Aggregates

PySQLite implements user-defined aggregates as Python classes. These classes must implement step() and finalize() methods. You register aggregates using Connection::create_aggregate(), which takes three arguments: the function's SQL name, the number of arguments, and the class name that implements the aggregate. Listing 8-16 implements a simple SUM aggregate called pysum.

Listing 8-16. *The pysum() Aggregate in PySQLite*

```
from pysqlite2 import dbapi2 as sqlite

class pysum:
    def init(self):
        self.sum = 0

    def step(self, value):
        self.sum += value

    def finalize(self):
        return self.sum

con = sqlite.connect("foods.db")
con.create_aggregate("pysum", 1, pysum)
cur = con.cursor()
cur.execute("select pysum(id) from foods")
print cur.fetchone()[0]
```

APSW

APSW is written and maintained by Roger Binns. Detailed information on APSW can be found at www.rogerbinns.com/apsw.html. Among the other information you will find there is a longer, more detailed list of differences between APSW and PySQLite.

Installation

Like PySQLite, building APSW requires that you have a working C compiler installed on your system, Python, and SQLite version 3. Similarly, once the source is unpacked, building with Python on POSIX systems can be performed by a single command.

```
python setup.py install
```

Building with MinGW on Windows is about as simple:

```
python setup.py build --compile=mingw32 install
```

This creates a single extension—apsw.so (Linux/Mac) or apsw.pyd (Windows)—which can either be installed in the Python site packages directory or simply dropped into the same directory as the scripts that use it.

Connecting

You create a database connection by instantiating a `Connection` object, passing it the name of the database file as the constructor's sole argument:

```
connection=apsw.Connection("foods.db")
```

All of the normal connection rules apply—the name follows the conventions for filenames on the system; a database name of :memory: creates an in-memory database; and so forth.

Query Processing

You execute commands using `Cursor` objects, which are obtained from `Connection.cursor()`. These are very similar to cursors in PySQLite. They are thin wrappers over SQLite statement handles. `Cursor.execute()` can be used as an iterator with which to traverse records in the result set:

```
import apsw

connection=apsw.Connection("foods.db")
cursor=connection.cursor()

for row in cursor.execute("SELECT * FROM foods LIMIT 10"):
    print row[2]
```

You can use a more traditional loop to obtain records through `Cursor.next()`, which returns a tuple containing the fields of the next record.

APSW automatically converts SQLite internal storage classes to similar Python types. Listing 8-17 illustrates this mapping.

Listing 8-17. *Type Mapping in APSW*

```
import apsw
connection=apsw.Connection(":memory:")
cursor=connection.cursor()

c = connection.cursor()
c.execute('create table types(i int, f float, t text, b blob, n)')
c.execute("insert into types values (1, 1.1, '1.1', X'01', NULL)")

for row in cursor.execute('SELECT * FROM types'):
    d = cursor.getdescription()
    i = 0
    for field in row:
        print "%s %5s %-6s %-10s" % ( d[i][0],
                                      d[i][1],
                                      str(field),
                                      type(field) )
        i += 1
```

This produces the following output:

```
i    int   1       <type 'int'>
f  float   1.1     <type 'float'>
t   text   1.1     <type 'str'>
b   blob           <type 'buffer'>
n   None   None    <type 'NoneType'>
```

User-Defined Functions and Aggregates

You create user-defined functions using Connection.createscalarfunction(), which takes two arguments: the SQL function name and the Python function name. The number of arguments is always variable. Listing 8-18 illustrates an example of hello_newman() using APSW.

Listing 8-18. *hello_newman() in APSW*

```
import apsw, string

connection=apsw.Connection(":memory:")

def hello_newman(*args):
    if len(args) > 0:
        return 'Hello %s' % string.join(args, ', ')
    return 'Hello Jerry'

connection.createscalarfunction("hello_newman", hello_newman)

c = connection.cursor()
print c.execute("select hello_newman()").next()[0]
print c.execute("select hello_newman('Elaine')").next()[0]
print c.execute("select hello_newman('Elaine', 'Jerry')").next()[0]
print c.execute("select hello_newman('Elaine', 'Jerry', 'George')").next()[0]
```

Aggregates

You register aggregates using a factory function that specifies the step and finalize functions. The best way to demonstrate this is by example. Consider the example shown in Listing 8-19.

Listing 8-19. *The pysum() Aggregate in APSW*

```
import apsw, string

connection=apsw.Connection("foods.db")

def step(context, *args):
    context['value'] += args[0]
```

```
def finalize(context):
    return context['value']

def pysum():
    return ({'value' : 0}, step, finalize)

connection.createaggregatefunction("pysum", pysum)

c = connection.cursor()
print c.execute("select pysum(id) from foods").next()[0]
```

The pysum function is used to define the step and finalize functions as well as initialize a context. The context here is a dictionary with one entry called 'value', whose initial value is 0. The step function adds to this value the first argument passed to the function. The finalize function simply returns the value built up over the step function iterations.

Ruby

The Ruby extension was written by Jamis Buck of 37 Signals. Detailed information on the extension as well as the source code can be obtained at http://rubyforge.org/projects/sqlite-ruby. There are extensions for both SQLite 2 and 3 databases. The complete documentation for the SQLite 3 extension can be found at http://sqlite-ruby.rubyforge.org/sqlite3/ whereas SQLite 2 is at http://sqlite-ruby.rubyforge.org/sqlite/.

Installation

The extension can be built in two ways: with or without SWIG. The Ruby configuration script will automatically figure out if SWIG is available on your system. You should build the extension with SWIG (the C extension), as that implementation is more stable.

At the time of this writing, the current version of sqlite-ruby is 1.1.0. To build from source, fetch the tarball from http://rubyforge.org/projects/sqlite-ruby. On POSIX systems, simply unpack the tarball and run three setup commands:

```
mike@linux $ tar xjvf sqlite3-ruby-1.1.0.tar.bz2
mike@linux $ cd sqlite3-ruby-1.1.0
mike@linux $ ruby setup.rb config
mike@linux $ ruby setup.rb setup
mike@linux $ ruby setup.rb install
```

If you have Ruby gems installed, you can get Ruby to do everything for you in one step:

```
mike@linux $ gem install --remote sqlite3-ruby
```

Connecting

To load the SQLite extension, you must import the sqlite3 module, using either load or require, as follows:

```
require 'sqlite3'
```

You connect to a database by instantiating a SQLite3::Database object, passing in the name of the database file. By default, columns in result sets are accessible by their ordinal. However, they can be accessed by column name by setting Database::results_as_hash to true:

```
require 'sqlite3'
db = SQLite3::Database.new("foods.db")
db.results_as_hash = true
```

Query Processing

The Ruby extension follows the SQLite API quite closely. It offers both prepared queries and wrapped queries.

Prepared queries are performed via Database::prepare(), which passes back a Statement object, which holds a sqlite3_stmt structure. You execute the query using Statement's execute method, which produces a ResultSet object. You can pass the Statement a block, in which case it will yield the ResultSet object to the block. If you don't use a block, then the Statement will provide the ResultSet object as a return value. ResultSet is used to iterate over the returned rows. Internally, it uses sqlite3_step(). You can get at the rows in ResultSet either through a block using the each() iterator, or by using a conventional loop with the next() method, which returns the next record in the form of an array, or nil if it has reached the end of the set. Listing 8-20 illustrates prepared queries in Ruby.

Listing 8-20. *Prepared Queries in Ruby*

```ruby
#!/usr/bin/env ruby

require 'sqlite3'

db = SQLite3::Database.new('/tmp/foods.db')

stmt = db.prepare('SELECT name FROM episodes')

stmt.execute do | result |
  result.each do | row |
    puts row[0]
  end
end

result = stmt.execute()
result.each do | row |
  puts row[0]
end

stmt.close()
```

It is important to call Statement.close() when you are done to finalize the query.

As a Statement object holds a sqlite3_stmt structure internally, each subsequent call to execute thus reuses the same query, avoiding the need to recompile the query.

Parameter Binding

The Ruby extension supports both positional and named parameter binding. You bind parameters using `Statement::bind_param()` and/or `Statement::bind_params()`. `bind_param()` has the following form:

```
bind_param(param, value)
```

If `param` is a `Fixnum`, then it represents the position (index) of the parameter. Otherwise, it is used as the name of the parameter. `bind_params()` takes a variable number of arguments. If the first argument is a hash, then it uses it to map parameter names to values. Otherwise, it uses each argument as a positional parameter. Listing 8-21 illustrates both forms of parameter binding.

Listing 8-21. *Parameter Binding in Ruby*

```ruby
require 'sqlite3'

db = SQLite3::Database.new("foods.db")
db.results_as_hash = true

# Named paramters

stmt = db.prepare('SELECT * FROM foods where name like :name')
stmt.bind_param(':name', '%Peach%')

stmt.execute() do |result|
  result.each do |row|
    puts row['name']
  end
end

# Positional paramters

stmt = db.prepare('SELECT * FROM foods where name like ? OR type_id = ?')
stmt.bind_params('%Bobka%', 1)

stmt.execute() do |result|
  result.each do |row|
    puts row['name']
  end
end

# Free read lock
stmt.close()
```

If you don't need to use parameters, a shorter way to process queries is using `Database::query()`, which cuts out the `Statement` object and just returns a `ResultSet`, as shown in Listing 8-22.

Listing 8-22. *Using the Database::query() Method in Ruby*

```ruby
require 'sqlite3'

db = SQLite3::Database.new("foods.db")
db.results_as_hash = true

result = db.query('SELECT * FROM foods limit 10')
result.each do |row|
  puts row['name']
end

result.reset()

while row = result.next
  puts row['name']
end
result.close()
```

Like Statement objects, Result objects are also thin wrappers over statement handles, and therefore represent compiled queries. They can be rerun with a call to reset, which calls sqlite3_reset() internally and reexecutes the query. Unlike Statement objects however, they cannot be used for bound parameters.

Other, even shorter, query methods include Database::get_first_row(), which returns the first row of a query, and Database::get_first_value(), which returns the first column of the first row of a query.

User-Defined Functions and Aggregates

User-defined functions are implemented using Database::create_function(), which has the following form:

```ruby
create_function( name, args, text_rep=Constants::TextRep::ANY ) {|func, *args| ...}
```

Here name is the name of the SQL function, args the number of arguments (-1 is variable), and text_rep corresponds to the UTF encoding. Values are UTF8, UTF16LE, UTF16BE, UTF16, and ANY. Finally, the function implementation is defined in the block. Listing 8-23 illustrates a Ruby implementation of hello_newman().

Listing 8-23. *hello_newman() in Ruby*

```ruby
require 'sqlite3'

db = SQLite3::Database.new(':memory:')

db.create_function('hello_newman', -1 ) do |func, *args|
  if args.length == 0
    func.result = 'Hello Jerry'
```

```
    else
      func.result = 'Hello %s' % [args.join(', ')]
    end
end

puts db.get_first_value("SELECT hello_newman()")
puts db.get_first_value("SELECT hello_newman('Elaine')")
puts db.get_first_value("SELECT hello_newman('Elaine', 'Jerry')")
puts db.get_first_value("SELECT hello_newman('Elaine', 'Jerry', 'George')")
```

This program produces the following output:

```
Hello Jerry
Hello Elaine
Hello Elaine, Jerry
Hello Elaine, Jerry, George
```

Aggregates

There are two ways to implement aggregates. One uses blocks, and the other a class. The block approach has embedded in it both the step function and the finalize function. Listing 8-24 illustrates this approach.

Listing 8-24. *The rubysum() Aggregate*

```
require 'sqlite3'

db = SQLite3::Database.new(':memory:')

db.create_aggregate( "rubysum", 1 ) do
    step do |func, value|
      func[ :total ] ||= 0
      func[ :total ] += value.to_i
    end

    finalize do |func|
      func.set_result( func[ :total ] || 0 )
    end
  end

puts db.get_first_value( "SELECT rubysum(id) FROM episodes " )
```

The class approach is similar to PySQLite and Perl, in which you create an aggregate class that has a step and a finalize method. You register the class using `Database::create_aggregate_handler()`. The class implements methods that provide all the needed information to register and run the aggregate. Two class methods and two instance methods are required. The class methods are

- `name()`: This specifies the name of the SQL function. The handler must implement this message.

- `arity()`: This is optional, and specifies the arity (number of arguments) of the function. If the handler does not respond to it, the function will have an arity of -1.

The instance methods are the step function and finalize function. Listing 8-25 illustrates this approach.

Listing 8-25. *A Class Implementation of rubysum()*

```
class RubySumAggregateHandler
  def self.arity; 1; end
  def self.name; "rubysum"; end

  def initialize
    @total = 0
  end

  def step( ctx, name )
    @total += ( name ? name.length : 0 )
  end

  def finalize( ctx )
    ctx.set_result( @total )
  end
end

db.create_aggregate_handler(RubySumAggregateHandler)
puts db.get_first_value("SELECT rubysum(id) FROM episodes")
```

Java

Several Java extensions are available for SQLite. The one covered here is written by Christian Werner, who wrote the SQLite ODBC driver as well. It includes both a JDBC driver and a native JNI extension, which closely shadows the SQLite C API. The extension can be downloaded from `www.ch-werner.de/javasqlite/overview-summary.html#jdbc_driver`.

The main class in the JNI extension is `SQLiteDatabase`. Most of its methods are implemented using callbacks that reference the following interfaces:

- SQLite.Callback

- SQLite.Function

- SQLite.Authorizer

- SQLite.Trace

- SQLite.ProgressHandler

The SQLite.Callback interface is used to process result sets through row handlers, as well as column and type information. SQLite.Authorizer is a thin wrapper over the SQLite C API function sqlite3_set_authorizer(), with which you can intercept database events before they happen. SQLite.Trace is used to view SQL statements as they are compiled, and wraps sqlite3_trace(). SQLite.ProgressHandler wraps sqlite3_progress_handler(), which is used to issue progress events after a specified number of VDBE instructions have been processed.

Installation

The current version requires JDK 1.1 or higher. The extension uses GNU Autoconf, so building and installing requires only three steps:

```
mike@linux $ javasqlite-20050608.tar.gz
mike@linux $ ./configure
mike@linux $ make
mike@linux $ make install
```

The configure script will look for SQLite and the JDK in several default locations. However, to explicitly specify where to look for SQLite and the JDK, use the command-line options --with-sqlite=DIR, --with-sqlite3=DIR, and --with-jdk=DIR. To specify the place where the resulting library should be installed (libsqlite_jni.so file), use the --prefix=DIR option. On POSIX systems, the default location is /usr/local/lib (i.e., the prefix defaults to /usr/local). To specify where the sqlite.jar is to be installed, use the --with-jardir=DIR option. On POSIX systems, the default is /usr/local/share/java. This file contains the high-level part and the JDBC driver. At runtime, it is necessary to tell the JVM both places with the -classpath and -Djava.library.path=.. command-line options.

For Windows, the makefiles javasqlite.mak and javasqlite3.mak are provided in the distribution. They contain some build instructions and use the J2SE 1.4.2 from Sun and Microsoft Visual C++ 6.0. A DLL with the native JNI part (including SQLite 3.2.1) and the JAR file with the Java part can be downloaded from the website.

Connecting

You connect to a database using SQLiteDatabase::open(), which takes the name of the database and the file mode, as shown in Listing 8-26. The file mode is an artifact from SQLite 2 API and is no longer used. You can provide any value to satisfy the function. The code in Listing 8-26 is taken from the example SQLiteJNIExample.java, which illustrates all main facets of database operations: connecting, querying, using functions, and so forth.

Listing 8-26. *The JavaSQLite Test Program*

```
import SQLite.*;

public class SQLiteJNIExample
{
    public static void main(String args[])
    {
        SQLite.Database db = new SQLite.Database();

        try
        {
            db.open("foods.db", 700);

            // Trace SQL statements
            db.trace(new SQLTrace());

            // Query example
            query(db);

            // Function example
            user_defined_function(db);

            // Aggregate example
            user_defined_aggregate(db);

            db.close();
        }
        catch (java.lang.Exception e)
        {
            System.err.println("error: " + e);
        }
    }

    ...
}
```

Query Processing

You perform queries using SQLiteDatabase::compile(). This function can process a string containing multiple SQL statements. It returns a VM (virtual machine) object that holds all of the statements.

The VM object parses each individual SQL statement on each call to compile(), returning true if a complete SQL statement was compiled, and false otherwise. You can therefore iterate through all SQL statements in a loop, breaking when the VM has processed the last statement.

When the VM has compiled a statement, you can execute it using VM::step(). This function takes a single object, which implements a SQLite.Callback interface. The example uses a class called Row for this purpose, which is shown in Listing 8-27.

Listing 8-27. *The Row Class*

```
class Row implements SQLite.Callback
{
    private String row[];

    public void columns(String col[]) {}
    public void types(String types[]) {}

    public boolean newrow(String data[])
    {
        // Copy to internal array
        row = data;
        return false;
    }

    public String print()
    {
        return "Row:    [" + StringUtil.join(row, ", ") + "]";
    }
}
```

The SQLite.Callback interface has three methods: columns(), types(), and newrow(). They process the column names, column types, and row data, respectively. Each call to VM::step() updates all of the column, type, and row information.

The use of VM is illustrated in the query() function of the example, which is listed in Listing 8-28.

Listing 8-28. *The query() Function*

```
public static void query(SQLite.Database db)
    throws SQLite.Exception
{
    System.out.println("\nQuery Processing:\n");

    Row row = new Row();
    db.set_authorizer(new AuthorizeFilter());

    Vm vm = db.compile( "select * from foods LIMIT 5;" +
                        "delete from foods where id = 5;" +
                        "insert into foods (type_id, name) values (5, 'Java');" +
                        "select * from foods LIMIT 5" );
    do
    {
        while (vm.step(row))
        {
            System.err.println(row.print());
        }
    }
    while (vm.compile());
}
```

The SQLite.Database::exec() performs self-contained queries and has the following form:

```
void exec(String sql, Callback cb, String[] params)
```

The params array corresponds to %q or %Q parameters in the SQL statement. An example is shown in Listing 8-29.

Listing 8-29. *The exec_query() Function*

```
public static void exec_query(SQLite.Database db)
    throws SQLite.Exception
{
    System.out.println("\nExec Query:\n");

    String sql = "insert into foods (type_id, name) values (5, '%q')";
    ResultSet result = new ResultSet();

    String params[] = {"Java"};
    db.exec(sql, result, params);

    System.out.println("Result: last_insert_id(): " + db.last_insert_rowid());
    System.out.println("Result:        changes(): " + db.changes());
}
```

Note that this is not the same thing as parameter binding. Rather, this is sprintf style substitution using sqlite3_vmprintf() in the SQLite C API.

User-Defined Functions and Aggregates

The SQLite.Function interface is used to implement both user-defined functions and user-defined aggregates. The hello_newman() function in Java is illustrated in Listing 8-30.

Listing 8-30. *hello_newman() in Java*

```
class HelloNewman implements SQLite.Function
{
    public void function(FunctionContext fc, String args[])
    {
        if (args.length > 0)
        {
            fc.set_result("Hello " + StringUtil.join(args, ", "));
        }
        else
        {
            fc.set_result("Hello Jerry");
        }
    }
```

```
    public void step(FunctionContext fc, String args[]){}
    public void last_step(FunctionContext fc)
    {
        fc.set_result(0);
    }

}
```

Notice that the step() and last_step() functions, while specific to aggregates, must also be implemented even though they do nothing in user-defined functions. This is because the SQLite.Function interface defines methods for both functions and aggregates. This class is registered using SQLite.Database.create_function(). The function's return type must also be registered using SQLite.Database.function_type(). Listing 8-31 illustrates using the Java implementation of hello_newman().

Listing 8-31. *The hello_newman() Test Code*

```
// Register function
db.create_function("hello_newman", -1, new HelloNewman());

// Set return type
db.function_type("hello_newman", Constants.SQLITE_TEXT);

// Test
PrintResult r = new PrintResult();
db.exec("select hello_newman()", r);
db.exec("select hello_newman('Elaine', 'Jerry')", r);
db.exec("select hello_newman('Elaine', 'Jerry', 'George')", r);
```

JDBC

The Java extension also includes support for JDBC. To use the driver, specify SQLite. JDBCDriver as the JDBC driver's class name. Also, make sure that you have sqlite.jar in your class path and the native library in your Java library path. The JDBC URLs to connect to a SQLite database have the format jdbc:sqlite:/path, where path has to be specified as the path name to the SQLite database, for example

```
jdbc:sqlite://dirA/dirB/dbfile
jdbc:sqlite:/DRIVE:/dirA/dirB/dbfile
jdbc:sqlite:///COMPUTERNAME/shareA/dirB/dbfile
```

Currently, the supported data types on SQLite tables are java.lang.String, short, int, float, and double. Some support exists for java.sql.Date, java.sql.Time, and java.sql. Timestamp although it is mostly untested. The data type mapping depends mostly on the availability of the SQLite pragmas show_datatypes and table_info. Enough basic database metadata methods are implemented such that it is possible to access SQLite databases with JDK 1.3 or higher and the iSQL-Viewer tool.

Listing 8-32 is a simple example (located in SQLiteJDBCExample.java) of using the JDBC driver to query the foods table.

Listing 8-32. *The SQLite JDBC Test Program*

```java
import java.sql.*;
import SQLite.JDBCDriver;

public class SQLiteJDBCExample {

public static void main ( String [ ] args )
{
    try
    {
        Class.forName("SQLite.JDBCDriver");
        Connection c = DriverManager.getConnection( "jdbc:sqlite://tmp/foods.db",
                                        "" // username (NA),
                                        "" // password (NA));

        Statement s = c.createStatement();
        ResultSet rs = s.executeQuery ("SELECT * FROM foods LIMIT 10");
        int cols = (rs.getMetaData()).getColumnCount();

        while (rs.next())
        {
            String fields[] = new String[cols];

            for(int i=0; i<cols; i++)
            {
                fields[i] = rs.getString(i+1);
            }

            System.out.println("[" + join(fields, ", ") + "]");
        }
    }
    catch( Exception x )
    {
        x.printStackTrace();
    }
}

static String join( String[] array, String delim )
{
    StringBuffer sb = join(array, delim, new StringBuffer());
    return sb.toString();
}

static StringBuffer join( String[] array, String delim, StringBuffer sb )
{
```

```
    for ( int i=0; i<array.length; i++ )
    {
        if (i!=0) sb.append(delim);
        sb.append("'" + array[i] + "'");
    }

    return sb;
}

}
```

This example produces the following output:

```
['1', '1', 'Bagels']
['2', '1', 'Bagels, raisin']
['3', '1', 'Bavarian Cream Pie']
['4', '1', 'Bear Claws']
['6', '1', 'Bread (with nuts)']
['7', '1', 'Butterfingers']
['8', '1', 'Carrot Cake']
['9', '1', 'Chips Ahoy Cookies']
['10', '1', 'Chocolate Bobka']
['11', '1', 'Chocolate Eclairs']
```

Tcl

SQLite's author wrote and maintains the Tcl extension. All of SQLite's testing code (more than 30,000 lines) is implemented in Tcl, and thus uses the SQLite Tcl extension. It is safe to say that this extension is both stable and well tested itself. The Tcl extension is included as a part of the SQLite source distribution. Complete documentation for this extension can be found on the SQLite website: www.sqlite.org/tclsqlite.html.

Installation

The SQLite GNU Autoconf script will automatically search for Tcl and build the Tcl extension if it finds it. So simply having Tcl installed before you build SQLite should provide you with the SQLite Tcl extension. Nevertheless, precompiled bindings for the Tcl extension for both Linux and Windows are available on the SQLite website.

Connecting

The SQLite extension is located in the sqlite3 package, which must be loaded using the package require directive. To connect to a database, use the sqlite3 command to create a database handle. This command takes two arguments: the first is the name of the database handle to be created and the second is the path to the database file. The following example illustrates connecting to a database:

```
#!/usr/bin/env tclsh

package require sqlite3

puts "\nConnecting."
sqlite3 db ./foods.db
```

The usual database connection rules apply: passing :memory: will create an in-memory database; passing in the name of a new file will create a new database; and so forth. The database handle returned corresponds to a connection to the specified database; however, it is not yet open—it does not open the connection until you try to use it. The database handle is the sole object through which you work with the database.

To disconnect, use the close method of the database handle. This will automatically roll back any pending transactions.

Query Processing

The extension executes queries using the eval method, which can process one or more queries at a time. eval can be used in several ways. The first way is to iterate through all records in a script following the SQL code. The script will be executed once for each row returned in the result set. The fields for each row are set as local variables within the script. For example:

```
puts "\nSelecting 5 records."
db eval {SELECT * FROM foods LIMIT 5} {
    puts "$id $name"
}
```

There is another form in which you can assign the field values to an array. To do this, specify the array name after the SQL and before the script. For example:

```
puts "\nSelecting 5 records."
db eval {SELECT * FROM foods LIMIT 5} values {
    puts "$values(id) $values(name)"
}
```

Both of the above code snippets produce the following output:

```
Selecting 5 records.
1 Bagels
2 Bagels, raisin
3 Bavarian Cream Pie
4 Bear Claws
5 Black and White cookies
```

eval will return the result set if no script is provided. The result set is returned as one long list of values, and you must determine the record boundaries. For example, consider the following statement:

```
set x [db eval {SELECT * FROM foods LIMIT 2}]
```

This will return a list in variable $x that is six elements long:

```
[1, 1, 'Bagels', 2, 1, 'Bagels, raisin']
```

This corresponds to two records, each of which has three fields (id, type_id, and name).

For non-SELECT statements, eval returns information regarding modified records, as illustrated in Listing 8-33.

Listing 8-33. *Examining Changes in Tcl*

```
db eval BEGIN

puts "\nUpdating all rows."
db eval { UPDATE foods set type_id=0 }
puts "Changes            : [db changes]"

puts "\nDeleting all rows."
# Delete all rows
db eval { DELETE FROM foods }

puts "\nInserting a row."
# Insert a row
db eval { INSERT INTO foods (type_id, name) VALUES (9, 'Junior Mints') }

puts "Changes            : [db changes]"
puts "last_insert_rowid() : [db last_insert_rowid]"

puts "\nRolling back transaction."
db eval ROLLBACK
```

The code in Listing 8-33 produces the following output:

```
Updating all rows.
Changes            : 415

Deleting all rows.

Inserting a row.
Changes            : 1
last_insert_rowid() : 1

Rolling back transaction.
Total records      : 415
```

Transaction scope can be automatically handled within Tcl code using the transaction method. If all code inside the transaction method's script runs without error, the transaction method will commit; otherwise, it will roll back. For example, if you wanted to perform the code from Listing 8-33 in a single transaction, you would have to check the status of each command after it is executed, and if it failed, then you would roll back the transaction and abort any further commands. The more commands you have to run in the transaction, the messier the code will get. However, all of this can be done automatically with the transaction method, as illustrated in Listing 8-34.

Listing 8-34. *Transaction Scope in Tcl*

```
db transaction {
puts "\nUpdating all rows."
db eval { UPDATE foods set type_id=0 }
puts "Changes            : [db changes]"

puts "\nDeleting all rows."
# Delete all rows
db eval { DELETE FROM foods }

puts "\nInserting a row."
# Insert a row
db eval { INSERT INTO foods (type_id, name) VALUES (9, 'Junior Mints') }

puts "Changes            : [db changes]"
puts "last_insert_rowid() : [db last_insert_rowid]"
}
```

Now, if any of the commands fail, transaction will roll back all commands without having to check any return codes. Furthermore, transaction also works with existing transactions. That is, if a transaction is already started, it will work within that transaction, and not attempt a commit or rollback. If an error occurs, it just aborts the script, returning the appropriate error code.

User-Defined Functions

User-defined functions are created using the function method, which takes the name of the function and a Tcl method that implements the function. Listing 8-35 illustrates an implementation of hello_newman() in Tcl.

Listing 8-35. *hello_newman() in Tcl*

```
proc hello_newman {args} {
    set l [llength $args]
    if {$l == 0} {
        return "Hello Jerry"
```

```
    } else {
        return "Hello [join $args {, } ]"
    }
}

db function hello_newman hello_newman
puts [db onecolumn {select hello_newman()}]
puts [db onecolumn {select hello_newman('Elaine')}]
puts [db onecolumn {select hello_newman('Elaine', 'Jerry')}]
puts [db onecolumn {select hello_newman('Elaine', 'Jerry', 'George')}]
```

This code produces the following output:

```
Hello Jerry
Hello Elaine
Hello Elaine, Jerry
Hello Elaine, Jerry, George
```

PHP

Starting with PHP version 5, SQLite became part of the PHP standard library. If you have PHP 5, you have SQLite installed on your system as well. As of PHP 5.1, there are three interfaces in PHP that allow you to work with SQLite.

The first extension—the SQLite extension introduced in version 5—is specific to SQLite version 2 and reflects its API. This extension provides two interfaces: a procedural interface and an object-oriented (OO) interface. For the most part, both interfaces are logically equivalent. The OO interface seems to help in writing simpler, cleaner code, but it doesn't encapsulate all of the functions of the procedural interface.

Since this extension is written explicitly around SQLite version 2 exclusively, there are some slight differences in the way this extension works compared to the other extensions covered in this book.

PHP 5.1 introduced a new database abstraction layer called PHP Data Objects, or PDO for short. This API uses drivers to support a standard database interface. PDO has drivers for both SQLite versions 2 and 3; therefore, SQLite version 3 is accessible via PHP. The PDO interface is an OO interface that is very similar to the OO interface in the SQLite extension. Since PDO is an abstraction layer, it is meant to accommodate many different databases and is therefore somewhat generic. Despite this, it is still possible for PDO drivers to provide access to database specific features as well. As a result, the PDO drivers provide a complete OO interface that works equally well with both SQLite version 2 and version 3.

Because this book is about using SQLite version 3, this section covers the PHP PDO extension for SQLite version 3.

Installation

Installation of PHP, while straightforward, is beyond the scope of this book. Detailed instructions on building and installing PHP can be found in the documentation on the PHP website: www.php.net.

Connections

There are two important issues to consider before you open a database: location and permissions. By default, the file path in PHP is relative to the directory in which the script is run (unless you provide a full path, relative to the root filesystem). So if you specify just a database name, you are opening or creating a database within the public area of your website, and the security of that database file depends on how the web server is configured. Since SQLite databases are normal operating system files just like HTML documents or images, it may be possible for someone to fetch them just like a regular document. This could be a potential security problem, depending on the sensitivity of your data. As a general security precaution, it may be a good idea to keep database files outside of public folders, so that only PHP scripts can access them.

With regard to permissions, the relevant file and folder permissions must allow the web server process running PHP both read and write access to the database files. Both of these are administrative details that must be addressed on a case-by-case basis.

In PDO, connections are encapsulated in the PDO class. The constructor takes a single argument called a data source name (DSN). The DSN is a colon-delimited string composed of two parameters. The first parameter is the driver name, which is either sqlite (which corresponds to SQLite version 3) or sqlite2 (which corresponds to SQLite version 2). The second parameter is the path to the database file. If the connection attempt fails for any reason, the constructor will throw a PDOException. The following example connects to a SQLite version 3 database (foods.db):

```php
<?php
try {
    $dbh = new PDO("sqlite:foods.db");
} catch (PDOException $e) {
    echo 'Connection failed: ' . $e->getMessage();
}?>
```

Queries

PDO is made up of two basic classes—PDO and PDOStatement. The first represents a connection, which internally contains a sqlite3 structure, and the other a statement handle, which internally contains a sqlite3_stmt structure. The query methods in the PDO class closely follow the methods in the SQLite C API. There are three ways to execute queries:

- exec(): Executes queries that don't return any data. Returns the number of affected rows, or FALSE if there is an error. This mirrors sqlite3_exec().

- query(): Executes a query and returns a PDOStatement object representing the result set, or FALSE if there is an error.

- prepare(): Compiles a query and returns a PDOStatement object or FALSE if there is an error. This offers better performance than query() for statements that need to be executed multiple times, as it can be reset, avoiding the need to recompile the query.

Additionally, transaction management in PDO can be performed through a method invocation using `beginTransaction()`, `commit()`, and `rollback()`. Listing 8-36 shows a basic example of using the PDO class to open a database and perform basic queries within a transaction.

Listing 8-36. *Basic Queries with PDO*

```php
<?php

try {
    $dbh = new PDO("sqlite:foods.db");
} catch (PDOException $e) {
    echo 'Connection failed: ' . $e->getMessage();
}

$dbh->beginTransaction();
$sql = 'SELECT * FROM foods LIMIT 10';
foreach ($dbh->query($sql) as $row) {
    print $row['type_id'] . " ";
    print $row['name']    . "<br>";
}

$dressing = $dbh->quote("Newman's Own Vinegarette");
$dbh->exec("INSERT into FOODS values (NULL, 4, $dressing)");
echo $dbh->lastInsertId();
$dbh->rollback();
?>
```

PDO uses the `setAttribute()` and `getAttribute()` methods to set various database connection parameters. Currently, the only parameter that applies to SQLite is `PDO_ATTR_TIMEOUT`, which sets the busy timeout.

The `prepare()` method uses a SQLite statement to navigate through a result set. It also supports both bound and positional parameters. To bind a SQL parameter, there must be some associated variable in PHP to bind it to. PHP variables are bound to parameters using `PDOStatement::bindParam()`, which has the following declaration:

```
nool bindParam ( mixed parameter, mixed &variable,
                 int data_type, int length,
                 mixed driver_options );
```

The `parameter` argument specifies the SQL parameter. For numbered parameters, this is an integer value. For named parameters, it is a string. The `variable` argument is a reference to a PHP variable to bind. The `data_type` argument specifies the data type of the variable. Finally, the `length` argument specifies the length of the value if the variable is a string. The value specifies the maximum length of the string to return. Listing 8-37 is a complete example of using positional parameters.

Listing 8-37. *Positional Parameters with PDO*

```php
<?php
$dbh     = new PDO("sqlite:foods.db");
$sql     = 'SELECT * from FOODS WHERE type_id=? And name=?';
$stmt    = $dbh->prepare($sql);
$type_id = 9;
$name    = 'JujyFruit';
$stmt->bindParam(1, $type_id, PDO_PARAM_INT);
$stmt->bindParam(1, $name, PDO_PARAM_STR, 50);
$stmt->execute();
?>
```

Named parameters work similarly. When you bind these parameters, you identify them by their names (rather than integers). Listing 8-38 is a modification of the previous example using named parameters.

Listing 8-38. *Named Parameters with PDO*

```php
<?php
$dbh     = new PDO("sqlite:foods.db");
$sql     = 'SELECT * from FOODS WHERE type_id=:type And name=:name;';
$stmt    = $dbh->prepare($sql);
$type_id = 9;
$name    = 'JujyFruit';
$stmt->bindParam('type', $type_id, PDO_PARAM_INT);
$stmt->bindParam('name', $name, PDO_PARAM_STR, 50);
$stmt->execute();
?>
```

PDO also allows you to bind columns of result sets to PHP variables. This is done using PDOStatement::bindColumn(), which has the following declaration:

```
bool bindColumn (mixed column, mixed &param, int type)
```

The column argument refers to either the name of the column or its index in the SELECT clause. The param argument is a reference to a PHP variable, and the type argument specifies the type of the PHP variable. The following example binds two variables $name and $type_id to a result set:

```php
<?php
$dbh = new PDO("sqlite:foods.db");
$sql = 'SELECT * from FOODS LIMIT 10';
$stmt = $dbh->prepare($sql);
$stmt->execute();
$name;
$type_id;
$stmt->bindColumn('type_id', $type_id, PDO_PARAM_INT);
$stmt->bindColumn('name', $name, PDO_PARAM_STR);
```

```
while ($row = $stmt->fetch()) {
    print "$type_id $name <br>";
}
```

User-Defined Functions and Aggregates

User-defined functions are implemented using sqliteCreateFunction(). Aggregates are implemented using sqliteCreateAggregate(). sqliteCreateFunction() has the following form:

```
void PDO::createFunction ( string function_name,
                           callback callback,
                           int num_args );
```

The arguments are defined as follows:

- function_name: The name of the function as it is to appear in SQL

- callback: The PHP (callback) function to be invoked when the SQL function is called

- num_args: The number of arguments the function takes

The following example is a PHP implementation of hello_newman():

```
<?php
function hello_newman() {
    return 'Hello Jerry';
}

$db = new PDO("sqlite:foods.db");
$db->createFunction('hello_newman', hello_newman, 0);
$row = $db->query('SELECT hello_newman()')->fetch();
print $row[0]
?>
```

You create aggregates in a similar fashion using the sqliteCreateAggregate function, declared as follows:

```
void PDO::createAggregate ( string function_name,
                            callback step_func,
                            callback finalize_func,
                            int num_args )
```

The following code is a simple implementation of the above SUM aggregate, called phpsum:

```
<?php
function phpsum_step(&$context, $value) {
    $context = $context + $value;
}

function phpsum_finalize(&$context) {
    return $context;
}
```

```
$db = new PDO("sqlite:foods.db");
$db->createAggregate('phpsum', phpsum_step, phpsum_finalize);
$row = $db->query('SELECT phpsum(id) from food_types')->fetch();
print $row[0]
?>
```

Summary

This has been a brief survey of several different language extensions and how they work with SQLite. While using SQLite with the C API is quite straightforward, using SQLite in language extensions is considerably easier. Many of the concepts are very similar. As you can see, there are many things in common even in cases where an extension conforms to a language-specific database API. All queries ultimately involve a connection object of some kind, which maps to an internal sqlite3 structure, and a statement or cursor object, which internally maps to a sqlite3_stmt structure.

These extensions, developed by the open source community, make using SQLite convenient and easy, making it accessible to many more applications ranging from system administration to website development. There are plenty more extensions for these and more languages with which to use SQLite. As mentioned earlier, you need only to look on the SQLite Wiki to find them: www.sqlite.org/cvstrac/wiki?p=SqliteWrappers.

CHAPTER 9

■ ■ ■

SQLite Internals

This chapter is a brief tour through SQLite's major subsystems. It was inspired from a SQLite presentation given by Richard Hipp at a convention I attended. Much of the material presented here was taken directly from the handouts. Even if you never look at SQLite's source code, you may find the material in this chapter quite interesting, as I did. While some of the material is apt to change with ongoing SQLite development, the major concepts presented here are not likely to change too dramatically.

By now, you should be familiar with the major components of SQLite's architecture. Chapter 1 provides a general description of each major component, and Chapter 5 elaborated a little on the B-tree and pager in the process of query execution and transaction management. Therefore, I will forgo any further introductions and dive right in. We will start with the virtual database engine, which is the heart of SQLite; proceed through the storage layer; and then finish with the compiler, which is perhaps the most complex part of the system.

The Virtual Database Engine

The VDBE is the center of the stack and is where execution takes place. To understand the system as a whole, it is easiest to start with the VDBE, as the modules above and below it essentially exist to serve it.

The VDBE is implemented in six source files: `vbde.c`, `vdbe.h`, `vdbeapi.c`, `vdbeInt.h`, and `vdbemem.c`. As explained in Chapter 5, a statement handle essentially represents a complete VDBE program to carry out a single SQL command. The statement holds everything needed to run the program, which includes the following:

- The VDBE program

- The program counter

- The names and data types of all result columns

- Bound parameter values

- The execution stack and a fixed number of numbered memory cells

- Other runtime state information, such as B-tree cursors

The VDBE is a virtual machine, and its program instructions resemble that of an assembly language. Each instruction in that language is composed of an *opcode* and three *operands*—P1, P2, and P3. The opcode, or operation code, it similar to a function. It performs a discrete task, and uses the operands as information needed to carry out that task. P1 is a 32-bit signed integer, P2 is a 31-bit unsigned integer, and P3 is a pointer to a string or structure. There are a total of 128 opcodes in SQLite at the time of this writing. The number and nature of opcodes are subject to change over time as they often adapt to support new features in SQLite. Unlike the C API, VDBE opcodes are always subject to change. Therefore, it is not safe for you to generate your own VDBE programs and try to run them across different versions of SQLite.

There are several C API functions that work directly with the VDBE:

- sqlite3_bind_xxx() functions

- sqlite3_step()

- sqlite3_reset()

- sqlite3_column_xxx() functions

- sqlite3_finalize()

Basically, all of the API calls used to execute a query and step through the results are associated with the VDBE. They all have one thing in common: they take a statement handle as an argument. This is because they all need either the VDBE code within the statement handle or its associated resources to carry out their job. Note that sqlite3_prepare() works with the front end (compiler) to produce the VDBE program. It has no part in execution.

The VDBE program for any SQL command can be obtained by prefixing the command with the EXPLAIN keyword. For example:

```
sqlite> .m col
sqlite> .h on
sqlite> .w 4 15 3 3 15
sqlite> explain select * from episodes;
addr  opcode            p1   p2   p3
----  ---------------   ---  ---  ---------------
0     Goto              0    12
1     Integer           0    0
2     OpenRead          0    2    # episodes
3     SetNumColumns     0    3
4     Rewind            0    10
5     Recno             0    0
6     Column            0    1
7     Column            0    2
8     Callback          3    0
9     Next              0    5
10    Close             0    0
11    Halt              0    0
12    Transaction       0    0
13    VerifyCookie      0    10
14    Goto              0    1
15    Noop              0    0
```

I included the first four commands in the listing for debugging and formatting. Also, I have compiled SQLite with the SQLITE_DEBUG option. This option provides more detailed information on the execution stack, such as including table names in the P3 operand as shown in the listing.

The Stack

A VDBE program is composed of different sections that accomplish specific tasks. In each section, there are usually a number of instructions that manipulate the stack, followed by an instruction that uses what is on the stack to carry out a task. Why is this so? Different instructions take different numbers of arguments. Some instructions only take one argument, and can use any of the operands to store it. Some instructions take no arguments. Some instructions take a variable number of arguments, in which case they cannot rely on just three operands to suffice.

In such cases, those instructions use the stack to supply their arguments. Thus, these instructions never operate by themselves, but with the help of other instructions that run before them, which load the stack with the needed arguments. In addition to the stack, the VDBE uses something called *memory cells* to hold intermediate values as well. This is useful for information that does not directly apply to the operation of subsequent instructions—such as record structures. Both stack entries and memory cells use the same underlying Mem data structure, defined in vdbeInt.h (*Int* is short for *internal*).

Program Body

For example, take the process of opening the episodes table for reading in the previous example. It is accomplished by a section of instructions, specifically instructions 1 through 3. The first instruction—Integer—prepares the stack for instruction 2. OpenRead takes the stack value and does something. Here's how it works.

As you know, SQLite can open multiple database files in the same connection using the ATTACH command. When SQLite opens a database, it assigns it an index. The main database is assigned index 0, the first attached database 1, and so on. The Integer instruction above OpenRead loads the database index on the stack. In this example, it loads 0 for the main database. The OpenRead instruction pulls this value off the stack and uses it to figure out which database to operate on. It uses the P2 operand to identify the location (the root page) of the table to open. It then opens a B-tree cursor on the given table within the given database. All of this is explained in the VDBE opcode documentation. For example, the OpenRead instruction is documented as follows:

Open a read-only cursor for the database table whose root page is P2 in a database file. The database file is determined by an integer from the top of the stack. 0 means the main database and 1 means the database used for temporary tables. Give the new cursor an identifier of P1. The P1 values need not be contiguous but all P1 values should be small integers. It is an error for P1 to be negative.

If P2==0 then take the root page number from off of the stack.

There will be a read lock on the database whenever there is an open cursor. If the database was unlocked prior to this instruction then a read lock is acquired as part of this instruction. A read lock allows other processes to read the database but prohibits any other process from modifying the database. The read lock is released when all cursors are closed. If this instruction attempts to get a read lock but fails, the script terminates with an SQLITE_BUSY error code.

The P3 value is a pointer to a KeyInfo structure that defines the content and collating sequence of indices. P3 is NULL for cursors that are not pointing to indices.

This documentation for OpenRead as well as all other instructions can be found directly in the source code, specifically in vdbe.c.

Finally, the SetNumColumns instruction sets the number of columns the cursor will hold, which corresponds to the number of columns in the table it points to. It uses operands P1 and P2. P1 specifies the cursor index (0 in this case, which is the index of the cursor just opened). P2 specifies the number of columns. The episodes table has three columns.

Continuing the example, the Rewind instruction places the cursor at the beginning of the table. It checks to ensure that the table is not empty (it has no records). If the table is empty, it will place the instruction pointer on the instruction specified in the P2 operand. In this case P2 is 10, so Rewind will jump to instruction 10 if the table is empty—in this example, the Close instruction (Figure 9-1).

Once Rewind has set the cursor position, the next section of instructions (instructions 5–9) takes over. This section's job is to iterate over all of the records in the table. Recno pushes the key value of the record onto the stack pointed to by the cursor identified in P1. The Column instruction pushes the value of the column with the ordinal given by P2 of the cursor given by P1. Together instructions 5, 6, and 7 place the id (primary key), season, and name fields onto the stack—all three fields of the episodes table—for the record that cursor 0 is pointing to. Notice that the P1 operand for all three instructions is 0. This refers to cursor 0. Next, the Callback instruction takes three values off the stack (specified by P1) and forms an array (or record) structure, which is stored in a memory cell. Callback will then suspend VDBE operation, yielding control back to sqlite3_step(), which will then return SQLITE_ROW.

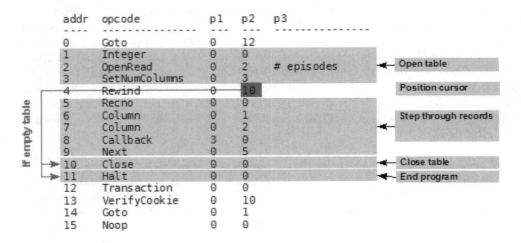

addr	opcode	p1	p2	p3	
0	Goto	0	12		
1	Integer	0	0		
2	OpenRead	0	2	# episodes	← Open table
3	SetNumColumns	0	3		
4	Rewind	0	10		Position cursor
5	Recno	0	0		
6	Column	0	1		Step through records
7	Column	0	2		←
8	Callback	3	0		
9	Next	0	5		
10	Close	0	0		← Close table
11	Halt	0	0		← End program
12	Transaction	0	0		
13	VerifyCookie	0	10		
14	Goto	0	1		
15	Noop	0	0		

Figure 9-1. *VDBE steps: Open and Read*

Once the VDBE has created the record structure, it too is associated with the statement handle. The program can then use the sqlite3_column_xxx() functions to retrieve the fields from the record structure. On the next call to sqlite3_step(), the instruction pointer will be pointing to the Next instruction. The Next instruction advances the cursor to the next row in the table. If there is another record, it jumps to the instruction given in P2, which in this case is instruction 5, which corresponds to the Recno instruction. Thus, it will go through another iteration, creating a new record structure, and sqlite3_step() will return SQLITE_ROW, indicating that there is another row to read. However, if there is not another row in the table, Next will fall through to the next instruction, which in this case is the Close instruction. Close will close the cursor and fall through to the Halt instruction, terminating the VDBE program, and sqlite3_step() will return SQLITE_DONE.

Program Startup and Shutdown

Now that we've seen the core of the program, let's look at the remaining sections, which relate to startup and initialization. These sections are shown in Figure 9-2. The first instruction is a Goto. Goto jumps to the instruction given in P2, which in this case is instruction 12.

Instruction 12 is a Transaction instruction, which starts a new transaction. It falls through to VerifyCookie, whose job is to ensure that the database schema has not changed since the VDBE program was compiled. This is an important concept in SQLite. Between the time SQL is compiled into VDBE code in sqlite3_prepare() and the time it is actually executed in sqlite3_step(), another SQL command could have run that changed the database schema (such as ALTER TABLE, DROP TABLE, or CREATE TABLE). When this happens, the schema version changes and it invalidates all statements that were compiled before the change. The current database schema is recorded at all times in the root page of the database file. Similarly, each statement object maintains a copy of the schema version it was compiled under for comparison. VerifyCookie's job is to check that they match, and if they don't, to take appropriate action.

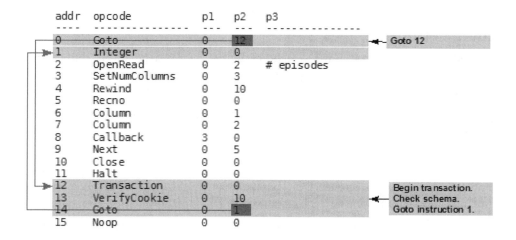

Figure 9-2. *VDBE steps: program startup*

VerifyCookie compares the database schema version on disk with the schema version given in P2—which corresponds to the statement's version referenced by the compiled code. If the schema has not changed since compile, the two will match. If they don't match, then the VDBE program (specifically the statement object that holds it) is no longer valid; it does not correspond to the most recent database schema. In this case, VerifyCookie will terminate the

VDBE program and arrange a SQLITE_SCHEMA error to be issued. In this case, the application needs to recompile the SQL statement, generating a new VDBE program based on the new schema. Recompiling could very well result in a different program. For example, what if someone dropped the episodes table and created a new table, which reused some of episodes' recycled pages? If the VDBE were to execute the invalid statement now, it would look for episodes (which no longer exists) starting at root page 2 (which has been recycled), and try to read records that no longer exist. The application would get junk for data.

However, when the schema versions do match, then the program counter steps from VerifyCookie to the following instruction—in this case Goto. Goto positions the program counter on instruction 1, which takes us to the main part of the program—opening the table and reading the records, as covered earlier. There are a few things to note here:

- The Transaction instruction doesn't acquire any locks in itself. It is the logical equivalent of a simple BEGIN. The actual shared lock is created by the OpenRead instruction. The lock is are freed when the transaction closes. This is determined by the Halt instruction, which cleans everything up. The action it takes depends on whether the connection is in autocommit mode or not.

- All of the storage space needed for the statement object (VDBE program) is determined before the start of the program. This is due primarily to two important facts. First, the depth of the stack is never greater than the number of instructions in the program. Second, the number of memory cells is never greater than the number of instructions (and is usually much less). Thus, even though SQL is dynamic in nature, SQLite can always compute how much memory a query will require and can allocate all of the resources before running the VDBE program.

Instruction Types

And this is how the VDBE works—one instruction at a time. Each instruction accomplishes a simple task and is often intertwined with instructions preceding or following it. If you look at the instruction set, you will see that opcodes fall into three general categories:

- **Value manipulation**: These instructions perform things like arithmetic operations (add, subtract, divide, etc.), logical operations (bitwise OR and AND), and string manipulation.

- **Data management**: These instructions manipulate data in memory and on disk. Memory instructions do things like stack manipulation and transfer data between stack entries and memory cells, and vice versa. Disk operations control the B-tree and pager modules—opening and manipulating cursors, beginning and ending transactions, and so forth.

- **Control flow**: Control instructions move the instruction pointer around both conditionally and unconditionally.

Once you become familiar with the instruction set, it is not hard to see what is going on. If nothing else, you can get a general feel for how the stack is used by some instructions to prepare the way for other instructions.

A Practical Example

Let's look at the example again, this time performing a VDBE trace on it. This will show us directly how the stack is being used between instructions. The first part of the program from startup to the first record is as follows:

```
sqlite> pragma vdbe_trace=on;
sqlite> select * from episodes;
VDBE Execution Trace:
SQL: [select * from episodes;]
    0 Goto              0    12
   12 Transaction       0     0
   13 VerifyCookie      0    10
   14 Goto              0     1
    1 Integer           0     0
Stack: i:0
    2 OpenRead          0     2 # episodes
    3 SetNumColumns     0     3
    4 Rewind            0    10
    5 Recno             0     0
Stack: i:0
    6 Column            0     1
Stack: NULL i:0
    7 Column            0     2
Stack:  s18[Good News Bad N](8) NULL i:0
    8 Callback          3     0
0||Good News Bad News
    9 Next              0     5
```

You can see the startup in the first four steps, followed by the Integer command, which specifies on the stack the database index upon which to open the cursor. OpenRead will pop it from the stack and open a cursor on the table with root page 2 (given by P2). Step down into the loop part and you see Recno and Column instructions pushing field values of the current record onto the stack. Callback then pops all of them off the stack and uses them to form a record structure, which is then stored in the statement handle. sqlite3_step() returns a SQLITE_ROW, indicating that a row is available for reading. The application accesses the data with sqlite3_column_xxx(), and proceeds to the next record by calling sqlite3_step() again. sqlite3_step() then resumes VDBE execution at the Next instruction, which moves on to the next record. And so on and so forth.

So not only can you see the stack at work, but you can also get some idea as to how the SQLite C API functions are intertwined within VDBE code. From here on out, it is a matter of just playing with the VDBE to see what the instructions do. For instance:

```
sqlite> explain BEGIN;

addr  opcode           p1   p2   p3
----  ---------------  ---  ---  ---------------
0     AutoCommit       0    0
1     Halt             0    0
2     Noop             0    0
sqlite> explain COMMIT;

addr  opcode           p1   p2   p3
----  ---------------  ---  ---  ---------------
0     AutoCommit       1    0
1     Halt             0    0
2     Noop             0    0
sqlite> explain ROLLBACK;

addr  opcode           p1   p2   p3
----  ---------------  ---  ---  ---------------
0     AutoCommit       1    1
1     Halt             0    0
2     Noop             0    0
```

You can see here that transactions work by toggling the AutoCommit instruction. This instruction must therefore be related to initiating the transfer of modified pages to disk. Try different things and see what happens. After a little practice, you may very well be able to recognize enough of the instruction patterns to use EXPLAIN to optimize queries.

The B-Tree and Pager Modules

The B-tree provides the VDBE with *O(logN)* lookup, insert, and delete as well as *O(1)* bidirectional traversal of records. It is self-balancing, and automatically manages both defragmentation and space reclamation. The B-tree itself has no notion of reading or writing to disk. It only concerns itself with the relationship between pages. The B-tree notifies the pager when it needs a page, and also notifies it when it is about to modify a page. When modifying a page, the pager ensures that the original page is first copied out to the journal file. Similarly, the B-tree notifies the pager when it is done writing, and the pager determines what needs to be done based on the transaction state.

Database File Format

All pages in a database are numbered sequentially, beginning with 1. A database is composed of multiple B-trees—one B-tree for each table and index (B+trees are used for tables, B-trees for indexes). Each table or index in a database has a root page that defines the location of its first page. The root pages for all indexes and tables are stored in the sqlite_master table.

The first page in the database—Page 1—is special. The first 100 bytes of Page 1 contain a special header (the file header) that describes the database file. It includes such information as the library version, schema version, page size, encoding, whether or not autovacuum is enabled—all of the permanent database settings you configure when creating a database along with any other parameters that have been set by various pragmas. The exact contents of the header are documented in btree.c. Page 1 is also the root page of the sqlite_master table.

Page Reuse and Vacuum

SQLite recycles pages using a free list. That is, when all of the records are deleted out of a page, the page is placed on a list reserved for reuse. When new information is later added, nearby pages are first selected before any new pages are created (expanding the database file). Running a VACUUM command purges the free list and thereby shrinks the database. In actuality, it rebuilds the database in a new file so that all in-use pages are copied over, while free-list pages are not. The end result is a new, compacted database. When autovacuum is enabled in a database, SQLite doesn't use a free list, and automatically shrinks the database upon each commit.

B-Tree Records

Pages in a B-tree are made up of B-tree records, also called payloads. They are not database records in the sense you might think—formatted with the columns in a table. They are more primitive than that. A B-tree record, or payload, has only two fields: a key field and a data field. The key field is the ROWID value, or primary key value that is present for every table in the database. The data field, from the B-tree perspective, is an amorphous blob that can contain anything. Ultimately, the database records are stored inside the data fields. The B-tree's job is order and navigation, and it primarily needs only the key field to do its work (although there is one exception in B+trees, which is addressed next). Furthermore, payloads are variable size, as are their internal key and data fields. On average, each page usually holds multiple payloads; however, it is possible for a payload to span multiple pages if it is too large to fit on one page (e.g., records containing BLOBs).

B+Trees

B-tree records are stored in key order. All keys must be unique within a single B-tree (this is automatically guaranteed as the keys correspond to the ROWID primary key, and SQLite takes care of that field for you). Tables use B+trees, which do not contain table data (database records) in the internal pages. An example B+tree representation of a table is shown in Figure 9-3.

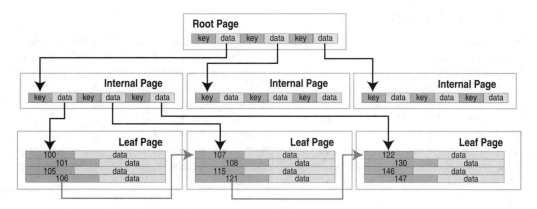

Figure 9-3. *B+tree organization (tables)*

The root page and internal pages in B+trees are all about navigation. The data fields in these pages are all pointers to the pages below them—they contain keys only. All database records are stored on the leaf pages. On the leaf level, records and pages are arranged in key order so it is possible for B-tree cursors to traverse records (horizontally), both forward and backward, using only the leaf pages. This is what makes traversal possible in *O(1)* time.

Records and Fields

The database records in the data fields of the leaf pages are managed by the VDBE (as in the Callback instruction described earlier). The database record is stored in binary form using a specialized record format that describes all of the fields in the record. The record format consists of a contiguous stream of bytes organized into a logical header and a data segment. The header segment includes the header size (represented as a variable-sized 64-bit integer value) and an array of types (also variable 64-bit integers), which describe each field stored in the data segment, as shown in Figure 9-4. Variable 64-bit integers are implemented using a Huffman code.

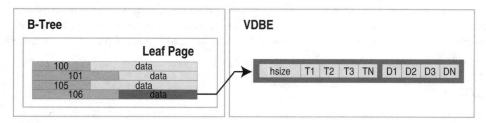

Figure 9-4. *Record structure*

The number of type entries corresponds to the number of fields in the record. Furthermore, each index in the type array corresponds to the same index in the field array. A type entry specifies the data type and size of its corresponding field value. The possible types and their meanings are listed in Table 9-1.

Table 9-1. *Field Type Values*

Type Value	Meaning	Length of Data
0	NULL	0
N in 1..4	Signed integer	N
5	Signed integer	6
6	Signed integer	8
7	IEEE float	8
8-11	Reserved for future use	N/A
N>12 and even	BLOB	(N-12)/2
N>13 and odd	TEXT	(N-13)/2

For example, take the first record in the episodes table:

```
sqlite> SELECT * FROM episodes ORDER BY id LIMIT 1;
id   season name
---  ------ --------------------
0    1      Good News Bad News
```

The internal record format for this record is shown in Figure 9-5.

Figure 9-5. *First record in the episodes table*

The header is 4 bytes long. The header size reflects this and itself is encoded as a single byte. The first type, corresponding to the id field, is a 1-byte signed integer. The second type, corresponding to the season field, is as well. The name type entry is an odd number, meaning it is a text value. Its size is therefore given by (49-13)/2=17 bytes. With the information, the VDBE can parse the data segment of the record and extract the individual fields.

Hierarchical Data Organization

Basically, each module in the stack deals with a specific unit of data. From the bottom up, data becomes more refined and more specific. From the top down, it becomes more aggregated and amorphous. Specifically, the C-API deals in field values, the VDBE in records, the B-tree in keys and data, the pager in pages, the OS interface in binary data and raw storage. This is illustrated in Figure 9-6.

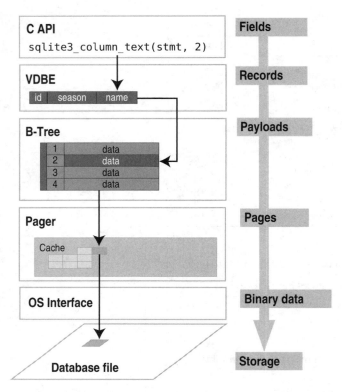

Figure 9-6. *Modules and their associated data*

Each module takes part in managing its own specific portion of the data in the database, and relies on the layer below it to supply it with a more crude form from which to extract its respective pieces.

Overflow Pages

As mentioned earlier, payloads and their contents can have variable sizes. However, pages are fixed in size. Therefore, there is always the possibility that a given payload could be too large to fit in a single page. When this happens, the excess payload is spilled out onto a linked list of overflow pages. From this point on, the payload takes on the form of a linked list of sorts, as shown in Figure 9-7.

The fourth payload in the figure is too large to fit on the page. As a result, the B-tree module creates an overflow page to accommodate. It turns out that one page won't suffice, so it links a second. This is essentially the way binary large objects are handled. One thing to keep in mind when you are using really large BLOBs is that they are ultimately being stored as a linked list of pages. If the BLOB is large enough, this can become inefficient, in which case you might consider dedicating an external file for the BLOB and keeping this filename in the record instead.

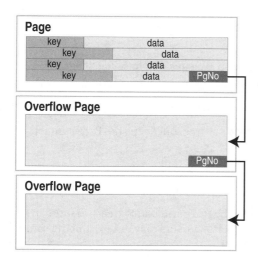

Figure 9-7. *Overflow pages*

The B-Tree API

The B-tree module has its own API, which is separate from and can be used independently of the C API. That is, you could use it as a standalone B-tree library, or access tables in a SQLite database directory, if you wish. An added benefit of SQLite's B-tree module is that it includes native support for transactions. Everything you know about the transactions, locks, and journal file are handled by the pager, which serves the B-tree module. The API can be grouped into functions according to general purpose.

Access and Transaction Functions

Database and transaction routines include the following:

- `sqlite3BtreeOpen`: Opens a new database file. Returns a B-tree object.

- `sqlite3BtreeClose`: Closes a database.

- `sqlite3BtreeBeginTrans`: Starts a new transaction.

- `sqlite3BtreeCommit`: Commits the current transaction.

- `sqlite3BtreeRollback`: Rolls back the current transaction.

- `sqlite3BtreeBeginStmt`: Starts a statement transaction.

- `sqlite3BtreeCommitStmt`: Commits a statement transaction.

- `sqlite3BtreeRollbackStmt`: Rolls back a statement transaction.

Table Functions

Table management routines include the following:

- `sqlite3BtreeCreateTable`: Creates a new, empty B-tree in a database file. Flags in the argument determine whether to use a table format (B+tree) or index format (B-tree).

- `sqlite3BtreeDropTable`: Destroys a B-tree in a database file.

- `sqlite3BtreeClearTable`: Removes all data from a B-tree, but keeps the B-tree intact.

Cursor Functions

Cursor functions include the following:

- `sqlite3BtreeCursor`: Creates a new cursor pointing to a particular B-tree. Cursors can be either a read cursor or a write cursor. Read and write cursors may not exist in the same B-tree at the same time.

- `sqlite3BtreeCloseCursor`: Closes the B-tree cursor.

- `sqlite3BtreeFirst`: Moves the cursor to the first element in a B-tree.

- `sqlite3BtreeLast`: Moves the cursor to the last element in a B-tree.

- `sqlite3BtreeNext`: Moves the cursor to the next element after the one it is currently pointing to.

- `sqlite3BtreePrevious`: Moves the cursor to the previous element before the one it is currently pointing to.

- `sqlite3BtreeMoveto`: Moves the cursor to an element that matches the key value passed in as a parameter. If there is no match, leaves the cursor pointing to an element that would be on either side of the matching element, had it existed.

Record Functions

Key and record functions include the following:

- `sqlite3BtreeDelete`: Deletes the record that the cursor is pointing to.

- `sqlite3BtreeInsert`: Inserts a new element in the appropriate place of the B-tree.

- `sqlite3BtreeKeySize`: Returns the number of bytes in the key of the record that the cursor is pointing to.

- `sqlite3BtreeKey`: Returns the key of the record the cursor is currently pointing to.

- `sqlite3BtreeDataSize`: Returns the number of bytes in the data record that the cursor is currently pointing to.

- `sqlite3BtreeData`: Returns the data in the record the cursor is currently pointing to.

Configuration Functions

Functions to set various parameters include the following:

- `sqlite3BtreeSetCacheSize`: Controls the page cache size as well as the synchronous writes (as defined in the `synchronous` pragma).

- `sqlite3BtreeSetSafetyLevel`: Changes the way data is synced to disk in order to increase or decrease how well the database resists damage due to OS crashes and power failures. Level 1 is the same as asynchronous (no `syncs()` occur and there is a high probability of damage). This is the equivalent to pragma `synchronous=OFF`. Level 2 is the default. There is a very low but non-zero probability of damage. This is the equivalent to pragma `synchronous=NORMAL`. Level 3 reduces the probability of damage to near zero but with a write performance reduction. This is the equivalent to pragma `synchronous=FULL`.

- `sqlite3BtreeSetPageSize`: Sets the database page size.

- `sqlite3BtreeGetPageSize`: Returns the database page size.

- `sqlite3BtreeSetAutoVacuum`: Sets the autovacuum property of the database.

- `sqlite3BtreeGetAutoVacuum`: Returns whether the database uses autovacuum.

- `sqlite3BtreeSetBusyHandler`: Sets the busy handler.

There are more functions, all of which are very well documented in `btree.h` and `btree.c`, but those listed here give you some idea of the parts of the API that are implemented in the B-tree layer, as well as what this layer can do in its own right.

The Compiler

So far, you have seen how things operate from the VDBE down the stack through the storage and OS layers. Now let's look at how the VDBE program is constructed to begin with. This is the job of the front end. The front end takes a single SQL command as an input and ends with a complete, optimized VDBE program. This happens in three stages: tokenizing, parsing, and code generation.

The Tokenizer

The first step of compilation is tokenizing the SQL command. The tokenizer splits a command into a stream of individual tokens. A token is simply a character or sequence of characters that has a specific meaning (in this case some meaning within SQL). Each token has an associated token class, which is simply a numeric identifier describing what the token is. For example, a left parenthesis token is classified as `TK_LP`, and the `SELECT` keyword is classified as `TK_SELECT`. All token classes are defined in `parse.h`. For instance, the SQL statement

```
SELECT rowid FROM foo where name='bar' LIMIT 1 ORDER BY rowid;
```

would be processed by the tokenizer as shown in part in Table 9-2.

In short, the tokenizer breaks up each unit of text, classifies it, and sends it to the parser (discarding white space).

Table 9-2. *A Tokenized SELECT statement*

Text	Token Class	Action
SELECT	TK_SELECT	Sent to parser
" "	TK_SPACE	Discarded
Rowid	TK_ID	Sent to parser
" "	TK_SPACE	Discarded
FROM	TK_FROM	Sent to parser
" "	TK_SPACE	Discarded
foo	TK_ID	Sent to parser
""	TK_SPACE	Discarded
WHERE	TK_WHERE	Sent to parser
" "	TK_SPACE	Discarded
name	TK_ID	Sent to parser
=	TK_EQ	Sent to parser

Keywords

The tokenizer is hand-coded and located in tokenize.c. While it is hand-coded, it does use generated code to classify SQL keywords, which are defined in keywordhash.h. This file is an optimization that compacts all SQL keywords into the smallest possible buffer by overlapping common character sequences in keywords. SQLite identifies keyword entries using arrays that define the offsets and size of each keyword. The method is a space optimization intended to help embedded applications. An example of the generated buffer is as follows:

```
static int keywordCode(const char *z, int n){
  static const char zText[537] =
    "ABORTABLEFTEMPORARYADDATABASELECTHENDEFAULTRANSACTIONATURALTER"
    "AISEACHECKEYAFTEREFERENCESCAPELSEXCEPTRIGGEREGEXPLAINITIALLYANALYZE"
    "XCLUSIVEXISTSTATEMENTANDEFERRABLEATTACHAVINGLOBEFOREIGNOREINDEX"
    "AUTOINCREMENTBEGINNERENAMEBETWEENOTNULLIKEBYCASCADEFERREDELETE"
    "CASECASTCOLLATECOLUMNCOMMITCONFLICTCONSTRAINTERSECTCREATECROSS"
    "CURRENT_DATECURRENT_TIMESTAMPLANDESCDETACHDISTINCTDROPRAGMATCH"
    "FAILIMITFROMFULLGROUPDATEIFIMMEDIATEINSERTINSTEADINTOFFSETISNULL"
    "JOINORDEREPLACEOUTERESTRICTPRIMARYQUERYRIGHTROLLBACKROWHENUNION"
    "UNIQUEUSINGVACUUMVALUESVIEWHERE";
```

The keywordhash.h file includes a routine sqlite3KeywordCode(), which allows the tokenizer to quickly match the keyword with its appropriate token class with minimal space. So, the tokenizer first tries to match a token with what it knows, and failing that, it resorts to sqlite3KeywordCode(), which will return either a keyword token class or a generic TK_ID.

The tokenizer and parser work hand in hand, one token at a time. As the tokenizer resolves each token, it passes the token to the parser. The parser takes the tokens and builds a parse tree, which is a hierarchical representation of the statement.

The Parser

The parser is generated from SQLite's custom parser generator—the Lemon parser generator. The parser uses grammar rules defined in parse.y to organize the tokens into a parse tree. The theory behind the parser is beyond the scope of this chapter—there are many textbooks that cover the topic. The point is that the parser converts a stream of tokens into a hierarchical data structure, called a parse tree, which represents the SQL command.

The parse tree is primarily composed of expressions and lists of expressions. An expression itself is a recursive structure that can contain subexpressions under it. For example, the WHERE clause in a SELECT parse tree is represented by a single expression. The SELECT clause, on the other hand, is represented as a list of expressions; each expression is a column that will be returned in the result set. For example, a very simplified representation of the statement

```
SELECT rowid, name, season FROM episodes WHERE rowid=1 LIMIT 1
```

might be arranged into a parse tree as shown in Figure 9-8.

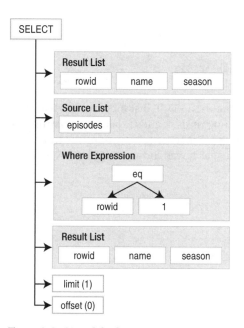

Figure 9-8. *Simplified parse tree representation*

Once the statement has been completely tokenized and parsed, the parse tree is passed to the code generator.

The Code Generator

The code generator is the largest and most complex part of SQLite. Unlike most other modules, the code generator does not have a well-defined interface, but is rather closely tied to the parser. It is made up of many source files, most of which are specific to SQL operations. For example, the code to generate SELECT statements is kept in select.c. Other source files include update.c, insert.c, delete.c, trigger.c, and so on.

The code generator takes the parse tree and produces the VDBE program to execute the statement. Each part of the tree more or less is handled by a specific routine that generates a sequence of VDBE instructions to accomplish a specific task. The values for the operands are taken from the data structures associated with the parse tree. For example, the function to open a table for reading is implemented as follows:

```
/*
** Generate code that will open a table for reading.
*/
void sqlite3OpenTableForReading(
  Vdbe *v,          /* Generate code into this VDBE */
  int iCur,         /* The cursor number of the table */
  Table *pTab       /* The table to be opened */
){
  sqlite3VdbeAddOp(v, OP_Integer, pTab->iDb, 0);
  sqlite3VdbeAddOp(v, OP_OpenRead, iCur, pTab->tnum);
  VdbeComment((v, "# %s", pTab->zName));
  sqlite3VdbeAddOp(v, OP_SetNumColumns, iCur, pTab->nCol);
}
```

The sqlite3vdbeAddOp function takes three arguments: a VDBE instance (to which it will add instructions), an instruction (or opcode), and two operands. It adds exactly one instruction to the VDBE instance's program. In this case, sqlite3OpenTableForReading adds the three instructions (1–3) to open a B-tree table for reading, just as it was shown in Figure 9-1, which are listed here again for convenience:

```
sqlite> explain select * from episodes;
addr  opcode           p1   p2   p3
----  ---------------  ---  ---  ---------------
0     Goto             0    12
1     Integer          0    0
2     OpenRead         0    2    # episodes
3     SetNumColumns    0    3
4     Rewind           0    10
5     Recno            0    0
6     Column           0    1
7     Column           0    2
8     Callback         3    0
9     Next             0    5
10    Close            0    0
11    Halt             0    0
12    Transaction      0    0
```

```
13    VerifyCookie    0    10
14    Goto            0    1
15    Noop            0    0
```

For example, the second line of sqlite3OpenTableForReading is

```
sqlite3VdbeAddOp(v, OP_OpenRead, iCur, pTab->tnum);
```

This creates instruction 3 in the program. The P2 value refers to the root page of the table to be opened. This is provided by the table data structure pointed to by pTab, specifically the tnum member, which holds the table's root page number. So whenever a parse tree calls for a table to be opened, it calls sqlite3OpenTableForReading to add the corresponding VDBE instructions to do so.

In short, code generation is done by many different routines across many different files in the code. The routines analyze a specific portion of the parse tree and create corresponding VDBE instructions to accomplish a specific task. The code generator contains a wide variety of routines for generating instructions. General functions are available that are used in many places; sqlite3ExprCode, for example, takes an expression and generates the instructions needed to evaluate it. Likewise, there are highly specific routines that accomplish unique tasks, such as sqlite3FinishTrigger, which generates the VDBE instructions to complete the process of building a trigger.

The Optimizer

The code generator does more than just code generation, however. It performs query optimization as well. The optimizer is part of the code generator, and lives in where.c. Code that creates the WHERE clause is shared by other modules, such as select.c, update.c, and delete.c. Each of these modules calls sqlite3WhereBegin() to generate the WHERE clause code to produce the search instructions, and then add their own VDBE code after it to process the rows that are returned. They then conclude that code with sqlite3WhereEnd(), which adds the VDBE instructions that concludes the WHERE clause code. The general structure is shown in Figure 9-9.

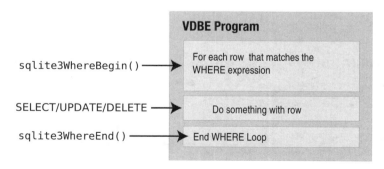

Figure 9-9. *WHERE clause VDBE code generation*

Optimizations take place in sqlite3WhereBegin(). Based on what is being done, it looks for indexes that might be used, expressions that can be rewritten, and so forth.

To get a feel for how this works, let's start with a simple SELECT with no WHERE clause, as shown in Figure 9-10.

```
sqlite> explain SELECT name FROM episodes;
addr   opcode              p1    p2    p3
----   --------------      ---   ---   ---------------
0      Goto                0     10
1      Integer             0     0
2      OpenRead            0     2     # episodes
3      SetNumColumns       0     3
4      Rewind              0     8                        ►► sqlite3WhereBegin()
5      Column              0     2                        ►► SELECT loop
6      Callback            1     0
7      Next                0     5                        ►► sqlite3WhereEnd()
8      Close               0     0
9      Halt                0     0
10     Transaction         0     0
11     VerifyCookie        0     14
12     Goto                0     1
13     Noop                0     0
```

Figure 9-10. *A SELECT statement with no WHERE clause*

By now, you can start to recognize the various code generation sections. Instructions 1–3 open episodes for reading, and instructions 4–9 iterate through all records, selecting the name column (identified here by the Column instruction). Even though there was no WHERE clause here, sqlite3WhereBegin() and sqlite3WhereEnd() are called and generate instructions. Here, the query calls for a table scan. sqlite3WhereBegin() adds the Rewind instruction, which places the cursor at the beginning of the table. Following that, instructions 5–6 are from the select code, and sqlite3WhereEnd() concludes with instructions 7–8. Instructions 0 and 10–13 are the standard prologue instructions for executing a command.

Next, let's look at what a WHERE clause does (Figure 9-11).

```
sqlite> explain SELECT name FROM episodes WHERE name='Soup Nazi';
addr   opcode              p1    p2    p3
----   --------------      ---   ---   ---------------
0      Goto                0     13
1      Integer             0     0
2      OpenRead            0     2     # episodes
3      SetNumColumns       0     3
4      Rewind              0     11
5      Column              0     2
6      String8             0     0     Soup Nazi           ►► sqlite3WhereBegin()
7      Ne                  296   10    collseq(BINARY)
8      Column              0     2
9      Callback            1     0
10     Next                0     5                        ►► sqlite3WhereEnd()
11     Close               0     0
12     Halt                0     0
13     Transaction         0     0
14     VerifyCookie        0     15
15     Goto                0     1
16     Noop                0     0
```

Figure 9-11. *Instructions relating to a WHERE clause*

Instructions 4–6, produced by sqlite3WhereBegin(), add the constraint name='Soup Nazi'. Everything else is unchanged. In both cases the WHERE clause performs a full table scan, as is evidenced by the Next instruction in the WhereEnd segment.

Now, create an index on the name column and see what happens (Figure 9-12).

Now, sqlite3WhereBegin() sees that there is an index it can use and writes in VDBE instructions to do so. This is essentially how the optimizer works: as the WHERE component of the code generator.

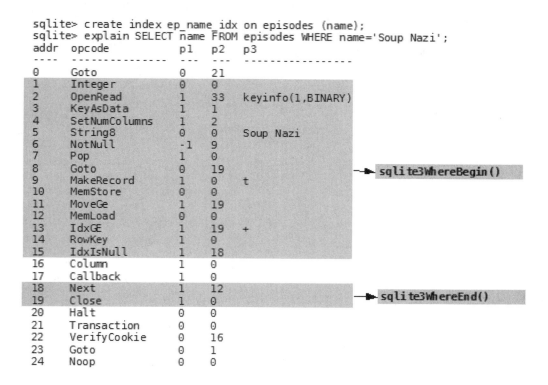

```
sqlite> create index ep_name_idx on episodes (name);
sqlite> explain SELECT name FROM episodes WHERE name='Soup Nazi';
addr    opcode            p1    p2    p3
----    --------------    ---   ---   ----------------
0       Goto              0     21
1       Integer           0     0
2       OpenRead          1     33    keyinfo(1,BINARY)
3       KeyAsData         1     1
4       SetNumColumns     1     2
5       String8           0     0     Soup Nazi
6       NotNull           -1    9
7       Pop               1     0
8       Goto              0     19                        → sqlite3WhereBegin()
9       MakeRecord        1     0     t
10      MemStore          0     0
11      MoveGe            1     19
12      MemLoad           0     0
13      IdxGE             1     19    +
14      RowKey            1     0
15      IdxIsNull         1     18
16      Column            1     0
17      Callback          1     0
18      Next              1     12                        → sqlite3WhereEnd()
19      Close             1     0
20      Halt              0     0
21      Transaction       0     0
22      VerifyCookie      0     16
23      Goto              0     1
24      Noop              0     0
```

Figure 9-12. *Instructions relating to index use in the WHERE clause*

Summary

And that concludes our journey through SQLite, not only in this chapter, but the book as well. I hope you have enjoyed it. As you've seen in Chapter 1, SQLite is more than merely a free database. It is a well-written software library with a wide range of applications. It is a database, a utility, and a helpful programming tool.

What you have seen in this chapter barely scratches the surface, but it should give you a better idea about how things work nonetheless. And it also gives you an appreciation for how elegantly SQLite approaches a very complex problem. You know firsthand how big SQL is, and you've seen the complexity of the relational model behind it. Yet SQLite is a small library and manages to put many of these concepts to work in a small amount of code. It does this by breaking query processing down into discrete tasks. Each of its modules accomplishes a specific task and works closely with the modules above and below it. This design keeps things simple, manageable, and reliable. Add to this a large and thorough testing suite and that is how SQLite packs a lot of relational power into a very small package.

From a programming standpoint, SQLite is not only useful in its own right, but there is a lot you can learn from it as well. Even though it is small, it employs quite a variety of different concepts: tokenizing, parsing, virtual machines, B-trees and B+trees, caching, locking, transactions, memory management, and more. Not only does it implement all of these things, it does so while also satisfying tough design constraints: portability, flexibility, simplicity, efficiency, and reliability. Therefore, by looking at SQLite's implementation, you can study not only a particular concept but also how it is implemented from this perspective. And if a particular implementation works for you, the code is yours for the taking.

■■■

SQL Reference

The SQLite library understands most of the standard SQL language. But it does omit some features while at the same time adding a few features of its own. This reference is an overview of the SQL syntax implemented by SQLite, taken directly from the original documentation on the SQLite website (www.sqlite.org/lang.html) and slightly edited. Many low-level productions are omitted. For detailed information on the language that SQLite understands, refer to the source code and the grammar file parse.y in the source distribution.

In all of the syntax diagrams that follow, literal text is shown in bold. Nonterminal symbols are shown in italic. Operators that are part of the syntactic markup itself are shown as regular, unformatted text.

ALTER TABLE

```
sql-statement ::= ALTER TABLE [database-name .] table-name alteration
alteration ::= RENAME TO new-table-name
alteration ::= ADD [COLUMN] column-def
```

SQLite's version of the ALTER TABLE command allows the user to rename or add a new column to an existing table. It is not possible to remove a column from a table.

ANALYZE

```
sql-statement ::= ANALYZE
sql-statement ::= ANALYZE database-name
sql-statement ::= ANALYZE [database-name .] table-name
```

The ANALYZE command gathers statistics about indexes and stores them in a special table in the database where the query optimizer can use them to help make better index choices. If no arguments are given, all indexes in all attached databases are analyzed. If a database name is given as the argument, all indexes in that one database are analyzed. If the argument is a table name, then only indexes associated with that one table are analyzed.

The initial implementation stores all statistics in a single table named sqlite_stat1. Future enhancements may create additional tables with the same name pattern except with the "1" changed to a different digit. The sqlite_stat1 table cannot be dropped, but all the content can be deleted, which has the same effect.

The RENAME TO syntax is used to rename the table identified by database-name.table-name to new-table-name. This command cannot be used to move a table between attached databases, but only to rename a table within the same database.

If the table being renamed has triggers or indexes, then these remain attached to the table after it has been renamed. However, if there are any view definitions, or statements executed by triggers that refer to the table being renamed, these are not automatically modified to use the new table name. If this is required, the triggers or view definitions must be dropped and re-created to use the new table name by hand.

The ADD COLUMN syntax is used to add a new column to an existing table. The new column is always appended to the end of the list of existing columns. column-def may take any of the forms permissible in a CREATE TABLE statement, with the following restrictions:

- The column may not have a PRIMARY KEY or UNIQUE constraint.

- The column may not have a default value of CURRENT_TIME, CURRENT_DATE, or CURRENT_TIMESTAMP.

- If a NOT NULL constraint is specified, then the column must have a default value other than NULL.

The execution time of the ALTER TABLE command is independent of the amount of data in the table. The ALTER TABLE command runs as quickly on a table with 10 million rows as it does on a table with 1 row.

After ADD COLUMN has been run on a database, that database will not be readable by SQLite version 3.1.3 and earlier until the database is vacuumed (see VACUUM).

ATTACH DATABASE

sql-statement ::= ATTACH [DATABASE] database-filename AS database-name

The ATTACH DATABASE statement adds a preexisting database file to the current database connection. If the filename contains punctuation characters it must be quoted. The names "main" and "temp" refer to the main database and the database used for temporary tables. These cannot be detached. Attached databases are removed using the DETACH DATABASE statement.

You can read from and write to an attached database and you can modify the schema of the attached database. This is a new feature of SQLite version 3.0. In SQLite 2.8, schema changes to attached databases were not allowed.

You cannot create a new table with the same name as a table in an attached database, but you can attach a database that contains tables whose names are duplicates of tables in the main database. It is also permissible to attach the same database file multiple times.

Tables in an attached database can be referred to using the syntax database-name.table-name. If an attached table doesn't have a duplicate table name in the main database, it doesn't require a database name prefix. When a database is attached, all of its tables that don't have duplicate names become the default table of that name. Any tables of that name attached afterward require the table prefix. If the default table of a given name is detached, then the last table of that name attached becomes the new default.

Transactions involving multiple attached databases are atomic, assuming that the main database is not :memory:. If the main database is :memory:, then transactions continue to be atomic within each individual database file. But if the host computer crashes in the middle of a COMMIT where two or more database files are updated, some of those files might get the changes where others might not. Atomic commit of attached databases is a new feature of SQLite version 3.0. In SQLite version 2.8, all commits to attached databases behaved as if the main database were :memory:.

The maximum number of databases that can be attached to a given session is 10. This is a compile-time limit: the limit can be increased by altering the value in the source code and recompiling SQLite.

BEGIN TRANSACTION

```
sql-statement ::= BEGIN [ DEFERRED | IMMEDIATE | EXCLUSIVE ] [TRANSACTION [name]]
sql-statement ::= END [TRANSACTION [name]]
sql-statement ::= COMMIT [TRANSACTION [name]]
sql-statement ::= ROLLBACK [TRANSACTION [name]]
```

Beginning in version 2.0, SQLite supports transactions with rollback and atomic commit.

The optional transaction name is ignored. SQLite currently does not allow nested transactions.

No changes can be made to the database except within a transaction. Any command that changes the database (basically, any SQL command other than SELECT) will automatically start a transaction if one is not already in effect. Automatically started transactions are committed at the conclusion of the command.

Transactions can be started manually using the BEGIN command. Such transactions usually persist until the next COMMIT or ROLLBACK command. But a transaction will also ROLLBACK if the database is closed or if an error occurs and the ROLLBACK conflict resolution algorithm is specified. See the documentation on the ON CONFLICT clause for additional information about the ROLLBACK conflict resolution algorithm.

In SQLite version 3.0.8 and later, transactions can be deferred, immediate, or exclusive. Deferred means that no locks are acquired on the database until the database is first accessed. Thus with a deferred transaction, the BEGIN statement itself does nothing. Locks are not acquired until the first read or write operation. The first read operation against a database creates a SHARED lock and the first write operation creates a RESERVED lock. Because the acquisition of locks is deferred until they are needed, it is possible that another thread or process could create a separate transaction and write to the database after the BEGIN on the current thread has executed. If the transaction is immediate, then RESERVED locks are acquired on all databases as soon as the BEGIN command is executed, without waiting for the database to be used. After a BEGIN IMMEDIATE, you are guaranteed that no other thread or process will be able to write to the database or do a BEGIN IMMEDIATE or BEGIN EXCLUSIVE. Other processes can continue to read from the database, however. An exclusive transaction causes EXCLUSIVE locks to be acquired on all databases. After a BEGIN EXCLUSIVE, you are guaranteed that no other thread or process will be able to read or write the database until the transaction is complete.

SHARED, RESERVED, and EXCLUSIVE locks are described in detail in Chapters 4 and 5.

The default behavior for SQLite version 3.0.8 is a deferred transaction. For SQLite version 3.0.0 through 3.0.7, deferred is the only kind of transaction available. For SQLite version 2.8 and earlier, all transactions are exclusive.

The COMMIT command does not actually perform a commit until all pending SQL commands finish. Thus if two or more SELECT statements are in the middle of processing and a COMMIT is executed, the commit will not actually occur until all SELECT statements finish.

An attempt to execute COMMIT might result in an SQLITE_BUSY return code. This indicates that another thread or process had a read lock on the database that prevented the database from being updated. When COMMIT fails in this way, the transaction remains active and the COMMIT can be retried later after the reader has had a chance to clear.

comment

```
comment     ::= SQL-comment | C-comment
SQL-comment ::= -- single-line
C-comment   ::= /* multiple-lines [*/]
```

Comments aren't SQL commands, but can occur in SQL queries. They are treated as white space by the parser. They can begin anywhere white space can be found, including inside expressions that span multiple lines.

SQL comments only extend to the end of the current line.

C comments can span any number of lines. If there is no terminating delimiter, they extend to the end of the input. This is not treated as an error. A new SQL statement can begin on a line after a multiline comment ends. C comments can be embedded anywhere white space can occur, including inside expressions, and in the middle of other SQL statements. C comments do not nest. SQL comments inside a C comment will be ignored.

COMMIT TRANSACTION

See "BEGIN TRANSACTION."

COPY

```
sql-statement ::= COPY [ OR conflict-algorithm ] [database-name .]
                     table-name FROM filename [ USING DELIMITERS delim ]
```

The COPY command is available in SQLite version 2.8 and earlier. The COPY command has been removed from SQLite version 3.0 due to complications in trying to support it in a mixed UTF-8/16 environment. In version 3.0, the command-line shell contains a new command .import that can be used as a substitute for COPY.

The COPY command is an extension used to load large amounts of data into a table. It is modeled after a similar command found in PostgreSQL. In fact, the SQLite COPY command is specifically designed to be able to read the output of the PostgreSQL dump utility pg_dump so that data can be easily transferred from PostgreSQL into SQLite.

The table-name is the name of an existing table that is to be filled with data. The filename is a string or an identifier that names a file from which data will be read. The filename can be the STDIN to read data from standard input.

Each line of the input file is converted into a single record in the table. Columns are separated by tabs. If a tab occurs as data within a column, then that tab is preceded by a backslash (\) character. A backslash in the data appears as two backslashes in a row. The optional USING DELIMITERS clause can specify a delimiter other than a tab.

If a column consists of the characters \N, that column is filled with the value NULL.

The optional conflict-clause allows the specification of an alternative constraint conflict resolution algorithm to use this one command. See the section "ON CONFLICT" for additional information.

When the input data source is STDIN, the input can be terminated by a line that contains only a backslash and a dot (\.).

CREATE INDEX

```
sql-statement  ::= CREATE [UNIQUE] INDEX [database-name .] index-name
                   ON table-name ( column-name [, column-name]* )
                   [ ON CONFLICT conflict-algorithm ]

column-name    ::= name [ COLLATE collation-name] [ ASC | DESC ]
```

The CREATE INDEX command consists of the keywords CREATE INDEX followed by the name of the new index, the keyword ON, the name of a previously created table that is to be indexed, and a parenthesized list of names of columns in the table that are used for the index key. Each column name can be followed by either the ASC or DESC keyword to indicate sort order, but the sort order is ignored in the current implementation. Sorting is always done in ascending order.

The COLLATE clause following each column name defines a collating sequence used for text entries in that column. The default collating sequence is the collating sequence defined for that column in the CREATE TABLE statement. Or if no collating sequence is otherwise defined, the built-in BINARY collating sequence is used.

There are no arbitrary limits on the number of indexes that can be attached to a single table, nor on the number of columns in an index.

If the UNIQUE keyword appears between CREATE and INDEX, then duplicate index entries are not allowed. Any attempt to insert a duplicate entry will result in an error.

The optional conflict-clause allows the specification of an alternative default constraint conflict resolution algorithm for this index. This only makes sense if the UNIQUE keyword is used since otherwise there are no constraints on the index. The default algorithm is ABORT. If a COPY, INSERT, or UPDATE statement specifies a particular conflict resolution algorithm, that algorithm is used in place of the default algorithm specified here. See the section "ON CONFLICT" for additional information.

The exact text of each CREATE INDEX statement is stored in the sqlite_master or sqlite_temp_master table, depending on whether the table being indexed is temporary. Every time the database is opened, all CREATE INDEX statements are read from the sqlite_master table and used to regenerate SQLite's internal representation of the index layout.

Indexes are removed with the DROP INDEX command.

CREATE TABLE

```
sql-command ::= CREATE [TEMP | TEMPORARY] TABLE table-name (
                column-def [, column-def]* [, constraint]* )

sql-command ::= CREATE [TEMP | TEMPORARY] TABLE [database-name.]
                table-name AS select-statement

column-def  ::= name [type] [[CONSTRAINT name] column-constraint]*

type        ::= typename | typename ( number ) | typename (number, number)

column-constraint ::= NOT NULL [ conflict-clause ] |
   PRIMARY KEY [sort-order] [ conflict-clause ] [AUTOINCREMENT] |
   UNIQUE [ conflict-clause ] |
   CHECK ( expr ) [ conflict-clause ] |
   DEFAULT value |
   COLLATE collation-name

constraint ::= PRIMARY KEY ( column-list ) [ conflict-clause ] |
   UNIQUE ( column-list ) [ conflict-clause ] |
   CHECK ( expr ) [ conflict-clause ]

conflict-clause ::= ON CONFLICT conflict-algorithm
```

A CREATE TABLE statement is basically the keywords CREATE TABLE followed by the name of a new table and a parenthesized list of column definitions and constraints. The table name can be either an identifier or a string. Table names that begin with sqlite_ are reserved for use by SQLite.

Each column definition is the name of the column followed by the data type for that column, then one or more optional column constraints. The data type for the column does not restrict what data may be put in that column. The UNIQUE constraint causes an index to be created on the specified columns. This index must contain unique keys. The COLLATE clause specifies what text collating function to use when comparing text entries for the column. The built-in BINARY collating function is used by default.

The DEFAULT constraint specifies a default value to use when doing an INSERT. The value may be NULL, a string constant, or a number. Starting with version 3.1.0, the default value may also be one of the special case-independent keywords CURRENT_TIME, CURRENT_DATE, or CURRENT_TIMESTAMP. If the value is NULL, a string constant, or number, it is literally inserted into the column whenever an INSERT statement that does not specify a value for the column is executed. If the value is CURRENT_TIME, CURRENT_DATE, or CURRENT_TIMESTAMP, then the current UTC date and/or time is inserted into the columns. For CURRENT_TIME, the format is *HH:MM:SS*. For CURRENT_DATE, it is *YYYY-MM-DD*. The format for CURRENT_TIMESTAMP is *YYYY-MM-DD HH:MM:SS*.

Specifying a PRIMARY KEY normally just creates a UNIQUE index on the corresponding columns. However, if the primary key is on a single column that has data type INTEGER, then that column is used internally as the actual key of the B-tree for the table. This means that the column may only hold unique integer values. (Except in this one case, SQLite ignores the data type specification of columns and allows any kind of data to be put in a column regardless of its declared data type.) If a table does not have an INTEGER PRIMARY KEY column, then the B-tree key will be an automatically generated integer. The B-tree key for a row can always be accessed using one of the special names ROWID, OID, or _ROWID_. This is true regardless of whether there is an INTEGER PRIMARY KEY. An INTEGER PRIMARY KEY column may also include the keyword AUTOINCREMENT. The AUTOINCREMENT keyword modified the way that B-tree keys are automatically generated. For additional information on AUTOINCREMENT, see the "Autoincrement Values" section later in this appendix.

If the TEMP or TEMPORARY keyword occurs in between CREATE and TABLE, then the table that is created is only visible to the process that opened the database and is automatically deleted when the database is closed. Any indexes created on a temporary table are also temporary. Temporary tables and indexes are stored in a separate file distinct from the main database file.

If a database-name is specified, then the table is created in the named database. It is an error to specify both a database-name and the TEMP keyword, unless the database-name is "temp". If no database name is specified, and the TEMP keyword is not present, the table is created in the main database.

The optional conflict-clause following each constraint allows the specification of an alternative default constraint conflict resolution algorithm for that constraint. The default is ABORT. Different constraints within the same table may have different default conflict resolution algorithms. If a COPY, INSERT, or UPDATE command specifies a different conflict resolution algorithm, then that algorithm is used in place of the default algorithm specified in the CREATE TABLE statement. See "ON CONFLICT" for additional information.

CHECK constraints are implemented in SQLite version 3.3.0 and later. As of version 2.3.0, only NOT NULL, PRIMARY KEY, and UNIQUE constraints are supported.

There are no arbitrary limits on the number of columns or on the number of constraints in a table. The total amount of data in a single row is limited to about 1MB in version 2.8. In version 3.0 there is no arbitrary limit on the amount of data in a row.

The CREATE TABLE AS form defines the table to be the result set of a query. The names of the table columns are the names of the columns in the result.

The exact text of each CREATE TABLE statement is stored in the sqlite_master table. Every time the database is opened, all CREATE TABLE statements are read from the sqlite_master table and used to regenerate SQLite's internal representation of the table layout. If the original command was a CREATE TABLE AS, then an equivalent CREATE TABLE statement is synthesized and stored in sqlite_master in place of the original command. The text of CREATE TEMPORARY TABLE statements is stored in the sqlite_temp_master table.

Tables are removed using the DROP TABLE statement.

Autoincrement Values

In SQLite, every row of every table has an integer ROWID. The ROWID for each row is unique among all rows in the same table. In SQLite version 2.8 the ROWID is a 32-bit signed integer. Version 3.0 of SQLite expanded the ROWID to be a 64-bit signed integer.

You can access the ROWID of a SQLite table using one of the special column names ROWID, _ROWID_, or OID. Unless you declare an ordinary table column to use one of those special names, the use of that name will refer to the declared column and not to the internal ROWID.

If a table contains a column of type INTEGER PRIMARY KEY, then that column becomes an alias for the ROWID. You can then access the ROWID using any of four different names, the original three names described earlier or the name given to the INTEGER PRIMARY KEY column. All these names are aliases for one another and work equally well in any context.

When a new row is inserted into a SQLite table, the ROWID can either be specified as part of the INSERT statement or it can be assigned automatically by the database engine. To specify a ROWID manually, just include it in the list of values to be inserted. For example:

```
CREATE TABLE test1(a INT, b TEXT);
INSERT INTO test1(rowid, a, b) VALUES(123, 5, 'hello');
```

If no ROWID is specified on the insert, an appropriate ROWID is created automatically. The usual algorithm is to give the newly created row a ROWID that is 1 larger than the largest ROWID in the table prior to the insert. If the table is initially empty, then a ROWID of 1 is used. If the largest ROWID is equal to the largest possible integer (9223372036854775807 in SQLite version 3.0 and later), then the database engine starts picking candidate ROWIDs at random until it finds one that is not previously used.

The normal ROWID selection algorithm described here will generate monotonically increasing unique ROWIDs as long as you never use the maximum ROWID value and you never delete the entry in the table with the largest ROWID. If you ever delete rows or if you ever create a row with the maximum possible ROWID, then ROWIDs from previously deleted rows might be reused when creating new rows and newly created ROWIDs might not be in strictly ascending order.

The AUTOINCREMENT Keyword

If a column has the type INTEGER PRIMARY KEY AUTOINCREMENT, then a slightly different ROWID selection algorithm is used. The ROWID chosen for the new row is 1 larger than the largest ROWID that has ever before existed in that same table. If the table has never before contained any data, then a ROWID of 1 is used. If the table has previously held a row with the largest possible ROWID, then new INSERTs are not allowed and any attempt to insert a new row will fail with a SQLITE_FULL error.

SQLite keeps track of the largest ROWID that a table has ever held using the special sqlite_sequence table. The sqlite_sequence table is created and initialized automatically whenever a normal table that contains an AUTOINCREMENT column is created. The content of the sqlite_sequence table can be modified using ordinary UPDATE, INSERT, and DELETE statements. But making modifications to this table will likely perturb the AUTOINCREMENT key generation algorithm. Make sure you know what you are doing before you undertake such changes.

The behavior implemented by the AUTOINCREMENT keyword is subtly different from the default behavior. With AUTOINCREMENT, rows with automatically selected ROWIDs are guaranteed to have ROWIDs that have never been used before by the same table in the same database. And the automatically generated ROWIDs are guaranteed to be monotonically increasing. These are important properties in certain applications. But if your application does not need these properties, you should probably stay with the default behavior since the use of AUTOINCREMENT requires additional work to be done as each row is inserted and thus causes INSERTs to run a little slower.

CREATE TRIGGER

```
sql-statement ::= CREATE [TEMP | TEMPORARY] TRIGGER trigger-name
  [ BEFORE | AFTER ] database-event ON [database-name .] table-name
  trigger-action

sql-statement ::= CREATE [TEMP | TEMPORARY] TRIGGER trigger-name
  INSTEAD OF database-event ON [database-name .] view-name
  trigger-action

database-event ::= DELETE | INSERT | UPDATE | UPDATE OF column-list

trigger-action ::= [ FOR EACH ROW | FOR EACH STATEMENT ]
  [ WHEN expression ]
  BEGIN
      trigger-step ; [ trigger-step ; ]*
  END

trigger-step ::= update-statement | insert-statement |
  delete-statement | select-statement
```

The CREATE TRIGGER statement is used to add triggers to the database schema. Triggers are database operations (the trigger-action) that are automatically performed when a specified database event (the database-event) occurs.

A trigger may be specified to fire whenever a DELETE, INSERT, or UPDATE of a particular database table occurs, or whenever an UPDATE of one or more specified columns of a table are updated.

At this time SQLite supports only FOR EACH ROW triggers, not FOR EACH STATEMENT triggers. Hence explicitly specifying FOR EACH ROW is optional. FOR EACH ROW implies that the SQL statements specified as trigger-steps may be executed (depending on the WHEN clause) for each database row being inserted, updated, or deleted by the statement causing the trigger to fire.

Both the WHEN clause and the trigger-steps may access elements of the row being inserted, deleted, or updated using references of the form NEW.column-name and OLD.column-name, where column-name is the name of a column from the table that the trigger is associated with. OLD and NEW references may only be used in triggers on trigger-events for which they are relevant, as follows:

- INSERT: NEW references are valid

- UPDATE: NEW and OLD references are valid

- DELETE: OLD references are valid

If a WHEN clause is supplied, the SQL statements specified as trigger-steps are only executed for rows for which the WHEN clause is true. If no WHEN clause is supplied, the SQL statements are executed for all rows.

The specified trigger time determines when the trigger-steps will be executed relative to the insertion, modification, or removal of the associated row.

An ON CONFLICT clause may be specified as part of an UPDATE or INSERT trigger-step. However, if an ON CONFLICT clause is specified as part of the statement causing the trigger to fire, then this conflict-handling policy is used instead.

Triggers are automatically dropped when the table that they are associated with is dropped.

Triggers may be created on views, as well as ordinary tables, by specifying INSTEAD OF in the CREATE TRIGGER statement. If one or more ON INSERT, ON DELETE, or ON UPDATE triggers are defined on a view, then it is not an error to execute an INSERT, DELETE, or UPDATE statement on the view, respectively. Thereafter, executing an INSERT, DELETE, or UPDATE on the view causes the associated triggers to fire. The real tables underlying the view are not modified (except possibly explicitly, by a trigger program).

For example, assuming that customer records are stored in the customers table, and that order records are stored in the orders table, the following trigger ensures that all associated orders are redirected when a customer changes his or her address:

```
CREATE TRIGGER update_customer_address UPDATE OF address ON customers
BEGIN
  UPDATE orders SET address = new.address WHERE customer_name = old.name;
END;
```

With this trigger installed, executing the statement

```
UPDATE customers SET address = '1 Main St.' WHERE name = 'Jack Jones';
```

causes the following to be automatically executed:

```
UPDATE orders SET address = '1 Main St.' WHERE customer_name = 'Jack Jones';
```

Note that currently triggers may behave oddly when created on tables with INTEGER PRIMARY KEY fields. If a BEFORE trigger program modifies the INTEGER PRIMARY KEY field of a row that will be subsequently updated by the statement that causes the trigger to fire, then the update may not occur. The workaround is to declare the table with a PRIMARY KEY column instead of an INTEGER PRIMARY KEY column.

A special SQL function RAISE() may be used within a trigger program, with the following syntax:

```
raise-function ::= RAISE ( ABORT, error-message ) |
  RAISE ( FAIL, error-message ) |
  RAISE ( ROLLBACK, error-message ) |
  RAISE ( IGNORE )
```

When one of the first three forms is called during trigger program execution, the specified ON CONFLICT processing is performed (either ABORT, FAIL, or ROLLBACK) and the current query terminates. An error code of SQLITE_CONSTRAINT is returned to the user, along with the specified error message.

When RAISE(IGNORE) is called, the remainder of the current trigger program, the statement that caused the trigger program to execute, and any subsequent trigger programs that would have been executed are abandoned. No database changes are rolled back. If the statement that caused the trigger program to execute is itself part of a trigger program, then that trigger program resumes execution at the beginning of the next step.

Triggers are removed using the DROP TRIGGER statement.

CREATE VIEW

```
sql-command ::= CREATE [TEMP | TEMPORARY] VIEW [database-name.]
               view-name AS select-statement
```

The CREATE VIEW command assigns a name to a prepackaged SELECT statement. Once the view is created, it can be used in the FROM clause of another SELECT in place of a table name.

If the TEMP or TEMPORARY keyword occurs in between CREATE and VIEW, then the view that is created is only visible to the process that opened the database and is automatically deleted when the database is closed.

If a database-name is specified, then the view is created in the named database. It is an error to specify both a database-name and the TEMP keyword, unless the database-name is "temp". If no database name is specified, and the TEMP keyword is not present, the table is created in the main database.

You cannot COPY, DELETE, INSERT, or UPDATE a view. Views are read-only in SQLite. However, in many cases you can use a TRIGGER on the view to accomplish the same thing. Views are removed with the DROP VIEW command.

DELETE

```
sql-statement ::= DELETE FROM [database-name .] table-name [WHERE expr]
```

The DELETE command is used to remove records from a table. The command consists of the DELETE FROM keywords followed by the name of the table from which records are to be removed. Without a WHERE clause, all rows of the table are removed. If a WHERE clause is supplied, then only those rows that match the expression are removed.

DETACH DATABASE

```
sql-command ::= DETACH [DATABASE] database-name
```

This statement detaches an additional database connection previously attached using the ATTACH DATABASE statement. It is possible to have the same database file attached multiple times using different names, and detaching one connection to a file will leave the others intact.

This statement will fail if SQLite is in the middle of a transaction.

DROP INDEX

```
sql-command ::= DROP INDEX [IF EXISTS] [database-name .] index-name
```

The DROP INDEX statement removes an index added with the CREATE INDEX statement. The index named is completely removed from the disk. The only way to recover the index is to reenter the appropriate CREATE INDEX command.

The DROP INDEX statement does not reduce the size of the database file in the default mode. Empty space in the database is retained for later INSERTs. To remove free space in the database, use the VACUUM command. If AUTOVACUUM mode is enabled for a database, then space will be freed automatically by DROP INDEX.

DROP TABLE

sql-command ::= **DROP TABLE** [**IF EXISTS**] [*database-name.*] *table-name*

The DROP TABLE statement removes a table added with the CREATE TABLE statement. The name specified is the table name. It is completely removed from the database schema and the disk file. The table cannot be recovered. All indexes associated with the table are also deleted.

The DROP TABLE statement does not reduce the size of the database file in the default mode. Empty space in the database is retained for later INSERTs. To remove free space in the database, use the VACUUM command. If AUTOVACUUM mode is enabled for a database, then space will be freed automatically by DROP TABLE.

The optional IF EXISTS clause suppresses the error that would normally result if the table does not exist.

DROP TRIGGER

sql-statement ::= **DROP TRIGGER** [*database-name* .] *trigger-name*

The DROP TRIGGER statement removes a trigger created by the CREATE TRIGGER statement. The trigger is deleted from the database schema. Note that triggers are automatically dropped when the associated table is dropped.

DROP VIEW

sql-command ::= **DROP VIEW** *view-name*

The DROP VIEW statement removes a view created by the CREATE VIEW statement. The name specified is the view name. It is removed from the database schema, but no actual data in the underlying base tables is modified.

END TRANSACTION

See "BEGIN TRANSACTION."

EXPLAIN

sql-statement ::= **EXPLAIN** *sql-statement*

The EXPLAIN command modifier is a nonstandard extension. The idea comes from a similar command found in PostgreSQL, but the operation is completely different.

If the EXPLAIN keyword appears before any other SQLite SQL command, then instead of actually executing the command, the SQLite library will report back the sequence of virtual machine instructions it would have used to execute the command had the EXPLAIN keyword not been present. For additional information about virtual machine instructions, see Chapter 9.

expression

```
expr ::= expr binary-op expr |
         expr [NOT] like-op expr [ESCAPE expr] |
         unary-op expr |
         ( expr ) |
         column-name |
         table-name . column-name |
         database-name . table-name . column-name |
         literal-value |
         parameter |
         function-name ( expr-list | * ) |
         expr ISNULL |
         expr NOTNULL |
         expr [NOT] BETWEEN expr AND expr |
         expr [NOT] IN ( value-list ) |
         expr [NOT] IN ( select-statement ) |
         expr [NOT] IN [database-name .] table-name |
         [EXISTS] ( select-statement ) |
         CASE [expr] ( WHEN expr THEN expr )+ [ELSE expr] END |
         CAST ( expr AS type )
```

```
like-op ::= LIKE | GLOB | REGEXP
```

This section is different from the others. Whereas the other sections discuss a particular SQL command, this section does not focus on a standalone command but on "expressions," which are subcomponents of most other commands.

SQLite understands the following binary operators, in order from highest to lowest precedence:

```
||
*    /    %
+    -
<<   >>   &    |
<    <=   >    >=
=    ==   !=   <>   IN
AND
OR
```

Supported unary operators include the following:

```
-    +    !    ~
```

Note that there are two variations of the equals and non-equals operators. Equals can be either = or ==. The non-equals operator can be either != or <>. The || operator is "concatenate"— it joins together the two strings of its operands. The operator % outputs the remainder of its left operand modulo its right operand.

The result of any binary operator is a numeric value, except for the || concatenation operator, which gives a string result.

A literal value is an integer number or a floating-point number. Scientific notation is supported. The . character is always used as the decimal point even if the locale setting specifies, for this role—the use of , for the decimal point would result in syntactic ambiguity. A string constant is formed by enclosing the string in single quotes ('). A single quote within the string can be encoded by putting two single quotes in a row—as in Pascal. C-style escapes using the backslash character are not supported because they are not standard SQL. BLOB literals are string literals containing hexadecimal data and are preceded by a single x or X character. For example:

```
X'53514697465'
```

A literal value can also be the token NULL.

A parameter specifies a placeholder in the expression for a literal value that is filled in at runtime using the sqlite3_bind() API. Parameters can take several forms, as Table A-1 shows.

Table A-1. *Parameter Forms*

Format	Meaning
?NNN	A question mark followed by a number NNN holds a spot for the NNN-th parameter. NNN must be between 1 and 999.
?	A question mark that is not followed by a number holds a spot for the next unused parameter.
:AAAA	A colon followed by an identifier name holds a spot for a named parameter with the name AAAA. Named parameters are also numbered. The number assigned is the next unused number. To avoid confusion, it is best to avoid mixing named and numbered parameters.
$AAAA	A dollar sign followed by an identifier name also holds a spot for a named parameter with the name AAAA. The identifier name in this case can include one or more occurrances of :: and a suffix enclosed in (...) containing any text at all. This syntax is the form of a variable name in the Tcl programming language.

Parameters that are not assigned values using sqlite3_bind() are treated as NULL.

The LIKE operator does a pattern matching comparison. The operand to the right contains the pattern, and the left-hand operand contains the string to match against the pattern. A percent symbol (%) in the pattern matches any sequence of zero or more characters in the string. An underscore in the pattern matches any single character in the string. Any other character matches itself or its lower/upper case equivalent (i.e., case-insensitive matching). (A bug: SQLite only understands upper/lowercase for 7-bit Latin characters. Hence the LIKE operator is case sensitive for 8-bit ISO8859 characters or UTF-8 characters. For example, the expression 'a' LIKE 'A' is true but 'æ' LIKE 'Æ' is false.)

If the optional ESCAPE clause is present, then the expression following the ESCAPE keyword must evaluate to a string consisting of a single character. This character may be used in the LIKE pattern to include literal percent or underscore characters. The escape character followed by a percent symbol, underscore, or itself matches a literal percent symbol, underscore, or escape character in the string, respectively.

The LIKE operator is not case sensitive and will match uppercase characters on one side against lowercase characters on the other.

The infix LIKE operator is implemented by calling the user function like(X,Y). If an ESCAPE clause is present, it adds a third parameter to the function call. The functionality of LIKE can be overridden by defining an alternative implementation of the like() SQL function.

The GLOB operator is similar to LIKE but uses the UNIX file globbing syntax for its wildcards. Also, GLOB is case sensitive, unlike LIKE. Both GLOB and LIKE may be preceded by the NOT keyword to invert the sense of the test. The infix GLOB operator is implemented by calling the user function glob(X,Y) and can be modified by overriding that function.

The REGEXP operator is a special syntax for the regexp() user function. No regexp() user function is defined by default and so use of the REGEXP operator will normally result in an error message. If a user-defined function named "regexp" is defined at runtime, that function will be called in order to implement the REGEXP operator.

A column name can be any of the names defined in the CREATE TABLE statement or one of the following special identifiers: ROWID, OID, or_ROWID_. These special identifiers all describe the unique random integer key (the "row key") associated with every row of every table. The special identifiers only refer to the row key if the CREATE TABLE statement does not define a real column with the same name. Row keys act like read-only columns. A row key can be used anywhere a regular column can be used, except that you cannot change the value of a row key in an UPDATE or INSERT statement. SELECT * ... does not return the row key.

SELECT statements can appear in expressions as either the right-hand operand of the IN operator, as a scalar quantity, or as the operand of an EXISTS operator. As a scalar quantity or the operand of an IN operator, the SELECT should have only a single column in its result. Compound SELECTs (connected with keywords like UNION or EXCEPT) are allowed. With the EXISTS operator, the columns in the result set of the SELECT are ignored and the expression returns true if one or more rows exist and false if the result set is empty. If no terms in the SELECT expression refer to value in the containing query, then the expression is evaluated once prior to any other processing and the result is reused as necessary. If the SELECT expression does contain variables from the outer query, then the SELECT is reevaluated every time it is needed.

When a SELECT is the right operand of the IN operator, the IN operator returns true if the result of the left operand is any of the values generated by the SELECT. The IN operator may be preceded by the NOT keyword to invert the sense of the test.

When a SELECT appears within an expression but is not the right operand of an IN operator, then the first row of the result of the SELECT becomes the value used in the expression. If the SELECT yields more than one result row, all rows after the first are ignored. If the SELECT yields no rows, then the value of the SELECT is NULL.

A CAST expression changes the data type of a column value into the type specified by type, which can be any non-empty type name that is valid for the type in a column definition of a CREATE TABLE statement.

Both simple and aggregate functions are supported. A simple function can be used in any expression. Simple functions return a result immediately based on their inputs. Aggregate functions may only be used in a SELECT statement. Aggregate functions compute their result across all rows of the result set.

The functions shown in Table A-2 are available by default. Additional functions may be written in C and added to the database engine using the sqlite3_create_function() API.

The aggregate functions shown in Table A-3 are available by default. Additional aggregate functions written in C may be added using the sqlite3_create_function() API.

Table A-2. *Built-in SQL Functions*

Function	Description
abs(X)	Return the absolute value of argument X.
coalesce(X,Y,...)	Return a copy of the first non-NULL argument. If all arguments are NULL then NULL is returned. There must be at least two arguments.
glob(X,Y)	This function is used to implement the X GLOB Y syntax of SQLite. The sqlite3_create_function() interface can be used to override this function and thereby change the operation of the GLOB operator.
ifnull(X,Y)	Return a copy of the first non-NULL argument. If both arguments are NULL then NULL is returned. This behaves the same as coalesce() above.
last_insert_rowid()	Return the ROWID of the last row insert from this connection to the database. This is the same value that would be returned from the sqlite_last_insert_rowid() API function.
length(X)	Return the string length of X in characters. If SQLite is configured to support UTF-8, then the number of UTF-8 characters is returned, not the number of bytes.
like(X,Y [,Z])	This function is used to implement the X LIKE Y [ESCAPE Z] syntax of SQL. If the optional ESCAPE clause is present, then the user function is invoked with three arguments. Otherwise, it is invoked with two arguments only. The sqlite_create_function() interface can be used to override this function and thereby change the operation of the LIKE operator. When doing this, it may be important to override both the two and three argument versions of the like() function. Otherwise, different code may be called to implement the LIKE operator depending on whether or not an ESCAPE clause was specified.
lower(X)	Return a copy of string X with all characters converted to lowercase. The C library tolower() routine is used for the conversion, which means that this function might not work correctly on UTF-8 characters.
max(X,Y,...)	Return the argument with the maximum value. Arguments may be strings in addition to numbers. The maximum value is determined by the usual sort order. Note that max() is a simple function when it has two or more arguments but converts to an aggregate function if given only a single argument.
min(X,Y,...)	Return the argument with the minimum value. Arguments may be strings in addition to numbers. The minimum value is determined by the usual sort order. Note that min() is a simple function when it has two or more arguments but converts to an aggregate function if given only a single argument.
nullif(X,Y)	Return the first argument if the arguments are different; otherwise return NULL.
quote(X)	This routine returns a string that is the value of its argument suitable for inclusion into another SQL statement. Strings are surrounded by single quotes with escapes on interior quotes as needed. BLOBs are encoded as hexadecimal literals. The current implementation of VACUUM uses this function. The function is also useful when writing triggers to implement undo/redo functionality.
random(*)	Return a random integer between -2147483648 and +2147483647.

Table A-2. *Built-in SQL Functions*

Function	Description
round(X), round(X,Y)	Round off the number X to Y digits to the right of the decimal point. If the Y argument is omitted, 0 is assumed.
soundex(X)	Compute the soundex encoding of the string X. The string "?000" is returned if the argument is NULL. This function is omitted from SQLite by default. It is only available if the -DSQLITE_SOUNDEX=1 compiler option is used when SQLite is built.
sqlite_version(*)	Return the version string for the SQLite library that is running. Example: "2.8.0"
substr(X,Y,Z)	Return a substring of input string X that begins with the Y-th character and that is Z characters long. The leftmost character of X is number 1. If Y is negative, then the first character of the substring is found by counting from the right rather than the left. If SQLite is configured to support UTF-8, then characters indexes refer to actual UTF-8 characters, not bytes.
typeof(X)	Return the type of the expression X. The only return values are "null", "integer", "real", "text", and "blob".
upper(X)	Return a copy of input string X converted to all uppercase letters. The implementation of this function uses the C library routine toupper(), which means it may not work correctly on UTF-8 strings.

In any aggregate function that takes a single argument, that argument can be preceded by the keyword DISTINCT. In such cases, duplicate elements are filtered before being passed into the aggregate function. For example, the function count(distinct X) will return the number of distinct values of column X instead of the total number of non-NULL values in column X.

Table A-3. *SQLite Built-in Aggregate Functions*

Function	Description
avg(X)	Return the average value of all non-NULL X within a group. String and BLOB values that do not look like numbers are interpreted as 0. The result of avg() is always a floating-point value even if all inputs are integers.
count(X), count(*)	The first form returns a count of the number of times that X is not NULL in a group. The second form returns the total number of rows in the group.
max(X)	Return the maximum value of all values in the group. The usual sort order is used to determine the maximum.
min(X)	Return the minimum non-NULL value of all values in the group. The usual sort order is used to determine the minimum. NULL is only returned if all values in the group are NULL.
sum(X), total(X)	Return the numeric sum of all non-NULL values in the group. If there are no non-NULL input rows, then sum() returns NULL but total() returns 0.0. NULL is not normally a helpful result for the sum of no rows but the SQL standard requires it and most other SQL database engines implement sum() that way so SQLite does it in the same way in order to be compatible. The nonstandard total() function is provided as a convenient way to work around this design problem in the SQL language.

The result of total() is always a floating-point value. The result of sum() is an integer value if all non-NULL inputs are integers and the sum is exact. If any input to sum() is neither an integer nor a NULL, or if an integer overflow occurs at any point during the computation, then sum() returns a floating-point value that might be an approximation to the true sum.

INSERT

```
sql-statement ::= INSERT [OR conflict-algorithm]
  INTO [database-name .] table-name [(column-list)] VALUES(value-list) |

  INSERT [OR conflict-algorithm] INTO [database-name .]
  table-name [(column-list)] select-statement
```

The INSERT statement comes in two basic forms. The first form (with the VALUES keyword) creates a single new row in an existing table. If no column-list is specified then the number of values must be the same as the number of columns in the table. If column-list is specified, then the number of values must match the number of specified columns. Columns of the table that do not appear in the column-list are filled with the default value, or with NULL if no default value is specified.

The second form of the INSERT statement takes its data from a SELECT statement. The number of columns in the result of the SELECT must exactly match the number of columns in the table if no column list is specified, or it must match the number of column named in the column list. A new entry is made in the table for every row of the SELECT result. The SELECT may be simple or compound. If the SELECT statement has an ORDER BY clause, the ORDER BY is ignored.

The optional conflict-clause allows the specification of an alternative constraint conflict resolution algorithm to use during this one command. See the section "ON CONFLICT" for additional information. For compatibility with MySQL, the parser allows the use of the single keyword REPLACE as an alias for INSERT OR REPLACE.

ON CONFLICT

```
conflict-clause ::= ON CONFLICT conflict-algorithm
conflict-algorithm ::= ROLLBACK | ABORT | FAIL | IGNORE | REPLACE
```

The ON CONFLICT clause is not a separate SQL command. It is a nonstandard clause that can appear in many other SQL commands. It is given its own section in the Appendix because it is not part of standard SQL and therefore might not be familiar.

The syntax for the ON CONFLICT clause is as shown for the CREATE TABLE command. For the INSERT and UPDATE commands, the keywords ON CONFLICT are replaced by OR, to make the syntax seem more natural. For example, instead of INSERT ON CONFLICT IGNORE we have INSERT OR IGNORE. The keywords change but the meaning of the clause is the same either way.

The ON CONFLICT clause specifies an algorithm used to resolve constraint conflicts. There are five choices: ROLLBACK, ABORT, FAIL, IGNORE, and REPLACE. The default algorithm is ABORT. Table A-4 shows what they mean.

When this conflict resolution strategy deletes rows in order to satisfy a constraint, it does not invoke delete triggers on those rows. But that may change in a future release.

Table A-4. *Conflict Resolution Algorithms*

Algorithm	Description
ROLLBACK	When a constraint violation occurs, an immediate ROLLBACK occurs, thus ending the current transaction, and the command aborts with a return code of SQLITE_CONSTRAINT. If no transaction is active (other than the implied transaction that is created on every command), then this algorithm works the same as ABORT.
ABORT	When a constraint violation occurs, the command backs out any prior changes it might have made and aborts with a return code of SQLITE_CONSTRAINT. But no ROLLBACK is executed so changes from prior commands within the same transaction are preserved. This is the default behavior.
FAIL	When a constraint violation occurs, the command aborts with a return code SQLITE_CONSTRAINT. But any changes to the database that the command made prior to encountering the constraint violation are preserved and are not backed out. For example, if an UPDATE statement encountered a constraint violation on the 100th row that it attempts to update, then the first 99 row changes are preserved but changes to rows 100 and beyond never occur.
IGNORE	When a constraint violation occurs, the one row that contains the constraint violation is not inserted or changed. But the command continues executing normally. Other rows before and after the row that contained the constraint violation continues to be inserted or updated normally. No error is returned.
REPLACE	When a UNIQUE constraint violation occurs, the preexisting rows that are causing the constraint violation are removed prior to inserting or updating the current row. Thus the insert or update always occurs. The command continues executing normally. No error is returned. If a NOT NULL constraint violation occurs, the NULL value is replaced by the default value for that column. If the column has no default value, then the ABORT algorithm is used.

The algorithm specified in the OR clause of an INSERT or UPDATE overrides any algorithm specified in a CREATE TABLE. If no algorithm is specified anywhere, the ABORT algorithm is used.

PRAGMA

```
sql-statement ::= PRAGMA name [= value] |
PRAGMA function(arg)
```

The PRAGMA command is a special command used to modify the operation of the SQLite library or to query the library for internal (non-table) data. The PRAGMA command is issued using the same interface as other SQLite commands (e.g., SELECT, INSERT) but is different in the following important respects:

- Specific pragma statements may be removed and others added in future releases of SQLite. Use with caution!

- No error messages are generated if an unknown pragma is issued. Unknown pragmas are simply ignored. This means that if there is a typo in a pragma statement the library does not inform the user of the fact.

- Some pragmas take effect during the SQL compilation stage, not the execution stage. This means if you are using the C-language `sqlite3_compile()`, `sqlite3_step()`, or `sqlite3_finalize()` API (or similar in a wrapper interface), the pragma may be applied to the library during the `sqlite3_compile()` call.

- The pragma command is not likely to be compatible with any other SQL engine.

The available pragmas fall into four basic categories:

- Pragmas used to query the schema of the current database

- Pragmas used to modify the library operation of the SQLite in some manner, or to query for the current mode of operation

- Pragmas used to query or modify the databases two version values, the `schema-version` and the `user-version`

- Pragmas used to debug the library and verify that database files are not corrupted

The pragmas that take an integer value also accept symbolic names. The strings "on", "true", and "yes" are equivalent to 1. The strings "off", "false", and "no" are equivalent to 0. These strings are case insensitive, and do not require quotes. An unrecognized string will be treated as 1, and will not generate an error. When the value is returned it is as an integer.

The following entries list all of the pragmas implemented in SQLite, arranged by category.

PRAGMA `auto_vacuum` (library operation)

`PRAGMA` auto_vacuum = 0 | 1;

Query or set the `auto_vacuum` flag in the database.

Normally, when a transaction that deletes data from a database is committed, the database file remains the same size. Unused database file pages are marked as such and reused later on, when data is inserted into the database. In this mode the `VACUUM` command is used to reclaim unused space.

When the `auto_vacuum` flag is set, the database file shrinks when a transaction that deletes data is committed. (The `VACUUM` command is not useful in a database with the `auto_vacuum` flag set.) To support this functionality the database stores extra information internally, resulting in slightly larger database files than would otherwise be possible.

It is only possible to modify the value of the `auto_vacuum` flag before any tables have been created in the database. No error message is returned if an attempt to modify the `auto_vacuum` flag is made after one or more tables have been created.

PRAGMA `cache_size` (library operation)

`PRAGMA` cache_size = *Number-of-pages*;

Query or change the maximum number of database disk pages that SQLite will hold in memory at once. Each page uses about 1.5K of memory. The default cache size is 2000. If you are doing UPDATEs or DELETEs that change many rows of a database and you do not mind if SQLite uses more memory, you can increase the cache size for a possible speed improvement.

When you change the cache size using the `cache_size` pragma, the change only endures for the current session. The cache size reverts to the default value when the database is closed and reopened. Use the `default_cache_size` pragma to check the cache size permanently.

PRAGMA `case_sensitive_like` (library operation)

`PRAGMA case_sensitive_like = 0 | 1;`

The default behavior of the `LIKE` operator is to ignore case for Latin1 characters. Hence, by default `'a' LIKE 'A'` is true. The `case_sensitive_like` pragma can be turned on to change this behavior. When `case_sensitive_like` is enabled, `'a' LIKE 'A'` is false but `'a' LIKE 'a'` is still true.

PRAGMA `count_changes` (library operation)

`PRAGMA count_changes = 0 | 1;`

Query or change the `count_changes` flag. Normally, when the `count_changes` flag is not set, `INSERT`, `UPDATE`, and `DELETE` statements return no data. When `count_changes` is set, each of these commands returns a single row of data consisting of one integer value—the number of rows inserted, modified, or deleted by the command. The returned change count does not include any insertions, modifications, or deletions performed by triggers.

PRAGMA `default_cache_size` (library operation)

`PRAGMA default_cache_size = Number-of-pages;`

Query or change the maximum number of database disk pages that SQLite will hold in memory at once. Each page uses 1KB on disk and about 1.5KB in memory. This pragma works like the `cache_size` pragma with the additional feature that it changes the cache size persistently. With this pragma, you can set the cache size once and that setting is retained and reused every time you reopen the database.

PRAGMA `default_synchronous` (library operation)

This pragma was available in version 2.8 but was removed in version 3.0. It is a dangerous pragma whose use is discouraged. To help dissuade users of version 2.8 from employing this pragma, the documentation will not tell you what it does.

PRAGMA `empty_result_callbacks` (library operation)

`PRAGMA empty_result_callbacks = 0 | 1;`

Query or change the `empty_result_callbacks` flag.

The `empty_result_callbacks` flag affects the `sqlite3_exec()` API only. Normally, when the `empty_result_callbacks` flag is cleared, the callback function supplied to the `sqlite3_exec()` call is not invoked for commands that return zero rows of data. When `empty_result_callbacks` is set in this situation, the callback function is invoked exactly once, with the third parameter set to 0 (NULL). This is to enable programs that use the sqlite3_exec() API to retrieve column names even when a query returns no data.

PRAGMA encoding (library operation)

```
PRAGMA encoding = "UTF-8";
PRAGMA encoding = "UTF-16";
PRAGMA encoding = "UTF-16le";
PRAGMA encoding = "UTF-16be";
```

If the main database has already been created, then this pragma returns the text encoding used by the main database, one of "UTF-8", "UTF-16le" (little-endian UTF-16 encoding), or "UTF-16be" (big-endian UTF-16 encoding). If the main database has not already been created, then the value returned is the text encoding that will be used to create the main database, if it is created by this session.

The second and subsequent forms of this pragma are only useful if the main database has not already been created. In this case the pragma sets the encoding that the main database will be created with if it is created by this session. The string "UTF-16" is interpreted as "UTF-16 encoding using native machine byte-ordering." If the second and subsequent forms are used after the database file has already been created, they have no effect and are silently ignored.

Once an encoding has been set for a database, it cannot be changed.

Databases created by the ATTACH command always use the same encoding as the main database.

PRAGMA full_column_names (library operation)

```
PRAGMA full_column_names = 0 | 1;
```

Query or change the full_column_names flag. This flag affects the way SQLite names columns of data returned by SELECT statements when the expression for the column is a table-column name or the wildcard (*). Normally, such result columns are named table-name/alias.column-name if the SELECT statement joins two or more tables together or simply column-name if the SELECT statement queries a single table. When the full_column_names flag is set, such columns are always named table-name/alias.column-name regardless of whether a join is performed.

If both the short_column_names and full_column_names are set, then the behavior associated with the full_column_names flag is exhibited.

PRAGMA fullfsync (library operation)

```
PRAGMA fullfsync = 0 | 1;
```

Query or change the fullfsync flag. This flag determines whether the F_FULLFSYNC syncing method is used on systems that support it. The default value is off. As of this writing only Mac OS X supports F_FULLFSYNC.

PRAGMA `page_size` (library operation)

PRAGMA page_size = *bytes*;

Query or set the page_size of the database. The page_size may only be set if the database has not yet been created. The page_size must be a power of 2 greater than or equal to 512 and less than or equal to 8192. The upper limit may be modified by setting the value of the macro SQLITE_MAX_PAGE_SIZE during compilation. The maximum upper bound is 32768.

PRAGMA `read_uncommitted` (library operation)

PRAGMA read_uncommitted = 0 | 1;

Query, set, or clear read uncommitted isolation. The default isolation level for SQLite is serializable. Any process or thread can select read uncommitted isolation, but serializable will still be used except between connections that share a common page and schema cache. Cache sharing is enabled using the sqlite3_enable_shared_cache() API and is only available between connections running the same thread. Cache sharing is off by default.

PRAGMA `short_column_names` (library operation)

PRAGMA short_column_names = 0 | 1;

Query or change the short_column_names flag. This flag affects the way SQLite names columns of data returned by SELECT statements when the expression for the column is a table or column name or the wildcard (*). Normally, such result columns are named table_name/alias. column_name if the SELECT statement joins two or more tables together or simply column_name if the SELECT statement queries a single table. When the short_column_names flag is set, such columns are always named column_name regardless of whether a join is performed.

If both the short_column_names and full_column_names are set, then the behavior associated with the full_column_names flag is exhibited.

PRAGMA `synchronous` (library operation)

PRAGMA synchronous = FULL; (2)
PRAGMA synchronous = NORMAL; (1)
PRAGMA synchronous = OFF; (0)

Query or change the setting of the synchronous flag. The first (query) form will return the setting as an integer. When synchronous is FULL (2), the SQLite database engine will pause at critical moments to make sure that data has actually been written to the disk surface before continuing. This ensures that if the operating system crashes or if there is a power failure, the database will be uncorrupted after rebooting. FULL synchronous is very safe, but it is also slow. When synchronous is NORMAL, the SQLite database engine will still pause at the most critical moments, but less often than in FULL mode. There is a very small (though non-zero) chance that a power failure at just the wrong time could corrupt the database in NORMAL mode. But in practice, you are more likely to suffer a catastrophic disk failure or some other unrecoverable hardware fault. With synchronous OFF (0), SQLite continues without pausing as soon as it has handed data off to the operating system. If the application running SQLite crashes, the data will be safe, but the database might become corrupted if the operating system crashes or the computer loses power before that data has been written to the disk surface. On the other hand, some operations are as much as 50 or more times faster with synchronous OFF.

In SQLite version 2, the default value is NORMAL. For version 3, the default was changed to FULL.

PRAGMA temp_store (library operation)

```
PRAGMA temp_store = DEFAULT; (0)
PRAGMA temp_store = FILE; (1)
PRAGMA temp_store = MEMORY; (2)
```

Query or change the setting of the temp_store parameter. When temp_store is DEFAULT (0), the compile-time C preprocessor macro TEMP_STORE is used to determine where temporary tables and indexes are stored. When temp_store is MEMORY (2), temporary tables and indexes are kept in memory. When temp_store is FILE (1), temporary tables and indexes are stored in a file. The temp_store_directory pragma can be used to specify the directory containing this file. When the temp_store setting is changed, all existing temporary tables, indexes, triggers, and views are immediately deleted.

It is possible for the library compile-time C preprocessor symbol TEMP_STORE to override this pragma setting. Table A-5 summarizes the interaction of the TEMP_STORE preprocessor macro and the temp_store pragma.

Table A-5. *Temporary Storage Pragma Options*

TEMP_STORE	PRAGMA temp_store	Storage Used for TEMP Tables and Indexes
0	any	file
1	0	file
1	1	file
1	2	memory
2	0	memory
2	1	file
2	2	memory
3	any	memory

PRAGMA temp_store_directory (library operation)

```
PRAGMA temp_store_directory = 'directory-name';
```

Query or change the setting of the temp_store_directory—the directory where files used for storing temporary tables and indexes are kept. This setting lasts for the duration of the current connection only and resets to its default value for each new connection opened.

When the `temp_store_directory` setting is changed, all existing temporary tables, indexes, triggers, and viewers are immediately deleted. In practice, `temp_store_directory` should be set immediately after the database is opened.

The value `directory-name` should be enclosed in single quotes. To revert the directory to the default, set the `directory-name` to an empty string, for example, `PRAGMA temp_store_directory =`. An error is raised if `directory-name` is not found or is not writable.

The default directory for temporary files depends on the OS. For Unix/Linux/Mac OS X, the default is the first writable directory found in the list of `/var/tmp`, `/usr/tmp`, `/tmp`, and the current working directory. For Windows NT, the default directory is determined by Windows, generally `C:\Documents and Settings\user-name\Local Settings\Temp\`. Temporary files created by SQLite are unlinked immediately after opening, so that the operating system can automatically delete the files when the SQLite process exits. Thus, temporary files are not normally visible through `ls` or `dir` commands.

PRAGMA database_list (database schema)

For each open database, invoke the callback function once with information about that database. Arguments include the index and the name the database was attached with. The first row will be for the main database. The second row will be for the database used to store temporary tables.

PRAGMA foreign_key_list(table-name) (database schema)

For each foreign key that references a column in the argument table, invoke the callback function with information about that foreign key. The callback function will be invoked once for each column in each foreign key.

PRAGMA index_info(index-name) (database schema)

For each column that the named index references, invoke the callback function once with information about that column, including the column name, and the column number.

PRAGMA index_list(table-name) (database schema)

For each index on the named table, invoke the callback function once with information about that index. Arguments include the index name and a flag to indicate whether the index must be unique.

PRAGMA table_info(table-name) (database schema)

For each column in the named table, invoke the callback function once with information about that column, including the column name, data type, whether the column can be `NULL`, and the default value for the column.

PRAGMA [database.] (database version)

```
PRAGMA [database.]schema_version;
PRAGMA [database.]schema_version = integer ;
PRAGMA [database.]user_version;
PRAGMA [database.]user_version = integer ;
```

The pragmas schema_version and user_version are used to set or get the value of the schema_version and user_version, respectively. Both the schema_version and the user_version are 32-bit signed integers stored in the database header.

The schema_version is usually only manipulated internally by SQLite. It is incremented by SQLite whenever the database schema is modified (by creating or dropping a table or an index). The schema_version is used by SQLite each time a query is executed to ensure that the internal cache of the schema used when compiling the SQL query matches the schema of the database against which the compiled query is actually executed. Subverting this mechanism by using PRAGMA schema_version to modify the schema-version is potentially dangerous and may lead to program crashes or database corruption. Use with caution!

The user-version is not used internally by SQLite. It may be used by applications for any purpose.

PRAGMA integrity_check (debugging)

The command does an integrity check of the entire database. It looks for out-of-order records, missing pages, malformed records, and corrupt indexes. If any problems are found, then a single string is returned which is a description of all problems. If everything is in order, "ok" is returned.

PRAGMA parser_trace (debugging)

```
PRAGMA parser_trace = ON; (1)
PRAGMA parser_trace = OFF; (0)
```

Turn tracing of the SQL parser inside the SQLite library on and off. This is used for debugging. This only works if the library is compiled without the NDEBUG macro.

PRAGMA vdbe_trace (debugging)

```
PRAGMA vdbe_trace = ON; (1)
PRAGMA vdbe_trace = OFF; (0)
```

Turn tracing of the virtual database engine inside of the SQLite library on and off. This is used for debugging. See the VDBE documentation for more information.

PRAGMA vdbe_listing (debugging)

```
PRAGMA vdbe_listing = ON; (1)
PRAGMA vdbe_listing = OFF; (0)
```

Turn listings of virtual machine programs on and off. When listing is on, the entire contents of a program are printed just prior to beginning execution. This is like automatically executing an EXPLAIN prior to each statement. The statement executes normally after the listing is printed. This is used for debugging. See the VDBE documentation for more information.

REINDEX

```
sql-statement ::= REINDEX collation name
sql-statement ::= REINDEX [database-name .] table/index-name
```

The REINDEX command is used to delete and re-create indexes from scratch. This is useful when the definition of a collation sequence has changed.

In the first form, all indexes in all attached databases that use the named collation sequence are re-created. In the second form, if [database-name.]table/index-name identifies a table, then all indexes associated with the table are rebuilt. If an index is identified, then only this specific index is deleted and re-created.

If no database-name is specified and there exists both a table or an index and a collation sequence of the specified name, then indexes associated with the collation sequence only are reconstructed. This ambiguity may be dispelled by always specifying a database-name when reindexing a specific table or index.

REPLACE

```
sql-statement ::= REPLACE INTO [database-name .]
  table-name [( column-list )] VALUES ( value-list ) |

  REPLACE INTO [database-name .] table-name [( column-list )] select-statement
```

The REPLACE command is an alias for the INSERT OR REPLACE variant of the INSERT command. This alias is provided for compatibility with MySQL. See the INSERT command documentation for additional information.

ROLLBACK TRANSACTION

See "BEGIN TRANSACTION."

SELECT

```
sql-statement ::= SELECT [ALL | DISTINCT] result [FROM table-list]
  [WHERE expr]
  [GROUP BY expr-list]
  [HAVING expr]
  [compound-op select]*
  [ORDER BY sort-expr-list]
  [LIMIT integer [( OFFSET | , ) integer]]

result ::= result-column [, result-column]*

result-column ::= * | table-name . * | expr [ [AS] string ]
```

```
table-list ::= table [join-op table join-args]*

table ::= table-name [AS alias] | ( select ) [AS alias]

join-op ::= , | [NATURAL] [LEFT | RIGHT | FULL] [OUTER | INNER | CROSS] JOIN

join-args ::= [ON expr] [USING ( id-list )]

sort-expr-list ::= expr [sort-order] [, expr [sort-order]]*

sort-order ::= [ COLLATE collation-name ] [ ASC | DESC ]

compound_op ::= UNION | UNION ALL | INTERSECT | EXCEPT
```

The SELECT statement is used to query the database. The result of a SELECT is zero or more rows of data where each row has a fixed number of columns. The number of columns in the result is specified by the expression list in between the SELECT and FROM keywords. Any arbitrary expression can be used as a result. If a result expression is * then all columns of all tables are substituted for that one expression. If the expression is the name of a table followed by .* then the result is all columns in that one table.

The DISTINCT keyword causes a subset of result rows to be returned, in which each result row is different. NULL values are not treated as distinct from each other. The default behavior is that all result rows be returned, which can be made explicit with the keyword ALL.

The query is executed against one or more tables specified after the FROM keyword. If multiple table names are separated by commas, then the query is against the cross join of the various tables. The full SQL-92 join syntax can also be used to specify joins. A subquery in parentheses may be substituted for any table name in the FROM clause. The entire FROM clause may be omitted, in which case the result is a single row consisting of the values of the expression list.

The WHERE clause can be used to limit the number of rows over which the query operates.

The GROUP BY clause causes one or more rows of the result to be combined into a single row of output. This is especially useful when the result contains aggregate functions. The expressions in the GROUP BY clause do not have to be expressions that appear in the result. The HAVING clause is similar to WHERE except that HAVING applies after grouping has occurred. The HAVING expression may refer to values, even aggregate functions, that are not in the result.

The ORDER BY clause causes the output rows to be sorted. The argument to ORDER BY is a list of expressions that are used as the key for the sort. The expressions do not have to be part of the result for a simple SELECT, but in a compound SELECT each sort expression must exactly match one of the result columns. Each sort expression may be optionally followed by a COLLATE keyword and the name of a collating function used for ordering text and/or keywords ASC or DESC to specify the sort order.

The LIMIT clause places an upper bound on the number of rows returned in the result. A negative LIMIT indicates no upper bound. The optional OFFSET following LIMIT specifies how many rows to skip at the beginning of the result set. In a compound query, the LIMIT clause may only appear on the final SELECT statement. The limit is applied to the entire query not to the individual SELECT statement to which it is attached. Note that if the OFFSET keyword is used in the LIMIT clause, then the limit is the first number and the offset is the second number. If a comma is used instead of the OFFSET keyword, then the offset is the first number and the limit is the second number. This seeming contradiction is intentional—it maximizes compatibility with legacy SQL database systems.

A compound SELECT is formed from two or more simple SELECTs connected by one of the operators UNION, UNION ALL, INTERSECT, or EXCEPT. In a compound SELECT, all the constituent SELECTs must specify the same number of result columns. There may be only a single ORDER BY clause at the end of the compound SELECT. The UNION and UNION ALL operators combine the results of the SELECTs to the right and left into a single big table. The difference is that in UNION all result rows are distinct where in UNION ALL there may be duplicates. The INTERSECT operator takes the intersection of the results of the left and right SELECTs. EXCEPT takes the result of left SELECT after removing the results of the right SELECT. When three or more SELECTs are connected into a compound, they group from left to right.

UPDATE

```
sql-statement ::= UPDATE [ OR conflict-algorithm ] [database-name .]
  table-name SET assignment [, assignment]* [WHERE expr]
```

```
assignment ::= column-name = expr
```

The UPDATE statement is used to change the value of columns in selected rows of a table. Each assignment in an UPDATE specifies a column name to the left of the equals sign and an arbitrary expression to the right. The expressions may use the values of other columns. All expressions are evaluated before any assignments are made. A WHERE clause can be used to restrict which rows are updated.

The optional conflict-clause allows the specification of an alternative conflict resolution algorithm to use during this one command. See the section "ON CONFLICT" for additional information.

VACUUM

```
sql-statement ::= VACUUM [index-or-table-name]
```

The VACUUM command is a SQLite extension modeled after a similar command found in PostgreSQL. If VACUUM is invoked with the name of a table or an index, then it is supposed to clean up the named table or index. In version 1.0 of SQLite, the VACUUM command would invoke gdbm_reorganize() to clean up the backend database file.

VACUUM became a no-op when the GDBM backend was removed from SQLite in version 2.0.0. VACUUM was reimplemented in version 2.8.1. The index or table name argument is now ignored.

When an object (table, index, or trigger) is dropped from the database, it leaves behind empty space. This makes the database file larger than it needs to be, but can speed up inserts. In time inserts and deletes can leave the database file structure fragmented, which slows down disk access to the database contents. The VACUUM command cleans the main database by copying its contents to a temporary database file and reloading the original database file from the copy.

This eliminates free pages, aligns table data to be contiguous, and otherwise cleans up the database file structure. It is not possible to perform the same process on an attached database file.

This command will fail if there is an active transaction. This command has no effect on an in-memory database.

As of SQLite version 3.1, an alternative to using the VACUUM command is autovacuum mode, enabled using the auto_vacuum pragma.

C API Reference

This appendix covers all functions in the SQLite version 3 API as covered in Chapter 6 and Chapter 7. Each function is indexed by its name, followed by its declaration, followed by the description of what it does.

Return Codes

Many of the API functions return integer result codes. There are 26 different return codes defined in the API, 23 of which correspond to errors. All of the SQLite return codes are listed in Table B-1. The API functions that return these codes are listed as follows:

```
sqlite3_bind_xxx()
sqlite3_close()
sqlite3_create_collation()
sqlite3_collation_needed()
sqlite3_create_function()
sqlite3_prepare()
sqlite3_exec()
sqlite3_finalize()
sqlite3_get_table()
sqlite3_open()
sqlite3_reset()
sqlite3_step()
sqlite3_transfer_bindings()
```

Table B-1. *SQLite Return Codes*

Code	Description
SQLITE_OK	The operation was successful.
SQLITE_ERROR	There is a general SQL error or missing database. It may be possible to obtain more error information depending on the error condition (SQLITE_SCHEMA, for example).
SQLITE_PERM	Access permission is denied. It is not possible to read or write to the database file.

Table B-1. *SQLite Return Codes (Continued)*

Code	Description
SQLITE_ABORT	A callback routine requested an abort.
SQLITE_BUSY	The database file is locked.
SQLITE_LOCKED	A table in the database is locked.
SQLITE_NOMEM	A call to malloc() has failed within a database operation.
SQLITE_READONLY	An attempt was made to write to a read-only database.
SQLITE_INTERRUPT	An operation was terminated by sqlite3_interrupt().
SQLITE_IOERR	Some kind of disk I/O error occurred.
SQLITE_CORRUPT	The database disk image is malformed. This will also occur if an attempt is made to open a non-SQLite database file as a SQLite database.
SQLITE_FULL	Insertion failed because the database is full. There is no more space on the file system, or the database file cannot be expanded.
SQLITE_CANTOPEN	SQLite is unable to open the database file.
SQLITE_PROTOCOL	There is a database lock protocol error.
SQLITE_EMPTY	(Internal only) The database table is empty.
SQLITE_SCHEMA	The database schema has changed.
SQLITE_CONSTRAINT	The operation is aborted due to constraint violation. This constant is returned if the SQL statement would have violated a database constraint (such as attempting to insert a value into a unique index that already exists in the index).
SQLITE_MISMATCH	There is a data type mismatch. An example of this is an attempt to insert noninteger data into a column labeled INTEGER PRIMARY KEY. For most columns, SQLite ignores the data type and allows any kind of data to be stored. But an INTEGER PRIMARY KEY column is only allowed to store integer data.
SQLITE_MISUSE	The library is used incorrectly. This error might occur if one or more of the SQLite API routines are used incorrectly. Examples of incorrect usage include calling sqlite3_exec() after the database has been closed using sqlite3_close() or calling sqlite3_exec() with the same database pointer simultaneously from two separate threads.
SQLITE_NOLFS	This value is returned if the SQLite library is compiled with large file support (LFS) enabled but LFS isn't supported on the host operating system.
SQLITE_AUTH	Authorization is denied. This occurs when a callback function installed using sqlite3_set_authorizer() returns SQLITE_DENY.
SQLITE_ROW	sqlite3_step() has another row ready.
SQLITE_DONE	sqlite3_step() has finished executing.

Glossary of Functions

sqlite3_aggregate_context

```
void *sqlite3_aggregate_context(sqlite3_context*, int nBytes);
```

Aggregate functions use this function to allocate a structure for storing state (for accumulating data). The first time this routine is called for a particular aggregate, a new structure of size nBytes is allocated, zeroed, and returned. On subsequent calls (for the same aggregate instance) the same buffer is returned. The buffer is automatically freed by SQLite when the aggregate is finalized.

sqlite3_bind

```
int sqlite3_bind_blob(sqlite3_stmt*, int, const void*, int n, void(*)(void*));
int sqlite3_bind_double(sqlite3_stmt*, int, double);
int sqlite3_bind_int(sqlite3_stmt*, int, int);
int sqlite3_bind_int64(sqlite3_stmt*, int, long long int);
int sqlite3_bind_null(sqlite3_stmt*, int);
int sqlite3_bind_text(sqlite3_stmt*, int, const char*, int n, void(*)(void*));
int sqlite3_bind_text16(sqlite3_stmt*, int, const void*, int n, void(*)(void*));

#define SQLITE_STATIC      ((void(*)(void *))0)
#define SQLITE_TRANSIENT   ((void(*)(void *))-1)
```

In a SQL statement, one or more literals can be replaced by a parameter (also called a *host parameter name*) of the forms ?, :name, and $var. The parameter of the form ? is called a *positional parameter*. The parameter of the form :name is called a *named parameter*, where name is an alphanumeric identifier. The parameter of the form $var is called a *TCL parameter*, where var is a variable name according to the syntax rules of the TCL programming language.

The sqlite3_bind_*xxx*() functions assign (or bind) values to parameters in a prepared SQL statement. (A prepared SQL statement is a string containing SQL commands passed to sqlite3_prepare() or sqlite3_prepare16()).

The first argument to sqlite3_bind_*xxx*() always is a pointer to the sqlite3_stmt structure returned from sqlite3_prepare().

The second argument is the index of the parameter to be set. All parameters are identified by an index or a number. Positional parameters, for example, are numbered using sequential integer values, starting with 1 for the first parameter. Take for example the following statement that uses positional parameters:

```
insert into foo values (?,?,?);
```

The first positional parameter (represented by the first question mark) is assigned index 1; the second, index 2; and the third, index 3. When it comes time to bind values to these parameters, they will be identified in the sqlite3_bind_*xxx*() functions using their index values. The index values for named parameters can be looked up using the sqlite3_bind_parameter_name(). The third argument to sqlite3_bind_*xxx*() is the value to bind to the parameter.

In those `sqlite3_bind_xxx()` variants that have a fourth argument, its value is the number of bytes (or the size) of the value. This is the number of characters for UTF-8 strings and the number of bytes for UTF-16 strings and blobs. The number of bytes does not include the zero-terminator at the end of strings. If the fourth parameter is negative, the length of the string is computed using `strlen()`.

The fifth argument to `sqlite3_bind_blob()`, `sqlite3_bind_text()`, and `sqlite3_bind_text16()` is a destructor used to dispose of the BLOB or TEXT after SQLite has finished with it. If the fifth argument is the special value `SQLITE_STATIC`, then the library assumes that the information is in static, unmanaged space and does not need to be freed. If the fifth argument has the value `SQLITE_TRANSIENT`, then SQLite makes its own private copy of the data before returning (and automatically cleans it up when the query is finalized).

The `sqlite3_bind_xxx()` routines must be called after `sqlite3_prepare()` or `sqlite3_reset()` and before `sqlite3_step()`. Bindings are not cleared by the `sqlite3_reset()` routine. Unbound parameters are interpreted as NULL.

sqlite3_bind_parameter_count

```
int sqlite3_bind_parameter_count(sqlite3_stmt*);
```

This function returns the number of parameters in the precompiled statement given as the argument.

sqlite3_bind_parameter_index

```
int sqlite3_bind_parameter_index(sqlite3_stmt*, const char *zName);
```

This function returns the index of the parameter with the given name (in zName). The name must match exactly. If there is no parameter with the given name, the function returns zero.

Note The string for the zName argument is always in UTF-8 encoding.

---

sqlite3_bind_parameter_name

```
const char *sqlite3_bind_parameter_name(sqlite3_stmt*, int n);
```

This function returns the name of the nth parameter in the precompiled statement. Parameters of the form :name or $var have a name that is the string :name or $var. In other words, the initial : or $ is **included** as part of the name returned. Positional parameters (parameters of the form ?) have no name.

If the value for argument n is out of range or if the nth parameter is nameless, then NULL is returned.

> **Note** The returned string is always in UTF-8 encoding.

sqlite3_busy_handler

```
int sqlite3_busy_handler( sqlite3 *db,        /* db handle */
                          int(*)(void*,int),  /* callback */
                          void*);             /* application data */
```

This function registers a callback function that can be invoked whenever an attempt is made by an API function to open a database table that another thread or process has locked. If a callback function is registered, SQLite may call it rather than having the API function return SQLITE_BUSY.

The callback function has two arguments. The first argument is a pointer to the application data passed in as the third argument to sqlite3_busy_handler(), and the second is the number of prior calls to the callback for the same lock. If the callback returns zero, then no additional attempts are made to access the database, and the blocked API call will return SQLITE_BUSY. If the callback returns non-zero, then another attempt is made by the API function to open the database for reading, and the cycle repeats itself.

If the callback argument in sqlite3_busy_handler() is set to NULL, then this will effectively remove any callback function (if one was previously registered). Then if an API function encounters a lock, it will immediately return SQLITE_BUSY.

The presence of a busy handler does not guarantee that it will be invoked whenever there is lock contention. If SQLite determines that invoking the busy handler could result in a deadlock, it will return SQLITE_BUSY instead. Consider a scenario where one process is holding a read lock that it is trying to promote to a reserved lock, and a second process is holding a reserved lock that it is trying to promote to an exclusive lock. The first process cannot proceed because it is blocked by the second and the second process cannot proceed because it is blocked by the first. If both processes invoke the busy handlers, neither will make any progress. Therefore, SQLite returns SQLITE_BUSY for the first process, hoping that this will induce the first process to release its read lock and allow the second process to proceed.

Since SQLite is re-entrant, the busy handler could in theory start a new query. However, the busy handler **may not close the database**. Closing the database from a busy handler will delete data structures out from under the executing query and will probably result in crashing the program.

sqlite3_busy_timeout

```
int sqlite3_busy_timeout( sqlite3 *db, /* db handle */
                          int ms);     /* time to sleep */
```

This function sets a busy handler that sleeps for a while when a table is locked. The handler will sleep multiple times until at least ms milliseconds have elapsed. After that time, the handler returns zero which causes the blocked API function to return SQLITE_BUSY. Calling this routine with an argument less than or equal to zero turns off all busy handlers.

sqlite3_changes

```
int sqlite3_changes(sqlite3*);
```

This function returns the number of database rows that were changed (or inserted or deleted) by the most recently completed INSERT, UPDATE, or DELETE statement. Only changes that are directly specified by the INSERT, UPDATE, or DELETE statement are counted. Auxiliary changes caused by triggers are not counted. To obtain the figure with these changes, use the sqlite3_total_changes() function. It provides the total number of changes **including** changes caused by triggers.

If called within a trigger, sqlite3_changes() reports the number of rows that were changed for the most recently completed INSERT, UPDATE, or DELETE statement within that trigger.

SQLite implements the command DELETE FROM table (without a WHERE clause) by dropping and recreating the table. This is an optimization that is much faster than going through and deleting individual records from the table. Because of this optimization, the change count for DELETE FROM table will be zero regardless of the number of records that were originally in the table. To obtain the actual number of deleted rows, use DELETE FROM table WHERE 1 instead, which disables the optimization.

sqlite3_clear_bindings

```
int sqlite3_clear_bindings(sqlite3_stmt*);
```

This function (re)sets all the parameters in the compiled SQL statement to NULL.

sqlite3_close

```
int sqlite3_close(sqlite3 *db);
```

This function closes the connection given by db. If the operation is successful, the function returns SQLITE_OK. If the db argument is not a valid connection pointer returned by sqlite3_open(), or if the connection pointer has been closed previously, sqlite3_close() will return SQLITE_ERROR.

If there are prepared statements that have not been finalized, sqlite3_close() will return SQLITE_BUSY.

sqlite3_collation_needed

```
int sqlite3_collation_needed(
  sqlite3*,
  void*,
  void(*)(void*,sqlite3*,int eTextRep,const char*)
);

int sqlite3_collation_needed16(
  sqlite3 *db,  /* database handle */
  void*,        /* application data */
  void(*crf)(void*,sqlite3*,int eTextRep,const void*)
);
```

This function allows the program to defer registration of custom collating sequences until they are actually needed at runtime.

It does this by registering a single callback function with the database handle whose job is to register undefined collation sequences (using sqlite3_create_collation()) when they are called upon at runtime.

From thereon out, when SQLite encounters an undefined collating sequence, it will call the callback function, pass it the name of the undefined collation sequence, and expect the callback to register a collating sequence by that name. Once complete, SQLite resumes the query requiring the custom collating sequence, using the function that the callback registered.

If sqlite3_collation_needed16() is used, the collating sequence name is passed as UTF-16 encoding in machine native byte order.

The callback function has the following declaration:

```
void crf( void*,        /* application data */
          sqlite3*,     /* db handle */
          int eTextRep, /* encoding */
          const void*)  /* collating sequence name */
```

The third argument is one of SQLITE_UTF8, SQLITE_UTF16BE, or SQLITE_UTF16LE, indicating the most desirable form of the collation sequence function required.

sqlite3_column

```
const void *sqlite3_column_blob(sqlite3_stmt*, int iCol);
int sqlite3_column_bytes(sqlite3_stmt*, int iCol);
int sqlite3_column_bytes16(sqlite3_stmt*, int iCol);
double sqlite3_column_double(sqlite3_stmt*, int iCol);
int sqlite3_column_int(sqlite3_stmt*, int iCol);
long long int sqlite3_column_int64(sqlite3_stmt*, int iCol);
const unsigned char *sqlite3_column_text(sqlite3_stmt*, int iCol);
const void *sqlite3_column_text16(sqlite3_stmt*, int iCol);
int sqlite3_column_type(sqlite3_stmt*, int iCol);
```

These functions return information about the value in a single column of the current row in a result set. In every case the first argument is a pointer to the SQL statement that is being executed (the statement handle returned from sqlite3_prepare()). The second argument (iCol) is the zero-based index of the column for which information should be returned. The left-most column has an index of zero.

If the statement handle is not currently pointing to a valid row, or if the column index is out of range, the result is undefined.

SQLite has five internal storage formats, also known as storage classes. These are defined in the API as follows:

```
#define SQLITE_INTEGER  1
#define SQLITE_FLOAT    2
#define SQLITE_TEXT     3
#define SQLITE_BLOB     4
#define SQLITE_NULL     5
```

The sqlite3_column_xxx() routines attempt to convert the internal format to the external *xxx* format requested in the respective function. For example, if the internal representation is FLOAT, and a TEXT result is requested (by sqlite3_column_text()), then sprintf() is used internally to do the conversion. SQLite's type conversion rules are listed in Table B-2.

Table B-2. *Type Conversion Rules*

Internal Type	Requested Type	Conversion
NULL	INTEGER	Result is 0
NULL	FLOAT	Result is 0.0
NULL	TEXT	Result is an empty string
NULL	BLOB	Result is a zero-length BLOB
INTEGER	FLOAT	Convert from integer to float
INTEGER	TEXT	ASCII rendering of the integer
INTEGER	BLOB	Same as for INTEGER to TEXT
FLOAT	INTEGER	Convert from float to integer
FLOAT	TEXT	ASCII rendering of the float
FLOAT	BLOB	Same as FLOAT to TEXT
TEXT	INTEGER	Use atoi()
TEXT	FLOAT	Use atof()
TEXT	BLOB	No change
BLOB	INTEGER	Convert to TEXT then use atoi()
BLOB	FLOAT	Convert to TEXT then use atof()
BLOB	TEXT	Add a \000 terminator if needed

If the result is a BLOB then the sqlite3_column_bytes() routine returns the number of bytes in that BLOB. No type conversions occur. If the result is a string (or a number, since a number can be converted into a string) sqlite3_column_bytes() converts the value into a UTF-8 string and returns the number of bytes in the resulting string. The value returned does not include the NULL (\000) terminator at the end of the string. The sqlite3_column_bytes16() routine converts the value into UTF-16 encoding and returns the number of bytes (not characters) in the resulting string. The NULL (\u0000) terminator is not included in this count.

sqlite3_column_count

```
int sqlite3_column_count(sqlite3_stmt *pStmt);
```

This function returns the number of columns in the result set returned by the prepared SQL statement. It returns zero if pStmt is an SQL statement that does not return data (an UPDATE statement for example).

sqlite3_column_database_name

```
const char *sqlite3_column_database_name(sqlite3_stmt *pStmt, int iCol);
const void *sqlite3_column_database_name16(sqlite3_stmt *pStmt, int iCol);
```

If the nth column returned by statement pStmt is a column reference, this function may be used to access the name of the database (either main, temp, or the name of an attached database) that contains the column. If the iColth column is not a column reference, NULL is returned.

See the description of function sqlite3_column_decltype() for exactly which expressions are considered column references.

Function sqlite3_column_database_name() returns a pointer to a UTF-8 encoded string. sqlite3_column_database_name16() returns a pointer to a UTF-16 encoded string.

sqlite3_column_decltype

```
const char *sqlite3_column_decltype(sqlite3_stmt *stmt, int iCol);
const void *sqlite3_column_decltype16(sqlite3_stmt*,int iCol);
```

This function returns the declared type of a column, as it is defined in the CREATE TABLE statement. The first argument is a statement handle (from a prepared SQL statement). The second argument is the column ordinal in the SQL statement. If the column does not correspond to an actual table column (but is, for example, a literal value, or the result of an expression) the function returns a NULL pointer.

The returned string is UTF-8 encoded for sqlite3_column_decltype() and UTF-16 encoded for sqlite3_column_decltype16(). For example, consider the following table:

```
CREATE TABLE t1(c1 INTEGER);
```

If you compile the following statement

```
SELECT c1, 1 + 1 FROM t1;
```

this routine would return the string INTEGER for the first column (iCol=0) and a NULL pointer for the second column (iCol=1).

sqlite3_column_name

```
const char *sqlite3_column_name(sqlite3_stmt*,int iCol);
const void *sqlite3_column_name16(sqlite3_stmt*,int iCol);
```

This function returns the column name in a prepared SQL statement. The first argument is the statement handle. The second argument is the column ordinal. The string returned is UTF-8 for sqlite3_column_name() and UTF-16 for sqlite3_column_name16().

sqlite3_column_origin_name

```
const char *sqlite3_column_origin_name(sqlite3_stmt *pStmt, int iCol);
const void *sqlite3_column_origin_name16(sqlite3_stmt *pStmt, int iCol);
```

If the nth column returned by statement pStmt is a column reference, these functions may be used to access the schema name of the referenced column in the database schema. If the iCol[th] column is not a column reference, NULL is returned.

See the description of function sqlite3_column_decltype() for exactly which expressions are considered column references.

Function sqlite3_column_origin_name() returns a pointer to a UTF-8 encoded string. sqlite3_column_origin_name16() returns a pointer to a UTF-16 encoded string.

sqlite3_column_table_name

```
const char *sqlite3_column_table_name(sqlite3_stmt *pStmt, int iCol);
const void *sqlite3_column_table_name16(sqlite3_stmt *pStmt, int iCol);
```

If the iCol[th] column returned by statement pStmt is a column reference. These functions may be used to access the name of the table that contains the column. If the nth column is not a column reference, NULL is returned.

See the description of function sqlite3_column_decltype() for exactly which expressions are considered column references.

Function sqlite3_column_table_name() returns a pointer to a UTF-8 encoded string. sqlite3_column_table_name16() returns a pointer to a UTF-16 encoded string.

sqlite3_column_type

```
int sqlite3_column_type(sqlite3_stmt*, int iCol);
```

Returns the storage class of a given column with ordinal iCol in the result set sqlite3_stmt. See also sqlite3_column.

sqlite3_commit_hook

```
void *sqlite3_commit_hook(
    sqlite3 *db,            /* db handle               */
    int(*xCallback)(void*), /* callback function ptr */
    void *pArg);            /* application data       */
```

This function registers a callback function (pointed to by xCallback) to be invoked whenever a new transaction is committed. The pArg argument is a pointer to application data which is passed back as the first and only argument of the callback function. If the callback function returns non-zero, then the commit is converted into a rollback.

If another function was previously registered, its pArg value is returned. Otherwise NULL is returned.

Registering a NULL function disables the callback. Only a single commit-hook callback can be registered at a time.

■**Note** sqlite3_commit_hook() is currently marked as experimental. However, it is unlikely to change at this point since it has been in the API for so long.

---

sqlite3_complete

```
int sqlite3_complete(const char *sql);
int sqlite3_complete16(const void *sql);
```

These functions return true if the given input string sql comprises one or more complete SQL statements. The argument must be a NULL-terminated UTF-8 string for sqlite3_complete() and a NULL-terminated UTF-16 string for sqlite3_complete16().

sqlite3_create_collation

```
int sqlite3_create_collation(
  sqlite3*,
  const char *zName,
  int pref16,
  void*,
  int(*xCompare)(void*,int,const void*,int,const void*)
);
```

```
int sqlite3_create_collation16(
  sqlite3*,
  const char *zName,
  int pref16,
  void*,
  int(*xCompare)(void*,int,const void*,int,const void*)
);
```

These functions register new collation sequences.

The second argument (zName) is the name of the new collation sequence. It is provided as a UTF-8 string for sqlite3_create_collation() and as a UTF-16 string for sqlite3_create_collation16().

The third argument must be one of the constants defined as follows:

```
#define SQLITE_UTF8      1
#define SQLITE_UTF16BE   2
#define SQLITE_UTF16LE   3
#define SQLITE_UTF16     4
```

It specifies the encoding to use when passing strings to the xCompare functions. The SQLITE_UTF16 constant indicates that text strings are expected in UTF-16 in the native byte order of the host machine.

The fourth argument is a pointer to application-specific data that is passed back as the first argument in the xCompare function.

The fifth argument is the comparison routine (xCompare). If NULL provides for this argument, it deletes the collation sequence (so SQLite cannot call it anymore). The comparison function has the following form:

```
int xCompare( void*,            /* application data */
              int, const void*, /* string 1 info */
              int, const void*) /* string 2 info */
```

The remaining four arguments after the application data argument correspond to the two strings, each represented by a [length, data] pair and encoded in the encoding specified in the pref16 (third) argument of sqlite3_create_collation(). The comparison function should return negative, zero, or positive if the first string is less than, equal to, or greater than the second string, respectively (i.e., string1-string2).

sqlite3_create_function

```
int sqlite3_create_function(
  sqlite3 *,
  const char *zFunctionName,
  int nArg,
  int eTextRep,
  void *pUserData,
  void (*xFunc)(sqlite3_context*,int,sqlite3_value**),
  void (*xStep)(sqlite3_context*,int,sqlite3_value**),
  void (*xFinal)(sqlite3_context*)
);

int sqlite3_create_function16(
  sqlite3*,
  const void *zFunctionName,
  int nArg,
  int eTextRep,
  void *pUserData,
  void (*xFunc)(sqlite3_context*,int,sqlite3_value**),
  void (*xStep)(sqlite3_context*,int,sqlite3_value**),
  void (*xFinal)(sqlite3_context*)
);
#define SQLITE_UTF8      1
#define SQLITE_UTF16     2
#define SQLITE_UTF16BE   3
#define SQLITE_UTF16LE   4
#define SQLITE_ANY       5
```

These functions register custom SQL functions and aggregates implemented in C.

The first argument is the database handle to which the new function or aggregate is to be registered. If a single program uses more than one database handle internally, then user functions or aggregates must be added individually to each database handle with which they will be used.

The second argument (zFunctionName) is the function or aggregate name, as it will be addressed in SQL. It is encoded in UTF-8 for sqlite3_create_function() and UTF-16 for sqlite3_create_function16() (in fact this is the only way in which the two functions differ).

The third argument (nArg) is the number of arguments that the function or aggregate takes. If this nArg is -1, then the function or aggregate may take any number of arguments.

The fourth argument, eTextRep, specifies what type of text arguments this function prefers to receive. Any function should be able to work with UTF-8, UTF-16le, or UTF-16be. But some implementations may be more efficient with one representation than another. Users are allowed to specify separate implementations for the same function. A specific implementation is called depending on the text representation of the arguments. SQLite will select the implementation that provides the best match for the given situation. If there is only a single implementation that works for any text representation, the fourth argument should be set to SQLITE_ANY.

The fifth argument is a pointer to application-specific data. The function implementations can gain access to this pointer using the sqlite3_user_data() function.

The sixth, seventh, and eighth arguments (xFunc, xStep and xFinal) are pointers to user-implemented C functions that implement the user function or aggregate. User-defined functions must provide an implementation for the xFunc callback only, and pass NULL pointers to xStep and xFinal arguments. Likewise, user-defined aggregates must provide implementations for xStep and xFinal, and pass NULL for xFunc.

If NULL is passed in all three function callbacks, it will delete (or unregister) the existing user-defined function or aggregate by that name.

sqlite3_create_function() will return SQLITE_ERROR if there is an inconsistent set of callback values specified, such as an xFunc and an xFinal, or an xStep but no xFinal.

sqlite3_data_count

```
int sqlite3_data_count(sqlite3_stmt *pStmt);
```

This function returns the number of values in the current row of the result set.

After a call to sqlite3_step() which returns SQLITE_ROW, sqlite3_data_count() will return the same value as the sqlite3_column_count() function.

If called before sqlite3_step() has been called on a prepared SQL statement, sqlite3_data_count() will return zero. Likewise, if called after sqlite3_step() has returned an SQLITE_DONE, SQLITE_BUSY, or an error code, sqlite3_data_count() will also return zero.

sqlite3_db_handle

```
int sqlite3_db_handle(sqlite3_stmt*);
```

This function returns the database handle corresponding to the prepared statement handle provided as the first (and only) argument. That is, this is the database handle used by sqlite3_prepare() to create the statement handle provided as the argument.

This function comes in handy when implementing query processing functions that have access to the statement handle, but not the database handle. If errors arise in the query processing, the query processing function will need the database handle in order to call `sqlite3_errmsg()` or `sqlite3_errcode()` for additional error information. This is where `sqlite3_db_handle()` helps out.

sqlite3_enable_shared_cache

```
int sqlite3_enable_shared_cache(int val);
```

This routine enables or disables the sharing of the database cache and schema data structures between connections to the same database. Sharing is enabled if the argument is true (val!=0) and disabled if the argument is false (val=0).

Cache sharing is enabled and disabled on a thread-by-thread basis. Each call to this routine enables or disables cache sharing only for connections created in the same thread in which this routine is called. There is no mechanism for sharing cache between database connections running in different threads.

Sharing must be disabled prior to shutting down a thread, or else the thread will leak memory. Call this routine with an argument of zero to turn off sharing. Or use the `sqlite3_thread_cleanup()` API.

This routine must not be called when any database connections are active in the current thread. Enabling or disabling shared cache while there are active database connections will result in memory corruption.

When the shared cache is enabled, the following routines must always be called from the same thread: `sqlite3_open()`, `sqlite3_prepare()`, `sqlite3_step()`, `sqlite3_reset()`, `sqlite3_finalize()`, and `sqlite3_close()`. This is due to the fact that the shared cache makes use of thread-specific storage so it will be available for sharing with other connections.

This routine returns `SQLITE_OK` if shared cache is enabled or disabled successfully. An error code is returned otherwise.

Shared cache is disabled by default for backward compatibility.

sqlite3_errcode

```
int sqlite3_errcode(sqlite3 *db);
```

This function returns the error code for the most recently failed API call associated with the database handle provided in the argument. If a prior API call fails but the most recent API call succeeds, the return value from this function is undefined.

Calls to many API functions set the error code and string returned by `sqlite3_errcode()`, `sqlite3_errmsg()`, and `sqlite3_errmsg16()` (overwriting the previous values). Note that calls to `sqlite3_errcode()`, `sqlite3_errmsg()`, and `sqlite3_errmsg16()` themselves do not affect the results of future invocations. Calls to API routines that do not return an error code (for example, `sqlite3_data_count()` or `sqlite3_mprintf()`) do not change the error code returned by this routine.

Assuming no other intervening API calls are made, the error code returned by this function is associated with the same error as the strings returned by `sqlite3_errmsg()` and `sqlite3_errmsg16()`.

sqlite3_errmsg

```
const char *sqlite3_errmsg(sqlite3*);
const void *sqlite3_errmsg16(sqlite3*);
```

This function returns a pointer to a UTF-8 encoded string (sqlite3_errmsg) or a UTF-16 encoded string (sqlite3_errmsg16) describing in English the error condition for the most recent API call. The returned string is always terminated by a 0x00 byte.

The string not an error is returned when the most recent API call is successful.

sqlite3_exec

```
int sqlite3_exec(
  sqlite3*,                /* An open database */
  const char *sql,         /* SQL to be executed */
  sqlite_callback,         /* Callback function */
  void *,                  /* 1st argument to callback function */
  char **errmsg            /* Error msg written here */
);
```

This function executes one or more statements of SQL contained in the second (sql) argument.

If one or more of the SQL statements are queries, then the callback function specified by the third argument is invoked once for each row of the query result. This callback should normally return zero. If the callback returns a non-zero value then the query is aborted, all subsequent SQL statements are skipped, and the sqlite3_exec() function returns the SQLITE_ABORT.

The fourth argument is an arbitrary pointer to application-specific data that is passed back to the callback function as its first argument.

The second argument to the callback function is the number of columns in the query result. The third argument to the callback is an array of strings holding the values for each column. The fourth argument to the callback is an array of strings holding the names of each column.

The callback function may be NULL, even for queries. A NULL callback is not an error. It just means that no callback will be invoked.

If an error occurs while parsing or evaluating the SQL (but not while executing the callback) then an appropriate error message is written into memory obtained from malloc(), and errmsg is made to point to that message. The calling function is responsible for freeing the memory that holds the error message, using sqlite3_free(). If errmsg is set to NULL, then no error message will be provided.

If all SQL commands succeed, the function returns SQLITE_OK, otherwise it will return the appropriate error code. The particular return value depends on the type of error. If the query could not be executed because a database file is locked or busy, then this function returns SQLITE_BUSY. This behavior can be modified somewhat using the sqlite3_busy_handler() and sqlite3_busy_timeout() functions.

sqlite3_expired

```
int sqlite3_expired(sqlite3_stmt*);
```

This function returns true (non-zero) if the statement supplied as an argument needs to be recompiled. A statement needs to be recompiled whenever the execution environment changes in a way that would alter the program that sqlite3_prepare() generates—for example, if new functions or collating sequences are registered, or if an authorizer function is added or changed.

sqlite3_finalize

```
int sqlite3_finalize(sqlite3_stmt *pStmt);
```

This function deletes a prepared SQL statement obtained by a previous call to sqlite3_prepare() or sqlite3_prepare16(). If the statement is executed successfully, or not executed at all, then SQLITE_OK is returned. If execution of the statement fails then the corresponding error code is returned.

All prepared statements must be finalized before sqlite3_close() is called, otherwise sqlite3_close() will fail and return SQLITE_BUSY.

This function can be called at any point during the execution of the virtual machine. If the virtual machine has not completed execution when this routine is called, it is like encountering an error or an interrupt (see sqlite3_interrupt()). In this case, incomplete updates may be rolled back and transactions canceled, depending on the circumstances, and sqlite3_finalize() will return SQLITE_ABORT.

sqlite3_free

```
void sqlite3_free(char *z);
```

This function frees memory obtained from sqlite3_mprintf(), sqlite3_vmprintf(), or error messages generated from sqlite3_exec().

sqlite3_get_table, sqlite3_free_table

```
int sqlite3_get_table(
  sqlite3*,              /* An open database */
  const char *sql,       /* SQL to be executed */
  char ***resultp,       /* Result written to a char *[]  that this points to */
  int *nrow,             /* Number of result rows written here */
  int *ncolumn,          /* Number of result columns written here */
  char **errmsg          /* Error msg written here */
);
void sqlite3_free_table(char **result);
```

This function is just a wrapper around sqlite3_exec(). Instead of invoking a user-supplied callback function for each row of the result, this function stores each row of the result in memory obtained from malloc(), and returns the entire result of the query.

For example, suppose the query result were the following:

```
Name         | Age
-------------+----------
Alice        | 43
Bob          | 28
Cindy        | 21
```

If the third argument is &azResult, for example, after sqlite3_get_table() returns, azResult will contain the following data:

```
azResult[0] = "Name";
azResult[1] = "Age";
azResult[2] = "Alice";
azResult[3] = "43";
azResult[4] = "Bob";
azResult[5] = "28";
azResult[6] = "Cindy";
azResult[7] = "21";
```

Notice that there is an extra row of data containing the column headers. But the *nrow return value is still 3. *ncolumn is set to 2. In general, the number of values inserted into azResult will be ((*nrow) + 1)*(*ncolumn).

After the calling function has finished using the result, it should pass the result data pointer to sqlite3_free_table() in order to release the memory that was allocated. Because of the way the malloc() happens, the calling function must not try to free the memory itself, but rather call sqlite3_free_table() to release the memory properly and safely.

The return value of this routine is the same as from sqlite3_exec().

sqlite3_get_autocommit

```
int sqlite3_get_autocommit(sqlite3*);
```

This function returns whether or not the database handle provided as the argument is in auto-commit mode. It returns true (non-zero) if it is and false (zero) if not.

By default, auto-commit mode is on. Auto-commit is disabled by a BEGIN statement and re-enabled by the next COMMIT or ROLLBACK.

sqlite3_global_recover

```
int sqlite3_global_recover();
```

This function is called to recover from a malloc() failure within the SQLite library. Normally, after a single malloc() fails the library refuses to function (all major calls return SQLITE_NOMEM). This function restores the library state so it can be used again.

All existing statement handles must be finalized or reset before this call is made. Otherwise, SQLITE_BUSY is returned. If any in-memory databases are in use, either as a main or a temp database, SQLITE_ERROR is returned. In either of these cases, the library is not reset and remains unusable.

This function is **not** thread safe. Calling this from within a threaded application when threads other than the caller have used SQLite is dangerous and will almost certainly result in malfunctions.

This functionality can be omitted from a build by defining the SQLITE_OMIT_GLOBALRECOVER at compile time.

sqlite3_interrupt

```
void sqlite3_interrupt(sqlite3*);
```

This function causes any pending database operation on a given database handle to abort and return at its earliest opportunity. This routine is typically called in response to a user action such as pressing Cancel or CTRL-C where the user wants a long query operation to halt immediately.

sqlite3_last_insert_rowid

```
long long int sqlite3_last_insert_rowid(sqlite3*);
```

This function returns the autoincrement primary key value generated from the last successful INSERT statement.

Each entry in a SQLite table has a unique integer key. (The key is the value of the INTEGER PRIMARY KEY column if there is such a column, otherwise the key is generated at random. The unique key is always available as the ROWID, OID, or _ROWID_ column.)

This function is similar to the mysql_insert_id() function from MySQL.

sqlite3_libversion

```
const char *sqlite3_libversion(void);
```

This function returns a pointer to a string, which contains the version number of the library. The same string is available in the global variable named sqlite3_version within SQL. This interface is provided since Microsoft Windows is unable to access global variables in DLLs.

sqlite3_mprintf

```
char *sqlite3_mprintf(const char*,...);
char *sqlite3_vmprintf(const char*, va_list);
```

These functions are variants of the sprintf() from the standard C library. The resulting string is written into memory obtained from malloc() so that there is never a possibility of buffer overflow. These routines also implement some additional formatting options that are useful for constructing SQL statements.

The strings returned by these routines should be freed by calling sqlite3_free().

All of the usual printf() formatting options apply. In addition, there is a %q option. This option works like %s in that it substitutes a NULL-terminated string from the argument list. But %q also doubles every single quote character ('). The %q option is designed for use inside a string literal. By doubling each single quote character, it escapes that character and allows it to be inserted into the string.

For example, say some string variable contains the following text:

```
char *zText = "It's a happy day!";
```

One can use this text in a SQL statement as follows:

```
sqlite3_exec_printf( db, "INSERT INTO table VALUES('%q')",
                     callback1, 0, 0, zText);
```

Because the %q format string is used, the single quote character in zText is escaped and the SQL generated is as follows:

```
INSERT INTO table1 VALUES('It''s a happy day!')
```

This is correctly formatted SQL. Had we used %s instead of %q, the generated SQL would have looked like this:

```
INSERT INTO table1 VALUES('It's a happy day!');
```

This would result in a SQL syntax error. As a general rule, you should always use %q instead of %s when inserting text into a string literal.

sqlite3_open

```
int sqlite3_open(
  const char *filename,    /* Database filename (UTF-8) */
  sqlite3 **ppDb           /* OUT: SQLite db handle */
);

int sqlite3_open16(
  const void *filename,    /* Database filename (UTF-16) */
  sqlite3 **ppDb           /* OUT: SQLite db handle */
);
```

This function opens the SQLite database file specified in filename. The filename argument is UTF-8 encoded for sqlite3_open() and UTF-16 encoded in the native byte order for sqlite3_open16(). A database handle is returned in the ppDb argument even if an error occurs. If the database is opened (or created) successfully, then SQLITE_OK is returned. Otherwise an error code is returned. The sqlite3_errmsg() or sqlite3_errmsg16() routines can be used to obtain an English language description of the error.

If the database file does not exist, then a new database will be created as needed. The encoding for the database will be UTF-8 if sqlite3_open() is called and UTF-16 if sqlite3_open16 is used.

Resources associated with the database handle should be released by passing it to sqlite3_close() when it is no longer required whether or not an error occurs when it is opened.

sqlite3_prepare

```
int sqlite3_prepare(
    sqlite3 *db,           /* Database handle */
    const char *zSql,      /* SQL statement, UTF-8 encoded */
    int nBytes,            /* Length of zSql in bytes. */
    sqlite3_stmt **ppStmt, /* OUT: Statement handle */
    const char **pzTail    /* OUT: Pointer to unused portion of zSql */
);

int sqlite3_prepare16(
    sqlite3 *db,           /* Database handle */
    const void *zSql,      /* SQL statement, UTF-16 encoded */
    int nBytes,            /* Length of zSql in bytes. */
    sqlite3_stmt **ppStmt, /* OUT: Statement handle */
    const void **pzTail    /* OUT: Pointer to unused portion of zSql */
);
```

This function prepares a SQL statement for execution by compiling it into a byte-code program readable by the SQLite virtual machine.

The first argument is an open SQLite database handle.

The second argument (zSql) is the statement to be compiled. The only difference between the two functions is that this argument is assumed to be encoded in UTF-8 for the sqlite3_prepare() and UTF-16 for sqlite3_prepare16().

If the third argument (nBytes) is less than zero, then zSql is read up to the first NULL terminator. If nBytes is not less than zero, then it should be the length of the zSql string in bytes (not characters).

The pzTail argument is made to point to the first byte past the end of the first SQL statement in zSql. This routine only compiles the first statement in zSql, so *pzTail is left pointing to what remains uncompiled.

The fourth argument (*ppStmt) is left pointing to a compiled SQL statement that can be executed using sqlite3_step(). If there is an error, *ppStmt may be set to NULL. If the input text contained no SQL (if the input is an empty string or a comment) then *ppStmt is set to NULL. The calling procedure is responsible for deleting this compiled SQL statement using sqlite3_finalize() after it has finished with it.

On success, sqlite3_prepare() returns SQLITE_OK. Otherwise the appropriate error code is returned.

sqlite3_progress_handler

```
void sqlite3_progress_handler(sqlite3*, int n, int(*)(void*), void*);
```

This function configures a callback function (the progress callback) that is invoked periodically during long running calls to `sqlite3_exec()`, `sqlite3_step()`, and `sqlite3_get_table()`. An example usage of this API would be to keep a GUI updated during a large query.

The progress callback is invoked once for every n virtual machine opcode, where n is the second argument to this function. The progress callback itself is identified by the third argument to this function. The fourth argument to this function is a void pointer passed to the progress callback function each time it is invoked.

If a call to `sqlite3_exec()`, `sqlite3_step()`, or `sqlite3_get_table()` results in less than n opcodes being executed, then the progress callback is not invoked.

To remove the progress callback altogether, pass NULL as the third argument to this function.

If the progress callback returns a result other than zero, the current query is immediately terminated and any database changes are rolled back. If the query is part of a larger transaction, the transaction is not rolled back and remains active. The `sqlite3_exec()` call returns SQLITE_ABORT.

■**Note** `sqlite3_progress_handler()` is currently marked as experimental. However, it is unlikely to change at this point since it has been in the API for so long.

---

sqlite3_reset

```
int sqlite3_reset(sqlite3_stmt *pStmt);
```

This function resets a prepared SQL statement obtained by a previous call to `sqlite3_prepare()` or `sqlite3_prepare16()` back to its initial state. The statement handle is then ready to be re-executed. Any SQL parameters that have values bound to them will retain their values on the subsequent execution.

sqlite3_result_*xxx*

```
void sqlite3_result_blob(sqlite3_context*, const void*, int n, void(*)(void*));
void sqlite3_result_double(sqlite3_context*, double);
void sqlite3_result_error(sqlite3_context*, const char*, int);
void sqlite3_result_error16(sqlite3_context*, const void*, int);
void sqlite3_result_int(sqlite3_context*, int);
void sqlite3_result_int64(sqlite3_context*, long long int);
void sqlite3_result_null(sqlite3_context*);
void sqlite3_result_text(sqlite3_context*, const char*, int n, void(*)(void*));
void sqlite3_result_text16(sqlite3_context*, const void*, int n, void(*)(void*));
void sqlite3_result_text16be(sqlite3_context*, const void*, int n, void(*)(void*));
void sqlite3_result_text16le(sqlite3_context*, const void*, int n, void(*)(void*));
void sqlite3_result_value(sqlite3_context*, sqlite3_value*);
```

These functions are used to set the return value for user-defined functions. The sqlite3_result_value() routine is used to return an exact copy of one of the arguments as the function return value.

The operation of these routines is very similar to the operation of sqlite3_bind_blob() and its cousins. Refer to the documentation of those functions for additional information.

sqlite3_rollback_hook

```
void *sqlite3_rollback_hook(sqlite3*, void(*)(void *), void*);
```

Register a callback to be invoked whenever a transaction is rolled back.

The new callback function overrides any existing rollback-hook callback. If there was an existing callback, then its pArg value (the third argument to sqlite3_rollback_hook() when it was registered) is returned. Otherwise, NULL is returned.

For the purposes of this API, a transaction is said to have been rolled back if an explicit ROLLBACK statement is executed, or an error or constraint causes an implicit rollback to occur. The callback is not invoked if a transaction is automatically rolled back because the database connection is closed.

sqlite3_set_authorizer

```
int sqlite3_set_authorizer(
  sqlite3*,
  int (*xAuth)(void*,int,const char*,const char*,const char*,const char*),
  void *pUserData
); */
```

This function registers a callback with the SQLite library, which can be used to monitor and control database events. The callback is invoked (at query compile-time, not at run-time) for each attempt to access a column of a table in the database. The callback should return SQLITE_OK if access is allowed, SQLITE_DENY if the entire SQL statement should be aborted with an error, and SQLITE_IGNORE if the column should be treated as a NULL value.

The second argument to the access authorization function will be one of the defined constants shown. These values signify the kind of operation to be authorized. The third and fourth arguments to the authorization function will be arguments or NULL, depending on which of the following codes is used as the second argument. These are listed in Table B-3.

Table B-3. *SQLite Authorization Events*

Event Code	Argument 3	Argument 4
SQLITE_CREATE_INDEX	Index name	Table name
SQLITE_CREATE_TABLE	Table name	NULL
SQLITE_CREATE_TEMP_INDEX	Index name	Table name
SQLITE_CREATE_TEMP_TABLE	Table name	NULL

Table B-3. *SQLite Authorization Events*

Event Code	Argument 3	Argument 4
SQLITE_CREATE_TEMP_TRIGGER	Trigger name	Table name
SQLITE_CREATE_TEMP_VIEW	View name	NULL
SQLITE_CREATE_TRIGGER	Trigger name	Table name
SQLITE_CREATE_VIEW	View name	NULL
SQLITE_DELETE	Table name	NULL
SQLITE_DROP_INDEX	Index name	Table name
SQLITE_DROP_TABLE	Table name	NULL
SQLITE_DROP_TEMP_INDEX	Index name	Table name
SQLITE_DROP_TEMP_TABLE	Table name	NULL
SQLITE_DROP_TEMP_TRIGGER	Trigger name	Table name
SQLITE_DROP_TEMP_VIEW	View name	NULL
SQLITE_DROP_TRIGGER	Trigger name	Table name
SQLITE_DROP_VIEW	View name	NULL
SQLITE_INSERT	Table name	NULL
SQLITE_PRAGMA	Pragma name	First argument or NULL
SQLITE_READ	Table name	Column name
SQLITE_SELECT	NULL	NULL
SQLITE_TRANSACTION	NULL	NULL
SQLITE_UPDATE	Table name	Column name
SQLITE_ATTACH	Filename	NULL
SQLITE_DETACH	Database name	NULL

The fifth argument is the name of the database (main, temp, etc.) if applicable. The sixth argument is the name of the inner-most trigger or view that is responsible for the access attempt, or NULL if this access attempt is directly from input SQL code.

The return value of the authorization function should be one of the constants SQLITE_OK, SQLITE_DENY, or SQLITE_IGNORE.

The intent of this routine is to allow applications to safely execute user-entered SQL. An appropriate callback can deny the user-entered SQL access to certain operations (e.g., anything that changes the database), or to deny access to certain tables or columns within the database.

sqlite3_sleep

```
int sqlite3_sleep(int ms);
```

This function sleeps for a little while. The argument is the number of milliseconds to sleep.

If the operating system does not support sleep requests with millisecond time resolution, the time will be rounded up to the nearest second. The number of milliseconds of sleep actually requested from the operating system is returned.

sqlite3_soft_heap_limit

```
void sqlite3_soft_heap_limit(int n);
```

This routine sets the soft heap limit for the current thread to n. If the total heap usage by SQLite in the current thread exceeds n, then sqlite3_release_memory() is called to try to reduce the memory usage below the soft limit.

Prior to shutting down a thread, sqlite3_soft_heap_limit() must be set to zero (the default) or else the thread will leak memory. Alternatively, use the sqlite3_thread_cleanup() API.

A negative or zero value for n means that there is no soft heap limit and sqlite3_release_memory() will only be called when memory is exhausted. The default value for the soft heap limit is zero.

SQLite makes a best effort to honor the soft heap limit. But if it is unable to reduce memory usage below the soft limit, execution will continue without error or notification. This is why the limit is called a "soft" limit. It is advisory only.

This routine is only available if memory management has been enabled by compiling with the SQLITE_ENABLE_MEMORY_MANAGMENT macro.

sqlite3_step

```
int sqlite3_step(sqlite3_stmt*);
```

This function executes a prepared query.

After a SQL query has been prepared with a call to either sqlite3_prepare() or sqlite3_prepare16(), this function must be called one or more times to execute the statement. The return value will be either SQLITE_BUSY, SQLITE_DONE, SQLITE_ROW, SQLITE_ERROR, or SQLITE_MISUSE.

SQLITE_BUSY means that the database engine attempted to open a locked database and there is no busy callback registered. Call sqlite3_step() again to retry the open.

SQLITE_DONE means that the statement has finished executing successfully. sqlite3_step() should not be called again on this virtual machine without first calling sqlite3_reset() to reset the virtual machine back to its initial state.

If the SQL statement being executed returns any data, then SQLITE_ROW is returned each time a new row of data is ready for processing by the caller. The values may be accessed using the sqlite3_column() functions. Subsequent rows are retrieved by calling sqlite3_step().

SQLITE_ERROR means that a run-time error (such as a constraint violation) has occurred. sqlite3_step() should not be called again in this situation. More information on the error may be found by calling sqlite3_errmsg().

SQLITE_MISUSE means that the function was called inappropriately. This could happen if it was called with a statement handle that had already been finalized or with one that had previously returned SQLITE_ERROR or SQLITE_DONE. Or it could be the case that the same database connection is being used simultaneously by two or more threads.

sqlite3_column_meta_data

```
int sqlite3_table_column_metadata(
    sqlite3 *db,                 /* Connection handle */
    const char *zDbName,         /* Database name or NULL */
    const char *zTableName,      /* Table name */
    const char *zColumnName,     /* Column name */
    char const **pzDataType,     /* OUTPUT: Declared data type */
    char const **pzCollSeq,      /* OUTPUT: Collation sequence name */
    int *pNotNull,               /* OUTPUT: True if NOT NULL constraint exists */
    int *pPrimaryKey,            /* OUTPUT: True if column part of PK */
    int *pAutoinc                /* OUTPUT: True if columns is auto-increment */
);
```

This routine is used to obtain meta information about a specific column of a specific database table accessible using the connection handle passed as the first function argument.

The column is identified by the second, third, and fourth parameters to this function. The second parameter is either the name of the database (i.e., main, temp, or an attached database) containing the specified table, or NULL. If it is NULL, all attached databases are searched for the table, using the same algorithm the database engine uses to resolve unqualified table references.

The third and fourth parameters to this function are the table and column name of the desired column, respectively. Neither of these parameters may be NULL.

Meta information is returned by writing to the memory locations passed as the fifth and subsequent parameters to this function, which are defined in Table B-4. Any of these arguments may be NULL, in which case the corresponding element of meta information is omitted.

Table B-4. *Out Parameters for sqlite3_column_meta_data*

Parameter	Output Type	Description
5	const char*	Declared data type
6	const char*	Name of the column's default collation sequence
7	int	True if the column has a NOT NULL constraint
8	int	True if the column is part of the PRIMARY KEY
9	int	True if the column is AUTOINCREMENT

The memory pointed to by the character pointers returned for the declaration type and collation sequence is valid only until the next call to any SQLite API function.

This function may load one or more schemas from database files. If an error occurs during this process, or if the requested table or column cannot be found, an error code is returned and an error message is left in the database handle (to be retrieved using sqlite3_errmsg()). Specifying an SQL view instead of a table as the third argument is also considered an error.

If the specified column is ROWID, OID, or _ROWID_ and an INTEGER PRIMARY KEY column has been explicitly declared, the output parameters are set for the explicitly declared column. If there is no explicitly declared INTEGER PRIMARY KEY column, then the data-type is INTEGER, the collation sequence is BINARY, and the primary-key flag is set. Both the not-NULL and the autoincrement flags are clear.

This API is only available if the library is compiled with the SQLITE_ENABLE_COLUMN_METADATA preprocessor directive defined.

sqlite3_thread_cleanup

```
void sqlite3_thread_cleanup(void);
```

This routine ensures that a thread that has used SQLite in the past has released any thread-local storage it might have allocated. When the rest of the API is used properly, the cleanup of thread-local storage should be completely automatic. You should never really need to invoke this API. It is provided to you as a precaution and as a potential workaround for future thread-related memory leaks.

sqlite3_total_changes

```
int sqlite3_total_changes(sqlite3*);
```

This function returns the total number of database rows that have to be modified, inserted, or deleted, since the database connection was created using sqlite3_open(). All changes are counted, including changes by triggers, and changes to temp and auxiliary databases. Changes to the sqlite_master table (caused by statements such as CREATE TABLE) are not counted. Changes counted when an entire table is deleted using DROP TABLE are not counted either.

SQLite implements the command DELETE FROM table (without a WHERE clause) by dropping and recreating the table. This is much faster than going through and deleting individual elements from the table. Because of this optimization, the change count for DELETE FROM table will be zero regardless of the number of elements that were originally in the table. To get an accurate count of the number of rows deleted, use DELETE FROM table WHERE 1 instead.

See also sqlite3_changes().

sqlite3_trace

```
void *sqlite3_trace(
    sqlite3*,                         /* database handle   */
    void(*xTrace)(void*,const char*), /* callback function */
    void*);                           /* application data  */
```

This function registers a callback function that will be called each time an SQL statement is evaluated on a given connection. The callback function is invoked on the first call to sqlite3_step(), after calls to sqlite3_prepare() or sqlite3_reset(). This function can be used (for example) to generate a log file of all SQL executed against a database. This can be useful when debugging an application that uses SQLite.

sqlite3_transfer_bindings

```
int sqlite3_transfer_bindings(sqlite3_stmt*, sqlite3_stmt*);
```

This function moves all bindings from the first prepared statement over to the second. This function is useful, for example, if the first prepared statement fails with an SQLITE_SCHEMA error. In this case, the same SQL can be prepared in the second statement. Then all of the bindings can be transferred to that statement before the first statement is finalized.

sqlite3_update_hook

```
void *sqlite3_update_hook(
    sqlite3*,
    void(*)(void* pArg,int ,char const *,char const *,sqlite_int64),
    void *pArg
);
```

Register a callback function with the database connection identified by the first argument to be invoked whenever a row is updated, inserted, or deleted. Any callback set by a previous call to this function for the same database connection is overridden.

The second argument is a pointer to the function to invoke when a row is updated, inserted, or deleted. The first argument to the callback is a copy of the third argument to sqlite3_update_hook. The second callback argument is one of SQLITE_INSERT, SQLITE_DELETE, or SQLITE_UPDATE, depending on the operation that caused the callback to be invoked. The third and fourth arguments to the callback contain pointers to the database and table name containing the affected row. The final callback parameter is the ROWID of the row. In the case of an update, this is the ROWID after the update takes place.

The update hook is not invoked when internal system tables are modified (i.e., sqlite_master and sqlite_sequence).

If another function was previously registered, its pArg value is returned. Otherwise NULL is returned.

See also sqlite3_commit_hook() and sqlite3_rollback_hook().

sqlite3_user_data

```
void *sqlite3_user_data(sqlite3_context*);
```

This function returns the application data specific to a user-defined function or aggregate. The data returned corresponds to the pUserData argument provided to sqlite3_create_function() or sqlite3_create_function16() when the function or aggregate was registered.

sqlite3_value_*xxx*

```
const void *sqlite3_value_blob(sqlite3_value*);
int sqlite3_value_bytes(sqlite3_value*);
int sqlite3_value_bytes16(sqlite3_value*);
double sqlite3_value_double(sqlite3_value*);
int sqlite3_value_int(sqlite3_value*);
long long int sqlite3_value_int64(sqlite3_value*);
const unsigned char *sqlite3_value_text(sqlite3_value*);
const void *sqlite3_value_text16(sqlite3_value*);
const void *sqlite3_value_text16be(sqlite3_value*);
const void *sqlite3_value_text16le(sqlite3_value*);
int sqlite3_value_type(sqlite3_value*);
```

This group of functions returns information about arguments passed to a user-defined function. Function implementations use these routines to access their arguments. These routines are the same as the sqlite3_column() routines except that these routines take a single sqlite3_value pointer instead of a sqlite3_stmt pointer along with an integer column number.

See the documentation under sqlite3_column_blob() for additional information.

sqlite3_vmprintf

```
char *sqlite3_vmprintf(const char*, va_list);
```

See sqlite3_mprintf().

APPENDIX C

■ ■ ■

Codd's 12 Rules

The following rules are taken directly from Codd's 1985 article, "Is your DBMS really relational?" in *Computerworld* magazine. They describe the essential characteristics of the relational model. All of these rules are covered in detail in Chapter 3.

0. Rule Zero:

For any system that is advertised as, or claimed to be, a relational data base management system, that system must be able to manage data bases entirely through its relational capabilities.

1. The information rule:

All information in a relational data base is represented explicitly at the logical level and in exactly one way—by values in tables.

2. The guaranteed access rule:

Each and every datum (atomic value) in a relational data base is guaranteed to be logically accessible by resorting to a combination of table name, primary key value, and column name.

3. Systematic treatment of null values:

Null values (distinct from the empty character string or a string of blank characters and distinct from zero or any other number) are supported in fully relational DBMS for representing missing information and inapplicable information in a systematic way, independent of data type.

4. Dynamic online catalog based on the relational model:

The data base description is represented at the logical level in the same way as ordinary data, so that authorized users can apply the same relational language to its interrogation as they apply to the regular data.

5. The comprehensive data sublanguage rule:

A relational system may support several languages and various modes of terminal use (for example, the fill-in-the-blanks mode). However, there must be at least one language whose statements are expressible, per some well-defined syntax, as character strings and that is comprehensive in supporting all the following items:

(a) Data Definition

(b) View Definition

(c) Data Manipulation (interactive and by program)

(d) Integrity Constraints, and Authorization

(e) Transaction boundaries (begin, commit, and rollback)

6. The view updating rule:

All views that are theoretically updatable are also updatable by the system.

7. High-level insert, update, and delete:

The capability of handling a base relation or a derived relation as a single operand applies not only to the retrieval of data but also to the insertion, update, and deletion of data.

8. Physical data independence:

Application programs and terminal activities remain logically unimpaired whenever any changes are made in either storage representations or access methods.

9. Logical data independence:

Application programs and terminal activities remain logically unimpaired when information-preserving changes of any kind that theoretically permit un-impairment are made to the base tables.

10. Integrity independence:

Integrity constraints specific to a particular relational data base must be definable in the relational data sub-language and storable in the catalog, not in the application programs.

11. Distribution independence:

A fully relational DBMS that does not support distributed data bases has the capability of being extended to provide that support while leaving application programs and terminal activities logically unimpaired, both at the time of initial distribution and whenever later redistribution is made.

12. The nonsubversion rule:

If a relational system has a low-level (single-record-at-a-time) language, that low level cannot be used to subvert or bypass the integrity rules and constraints expressed in the higher level relational language (multiple-records-at-a-time).

Index

Find it faster at http://superindex.apress.com

You Need the Companion eBook

Your purchase of this book entitles you to its companion eBook for only $10.

We believe this Apress title will prove so indispensable that you'll want to carry it with you everywhere, which is why we are offering the companion eBook for $10 to customers who purchase this book now. Convenient and fully searchable, the eBook version of any content-rich, page-heavy Apress book makes a valuable addition to your programming library. You can easily find, copy, and apply code—and then perform examples by quickly toggling between instructions and the application. Even simultaneously tackling a donut, diet soda, and complex code becomes simplified with hands-free eBooks!

Once you purchase this book, getting the $10 companion eBook is simple:

❶ Visit **www.apress.com/promo/tendollars/**.

❷ Complete a basic registration form to receive a randomly generated question about this title.

❸ Answer the question correctly in 60 seconds and you will receive a promotional code to redeem for the $10 eBook.

2560 Ninth Street • Suite 219 • Berkeley, CA 94710

eBookshop

THE EXPERT'S VOICE™

Offer valid through 11/29/06.